CONVERSATIONS WITH WOMEN IN MUSICAL THEATRE LEADERSHIP

Many writers, composers, librettists, and music directors who make their careers in musical theatre do so without specific training or clear pathways to progress through the industry. *Conversations with Women in Musical Theatre Leadership* addresses that absence by drawing on the experiences of these women to show the many and varied routes to successful careers on, off, and beyond Broadway.

Conversations with Women in Musical Theatre Leadership features 15 interviews with Broadway-level musical theatre music directors, directors, writers, composers, lyricists, stage managers, orchestrators, music arrangers, and other women in positions of leadership. Built around extensive interviews with women at the top of their careers in the creative and leadership spheres of musical theatre, these first-hand accounts offer insight into the jobs themselves, the skills that they require, and how those skills can be developed.

Any students of musical theatre and stagecraft, no matter what level and in what setting from professional training to university and conservatory study, will find this a valuable asset.

Amanda Wansa Morgan is the Coordinator of Musical Theatre and an Associate Professor of Theatre and Performance Studies at Kennesaw State University, USA.

CONVERSATIONS WITH WOMEN IN MUSICAL THEATRE LEADERSHIP

Edited by Amanda Wansa Morgan

LONDON AND NEW YORK

Designed cover image: © Fer Gregory/Shutterstock.

First published 2024
by Routledge
4 Park Square, Milton Park, Abingdon, Oxon OX14 4RN

and by Routledge
605 Third Avenue, New York, NY 10158

Routledge is an imprint of the Taylor & Francis Group, an informa business

© 2024 selection and editorial matter, Amanda Wansa Morgan; individual chapters, the contributors

The right of Amanda Wansa Morgan to be identified as the author of the editorial material, and of the authors for their individual chapters, has been asserted in accordance with sections 77 and 78 of the Copyright, Designs and Patents Act 1988.

All rights reserved. No part of this book may be reprinted or reproduced or utilised in any form or by any electronic, mechanical, or other means, now known or hereafter invented, including photocopying and recording, or in any information storage or retrieval system, without permission in writing from the publishers.

Trademark notice: Product or corporate names may be trademarks or registered trademarks, and are used only for identification and explanation without intent to infringe.

British Library Cataloguing-in-Publication Data
A catalogue record for this book is available from the British Library

Library of Congress Cataloging-in-Publication Data
Names: Morgan, Amanda Wansa, editor.
Title: Conversations with women in musical theatre leadership / edited by Amanda Wansa Morgan.
Description: [1.] | New York : Routledge, 2024. | Includes index.
Identifiers: LCCN 2023024765 (print) | LCCN 2023024766 (ebook) | ISBN 9781032349640 (hardback) | ISBN 9781032349626 (paperback) | ISBN 9781003324652 (ebook)
Subjects: LCSH: Musical theater--Vocational guidance. | Music trade--Vocational guidance. | Women theatrical producers and directors--Interviews. | Women dramatists--Interviews. | Women composers--Interviews. | Women lyricists--Interviews. | Women conductors (Music)--Interviews. | Women theatrical managers--Interviews. | LCGFT: Interviews.
Classification: LCC ML3795 .C658 2024 (print) | LCC ML3795 (ebook) | DDC 780.23--dcundefined
LC record available at https://lccn.loc.gov/2023024765
LC ebook record available at https://lccn.loc.gov/2023024766

ISBN: 978-1-032-34964-0 (hbk)
ISBN: 978-1-032-34962-6 (pbk)
ISBN: 978-1-003-32465-2 (ebk)

DOI: 10.4324/9781003324652

Typeset in Times New Roman
by KnowledgeWorks Global Ltd.

*For my mother, Barbara Ann (1952–1995).
A very smart woman.*

CONTENTS

Preface   *x*
About the Author   *xiii*
Acknowledgments   *xv*

1 The State of Things   1

   Data and Statistics on Gender Representation in Regional Theater 2
   Takeaways and Thoughts on Leadership 5

2 The Writers   7

   Introduction 7
   References, Terms, and Concepts 8
   The BMI Lehman Engel Musical Theatre Workshop (New York, NY) 9
   Notable Women Who Write Musical Theatre 9
   INTERVIEWS 11
   Kristen Anderson-Lopez Biography 11
   Interview with Kristen Anderson-Lopez, December 13, 2022 via Zoom 12
   Zina Goldrich Biography 28
   Interview with Zina Goldrich and Amanda Wansa Morgan, November 11, 2022 via Zoom 29
   Georgia Stitt Biography 45

Interview with Georgia Stitt and Amanda Wansa Morgan, January 10, 2023 via Zoom 46
Kate Anderson & Elyssa Samsel Biography 63
Interview with Elyssa Samsel and Kate Anderson, November 10, 2022 on Zoom 63

3 The Music Team   78

A Personal Perspective 78
Notable Figures 79
Job Descriptions 80
Music Glossary 85
INTERVIEWS 87
Kimberly Grigsby – Biography 87
Interview with Kimberly Grigsby, Zoom, October 13, 2022 87
Mary-Mitchell Campbell – Biography 100
Interview with Mary-Mitchell Campbell, January 9, 2022 via Zoom 101
Meg Zervoulis – Biography 114
Interview with Meg Zervoulis, November 5, 2022 via Zoom 114
AnnMarie Milazzo – Biography 122
Interview with AnnMarie Milazzo, October 25, 2022 via Phone 122

4 Director/Choreographers   141

Introduction 141
Additional Directing Team Members 142
Important Figures 143
INTERVIEWS 145
Graciela Daniele Biography 146
Interview with Graciela Daniele, October 17, 2022, via Phone, 10/17/22 146
Susan Stroman Biography 157
Interview with Susan Stroman, October 25, 2022, via Zoom 158
Baayork Lee Biography 171
Interview with Baayork Lee, November 21, 2022 via Zoom 172

5 The Producers   186

What Does a Producer Do? 186
Notable Figures 188
INTERVIEWS 189
Jenny Gersten Biography 189
Interview with Jenny Gersten, December 1, 2022,
   via Zoom 190
Dori Berinstein Biography 203
Interview with Dori Berinstein, via Zoom, October 17,
   2022 204

6 Management   218

Introduction 218
Job Descriptions 219
Notable Figures 220
INTERVIEWS 221
Beverly Jenkins Biography 221
Interview with Beverly Jenkins, via Zoom, November 15,
   2022 221
Amanda Spooner Bio 236
Interview with Amanda Spooner, November 15,
   2022 via Zoom 236

7 The Resources   257

Introduction 257
Training: Graduate School 257
Non-Graduate Training Opportunities 260
Workshops and Training Programs Outside of New York
   City 261
Additional Resources 261
Organizations That Support Women in Musical
   Theatre 261

Index   *264*

PREFACE

Hi, I'm Amanda. I am a professional theatre artist and a university professor. I am a music director, director, composer, musician, music arranger, orchestrator, sound designer, and educator. The term is "multi-hyphenate artist," but that sounds pretentious; I don't self-identify as pretentious.

While some of the facets of my artistry had a clear path of training, many did not. I didn't have any resources growing up as to how to become a music director, nor did I see many examples of women working as directors, music directors, producers, and other leaders. Furthermore, I was unable to distinguish the path to becoming a creative leader as a woman at the Broadway level. The visible figures were Susan Stroman (whom I was able to interview for this book) as a director, Lucy Simon and Mary Rodgers as composers, and Lynn Ahrens as a lyricist. Much of this is aided nowadays by the development of the internet; however, the musical theatre history books still prioritize men as "the greats": Jerome Robbins, Stephen Sondheim, and Hal Prince. This has relegated women and their contributions, to special book chapters (or issues, in the case of magazines such as *The Dramatist*).

Once I established myself and started to work with artists from the Broadway arena, I discovered that not only was I doing things the same way that they were, but our paths were similar. We connected over having a lack of role models (or access to them) in musical theatre leadership, particularly women. I discovered this through conversation.

Groups of marginalized individuals often find community through conversation. Groups in power stay in power when those whom they are aiming to suppress are in isolation. Through community comes conversation and with conversation comes understanding. Conversation provides context, power, and connection.

I have often found myself as the only woman in the room in a position of leadership as a music director, musician, or director. That isolation has certainly bred self-doubt, ignorance, and delay in professional development; however, it has also fueled passion and drive for success, like many of the subjects in this book. My mother raised me on Meryl Streep movies and television shows like *Murphy Brown*. She engrained in my brain that I could go to Yale, if I wanted, from a very young age. She established intelligence as an unquestionable part of my identity, for better or for worse.

Gender is one of many facets of identity; however, as the musical theatre industry continues to attempt to reinvent itself and expand the canon of stories, many agree that more stories written by women and non-binary artists deserve to be seen and heard. This book is part of that storytelling; I want to help tell the stories of artists themselves. One can find information on our subjects through interviews, articles, and podcasts on the internet; however, their stories deserve to be in print, in libraries, and databases alongside Jerome Robbins, Steven Sondheim, and Harold "Hal" Prince.

Artists need examples, mentors, and guidance. This book features interviews with Broadway-level musical theatre women in positions of leadership. They speak about their work in the field, their careers, their upbringings, their politics, their dreams, and their jobs. We discuss how to get the job, how to do the job, and how to survive the job. This book is about leadership, gender roles, professional skills, and personal experience. It is also a documentation that differs from interviews given by journalists because I myself am a woman in musical theatre leadership and will facilitated candid conversations. I asked my subjects questions that I wanted to know about, or what I think a young artist – particularly a female-identifying one – would want to know about. I approached the interviews with my gender in mind as well as my own experiences. I wanted to know about their paths to success, the people that helped them along the way, and their viewpoints on the industry in 2022–2023.

I must give credit where credit is due. The format for this book was most inspired by the book *I Got Thunder: Conversation with Black Singer-Songwriters*, edited by LaShonda Katrice Barnett. I came across it when I was completing initial research for a different scholarly project. The format of that book is riveting, containing conversations, rather than just interviews, where the Editor included her own point of view and asked specific and poignant questions of the subjects – like a podcast, but in print; old school. It's an amazing book.

A Few Disclaimers

This book focuses on women working in different areas of creative leadership in the specific industry of musical theatre at the Broadway/New York level. While I would love to include discussions with women who work in the regional theaters of the United States (outside of the New York market), my editors and I agreed that starting with the Broadway-level artists would be a good idea.

There is a collection of female-identifying theatrical designers working in musical theatre; however, I am not including those conversations in this book. While

I am a sound designer, I have less experience in scenic, costume, and lighting design and hesitated to lead conversations with designers in those fields at this time. Therefore, I would want to work with a collaborator in that area to bring those interviews and that research into the fold. There exists a possibility of doing a second edition of this book that would include designers and explore additional production personnel such as, but not limited to, general managers, technicians, production assistants, educators, arts managers, and more.

The subjects interviewed in this book were included because I asked, and they said yes. There are many women of importance in our industry who are mentioned in the book and still living today, but not featured with interviews. I contacted many subjects, and many were too busy. I am truly thankful that they are all busy with fruitful work and projects and support them in those endeavors. I also had a word count limit. Cheers to a future edition!

Lastly, conversations around identity and intersectionality are important. The musical theatre industry is built on and steeped in white supremacy. Therefore, the progress made in providing opportunities for people of color at the commercial level of theatre production is not nearly far enough along (as of 2023), and therefore, the representation among the highest positions in leadership is still filled with a disproportionate amount of white people. Since this book provides resources on navigating this harsh industry, I hope that young people of all racial backgrounds, but particularly the Global Majority, find themselves in the rooms where the art is happening, sharing their stories, contributing their valuable talent and skills, and feeling (and being) supported while doing so. Women of color face significant obstacles in the United States, particularly in capitalist structures and on ladders of leadership. We must uplift them, support them, and listen to them. Hopefully, a future edition of this book will welcome more of their stories.

In the meantime, I hope this book will inspire young women who want to see themselves on a podium, in a pit, on the front cover of a script or score, at production meetings, behind the tech table, and in the "room where it happens" (*Hamilton*, 2015).

I hope this book will inspire students to train; prod professors to dig into the resources to lead; and nudge practitioners to reengage with study, or create new opportunities for others.

ABOUT THE AUTHOR

Amanda Wansa Morgan (she/her) is an Atlanta-based music director, composer, director, and actor who serves as Coordinator of Musical Theatre & Associate Professor at Kennesaw State University (KSU). At KSU, she teaches classes in musical theatre performance, voice, acting, and musical theatre history and literature. Amanda previously served as a faculty at the University of Mississippi and also as the Director of Music Education at Charleston Stage. Additionally, she has professionally served as a music director for The Alliance Theatre, Six Flags Over Georgia, The Atlanta Lyric Theatre, Jennie T. Anderson Theatre, Actor's Express, Synchronicity Theater, Wallace Buice Theatre Company & Buicentennial Productions, Playhouse on the Square, Post Playhouse, and Osceola Center for the Arts. She occasionally serves as a Teaching Artist for the Alliance Theatre, the Atlanta Lyric Theatre, and the Jennie T. Anderson Theatre. She has composed original music for productions of *A Christmas Carol*, *Thumbelina*, *The Velveteen Rabbit*, *A Midsummer Night's Dream*, *Mary Had a Little Ham*, *Polaroid Stories*, *We Made History: A TYA Musical*, *Twelfth Night*, and additional projects. Favorite professional music direction credits include *The Color Purple* (2018 Suzi Bass Award for Music Direction, 2018 BroadwayWorld Atlanta Award in Music Direction), *Jesus Christ Superstar*, *Songs for a New World*, *Hairspray*, *Matilda*, *Avenue Q*, *Always Patsy Cline*, and *The 25th Annual Putnum County Spelling Bee*. Direction credits include *Next to Normal*, *Rent*, *The Spongebob Musical*, *Ragtime*, *The Mystery of Edwin Drood*, *Heathers*, and *A Man of No Importance*.

Amanda has an MFA in Acting from the University of Central Florida and undergraduate degrees in Music and Theatre from Florida State University. Amanda has a Certificate of Figure Proficiency from Estill Voice Systems and is a member of Musical Theatre Educators Alliance (MTEA), National Association of Teachers of Singing (NATS), The Dramatist's Guild, American Society of Composers,

Authors, and Publishers (ASCAP), and Maestra. Amanda is the author of the chapter "Women in CCM (Contemporary Commercial Music)" in the Rowan & Littlefield book *So You Want to Sing Music by Women,* the creator and arranger of the original concert tribute show *She's a Rebel* (2021), and is available for booking through Buicentennial Productions out of Atlanta, GA. For further information please visit www.amandawansamorgan.com

ACKNOWLEDGMENTS

Thank you to the subjects of this book: Kristen, Dori, Mary-Mitchell, Grazi, Jenny, Zina, Kimberly, Miss Beverly, Baayork, AnnMarie, Kate, Elyssa, Spooner, Georgia, Susan, and Meg. Thank you for your time, patience, wit, wisdom, and generosity; also for your emails of edits, patience with logistics, and swift correspondence.

My heartfelt thanks to Kennesaw State University; specifically, The College of the Arts, the Department of Theatre and Performance Studies (TPS), and Academic Affairs. This work was made possible in part with the support of the Center for Excellence in Teaching and Learning at Kennesaw State University and the support of my work with a Tenured Faculty Enhancement Leave in Fall 2022 to complete the bulk of this project. I'm grateful to my TPS colleagues whom I love, laugh with, vent to, and share all things with. Special thanks to my Chair Chuck Meacham for his constant support and pragmatism; to Dr. Tom Fish and Dr. Charles Parrott for being my hallway sounding boards; and to Timothy Ellis – my partner in musical theatre adventures. To my dear students: Thank you for teaching me every day and for bringing the joy, curiosity, and drama into the room. You make life worth living.

Thank you to my colleagues at the Musical Theatre Educators Alliance (MTEA), particularly Matty Miller for check-ins and Elizabeth Ann Benson for consultation on the interview process and writing a book. To the following friends for helping me to reach some of these amazing subjects: Rose Van Dyne, Morgan Rose-Johnson, Courtenay Collins, Rick Edinger, and Lauren Haughton-Gills.

Thank you to Routledge for being so enthusiastic about this project for two years – particularly Ben Piggott and Steph Hines. My deepest gratitude to my colleague and mentor Karen Robinson for her eagle eye proofreading and for being a role model to me since 2015.

A resounding thanks to my Wansa family – Karen, Bill, Jenna, Clint, and Kinzie – for their support through the years; enduring all things theatrical (including me). To my sister-in-law, Alli Morgan, for being particularly supportive in recent years and through this process. To Schroeder and Edgar, for emotional support and for being (fairly) well-behaved dogs when mom was on Zoom with fancy Broadway people. To my dearest friends: You know who you are; I am deeply grateful for your love and support.

I give huge thanks and credit to a selection of smart and savvy women in my life who have served as my role models, sounding boards, and greatest influences: Margaret Baldwin, Jen Lowe, Mary Nye Bennett, Stephanie Polhemus, Bethany Irby Okie, Dr. Angela Farr Schiller, Dr. Susan Belangee, Rachel May, Rene Pulliam, Stacy Alley, Carey Hanson, Marybeth Clark, Anne Hering, Anita Anderson Endsley, Dr. Julia Listengarten, and Kate Ingram.

Thank you David Morgan for being my person through all things and for loving me for the strong, stubborn woman that I am.

1
THE STATE OF THINGS

Tony-Award-winning director Rachel Chavkin said in her 2019 acceptance speech for the Tony for Best Direction of a Musical (*Hadestown*): "[Gender parity on Broadway] is not a pipeline issue. It is a failure of imagination by a field whose job is to imagine the way the world could be."[1]

The year is 2023. Approximately sixty years after the women's rights movement in America began that sparked debate on equal rights for women, especially in the workplace, there is still a distinguishable gap in the number of women in professional leadership in the theatre industry, and the number of men. There is also a distinguishable pay gap between the salaries of women and men. Some studies may link this to the time that the average woman takes away from work for caregiving (either children or otherwise) and others link this to the lack of opportunities for women to ascend to leadership throughout training as well as early levels of career.[2] Nonetheless, the data exists, thanks to The Lillys organization, The Dramatists Guild, as well as researchers and scholars who have made it their mission to uncover the statistics in real time.

Why is it important to have women in the rooms where decisions are made? Theatre is about presenting life onstage, either with a magnifying glass or a mirror. If women are present in the stories onstage, shouldn't the storytellers have perspective on how the stories get told, from the writing to the design? Musical theatre heightens these circumstances through song, dance, and music. If we are going to augment the situation at hand, unpacking emotion with melody and high kicks, shouldn't we dive into that emotion from a first-hand perspective? I share this sentiment regarding pieces that are specific to race, gender identity, religion, and other facets of identity and representation. We have seen, throughout the history of producing musical theatre, the problems that have arisen in the creation and presentation of musicals without women in the room to raise questions and make

DOI: 10.4324/9781003324652-1

valuable points regarding the painting of these stage pictures. There is value to having multiple perspectives in the room to discuss shared experiences, and empathy can go a long way; however, there are musicals that have debuted on Broadway exploring women's stories that haven't had a woman on or near the creative or writing team *at all*. *Chicago* – the John Kander and Fred Ebb musical about the stories of women caught up in the criminal justice system and media frenzy of America in the 1920s – was written by two men in the 1970s and was mounted on Broadway by an *almost* entirely male creative team. According to the *Internet Broadway Database*, the Broadway production featured costume design by Patricia Zipprodt, a woman, and a few female-identifying assistants, including Graciela Daniele as the original Dance Captain.[3]

While this book is more about representation through conversation and storytelling than it is about arriving at a solution to a problem, it is worth laying out the challenges and realities of the industry as it currently exists, as move through these stories.

Data and Statistics on Gender Representation in Regional Theater

The Lillys is a non-profit organization dedicated to "celebrating, funding, and fighting for women by promoting racial and gender parity in the American theater since 2010." It has worked over the past decade to collect and share data surrounding the demographics of humans working on Broadway. It is a grantee of The New York Women's Foundation and has a collection of supporters. It has developed a series of awards that include the Stacey Mindich "Go Write a Musical" Award, the Stacey Mindich "Go Work in Theater" Award, and the Daryl Roth Creative Spirit Award.

From The Lillys Website:

> The Lillys began in the Spring of 2010 as The Lilly Awards, an outlet to honor the work of women in the American theater. The founders are: Julia Jordan, Marsha Norman, and Theresa Rebeck. The organization is named for Lillian Hellman, a pioneering American playwright who famously said, "You need to write like the devil and act like one when necessary."
>
> In 2015, through a partnership with the Dramatists Guild, we have gathered our resources and conducted a national survey simply called The Count, proving that BIPOC[4] women were by far the least represented demographic on our stages. The Lillys spread that information far and wide and have devoted the majority of their funds and efforts to women of color ever since.
>
> One hundred percent of our financial awards in directing, design, tech and composing, and the majority of our writing awards been given to women of color.

Most important to this work is the data that The Lillys periodically provides on its website called The Count, which is an ongoing study by The Lillys in partnership with The Dramatists Guild.[5] Interestingly enough, The Lillys keeps the previous "Counts" available on its website. As of January 2023, the record available is "The Count 3.0."

From The Lillys Website regarding The Count 3.0:

The Count 3.0 gathered production data from a diverse sample of 147 not-for-profit theaters nationwide as chosen by The Dramatists Guild regional representatives. The focus is on theaters that produce contemporary work. The Count studies gender, race, and nationality of the creators of plays and musicals. Due to the size of the data set and intersectionality, we could only reliably break down race into two groups, BIPOC and white. The Count collects national statistics and breaks them down by region and city. Findings are presented in three-year installments, in hopes of creating a dynamic record of change over time.

In this third installment and ninth year of this project, it's clear that, although the American theater has continued to add to the diversity of its playwrights, neither gender nor racial parity has yet been achieved in terms of production. Anecdotally, it appears that women over the age of 50, especially BIPOC women, who led the push for the diversity we now enjoy, do not appear to have directly benefitted. As information on playwrights' ages is not widely available, we cannot show national statistics. The Lillys has begun a study of the stages of NYC, and will announce our findings in the near future.

The facts and findings of The Count 3.0, while improved from The Count 2.0, are still disheartening. Note that the term "play" includes musicals in this study. The Lillys produce a new "Count" set of data every three years. "See Figure 1.1."

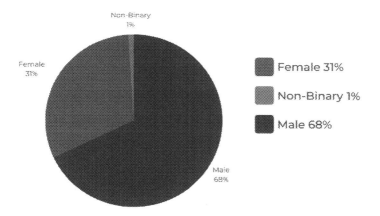

FIGURE 1.1   Produced playwrights.

4 The State of Things

According to The Count 3.0:

- Thirty-nine percent of new plays written and produced were by female-identifying writers while 61% were written by males.
- Thirty-one percent of produced playwrights identified as female while 68% are male.
- Each city analyzed – Philadelphia, New York City, the Bay Area, Seattle, Minneapolis–St. Paul, Washington DC and Baltimore region, Chicago, Kansas City, and Los Angeles – demonstrated a rise in percentage of plays produced and written by women. Interestingly enough, excluded from this study are cities in the American South, including Atlanta, Orlando, Nashville, Memphis, and Birmingham.

I'm going to zoom out from the theatre industry for a moment. The Center for American Progress published a study in 2018 called *The Women's Leadership Gap: Women's Leadership by the Numbers* by Judith Warner, Nora Ellmann, and Diana Boesch. There are some startling points made, comparing population statistics to representation of those populations in leadership:

- Women are 50.8% of the US population.
- They earn 57% of undergraduate degrees and 59% of master's degrees.
- Women earn 48.5% of law degrees and represent 45% of associates; however, they only make up 22.7% of partners and 19% of equity partners.
- Women earn 47.5% of medical degrees awarded and represent 40% of all physicians and surgeons but only make up 16% of medical deans.
- As of 2017, women accounted for 18% of directors, executive producers, writers, cinematographers, and editors in Hollywood who worked on the top-grossing 250 domestic films.[6]
- As of 2020, female CEOs represented 7.4% of the companies on The Fortune 500 list – or 37 out of 500.[7]

To suggest that the personnel simply aren't out there and aren't qualified is bogus. I have been in many rooms where decisions are being made and heard statements justifying why there aren't more women in the room and participants leaning on the myth that qualified individuals aren't out there. I vehemently disagree.

Check out the Broadway Women's Fund "Women to Watch" website. As of January 2023, there are thirty individuals on their list (varying in skill sets from writers to designers and in between) and this is simply scratching the surface.[8]

Tokenism is not the answer. No one is asking to be placed in a room without appropriate qualifications. However, the conversations unfolding between women in our industry suggest that many years of bias and assumptions plague young women when they're in early career pivot points, on the verge of getting an opportunity that might open a bevy of doors, or at the precipice of learning a slew of new skills from an educator or training program. Musical theatre training programs in this country have demonstrated problematic procedures in admission processes. Many educators are more focused on what skills the students are bringing into the program versus what skills the educators are able to provide. This is demonstrated by the application and audition procedures, which establish rigid standards of expectation, use unclear definitions of potential, and ignore students who lack a particular amount of resources and training in their secondary education. This must change, and there are a few organizations and institutions that are poised to help. This will be discussed more in Chapter 7.

There are a few books that feature the work of women in the musical theatre industry; however, the few that do either showcase the work and words of performers or are essays *about* women in leadership. The most substantial source currently in print that informs this book is *Women in Musical Theatre*, edited by Bud Coleman and Judith A. Sebesta. This book is a wonderful, comprehensive *dig* into the histories of the women who visibly, and not so visibly, created the canon of musical theatre. Some of them are mentioned in this book, but if this subject is of interest to you, Coleman and Sebesta's book has a lot of information as well as starting points for further research.

Takeaways and Thoughts on Leadership

What do we do about this disparity? How does a woman become a leader and succeed in a system not originally built for her to thrive? There are clear commonalities between the interviews in this book and the experiences of the women in positions of leadership. Thoughts on leadership collide with concepts of collaboration, communication, empathy, grace, perseverance, positivity, and community. There are links between these interviews around sexism, inequality, insecurity, lack of representation, and struggle. These women are smart and strong; they are also sensitive and generous. They demonstrate all of the qualities of leadership that experts in leadership training spout in books and lectures without having officially "studied" any of it. Not one interviewee listed a "leadership guru" in their role models. They listed their mentors in the field, their parents, and perhaps some of the least expected humans in their sphere like a hotel bar server and a civics teacher. There is also a clear division of perspective between generations (even though the generation lines are blurry) on what a woman had or has to do to gain traction in such a competitive career. The Baby Boomers had to fight, stand their ground, and persevere with laser focus as often the only woman at the leadership table. The Millennials are speaking openly about working in collaboration with others to ascend as a team. The Gen Xers – not surprisingly – are a little bit of both. A common theme that runs through these interviews is that I spoke to women who stick to their values, consciously or unconsciously. Brené Brown writes, "Integrity is choosing courage over comfort; it's choosing what's right over what's fun, fast, or easy; and it's practicing your values, not just professing them."[9] Leadership is about gathering support around values and ideals from a group of people in order to move a project, a vision, or a community forward. A director leads the production process, a stage manager leads a rehearsal room, a music director leads an orchestra, and a producer leads an entire company. When leaders seek buy-in from the entire community by involving constituents in the process, those participants can speak freely about the process and contribute toward the movement to the goal.[10] This requires establishing shared values. One cannot establish shared values without defining their own. Therefore, the most common of traits among these lady bosses is a strong sense of values, whatever they may be. Whether conscious or not, the common thread is a sense of value and a sense of truth. These subjects – these women – stand in their truths, and their truths are present in these stories.

Notes

1. Nancy Coleman, "'Hadestown' Director Rachel Chavkin: Diversity 'Is Not a Pipeline Issue'," *The New York Times*, June 9, 2019. See https://www.nytimes.com/2019/06/09/theater/hadestown-rachel-chavkin-tony-awards.html.
2. Dubner, Stephen J., "The True Story of the Gender Pay Gap," *Freakonomics*, podcast audio, January 7, 2016. See https://freakonomics.com/podcast/the-true-story-of-the-gender-pay-gap/.
3. "Chicago (1975)," *Internet Broadway Database*, Accessed December 12, 2023. See https://www.ibdb.com/broadway-production/chicago-3748.
4. Black, Indigenous, and People of Color.
5. "The Count 3.0," *The Lillys,* Accessed January 20, 2023. See https://the-lillys.org/the-count-3.
6. "The Women's Leadership Gap: Women's Leadership by the Numbers," *Center for American Progress,* November 20, 2018. See https://www.americanprogress.org/article/womens-leadership-gap-2/#:~:text=Although%20they%20hold%20almost%2052,19%20percent%20of%20equity%20partners.
7. Tacy Byham, "Women CEOs' Highest Representation on the Fortune 500 List Still Isn't Enough," *Forbes,* August 3, 2020. See https://www.forbes.com/sites/forbescoachescouncil/2020/08/03/women-ceos-highest-representation-on-the-fortune-500-list-still-isnt-enough/?sh=1ba75a255aa8.
8. "Women to Watch," *The Broadway Women's Fund* website, Accessed January 20, 2023. See https://www.broadwaywomensfund.com/womentowatch/.
9. Brené Brown, *Dare to Lead* (New York: Random House, 2018).
10. James M. Kouzes and Barry Z. Posner, *The Leadership Challenge*, 6th ed. (New Jersey: John Wiley and Sons, 2017), 65.

2
THE WRITERS

Introduction

I started writing music in college. In fact, I was sent a children's book by a family member. When I called to thank them, they said, "Wouldn't that book make a great musical?" I agreed, sat down at my 76-key Casio keyboard in my Tallahassee apartment, and wrote three little songs on some scratch notebook paper. At the time, I was just learning how to use Finale™ and was somewhere between harmonic dictation and sonata form in music theory. I put the notebook papers in the book and shut it, thinking, "I'm not a composer. I don't know how to do that." Two years later, in graduate school, I was approached by the director of a play to arrange some music for it. Additional opportunities to compose or arrange music followed, once everyone heard my ideas and my work. Often, I was saying yes to projects that I felt unqualified to do; however, I was interested in trying. I composed music for Shakespeare plays and edited pre-existing music into fully fleshed-out sound designs. I kept saying yes, learning how to do the jobs as I went, and I was grateful to the professors and supervisors who were taking chances on me and allowing me to try. However, there wasn't a clear path on how to get better other than to keep trying. The first two full-length shows I wrote were on commission for companies I was working for. When I agreed to pen the music for these projects, I didn't realize that the commissioning companies would then legally own those royalties. When I set out to write a passion project, I had no idea where to start. How do I option the rights to a pre-existing work? What kind of contract do I need in order to work with a collaborator? I joined The Dramatist's Guild and was able to obtain legal templates for contracts and get some answers to my questions. I had no money to afford an entertainment lawyer nor knew where to find an agent or a manager. I really didn't know who to talk to, especially since I wasn't living

DOI: 10.4324/9781003324652-2

in New York, where so many resources are. Most of my personal friends that were in New York were performers and didn't have helpful information. I had one friend who was a producer, but his suggestions involved hiring lawyers that I could not afford. I even submitted a script I wrote to the now-defunct Next Link Project at New York Musical Festival (NYMF) and it was a Finalist, only for me to find out that I would need at least $50,000 to produce it myself. How would I do that from Oxford, Mississippi, where I was a junior professor at the time? What was the next step, beyond hosting readings of my musicals with students, or praying that a company commission me to write something? Should I just start writing things and pedal them to whoever would listen?

Come to find out through these interviews, all of our amazing women writers had to start somewhere as well, without clear guidance on how to ascend the writing chain. They all experienced significant moments of self-doubt. Many of them speak of moments where they gained permission to self-identify as a writer or a composer. Many of them share the same role models – Betty Comden, Mary Rodgers, Lynn Ahrens. Most of them agree to simply just start. Prioritize *story*. When working with a collaborator – a writing partner – communication is successful if it is second nature, like in a professional marriage. Develop a shorthand of finishing each other's thoughts. Research the legality of intellectual property, optioning, and collaboration agreements; and get things in writing before you go sharing your ideas openly.

References, Terms, and Concepts

Composers write the music. Lyricists write the lyrics. Librettists write the dialogue or the "book."

How composers write varies drastically. Some write by ear, some notate, and some simply press record on a device and start making music. Some work in Digital Audio Workstations (DAWs) like Garageband™ or Logic™. Some input their ideas directly into music notation software like Finale™ or Sibelius™. Some record their ideas into audio files via a computer or device (previously, tapes) as live demos.

While some composers start with lyrics, and some do not, all of our composers in musical theatre begin their process with story, for story is at the center of what we do.

A Librettist can also be known as a Book Writer or a Playwright. They are known as the creators or commanders of spoken dialogue. A "libretto" means "little book," which harkens back to the days of opera and operetta, when it was easier for a performer to carry around a smaller book of all of the words, rather than the entire hefty musical score. When musicals began to emerge as a genre, the term "libretto" seemed most appropriate, given that many musicals combine spoken dialogue with sung lyrics. Libretto is the word we use today for the script that contains *all* of the words together. However, to distinguish lyrics from dialogue, we call the dialogue the "book" and those who write it "book writers." One might say that a musical could have wonderful lyrics but a weak "book," which refers to the story, the dialogue, and the scenes.

Some writers write both music *and* lyrics. Some writers write lyrics and dialogue. Some writers write the music and lyrics together. The division of labor can sometimes be muddy, which requires more specifically written contracts to handle the dissemination of profits.

Writing for musicals happens in a variety of ways. There are commissioned pieces and passion projects. There are many ways in which a piece can be developed and a variety of timelines that a developing musical can undergo. Lin-Manuel Miranda has stated publicly many times that it took him seven years to write the hit musical *Hamilton*. Stephen Sondheim debuted six musicals on Broadway in the 1970s alone.

Suggested reading for the development of a new musical(s) includes: *Performing in Contemporary Musicals* by David Sisco and Laura Josepher, *The Secret Life of the American Musical: How Broadway Shows are Built* by Jack Viertal, and *The Musical as Drama* by Scott McMillin.

The BMI Lehman Engel Musical Theatre Workshop (New York, NY)

For many years, the "BMI Workshop" was one of the only development programs for new musicals available. Many of the subjects in this book found each other through this program or worked through this program in other ways. It was founded in 1961 by Broadway music director Lehman Engel through BMI – the music production agency – with the intent to create a free-standing training ground for musical theatre writers. The program typically runs September through June in New York City with weekly workshop classes and is free to participants; however, they must plan to live near or within commuting distance of New York City while participating.

When participants apply, they apply under a specific status: Composer, Lyricist, Composer/Lyricist, or Librettist. They then work with different writers in their "class" to find writing partners. Some teams are asked to participate in an "advanced workshop" after the main process is finished. The librettist workshop has a slightly different structure; however, there are some activities that group all of the participants together.

Many subjects of this book – as well as many other successful musical theatre writers – have attended this workshop or have worked with and been mentored by former participants. The workshop has served as a model for additional development programs in existence and remains in operation to this day (2023).[1]

Notable Women Who Write Musical Theatre

Clare Kummer (1873–1958) was a composer who wrote songs for dozens of musicals as early as 1905 with *Sergeant Blue*, in addition to songs for films and television programs.

10 The Writers

Kay Swift (1897–1993) was a composer who was the first known woman to compose a full-length musical of note – *Fine and Dandy* (1930). Swift composed popular music of the 1920s and 1930s and also worked on music arrangements for George Gershwin's music after his death.

Dorothy Fields (1904–1974) wrote lyrics for over 400 songs for musicals and films, in addition to librettos. She is noted as one of the first successful female-identifying songwriters for Hollywood, Broadway, and Tin Pan Alley.

Betty Comden (1917–2006) was a prolific lyricist, playwright, and screenwriter who worked exclusively in partnership with Adolph Green for sixty years on Broadway musicals and films. She also had a career as a performer in her youth. Comden and Green wrote lyrics and/or books for eighteen full-length musicals as well as hit films such as *Singin' in the Rain*, *Good News*, and *The Band Wagon*.

Mary Rodgers (1931–2014) was the daughter of musical theatre composer Richard Rodgers and the mother of musical theatre composer Adam Guettel. Rodgers was a composer in her own right, creating music for *Once Upon a Mattress*, *The Mad Show*, and *Free to Be... You and Me*. In 2022, a riveting memoir came out about her life: *Shy: The Alarmingly Outspoken Memoirs of Mary Rodgers* (Rodgers and Green) and is an intimate look into her professional and personal life, during a robust era of musical theatre history and development. Rodgers wrote songs for Golden Records, penned the novel *Freaky Friday*, and served as a philanthropist for many years in New York.

Lucy Simon (1940–2022) was a composer famous for *The Secret Garden* (1991), *Doctor Zhivago* (2011), and popular music.

Carolyn Leigh (1926–1983) was a lyricist for Broadway shows and films, best known for her lyrics in *Peter Pan*, *How Now Dow Jones*, and *Smile*.

Lynn Ahrens (b. 1948) is a lyricist and librettist for musical theatre, television, and film, known for her collaboration with composer Stephen Flaherty and their many influential and successful Broadway musicals. These hits include: *Ragtime, A Man of No Importance, Suessical, Dessa Rose, Anastasia, and Once on This Island*. Ahrens also penned many songs for the famous television series *Schoolhouse Rock!*

Jeanine Tesori (b. 1961) is a prolific and respected Tony-award-winning composer of Broadway musicals with multiple hit shows and Tony-award nominations. Her hits include *Thoroughly Modern Millie*, *Fun Home*, *Shrek*, *Violet*, *Kimberly Akimbo*, and *Caroline, or Change*.

Marsha Norman (b. 1947) is a playwright who has penned books for hit musicals that include *The Color Purple*, *The Secret Garden*, and *The Bridges of Madison County*.

Brenda Russell is a singer–songwriter, producer, and musician famous in the musical theatre world for co-writing music and lyrics for *The Color Purple* (2005).

Irene Sankoff collaborated on the book, lyrics, and music for *Come from Away* (2017).

Barbara Anselmi wrote the music for *It Shoulda Been You* (2011) and also works as a Broadway music director.

Sara Bareilles penned the music to *Waitress* (2016) and also enjoys a successful career as a pop singer–songwriter and performer.

Lisa Lambert collaborated with Greg Morrison on the music and lyrics for *The Drowsy Chaperone* (Broadway, 2006).

Carol Hall (1936–2018) was a composer and lyricist, best known for her work on *The Best Little Whorehouse in Texas*.

Kirsten Childs is a librettist and playwright known for *The Bubbly Black Girl Sheds her Chameleon Skin, Funked up Fairy Tales,* and *Miracle Brothers*. She is also a writer for the Sesame (Street) Workshop.

Masi Asare is a composer, lyricist, and book writer, most recently known for her work on the lyrics for *Paradise Square* (2022).

Micki Grant (1929–2021) wrote lyrics for fourteen Broadway shows, including *Don't Bother me I Can't Cope* (1971).

Nell Benjamin has written lyrics for Broadway hits *Legally Blonde* and *Mean Girls*.

Amanda Green has written lyrics for shows such as *Bring It On, Hands on a Hardbody, High Fidelity,* and *Mr. Saturday Night*.

Lisa Kron penned the Tony-award-winning book *Fun Home* (2015) along with many successful plays.

Marcy Heisler is a lyricist who works with Interviewee Zina Goldrich on full-length musicals and cabaret songs. Hits include *Ever After, Dear Edwina,* and *Junie B. Jones*.

Kait Kerrigan is the lyricist of the duo Kerrigan & Lowdermilk, having written lyrics to *The Unauthorized Autobiography of Samantha Brown* and a number of successful musical theatre albums.

Patricia Resnick – Librettist for *9 to 5* (2009).

Heather Hach – Librettist for *Legally Blonde* (2007).

Katori Hall – Librettist for *Tina: The Tina Turner Musical* (2019).

Tina Fey – Librettist for *Mean Girls* (2018).

Jennifer Lee – Librettist for *Frozen* (musical, 2018) and a screenwriter for *Frozen* (film) and *Frozen 2* (film).

Quiara Alegría Hudes – Librettist for *In the Heights* (2008) and playwright.

Winnie Holzman – Librettist for *Wicked* (2003) and screenwriter.

Catherine Johnson – Librettist for *Mamma Mia* (West End, 1999).

INTERVIEWS

Kristen Anderson-Lopez
Zina Goldrich
Georgia Stitt
Kate Anderson & Elyssa Samsel

Kristen Anderson-Lopez Biography

KRISTEN ANDERSON-LOPEZ is an Oscar and Grammy award-winning songwriter. She is the co-writer of *Frozen* on Broadway as well as the Disney's *Frozen* (Oscar and Grammy wins), *Frozen 2*, and "Remember Me" from Pixar's *Coco* (Oscar win). She is also the co-writer of In Transit, the first-ever all a cappella musical on Broadway, *Finding Nemo the Musical*, running at Disney World since 2006, Disney's *Winnie the Pooh*, and Emmy-nominated songs for TV's 87th Academy Awards and *The Comedians*. A recipient of the BMI Harrington Award and the 2014 Lilly Award, Anderson-Lopez serves on the Council for the Dramatists Guild and on the Advisory Board for the Brooklyn Children's Theatre. She resides in Brooklyn with her husband and two daughters.[2]

Interview with Kristen Anderson-Lopez, December 13, 2022 via Zoom[3]

MORGAN: Kristen Anderson-Lopez. One of the most important and prolific lyricists in our current day, currently working. You're doing some amazing work.

ANDERSON-LOPEZ: Thank you.

MORGAN: I really appreciate female-identifying lyricists because of the stories that they're able to tell and the firsthand perspective. I was really drawn to the work of Betty Comden growing up. As a youngster, I was a lover of Sondheim and deeper, more contemporary works, so I wasn't that connected to Golden Age material except for the work of Betty Comden, and I didn't know why [as a kid]. As I got older, I realized it was because those lyrics and stories were being influenced and written by a woman. I also appreciate that your work is so rooted in family relationships and that some of the work even passes The Bechdel Test![4] I've also really enjoyed watching your other interviews and the way that you put story at the front of your writing. It's really beautiful and authentic.

ANDERSON-LOPEZ: Thank you. I appreciate it. I don't know how pop singers just sit down and write something because, for me, all inspiration comes from story and the heat that comes from how I resonate emotionally with that story. I really can't separate my work from story. It has to be about how the character is reacting within that story and the drama that drives not only the words you're going to pick, but the tempo, the energy of the music, and the key of the music. For me to create, I have to know what function I'm serving before I write the form.

MORGAN: Yes; the container. Otherwise, it's truly a blank page. At that point, we are writing songs about feelings. I try to analyze that with my students. What's the difference between a composer and a songwriter? I think it's the breadth of what you're doing. I think it's the timeline or the breadth of the piece. Also, when someone's writing a stand-alone song in a pop context, I think emotion gets privileged over story a little bit. If you're listening to "Someone Like You" by Adele, the story line is "we broke up." However, the emotion gets unpacked in an aria that puts emotion over story.

ANDERSON-LOPEZ: Totally. A pop song has the permission to swim around in repetition and rhythm; you can only say the same thing over and over again in a stage piece before you're going to get the audience squirming and coughing. You must forward the story.

MORGAN: Only Hansen gets away with a song literally called "MMM-Bop" that makes very little sense. It's gibberish that made millions of dollars!

Tell me a little bit about your upbringing and your journey from childhood to where you are now in your career.

ANDERSON-LOPEZ: I spent the first fourteen years of my life in Westchester, and we had a next-door neighbor who babysat for me who happened to be in the high school play… I think it was *Shenandoah* (1974). When I was two (years old) they brought me down to watch them rehearse. For some reason, they were on a football field rehearsing. I remember my eyes opening and falling in love with the idea of pretending and being a character and singing and telling a story, really early. I loved anything where somebody sang and told a story. I was obsessed. I think my first Broadway show that I got to see was *Annie* (1976) or *Peter Pan* (1954) – they were both running right around the same time. After that, I would ask to see a Broadway show for every birthday and Christmas. At the same time, I lived in a neighborhood where three houses all shared the same big backyard space with few fences. What that meant was: I had my own company. This was before kids were overscheduled all the time. During the summer, you could send the kids out to play with each other and come home for lunch and dinner. So, I had my own theater company that I'd say, "What are we putting on today?" We had a patio that was a perfect theatrical space off the side of my house, which had a staircase for entrances, exits, and costume changes. I would like write, direct, and make up a play once a week; and star in it. You'd think that would have pointed out that I'm

	a director or writer, but I downloaded this narrative that I liked theater so I'm an actress. Very early, I got a little obsessed with the idea that I had to be a Broadway actress, and I wrote papers about being a Broadway actress. Around that time, I saw *My Fair Lady* (1956) at some community theater; in the fourth grade. My mom took me to see it on a Friday, and by Monday I had written my own version of *My Fair Lady*.
MORGAN:	Perhaps one where she *leaves*!?
ANDERSON-LOPEZ:	Yes, she does. She leaves. She goes and teaches the Cockney children how to speak proper English; right back to the neighborhood. Pay it forward!
MORGAN:	Bartlett [Sher] stole from *you*[5]!
ANDERSON-LOPEZ:	I also wrote a whole scene of Eliza as a child in class, sort of replicating dynamics I'd seen in my own classroom. Bobby wants me to do a 54 Below show called *Eliza, You Dingaling!* where we just really just put on my fourth-grade version. My friend happened to hold on to the script and I have it; which would be so fun. I rewrote *My Fair Lady* and my fourth-grade teacher was my first producer: Mrs. Priscilla Leibowitz. She actually cleared time during the whole spring semester, and she got the music department to teach us all the music, and she got the art department to help us do all the costumes. We put it on for the school with the fourth and fifth grade. It was = the 1980s, so it was an open classroom, and we had a blended fourth and fifth-grade class. So, there were probably about sixty kids that we put it on with. I look back at that experience and realize that I was always a maker. I was always going to have a passion to build the thing probably more than I like acting in the thing.
MORGAN:	Do you think part of that assumption to be an actor was based in not seeing the other pathways?
ANDERSON-LOPEZ:	Yeah. I have a whole schtick where I talk about how all the cast albums just had photos of old men hanging around a piano, looking really worried and grumpy, smoking cigarettes. On all the old cast albums, that guy looks like my grandpa, and he's pissed. I'd watch the Tonys every year, and there weren't a whole lot of women up there unless they were winning for acting. Interestingly enough, my dad really should have been a songwriter. This genetic mutation that exists in our family, and it comes from my dad.

MORGAN: Right. You *and* your sister [Kate Anderson]. Kate talked mostly about you as her inspiration.

ANDERSON-LOPEZ: Well, my sisters weren't born until I was fifteen, so my dad is mine. My dad always made parodies of when my friends would call. One of my best friends was named Maria. He'd always sing, "Maria. I just got a call from Maria. She wants to go and skate…." [to the tune of "Maria" from *West Side Story*] or whatever. He spontaneously makes parodies! He gets inspired and sends them – even to this day – to the whole group chat.

MORGAN: That's adorable.

ANDERSON-LOPEZ: He's always writing parodies. I mean, there's my sister Kate, *and* my sister Lindsay [Kate's twin] who is also a lyricist and climbing the ladder. We all have the mutation where we want to put words on music. Lynn Ahrens is the one who said she once heard that it might be a form of OCD, which tracks. We hear the chaos that is music, and we want to pin it down to something we can control through language. We want to take it, label it, and define it in some way so that we can understand it better.

MORGAN: So, you were performing in high school…?

ANDERSON-LOPEZ: Right. I did commercials for a brief second in the 1980s, right before my parents moved from New York to North Carolina. I did a lot of musicals in North Carolina.

MORGAN: Did that make you sad to move away from New York City, since you wanted to be a performer?

ANDERSON-LOPEZ: Oh, one of the heartbreaks of my life was moving away from New York. Although I think it built a lot of resilience in me, I think that my life might have been a little different. I might not have been tough enough to handle show business if I hadn't had to survive the move to North Carolina. My parents had twins and we moved from the bluest state to a rather red state, and we all had to navigate that.

MORGAN: I understand. I've lived in Mississippi… Charleston, South Carolina… I currently live in Georgia… and I'm from San Diego. It's a thing. I understand.

ANDERSON-LOPEZ: Right? Beautiful landscapes… kind people… sometimes just different vibes. I had to learn how to navigate being a big creative girl in a place I was supposed to be small and blonde.

MORGAN: You know, Mary-Mitchell Campbell is from North Carolina. So is Beth Leavel, I think. There's a bunch of Broadway ladies from North Carolina.

ANDERSON-LOPEZ: Lauren Kennedy. There's a whole bunch of us. Though, I really consider myself "half New Yorker, half North Carolinian."

MORGAN: I moved to Florida when I was fifteen but when people ask where I'm from, I say California. That was my childhood, really.

ANDERSON-LOPEZ: Right. You're already built. The architecture's there already.

So, I have to tell you that I did all the "Jesus musicals" in high school. I did *Godspell* three times. I did *Jesus Christ Superstar* (1971) … and I did *Joseph* [*and the Amazing Technicolor Dreamcoat*] twice. North Carolina was the land of Jesus musicals. Then I went to Williams [College] and I majored in theatre and psychology because my parents insisted that I get something to fall back on. I'm actually glad they did because I use my psychology degree all the time.

MORGAN: I'm sure. When my students want to double major, I encourage them to consider psychology, sociology, marketing, business, or another language.

ANDERSON-LOPEZ: Yes, that's good advice! I graduated from college and came to New York to start auditioning. I discovered that while I learned a lot in college – I could write a great paper on Pinter versus Beckett, and I could collaborate with very bright people on a devised piece – that I was not prepared to walk into an open call and get a job acting. It's just not what the theater major at Williams College in the nineties was training us to do – they were training us to think critically about what, how and why we create – which has been hugely helpful in my career – but not when I was auditioning for *Oklahoma* at a LORT theatre. I did get a job at the Jupiter Theater in Florida. I was like basically an indentured servant. I was in the Apprentice program from 1994 to 1995. They did thirteen shows, six children's shows… I did a lot of theatre. We lived right on the beach and some of us had a lot of sex. We also almost burned down the entire theater during a kids' show of *Jack and the Beanstalk*.

MORGAN: Yes! I did my apprenticeship at Seaside Music Theater in Daytona. That kind of experience grows one up fast into a … well-rounded human.

Were you able to write at all? When I did an apprenticeship, they used me to write a musical for them while my peers were doing office work or teaching. It was wild but a good experience.

ANDERSON-LOPEZ:	That *is* wild. I didn't get to do that. Nobody was trying to do anything original down there, but we would rewrite all the lyrics backstage – parodies and stuff – and there was a parody show at the end of the year that a bunch of us created and performed. One thing I did was: for every person's birthday, I would write a poem… like a roast poem that was for each person. So, there were like forty different roast poems I wrote over the course of that summer. They were just rhymes because I had not realized I was a songwriter yet. I'm going to skip through all the years that I was a temp and did a lot of shows where I played a nun in New Hampshire. You know… *Nunsense… Nunsense Two… The Sound of Music…*
MORGAN:	This is hilarious. What is it with you and all the religious stuff? You did all of the Jesus shows in high school and then all the nun shows as an adult? What's happening?
ANDERSON-LOPEZ:	I wasn't a good archetype, really.
MORGAN:	Oh, me neither. There was no pathway for women who weren't who were in their twenties but weren't ingenues.
ANDERSON-LOPEZ:	Right. Yeah. I could be funny and I could read music and hold harmonies really well; I had been in a capella groups and stuff. So, the nuns in *The Sound of Music* were holding it down with the liturgical music. In *Nunsense Two*, if you play Sister Robert Anne, you get to basically write your own script. It'll say, "insert joke about car here." So, I was still doing parodies and stuff and I came back and I did a cabaret to try and get an agent or something and I re-wrote "Opening Doors."
MORGAN:	From *Merrily We Roll Along* (1981)?
ANDERSON-LOPEZ:	Yep. Jeff Hardy was our pianist, and he had been through BMI.[6] He said, "You're a lyricist." I said, "What do I do with that?" Later, I was in the original production *Urinetown* and Mark Hollman, who wrote that, also told me I was a lyricist. I was hearing from other people that I was a lyricist. I was at my temp job and wrote three [sets of] lyrics in order to audition for BMI in August, and I had like a week to do it. So, my first one was about auditioning for *Cats* (1981) called "Allergic to Cats." My second one was about whether it was worth it to shave my legs for an audition. The third one was about taking a quiz in Cosmo magazine and realizing that you were in a terrible relationship and you had to break up with them. Luckily, Lynn Ahrens was at the table that day because I was

singing these things to a bunch of older men who I could tell were perplexed. Lynn asked to hear my third piece, and I got into BMI. The first song I did for BMI, the sky opened, and it was "THIS is what you're supposed to do!" Even though it wasn't the best song – it was called "How to Say Goodbye to Randall High" – and it was a "sad hello/happy goodbye" song. It was from a smart, not very popular valedictorian who hated her high school and was telling everyone of her fellow students to f*&k off. It was a life-changing moment for me to realize that if I put myself on paper and I just tell my truth, and I work with someone who can set it to music, I can connect with people. It felt amazingly good.

MORGAN: Did you receive responses to that song right away that also influenced that feeling, or were you so self-secure that you knew it when you heard it?

ANDERSON-LOPEZ: I sure was not self-secure. I mean, there was nothing more terrifying in those days, that first year of BMI. It felt so raw and so vulnerable to put myself out there, especially at age twenty-seven. I hadn't studied to be a writer. But by that point, the alternative was worse than the risk that it took. Temping for people who are starting to get younger than you; like, temping in an investment bank when suddenly the associates and the analysts are right out of school and you're there floundering. The days just ticked by so painfully and you had no idea what your future was going to be. That was far worse than the risk of putting myself out there trying to move forward. That was a big part of it. The other part is, I think I was incredibly lucky in that Skip Kennon [composer, lyricist] was my BMI teacher. He was a wonderful first-year BMI teacher because he is so sensitive. He was really committed to creating a safe space for everyone. There were rules in place not allowing folx to comment on songs unless they were presenting. You weren't allowed to try and write your own show; you have to comment on what *they've* done. He was really good about boundaries around how we speak to people. I was really lucky that, in this moment where I finally was learning how to create, I was in a space that took the beginner's mind of the first year very seriously. I'll always be grateful to Skip Kennon for that. At the end of that year, we had to do a ten-minute musical. During

	that year, I had met James-Allen Ford [composer], who I ended up writing *In Transit* (Off-Broadway 2010/ Broadway 2016) with. He was the first person I met at BMI. We founded an a cappella group that Christmas.
MORGAN:	I have a little bit of experience with contemporary a cappella. It was a big thing at my college, and I went to a few conferences. There's some great material out there.
ANDERSON-LOPEZ:	It's a great way to have a community and find your "found family." It's helpful to have, essentially, the equivalent of a repertory company. What I ended up doing was using that acapella group to do my ten-minute musical, which was *Oedipus Acapella*. It was a ten-minute, postmodern re-telling of *Oedipus [Rex]*. A significant and critical moment that happened that year is that I had broken up with the apprentice from Jupiter… and I was single… and then I met Robert Lopez. It was the first night he and Jeff Marx presented the first song from *Avenue Q* (2003). He had been bitten by a dog. Usually he was at the piano, but he couldn't play the piano. His hand had stitches in it, so he ended up playing Kate Monster.
MORGAN:	In her octave?
ANDERSON-LOPEZ:	Yeah! He's a tenor; he could do it. So, the night I met him, there were instant sparks and I'm like, "I'm going to marry this person." Keep in mind, we had graduated into a time when the pendulum had swung from big, earnest mega musicals. People kind of hated musicals and we had to figure out how to take our love of story and penetrate this culture where irony and critical detachment was king. I was so much a product of the acapella worlds in high school and college; I had never seen an acapella musical before. And I sort of played on the idea that a cappella was the cheesiest form of music you could make – but pushed it to the ridiculous (and therefore ironic) by having a dorky a cappella group perform a Greek tragedy in a post-modern 10-minute form. That actually got me my first job at Theatreworks USA [producing company based out of New York specializing in Theatre for Young Audiences],[7] where we used the a capella model and took four literary works, usually taught in secondary schools, and put them in to a contemporary a capella group in a high school situation.

MORGAN: I learned huge amounts from that experience, like how stressed you get during rehearsals and the manic thing of being in production [while writing], which is a psychology game. I had to learn how to play, work, write, and when to sleep.

MORGAN: Right? I've served on music teams of original musicals… and most people don't understand that when you're a writer, you have to be *in* rehearsal to hear things and to take notes; but then you have to go home and do the work overnight to get things back the next day. Now, we have Dropbox and stuff, but I can't imagine doing all that by hand. It's very sleepless. Then, how do you produce with full creative juices on very little sleep.

ANDERSON-LOPEZ: You need to see it in front of a bunch of kids. There's nothing more brutal than being in a cafetorium of kids. That ballad you put in the last third of the piece is just not going to work because [the kids are] talking and squirming. Oh my.

MORGAN: Yep. Oh my God.

ANDERSON-LOPEZ: You've got to rewrite it tonight and try it in the show tomorrow. It was the same process I've had to face Off-Broadway or on Broadway. You have to power through.

MORGAN: What is that writing process like for you and Robert? Sounds like you call him Bobby.

ANDERSON-LOPEZ: He's Bobby. Robert is for people who don't know him. What is the process like for us? It's so great because we have such seamless communication and trust. Huge trust has to be there. But it can get brutal if things are going badly and you're really stressed. You never leave your job. You never get to go home and blow off steam with someone who has different perspective or to leave it. Like this summer, after 16-hour days on our original musical for Hulu, we started pretending we were going home to other spouses. We would take turns trying to be the spouse that had a normal job and wasn't caught in the vortex of creating TV. The pace and relentlessness of TV production was really hard on us. I think it'll be different if we have to do it again. This was one where we were executive producing and wrote every song and helped create the whole show, so it never stopped. We enjoyed our glass of wine at the end of the day.

MORGAN: That'll get you *great* lyrics! Do you get into the same room to write, or do you need your space? Kate

[Andrson] and Elyssa [Samsel] were talking about how they start with a hook, they expand, and then they're able to work apart a little bit. It's a different working relationship, obviously. Where do you start?

ANDERSON-LOPEZ: Well, we always start in stories; we start in talking about the characters, talking about tempo, and talking about how we could approach it. Even color... I'm really visual. I'll say "I think this is more of a primary colors thing..." or we will talk about energy... talk about the psychology... how to improve the inner monologue of the character. On one level, it is playing pretend with your best friend and then your best friend just happens to be an incredible Broadway composer who can sit at the piano and start riffing with you, like doing an improv musical. At a certain point over the years, we've found probably 99% of our songs start with those conversations. Then often I'll go off on my own. I like to write in bed, lying down, where I can just sort of not feel like I'm working, but feel like I'm napping or relaxing.

MORGAN: Do you just use voice memo or voice dictation?

ANDERSON-LOPEZ: No, no. I'll take a yellow pad and a pen. I've started to use an iPad – still getting used to that. What's nice about that is that I can hold on to those notes and always go back to them because I have yellow pads and scraps of paper everywhere from things that I've written. I'll usually start and just get somewhere; just throw some spaghetti at the wall, so we have some kind of foothold. I'm a starter and Bobby is a finisher. One of the strengths is that I can live with the unknowing and live with the imperfect. I am okay with: if all we get out of it is a riff or rhythm, I don't mind. I'll keep writing to find it. Bobby likes to have more certainty before starting. Bobby wants to know what it is because...

MORGAN: He's a musician! It's called the perfect authentic cadence for a reason. Musicians are trained to really feel resolution or resolve a phrase. When we have dissonance, it should eventually resolve. Or, if it's unresolved, it has to be for a reason. I can understand it since I do both. If I'm working on the music aspect, I really feel like I have to know something in order to record it. I'll feel better if I know what that chord structure is going to be. With lyrics, I can absolutely be flexible and keep working until I find it. We'll figure it out as long as the structure is there.

ANDERSON-LOPEZ: Bobby and I benefit from our different approaches for sure. At the end of the songwriting process, after we've recorded it and mixed it… that's when I never want to hear the song again. I'm bored of it, and I just can't iterate over and over again. I can't invest my energies in listening to the tiny differences in a mix or a mastering process. Bobby can really sweat the details on it at a time that I run out of endurance, which is really great that we've discovered that. I like to generate, and, among other incredible strengths, Bobby is great at pushing until the end for perfection.

MORGAN: Do you like to cook or bake? Do you like gardening?

ANDERSON-LOPEZ: He likes to bake, he's a perfectionist about making pizza. I'm not a great cook, but I don't mind cooking. I like to put together spaces, I like to dream about and research real estate and places we could live; and I like to plan experiences for my family.

MORGAN: Who are the writers that really inspire you or have inspired you?

ANDERSON-LOPEZ: Sondheim. Everyone says Sondheim but I *did* go to Williams and every year my car-ride to Williams was Sondheim-heavy. I would always, make it a ritual thinking, "I'm going to the place that inspired Sondheim." If I had to guess, the writer that used a similar approach to how I approach things is Howard Ashman.[8] From what I know about Howard Ashman, he was all about story and really liked to approach the musical architecture of the story as a whole. I really think like an architect when I'm attacking songs… I'm plotting and want to make sure that the first song is in dialogue with the last song, which should be in dialogue with all the major tentpoles holding up the circus tent of the story.

MORGAN: Do you work on things visually in that way? Do you do post-its and big whiteboards and stuff like that?

ANDERSON-LOPEZ: Yeah. I also have this weird, multidimensional chart that I make. I'll make a table in [Microsoft] Word where I'll put the hook and then I'll put a theme… motifs… I do like the old school Gen-X table. Columns… rows…

MORGAN: I can hear that in your work. I recently went back and watched *Frozen 2*. My mom passed away when I was a little girl, so *Frozen 2* gets to me.

ANDERSON-LOPEZ: Bobby's mom died in 2017. It was definitely informed by the loss of a beloved mom.

MORGAN: That beautiful theme that the Norwegian singer sings out of the forest... and the themes throughout both movies really connect. You all are really adept at bringing things back and connecting all of the metaphors. It does speak to the qualities of the Disney Renaissance.[9] The work of Alan Menken, Howard Ashman, and Elton John and all those guys was so impactful. There's a lull in success of the material of Disney movie musicals... but then... *Frozen*! *Frozen* felt like a revival. I think about trends, and if *Frozen* had come out five years earlier or five years later, would it have been as successful? Xennials like me were in elementary school when the Disney Renaissance happened; then, we were in our mid-twenties when *Frozen* came out and we were ready to buy things as consumers. A lot of my generation really loves *Frozen* because it felt like the Disney Renaissance movies in terms of quality, comprehensiveness, thoroughness, depth of story, and emotional connections.

ANDERSON-LOPEZ: Thank you. I'm fascinated by the fact that culturally, we were at this tipping point where the Gen-Xers were having kids. We learned to *not* digest the princess myth and the idea that true love is a handsome prince who is going to kiss you and solve everything. I was raising my own kids and dealing with the problem of my two girls loving to wear Cinderella and Snow-White costumes. The success of *Frozen* may be related to the difference in who was telling the story. There were two women at the table whose voices really mattered – mine and Jennifer Lee [screenwriter]. We were empowered by John Lasseter.[10] He told us to drive this story, which was just fate and luck. I was ready for it because I had been doing it through my own work a lot and I had been a secret voice at the table through a lot of Bobby's work. If you talk to any married couple, they're weighing in on each other's work. If I wasn't at the table, I was certainly a private consultant as Bobby navigated some high-pressure career moments. I learned a lot through that, so I was ready for it at the time that the table became available. It was a big, big deal that Jenn was there, too. There was a difference between being the *only* woman at the table, and being able to speak up and say, "That's not my experience. She wouldn't want to kill your sister over a man if there aren't deeper wounds." It *seemed*

	easiest to solve plot problems by having them both be in love with Hans or whatever. But we kept saying, "No, that's not what this is…"
MORGAN:	That was an option?!
ANDERSON-LOPEZ:	It would often be brought up when we were trying to solve plot problems, because the thing about these musicals is that they aren't written. It's not like you show up as a songwriter and it's like all the songs are slotted for you. They're ideas…
MORGAN:	As crisis points…
ANDERSON-LOPEZ:	When we showed up, there was an ending and the story had two sisters, but everything else was totally different than how it ended up. It's just how it works at Disney Animation. We had to work and build it and *rebuild* it every three months. It's like you are building a Lego city in a gymnasium for three months and then, after three months, you invite people you really care about and trust them. They come and smash everything that doesn't work with a baseball bat. It's really the best metaphor I can give to understand the intensity and huge amount of work that goes into the iterations of each musical movie. It takes like six versions… all of which have been storyboarded. Songs that have been written get thrown on the floor. It's brutal. It's not for the weak.
MORGAN:	Not for the weak! When did the story for *Frozen 2* come to light? Was that a part of thinking about the first one? The Harry Potter movies were made knowing this seven-part saga and all this background. Was it later on you had to dig back in, after the success of *Frozen*?
ANDERSON-LOPEZ:	It was really scary to have to live up to the success of *Frozen*. We really all promised ourselves that we were not going to look at it like that. We had to all find the heat of what our characters needed next. I figured out how I wanted to approach the sequel by discovering that the original purpose of *Frozen* was opening the lens of true love. Its purpose was to expand the power of true love to familial relationships. True love was in the form of the sister who was going to be there for her loved one paralyzed in crisis and shame. True love is a version of compassion for people who care. *Then*, I think we found footing with *Frozen 2* when we figured out that there was unfinished business for Elsa. Elsa building ice rinks back at Arendelle didn't feel like the right happy ending

for her. That was where we began. Is Kristoff really happy in the castle? Is Elsa really happy being an ice decorator? We talked about the whole idea of true love as our kids were getting older. Jenn and Bobby and I have kids around the same age. Once we addressed how family can be true love, we realized that there's also this version of love in the form of an individual finding their purpose and place in the world. Once it was about that, then I knew what could fuel our songs. I really believe it very, very strongly that in order to truly be happy and find peace, you need to be engaged with and find self-love in your purpose and place in the world.

MORGAN: Right? A love of self… maybe love of God or the universe. Trust? It's a trust thing and a faith thing, too. Why am I here? What am I doing? Deep stuff.

ANDERSON-LOPEZ: Right. We knew that we were going to look at that. Jenn also is a brilliant, prolific generator, so some tossed ideas around like going into the forest… going into the woods… going into the unknown… testing your love….

MORGAN: I'm so sorry to interrupt, but I *love* "Into the Unknown." It's so singable. You're really great at writing considerate vowels for singers. You set your lyrics in a way that is considerate of where the note is in the singer's range, using "call vowels"[11] when appropriate. As a vocal technician, I think the placement of some of those notes are so singable. Do you think about that? Is it because you're a singer? So, you sing it and can figure out what works, hurts, etc.?

ANDERSON-LOPEZ: Yeah. I think it's because we do all our demos. Bobby and I sing every one of our demos. It's a vital part of our process beyond just writing the song and polishing it. There's a part of the process where we sit around the piano, singing the verses, choruses, and bridges before we ever get to a computer. When we get to a computer, we're also rewriting and changing things up when they don't feel good. I have a pretty big [singing] range and over the years I've learned to take my mix pretty high, so that's perhaps why we can be known to let the emotion of a song lead to some serious "screlts."[12] We're trying to get a little more mindful around voice parts in our most recent project. We were trying to write a little less rangy. With Idina [Menzel, original voice of Elsa] we always knew who we were writing for. If you know

MORGAN:	their range, *use* their range; but, when you don't know who is going to be singing your parts, we have to be a little more cautious around range. Bobby has his tricks. How about "Remember Me"? [song from the 2017 feature film *Coco*, written by Anderson-Lopez and Lopez]. It's sung by a guy. Gosh, what a beautiful song.
ANDERSON-LOPEZ:	We wrote "Remember Me" shortly after we wrote "Let It Go." We were working on *Coco* for a while. We had this job with Pixar, and they asked this question of: "Do you know of any songs in which their meaning changes? It can be the exact same song but the meaning changes based on arrangement." We thought about "It's a Small World." If you've ever heard the original, it was written as this beautiful prayer for peace that's almost like a hymn written by someone who had fought in World War II. If you think about the lyrics… "It's a world of laughter" … it's a world of someone who had seen the world fall apart and who goes on to sing that it's a small world, after all. It's this beautiful thing that gives you chills when you hear it that way. Then, you go on the ride…
MORGAN:	…and it's a nightmare. It's a literal fever dream. Terrifying.
ANDERSON-LOPEZ:	We were inspired by that. We used to live in a loft of an old clock factory, and our piano was in our kitchen. Bobby was in his boxers cooking breakfast, and then ran over to the piano and was just noodling and played this tune. I recorded it into my phone. I had to go to a rehearsal for *In Transit*. I got onto the F-train and totally channeled what I was feeling as a mother. I was having to travel so much. We would actually write little lullabies that [our kids] could sing when we had to travel. We had all of these little quirky lullabies that they could sing at bedtime with Aunt Kate or Aunt Lindsay, and it'll be like we're there. So, I just channeled that into "Remember Me."
MORGAN:	Oh God, you're going to make me cry on Zoom! Do your kids like to write music?
ANDERSON-LOPEZ:	Yeah. Our daughter Katie is turning into an incredible composer. She writes cool singer–songwriter pop lyrics that are really good, and she can do both. She's obsessed with music theory right now. Our daughter, Annie, is younger and super musical too. She's a creator and wrote a little parody the other night. She is also writing little weird songs, too.

MORGAN: How have you juggled this whole parenting thing through this career? Can you also talk about your own self-care and your own boundaries?

ANDERSON-LOPEZ: I think one of the things that really worked for us and for me is that at a certain point, Bobby and I realized juggling multiple projects was really stressful; for us to have two careers in that way. We were both up for the same award season – I was doing *In Transit* off-Broadway and he was up for *Book of Mormon* (2011), which was obviously going to win. There was a moment in time we realized that we had to put raising our children first in our list of priorities. What really helped make that a reality is combining our careers, so we only were juggling one schedule rather than two competing schedules. It was a really painful time before we did that. Having to decide what to do when our youngest had the chickenpox, our nanny has not had chickenpox... I've got the first rehearsals for *In Transit* off-Broadway, but Bobby was in a workshop for *The Book of Mormon*. Whose career is more important?

MORGAN: Gosh, that's hard.

ANDERSON-LOPEZ: Who's staying home and who gets to be where they need to be? If we kept having to have those conversations, I don't know that we would've been able to stay together because it was just too painful and full of lots of tough questions. Why do people take a risk on male writers when women writers have to prove themselves first? How do you prove yourself if everyone is taking the risk on the male writers? It's statistically shown that they'll give male writers the benefit of the doubt because of unconscious bias, but that women have a track record. Bobby was a little bit ahead of me, so how was I ever going to get anywhere while always making the family sacrifices? We decided to combine forces. To my husband's credit, he very easily could have turned *Avenue Q* into a TV show and worked on that for the rest of his career or gone to work with the *South Park* [Trey Parker and Matt Stone] guys for the rest of his career. But Bobby continues to keep reinventing himself. We could have maybe moved to California and joined forces with a studio? Who knows? But in reinventing and exploring new mediums every couple of years, we keep things fresh, and we also keep our children at the

MORGAN: center of that. We sit down and say, "Okay, we did that. Now what can we do that's also going to be sustainable for our family?" As the kids grow, we can commit to dipping our toes into situations that are less family-friendly (ahem TV.) We have four more years where we've got a child under our roof. Then, it'll be an interesting moment of, "Now what do we do?"

MORGAN: I think it's really beautiful that you found a way to put your priorities at the core of what you're doing in a way that works.

ANDERSON-LOPEZ: Yeah, I appreciate that. To somebody female-identifying reading this book: I definitely had a moment where I was terrified to get married to another composer. Especially a composer who had already gotten a firm toehold [in the industry]. I was so terrified of what that would mean, and the way people would see me. I didn't want them to think that I was just there because I married him. I was also terrified to have children and what that would mean to my career. However, in both cases I just grew as a person and had more to write about! Falling in love and choosing to share your life with someone gives you so much to say about love and relationships. *Then*, choosing to raise a human being and learning every step of their development and thinking about what a human is in the world. What is the world you want to make for your humans? It fills with you so much and gives you so much to say, so you're not just writing musicals about your temp job…

MORGAN: Or your time in theatre school! The best way to become a well-rounded artist is to go hang out with people who don't do theatre. Go get some life experience so you can write about it and create art about it. That's a really wonderful lesson for all of the readers. I could talk to you for hours but thank you so much for your time!

ANDERSON-LOPEZ: Thanks for your great questions!

Zina Goldrich Biography

Zina Goldrich won the 2009 Fred Ebb Award for excellence in songwriting with longtime collaborator, Marcy Heisler. Their musical *Ever After* finished a sold-out run in 2018, and was the first production on the brand new Coca Cola Stage at the Alliance Theatre in Atlanta. They are also currently developing *Hollywood Romance*, a new musical with Emmy Award-winning writers Gabrielle Allan and

Jen Crittenden. Goldrich and Heisler's musical, *The Great American Mousical*, directed by Julie Andrews, premiered in 2012 at Goodspeed's Chester Theatre in Connecticut. Goldrich and Heisler's songs have been sung by many Broadway stars, including Audra McDonald, Kristin Chenoweth, Meghan Hilty and Alan Cumming. Ms. Goldrich composed music for *Dear Edwina* (Drama Desk Nomination) and *Junie B. Jones* (Lucille Lortel Nomination) which ran successfully Off-Broadway. "Snow White, Rose Red (and Fred)" (Helen Hayes Nomination) was commissioned by the Kennedy Center and is licensed by MTI. On television, Goldrich has composed for ABC's "The Middle," "Wonderpets," "Johnny and the Sprites," "Pooh's Learning Adventures," and "Peg + Cat" on PBS. She is the recipient of the ASCAP Richard Rodgers New Horizons Award, a Larson grant, and is a Seldes-Kanin Fellow. She has played keyboards on Broadway for *Avenue Q*, *Bombay Dreams*, *Oklahoma*, and *Titanic*, where she also conducted. www.marcyandzina.com

Interview with Zina Goldrich and Amanda Wansa Morgan, November 11, 2022 via Zoom[13]

MORGAN: Zina Goldrich! One of the wonderful lady composers who is currently writing in today's world, currently inspiring all the great stuff. I've been such a fan of yours since I saw *Dear Edwina* at Seaside Music Theater in the year 2001. I immediately found the sheet music to "Sing Your Own Song" and put it in my audition book. It was so darling. When I started to write musicals myself, I was very much inspired by the work of you and your writing partner, Marcy [Heisler]. I would characterize your music as light… bright… and with a jazzy swing to it. It's accessible, it's hummable, and it's authentic in being itself versus trying to imitate anybody else. I'll start with the compliments because this is exciting.

GOLDRICH: Thank you. All of those compliments are quite lovely.

MORGAN: Please tell me about your upbringing and your journey from childhood to where you are in your career. We can go up to the moment that you met Marcy, and then we can talk about your writing process together.

GOLDRICH: I grew up in Kings Point, which is in the North Shore of Long Island; a suburb of Manhattan. My dad's an obstetrician and my mom was a housewife at the time. My dad loved jazz; that was his thing. He moved to New York for his residency, met my mother, and then they had me and my older sister, who is an art lawyer. When my dad came to New York for his residency, he would go play a mid-day jazz gig on a Thursday or Friday, and some of the great jazz artists would come. At one of these gigs, Thad Jones of

"The Thad Jones/Mel Lewis Jazz Orchestra[14]" invited my dad to come play with them. My dad started to sit in with them, and he ended up playing with them for seven years every Monday night at the Village Vanguard.[15] So, I grew up with all these jazz musicians in the house: Billy Taylor, Grady Tate, Eddie Daniels, Ben Tucker, Jerome Richardson… they would have these jam sessions at our house on the weekends. That's where I learned about ear training and what groove feels like. I would go to the Village Vanguard with them I started to learn about form. What it really did for me was open up my ears.

MORGAN: Right? Because Western classical music training isn't going to teach you that until later semesters of theory, if at all.

GOLDRICH: Right. The groove is a very specific thing to me. Really good music has to be "in the pocket." That is to say, it has to be the absolute perfect tempo. I learned to feel where the pocket is, based on what I listened to when I was growing up.

MORGAN: I grew up with 1990s R&B and most people hire me in town for pop-rock musicals, because I play with groove. I grew up with Boyz II Men and my mom listened to Motown music. Then, I liked musical theatre and trained classically.

GOLDRICH: Same as me. I started studying music when I was three years old… Dalcroze Education.[16] It's theory and Eurythmics… the first half of it was feeling the rhythm in your body and transcription, ear training, and theory was taught at a very young age. My dad and I have perfect pitch and my kids have it too, actually. I started Dalcroze at age three and I started piano at age five. I was fortunate enough to have a really amazing piano teacher named Edith Wax. She constantly encouraged me to improvise. She would give me an exercise asking me to play "Twinkle, Twinkle, Little Star" like Bach, then like Mozart… Liszt… different composers. She was a wonderful teacher. If I had a great lesson, she would reward me by playing four-handed duets together.

MORGAN: I initially learned to play by ear at first and then I learned the basics from a Nintendo program called The Miracle Keyboard.[17]

GOLDRICH: Wow.

MORGAN: It was almost like those typing programs where like if you messed up, the little guy fell down – same thing with notes and chords. I learned scales on that program. You can watch videos about it on YouTube now where a guy sets it up. It came with a 66-keyboard that you plugged in like a controller into the *original* Nintendo. As I got older, it lived under my bed, and I would bring it out to listen to the radio and play along by ear. By the time I got to formal training, I was hungry to learn the "why" of the theory.

GOLDRICH: You were motivated. I learned to play by ear first. My teacher found me out because I'd ask her to play something first – so I could listen – then, I'd play the whole thing back by ear. She figured it out and wouldn't do that anymore, so I really had to learn how to read. It was painstaking, but it was worth it.

MORGAN: I never really did concert pianist classical stuff because it frustrated me if I couldn't get it as quickly as the pop or the musical theatre stuff. I just practiced on my own time. Over the years, it all became second nature. Now, I can look at a chord and my fingers know what to do. I practiced with discipline because I was motivated to get it right.

GOLDRICH: Same for me. When I got to New York and started to play piano for auditions or rehearsal, I realized that I needed to be a much better reader. There are some people who are machines. They can read anything, *and* they can play it by ear. Some people rely exclusively on the sheet music. I worked hard to do both well. As far as influences go, I grew up with classical training and jazz in the household, and I was listening to the radio… listening to pop and Motown, R&B, and everything. Some of my bigger influences back then were Stevie Wonder and Billy Joel and a lot of the singer songwriters, actually.

MORGAN: That makes sense because a lot of your songs feel like they're really coming from you. They have a feminine perspective and drive. I can tell that the songs in the songbook are from you, as opposed to writing from someone else's perspective, which is ingrained in the work of singer–songwriters, because it's all first-person perspective.

GOLDRICH: Thank you. Well, we really did start out by writing a lot of personal songs, a lot of songs from Marcy's diaries, some were from my experiences…

MORGAN: So, what or who was the inspiration for "I Want Them Bald?"[18]

GOLDRICH: Marcy had a boyfriend who was "follicly challenged." She loved it. We still do that song, and it kills every time. A lot of these ideas came from our younger years.

MORGAN: So, how did you get together with Marcy?

GOLDRICH: I met Marcy in the BMI workshop. I was working at Disney Feature Animation, and I came back to visit. We hit it off immediately. The BMI Workshop is also where I met Maury Yeston. He was a big mentor for me.

MORGAN: He writes beautiful music.

GOLDRICH: I love his music. Before I got to New York, we had taken a trip there and I had seen *Nine*.[19] I had the album, and I warped that thing. I just could not stop listening to it.

MORGAN: I got to stick conduct it as a concert last year. So much fun. He's a beast.

GOLDRICH: It's great stuff. So, I was in the BMI Workshop for a while, and I did not end up finding anybody to write with there. That's when I got my first job playing in [orchestra] pits – I got the world tour of *A Chorus Line*. I was the assistant conductor, working with Michael Kosarin.[20] I got to travel, see the world, play a show in an orchestra… actually, it was a band.

MORGAN: What do you think the difference between an orchestra and a band is?

GOLDRICH: I think of an orchestra as having strings.

MORGAN: So, *Spring Awakening*[21] has an orchestra, not a band?

GOLDRICH: You *could* say it's a "pit orchestra." For *A Chorus Line*, I think we had 12–14 people traveling in the band. I loved that job. I loved playing the show and seeing the world. I came back to the BMI Workshop, and I had not found my person, writing-wise. I told Maury that I didn't know what to do. I hadn't really found someone who I really connected with, and he said that I should write lyrics myself. I had been in that class long enough to know what a good lyric contained. So, I started to write a musical based on *Moonstruck*. I could not get the rights, but I tried to. One day, somebody from Disney came and I was playing some music that I wrote for *Moonstruck*. I got offered a job to write three songs for a *Mickey Mouse/Robin Hood* featurette. So, I spent some time in L.A. and wrote a few songs for them. Ultimately, they hired me as a staff songwriter. Just before that, I was working on *Grand Hotel* in the pit…

MORGAN: You did a lot of pit work, right?

GOLDRICH: My first Broadway show was *Grand Hotel*.[22] I had done an Off-Broadway show for Maury. When I came back from the *Chorus Line* tour, I needed to get work and I knew Maury's show was going up at Manhattan Theatre Club. One day after class, I came up to him and asked him if he needed any kind of help with his upcoming show. In my family, my mother always said, "If you don't ask; you don't get." To point out the obvious, there were not a lot of women in Broadway pits at the time, and if they were, they were usually string players. Maury was open to it and asked me to learn some songs and come back and play for him. I was very lucky because Maury's music really fit into my hands. There are also similarities, things that we both like harmonically… musically, we are kindred spirits.

MORGAN: Yes! For small hands, it's great because it's a lot of close patterns. Do you like playing Maltby & Shire with all that jazz music background?

GOLDRICH: Oh yeah, I like their songs. Everything fits. For some reason, the way Maury wrote his piano charts really fit for me. He brought me on, and I was his assistant for a show called *1-2-3-4-5* at Manhattan Theatre Club, with a book by Larry Gelbart,[23] who was one of the greatest comedy writers of the modern era. I played that show and conducted from the piano.

MORGAN: Had you worked with voices at that point? Did you have experience in that area? You sing too, right?

GOLDRICH: Yes. I performed a bit in high school. I actually went to high school with Tina Landau and Tina wrote a musical [in high school] and I played for it. At the time, I was studying performance and piano. I didn't know I was going to be a composer yet, but I was writing music. I wrote a song in sixth grade called "The American March," and I orchestrated it for my band. For a sixth grader, it was pretty advanced. I was very proud of that. By high school, I started writing songs with a friend's daughter who wrote lyrics.

MORGAN: So, when you got into that conductor chair, and eventually the music director chair, did you feel like you already had the whole set of skills? Music directing has its own set of skills.

GOLDRICH: Yes. It took me a while to realize it, but I had developed some while performing. When I got to New York, I was still performing. I went to an open call as an actor–singer. They were typing people out (they weren't letting everybody sing). There were fifty actors auditioning in the room, in a long line like in *A Chorus Line*. The casting person was walking down the line looking at everybody and everybody was just standing there, silent. They came up to me and I said "Hi!"

They looked at me oddly because I guess nobody had talked before that. If someone is looking me up and down, I'm the type of person who's going to say hi if you're looking at me!

MORGAN: Me too! What do we have to lose?

GOLDRICH: I had nothing to lose. They looked at me kind of funny, and then they asked for my resumé. All it had were credits from school. After that, everybody else down the rest of the line started saying hello after I broke the ice. But here's what I discovered that day. I looked around that room and I thought… I'm fairly certain I can sing better than most of the people in this room… I am an average actress and I'm an average dancer. I'm not going to get much work. If I look at the turning points in my life… I'm so grateful that I looked at myself with a critical eye and said: "I can write songs better than a lot of people. I'm not as good a performer as other people." Nobody really tells you what you should do with your life. I've spoken to a lot of colleagues who are women and they said that a lot of people told them that they can teach or play at the church. They were never supported in aiming for something different.

MORGAN: Writing partners Kate Anderson and Elyssa Samsel[24] were told that they should connect with a male writing partner in order to make it.

GOLDRICH: I'm grateful for everything that Marcy and I have written together because we really have a very specific voice and I put it up against anybody's writing. As I look back, I imagine that it would have been easier for both of us if either of us had a male partner; not based on talent or anything, just based on hiring practices and all that other stuff. Anyway, back to the journey. After writing for Disney for a year, I went to do the USC Film Scoring program.

MORGAN: So, you were a Disney *staff* writer?

GOLDRICH: That's when I was at feature animation. I was one of the last of the staff songwriters.

MORGAN: How did that job affect your creative juices? Do you like deadlines? Did it help you to have those kinds of guidelines like deadlines and specific topics?

GOLDRICH: I like having a certain kind of structure in my life. Usually, you were working up to a pitch. Instead of needing a certain song by a certain day, we had a deadline to show a pitch in a meeting in two weeks. I remember we worked on this Mickey Mouse/Robin Hood thing for almost six months, developing it. We finally pitched it to Jeffrey Katzenberg and he said, "I don't want to do Robin Hood." Well, there you go. Six months' worth of work. That's the development process!

MORGAN: So, it probably thickened your skin as a writer. It's easy to be precious.

GOLDRICH: Exactly. There were definitely interesting things. For the rest of the time there, we weren't working on that piece; we were doing other things. I still had a yearlong contract, so we had to come up with other fun stuff. I was at the meeting where *Pocahontas* was pitched. The word went out that they were looking for another big title to do and they didn't know what they wanted. They called a big meeting with a lot of the creative people. They called in animators, some of the writers, and all sorts of people in this room. The meeting was with all the bigwigs – Michael Eisner, Roy Disney and Jeffrey Katzenberg. We had pitched something based on Baba Yaga, I think. Everyone had to pick folktales and things like that. When I was there, *The Little Mermaid* had already come

	out and *Beauty and the Beast* was in the process of being made. *Aladdin* was also being made at the same time, so you'd walk into a certain building and hear Robin Williams voice and see big storyboards all over the place. Remember, it wasn't digital yet, so it was very different. It was a very exciting place to be.
MORGAN:	Of course! The Disney Renaissance essentially revived musicals in popular culture! They raised Xennials and Millennials into being musical-lovers. I got to see those movies *in* the theaters. I think it really cultivated an audience for what has been the movie musical resurgence that started with *Chicago* in 2002… *Glee* … and all that followed.
GOLDRICH:	Yes, that's the thing. My mom got her Master's in Cinema Studies at NYU, and so we watched movies all the time; particularly movie musicals. I grew up with jazz in the city and movie musicals. That is part of who I am and where I came from.

So, we are at this meeting and going around the table hearing all of these ideas; they were all fine ideas. But the director, Mike Gabriel, has this 8.5 × 11 or 10 × 13 drawing with tracing paper over it, so you couldn't see what it was. He was sitting next to me and, dramatically lifts the tracing paper up and he just says, "Pocahontas" and it was basically what that poster looked like later on. They greenlit it right there. Being there was really exciting. I went to USC afterwards to do the film scoring program because I thought if I want to continue to work in film or anything like that, I've got to learn the rest of these skills. I studied with Jerry Goldsmith there and he was an amazing teacher. We got to score whatever movies he was working on, we used his music editor, and we recorded at Sony, with their live musicians. We learned so many valuable skills. We were doing orchestrations, conducting music, copying… these were the very *early* days of Finale®. When I finished it, I came back to visit the BMI Workshop and people knew me because I was the one who "got the Disney job" from being at BMI. Pat Cook, who now runs the BMI Workshop, was there and he was a good friend of mine. He was sitting next to Marcy and I didn't know her, so he introduced us. We complimented each other's dresses and we started talking. We spent the next three or four days while I was in the city talking, walking, eating, and having fun. We became friends. I was still living in L.A. It's interesting because we didn't write together until a year later. She was writing with somebody else, and I was writing my own lyrics, but we just really hit it off. As soon as I heard that she was maybe not going to be writing with her other friend…

MORGAN:	Wow, this sounds like a dating story! It's like choosing someone else.
GOLDRICH:	Oh, yeah, she was "seeing" someone else. I thought her lyrics were really good and when I saw that there was an opening, I suggested that we try writing a song together. Very casual. We wrote

this song "RSVP," which was eventually cut from *Dear Edwina*, about responding to birthday party invitations. It was very obvious from the first time we wrote a song together that it was easy. They say that about when you meet your spouse or that kind of thing. You start talking and they know exactly what you're talking about... the same frame of reference. We were immediately one voice in the song. I came to New York after I graduated [from USC] and we started to write some songs together. We were looking to do something like *Schoolhouse Rock*.

MORGAN: Ah, like Lynn Ahrens.

GOLDRICH: She's fantastic. I admire her so much and what she's been able to do all these years. Since Marcy and I were trying to write something similar to *Schoolhouse Rock*, we came up with a few songs about like having good manners... being a good kid... that kind of thing. We went to pitch it out in L.A. We called it *Rock and Rules* at the time. We had a number of meetings and people liked it; but nobody was going to dump all this money into animation and do that kind of thing with people who are completely unknown. So, we decided to turn it into a musical, and that's where *Dear Edwina* came from.

MORGAN: Right, that was at a time when "Children's Theater" was transitioning into this field called TYA—Theatre for Young Audiences. There weren't a *lot* of great titles out there. Everybody was doing the same five titles in rotation. There's always an audience with kids. Most kids like theatre, art, and music because their imaginations are still vibrant enough to digest and accept new things. I'm curious how you and Marcy really steered into that. Did you mean to?

GOLDRICH: It was a way to get productions. When we came up, they were not hiring young people nor were they particularly looking for women. Kander and Ebb were still writing... Steven Sondheim... Andrew Lloyd Webber... Maury [Yeston]... all of these big people were writing but you didn't see a whole lot of women's names up there. I mean, I cannot say that there was anybody I knew other than Gretchen Cryer or Nancy Ford... and that was Off-Broadway. There weren't any teams of women gaining traction. A lot of people got their first job at Theatreworks because the shows get up and you're able to make a little money. That's a big deal when you're starting out as a writer. Marcy and I were working on *Dear Edwina* while I was assisting Maury [Yeston]. When he saw *Dear Edwina*, he recommended that we do it for Freddie Gershon, who was the head of Music Theatre International [MTI]. We took the whole reading – the whole team – all the actors – and we did

	it at the MTI offices. At the time, Freddie was just starting Broadway Junior. It was the first year of it, so he didn't have a lot in the catalog yet. After the reading, he basically said he'd take it and license it and he gave us money. We were finally paid as writers!
MORGAN:	Right. Regional theaters were doing it before it was Off-Broadway.
GOLDRICH:	It was like "direct to video." He decided to take it, even though it had never been on Broadway or even Off-Broadway, and make it one of the Broadway Junior titles, which was a huge deal. Our timing on that was unbelievable. [MTI] would push it because one of the nice things about *Dear Edwina* is you can do with a cast of sixty or you can do with a cast of six.
MORGAN:	Which was inspiring to me when I wrote a musical called *Mary Had A Little Ham*, which is based on a book about a pig named Stanley who goes to Broadway to make it…
GOLDRICH:	Oh, that's hilarious. I love it.
MORGAN:	It also can be done by six or sixty people. That flexibility was inspired by shows like yours.
GOLDRICH:	Well, thank you. That is how we started into the children's theatre thing. Barbara Pasternak at Theatreworks USA called us up and said she had the book *Junie B Jones* and she thought we were really right for [writing] it. I thought the book was really charming and funny. So, not knowing anything about these books or how popular they were, we just wrote the show. We had a great time doing it. It was really a great process. The show kept on going out and it was the best thing that ever happened to us as writers, because all of a sudden, we had a little bit of income coming in so that we weren't doing our day jobs all the time. We could actually focus on writing.
MORGAN:	Did you have any feelings about how that steered you into that particular brand or were you okay because you knew you had other adult material; like, your cabaret and songbook songs are about adults and relationships, right?
GOLDRICH:	We never thought of ourselves as "children's writers." We were writing children's theatre. But all this stuff that we wrote never pandered *to* children. We just wrote adult pieces that were appropriate *for* kids. We always wanted it to be fun for adults to see, and having my own kids, I can tell you, I've seen a lot of theatre where I really struggled to enjoy it because it can be quite juvenile.
MORGAN:	Agreed. You want it to be like *Shrek*, where it works on two levels.
GOLDRICH:	Bugs Bunny always worked on two levels.
MORGAN:	Yeah! And *Peanuts*.
GOLDRICH:	All of that stuff. The best children's entertainment is funny for adults, too, because adults are just big kids, right?

MORGAN: This has been very inspiring to me in my writing. Pixar successfully taps into material that evokes nostalgia in the adults; it tugs at our heartstrings and creates new love for that sentiment in the young people.

GOLDRICH: Totally. All of this was going on as we were pursuing our adult songs. At first, we were pegged as "just cabaret writers" because we had standalone songs like "Taylor the Latte Boy." We got the opportunity to do show based on all of our romantic songs at the Ordway [Center for the Performing Arts, in Minneapolis] called *Adventures in Love*. We put that song in that show and wrote a lot of other new songs in that style like "The Morning After."

MORGAN: Was that before or after all those shows like *I Love You, You're Perfect Now Change...Edges... I Love you Because...* those relationship shows...?

GOLDRICH: It was in 2000. It was around that time everybody was trying to do that kind of thing but that was our first real production other than the children's stuff. I did not imagine myself becoming a "children's writer;" I thought I was simply a writer. Then, all of a sudden, we were "children's writers" because we were doing *Dear Edwina* and *Junie B. Jones*. After we did *Adventures in Love,* we got a job to write *Ever After*. Once people started to hear our *Ever After* stuff, they realized that we do that, too. For a long time, it was very difficult for people to take us seriously in order to invest $12 million dollars in a musical. Even in a review for *Ever After* in Atlanta, they called us "children's writers Marcy Heisler and Zina Goldrich"... But look... Jeff Marx and Bobbie Lopez also did a show for Theatreworks. Nobody called *them* "children's writers." Almost every successful team I know did shows for Theatreworks, and nobody else was called "children's writers" for the rest of their career. It's an interesting thing. I'm proud of the work that I've done, but I don't like being pegged as anything. I never changed *how* I wrote. I just felt that kids could handle any kind of music I could throw at them. There's a lot of jazz in there. There's a lot of groove in there, and that's the fun part.

MORGAN: That's interesting. Complicated content and appropriateness don't necessarily go hand-in-hand with the complicated nature of the music itself. That doesn't mean that it's simple.

GOLDRICH: There's a big difference between simple and simplistic. I think being simple is really difficult. You want to find something that's simple, elegant, and really encapsulates a musical idea that is concise, memorable, and makes you feel things. I teach now and I tell my students, "Your job is to make me feel things. Music needs to make people feel things."

MORGAN:	One of my favorite songs is "Smile" by Charlie Chaplin.
GOLDRICH:	It's gorgeous. Who doesn't cry?
MORGAN:	I totally cry every time I hear that song.
GOLDRICH:	Every single time. Ironically, a song called "Smile." You know, that's the beautiful thing about music. My dad is ninety-three and he and I can sit and listen to some music together and our eyes will fill with tears because music makes us so content, so fulfilled. It is such a basic joy that everyone can experience across the world. It's a language unto itself. It communicates completely and thoroughly to our hearts. That's why I feel so fortunate to be doing what I get to do. I never really imagined the power of what music can do. When my grandmother was eighty-two, she had terminal lung cancer and she came to live with us. She was in hospice during this time. One night, we decided we were going to have a concert, so we all came out – my uncle, my mom, my sister, my dad, and my grandmother, who was quite ill. I played whatever songs anybody wanted. I played songs from her childhood and whatever she wanted. I played, we all sang, and we just had a beautiful evening of memories and stories and music, but mostly music. So, the next morning the nurse comes in after taking her vitals and she's asked, "What happened?" Everything [with her health] was noticeably better. Her cancer wasn't cured, but all of her vitals – her breathing, her skin tone, her pulse – everything had improved. I saw how she felt the next day from having music in her life just for that evening.
MORGAN:	There's such a commonality between some of these artists' stories… of their upbringing and what young people grow up with in their ears and how they take in the world. It matters.
GOLDRICH:	I'll tell you, it really helped to have such supportive parents. They always said, "You can do whatever you set your mind to. You have the talent. We are behind you 100%. We think you write pretty great music. We really love how you play." They never told me to have a backup. I knew what I wanted very early on, since my teenage years, and that was to write for Broadway.
MORGAN:	Sixth grade with the "The American March"!
GOLDRICH:	Yes. I had all of these big numbers in my head… I could hear people singing. There were not a lot of women working and doing what I was doing when I moved to the city. I tried to downplay my femininity, so I rarely wore skirts or dresses. I always wanted people to forget that I was a woman because that seemed to be a big deal for everybody else. I just wanted them to listen to what I could do.
MORGAN:	It was purposeful, right?

GOLDRICH: It was purposeful. I mean, I think about it now and I really don't have to hide my femininity anymore. I feel so much better that there are groups like Maestra and that we are not so invisible anymore. I think there have been tremendous strides in the past few years. I have to tell you that in my "prime writing years," a lot of men were getting ahead. There's nothing you can really blame it on. I've had to fight for visibility.

MORGAN: I wrote a whole book chapter about women in pop rock music. It ended up being about how they couldn't get their music that they wrote on the air, so they had to perform it. It makes total sense… the visibility thing. If you couldn't get it played or produced by male producers or DJs, it's going to sit on the shelf. Now, with the internet, you can get it heard.

GOLDRICH: When I was working on *Titanic*,[25] I was subbing a lot over there and then somebody was leaving, and I was offered the job. However, I had found out that I was pregnant with my first child. I had to tell them. I didn't think it was fair for me to hide it. I was probably already like four months pregnant. I said, listen, I would love to take this job. I need to let you know that I'm pregnant. They said, that's fine. I'm not totally sure of this, but I believe I am the first woman to conduct nine months pregnant on Broadway. Each week, I was getting bigger on the monitor. I was subbing as conductor, and I was playing the show most of the time. Every time it got up to the iceberg, my daughter would start to move around to the music. It was so funny. There it was in full display and I'm very proud of that.

There are also a few things we did because people said no to us, and we wanted to do those things anyway. Kristin Chenoweth sang "Taylor, the Latte Boy" on *The Rosie O'Donnell Show*. That is what broke that song through. All of a sudden, everybody wanted that song. Remember, this was before YouTube. Marcy and I would do our shows at Don't Tell Mama[26] and other clubs. After the shows, we would sit there and sell sheet music. There wasn't even an anthology yet. We were selling individual copies. We would print out music before our shows, and folks would buy the sheet music afterwards. It was a great way for people to get to know our work. We started talking to publishers and we really wanted to have a book. We said, "Look, we have a song that people actually want, but I don't want to print just the song by itself. We want people to know us as writers." We got a lot of rejections because it costs money to print a book. At that time, books didn't usually sell well. If it was a vanity book, you could print a thousand books and they could sit in your folks' garage. So, we decided to print a book and put "Taylor…" in it, along with all of our other songs. I worked on getting all the music perfect and beautiful – formatted and copied properly. We hired a graphic designer. We got an estimate from the printer. Before we knew it, we had it! It said "contains 'Taylor, the Latte Boy'" on the front of it. That was *Goldrich and Heisler: Volume One.* It was heavy and we charged $39.99 for it because it was expensive for us to do; however, we were including thirty-five songs. That was a good deal! We dragged those heavy books over to Colony Music. I talked to the guy–Rob–and I said, "Hey, we have a song that people want and we do have these books. And we were wondering if you would try to see if you could sell any of them… carry the book…" He took five of them to sell and said, "Let's see what happens." They put us at the end of the row, on a display. But when you're at the end of the row, you really stick out. Within about a week or two, he called back and he said, "We'd like some more books, please." So, there I am, dragging these boxes of books to Colony Music. We were also at Hollywood Sheet Music in Los Angeles. We did it all ourselves and, believe it or not, we went through the one thousand books and so we reprinted again. Finally, a few years later, when we were on our fourth printing, we met somebody at Hal Leonard and they made a deal with us. By that time, digital music was starting to come in. So, it happened, but it only happened because "if you don't ask, you don't get." We didn't wait for anybody. We did it. I'm really proud of that fact because it took a lot of gumption to do that. Then, we did a second book!

MORGAN: I have both of them in my office.

GOLDRICH: As the lyric goes to a song that we do when we open up our show, "Sometimes you got to make your own party." That's been kind of our philosophy for a long time.

MORGAN: Can you tell me about your writing process with Marcy? What comes first?

GOLDRICH: We like to work "lyrics first" 85 to 90% of the time. I really prefer to work that way because I like to know what I'm writing about. I think of better melodies when I know what the natural line of the lyric is. I can highlight certain words and I can downplay certain words. That's worked better for me over the years. But there are certain songs, if it has to be a really great ballad or something where it's really stylistically specific… For example, "Right Before My Eyes" from "Ever After" was music first. Some of them happen when we're both in the room at the same time. We do have a couple of rules. If there's something we're disagreeing about, she has the final word on lyrics. Pardon the pun.

If there's a music thing and I want to set it a certain way and she doesn't like it, but that's the way I want to do it, I have the final say on music. A lot of the time, I'm not happy unless she's happy, and she's not happy unless I'm happy. Sometimes it's not A or B, it becomes C. Oddly, if something doesn't come to me fairly quickly, we know we haven't hit it because usually I'm pretty fast. A lot of the time, I'm thinking about something for three days, so when I sit down at the piano, it's ready to go. Sometimes, if we have a deadline, and it has to be done in one hour; that can happen. That's being a professional; speeding it up if you have to.

MORGAN: I was commissioned to write a musical in the shut-down by a local producing company because the county schools wanted some content to show their kids. They asked me to write a 45-minute musical about historical figures in Georgia. I spent most of my time devouring the books I could from the library on those folks. I watched any media I could. Then, I actually did it in a weekend by myself, in my studio, churning it out because I like to digest, think, then spit it out.

GOLDRICH: Marcy calls that process "puke and revise." The worst thing you can do is edit yourself as you're writing. You just have to let it out and then edit later. Otherwise, you're going to stop up the pipes or stop up the process and that's no good. Just let it flow. Generally, the way I like to write is: I always have a recording device on because I'll just start. If I have a lyric from Marcy, I will sit down at the piano and start playing and singing. I just wander off into another world. I'm not in that conscious place. I'm not thinking about "going to the minor third here" or there. I never think that way. I start to sing the lyrics and I see where it leads me. I'm trying to figure something out and playing something and I'm not really conscious of it, and I'll say, "That was it! I know that was good." But I'll have no idea what I did. That's why I have the recorder; because I can go back and hear what I did. I really get lost in the feelings of it, and I think that's the most important part. I remember we wrote something for "The Great American Mousical" called "What Do You Think of That?" The show is about mice who live under a Broadway theatre. The song is about a young mouse who gets to be an intern and he meets the big star. The character's name is Pippin. We got to the end of it, to the place where the lyric goes "Someday they'll say, 'Pippin was here. Theater was made. That's what he did. Here's where he sat. What do you think of that?" I remember when we got up to that part (and I just had my recorder on while I was playing) and all of a sudden, I was saying those words and I'm literally crying. I was feeling the thing I should be feeling and that's how you know. I'm not always crying when I'm writing, but I know that if I get that lump in my throat while I'm coming up with it, I will not be alone in that. Somebody else is going to feel that, too. That's the goal. I get really excited if I cry... if I actually feel something like that when I'm writing.

MORGAN: How'd you get into liturgical music?

GOLDRICH: Interesting story. I was not raised religiously at all, so it's super ironic that I ended up doing some of this stuff. My parents are agnostic. My ex-husband was far more observant, and I agreed that the kids should have education and then they could do whatever they wanted. For many years, I was taking them to Hebrew school and taking them to all these activities and I got to know the clergy. The cantor knew I was a professional songwriter and once asked me if I would ever consider doing something for the synagogue. I figured: why not? I told them that I don't speak Hebrew at all, though.

MORGAN: You didn't have a Bat Mitzvah?

GOLDRICH: Oh, no. We were culturally Jewish. I lived in areas that had a lot of Jewish people. I went to a lot of my friends' bar mitzvahs and bat mitzvahs. I didn't grow up with any of that stuff. To be honest, it was very difficult to be involved with the synagogue when I struggled with what's "out there." I felt like a big phony.

MORGAN: Oh yeah; I've played a lot of church gigs and there are some that I would have to withdraw from just because I didn't like mixing spirituality and work. Sometimes, you go to work, especially the music team, and you're admittedly clocking in and clocking out… you can go on autopilot and play from muscle memory after four weeks of playing a show. I don't want to do that with something related to my faith!

GOLDRICH: Yeah, exactly. That makes a lot of sense. So, the next cantor came in and asked me to write a song and I did. Then, Azi Schwartz came to us at Park Avenue Synagogue in New York City. He was from Israel, and he was a pretty well-known cantor and we became very good friends. He told me he would like for me to write one for him. I asked him not only to translate; I told him I wanted to know what every syllable means, even if it doesn't make sense as a sentence. I needed to know what each word means. Then, I was able to highlight the words I want to highlight and find a flow, so they get the emphasis and pronunciation right. Now, I have done over a dozen for him. When the pandemic hit, everything went on Zoom, and so the synagogue started to do a lot of filmed services, meaning the songs have a far wider reach. That's how I got into liturgical writing. I never really thought I would do it, but I enjoy facilitating other people's faith.

MORGAN: I've gone to different churches my whole life and I've played in all of them in different ways because I can play a variety of styles, but I so I get easily distracted if the church music is poorly executed. It ruins my experience – my connection to God – because it's *my* church service. I played in a mega church band who had a worship pastor who made it clear that it was less about who could show off musically and that the number one objective was to facilitate the experience of the congregation to connect to God in their way. It is not about us. "The minute any of you make it about *you*, then you are making music in the wrong space." It taught me a lot about transitions between songs, sermons, and segments. There was storytelling involved because I, as a parishioner, had great experiences by having a really solid worship team lead us between the sermon, the songs, and back.

GOLDRICH: You're so right. It's so interesting you bring up the transitions. My experience as someone who works in the live theatrical medium is that a worship service is *still* a live theatrical experience; therefore, being aware of why a song is working or not working… why aren't people singing… what's happening here? Chances are people are not singing because they don't know they're allowed to sing. If you tell them that it's okay to sing, they will sing.

MORGAN: Yes. It's performing rituals… performance studies. That same worship pastor would sit down with the preacher to find out the sermon topic, and determine how it would impact the music selections during offering. People are going to be in a particular emotional state for this song to facilitate that. So, it is absolutely storytelling from the minute you walk in the door to the end, and it can be done in a way that's compassionate and not manipulative.

GOLDRICH: I've talked about manipulating people's emotions with music and I say that in the gentlest form. I want to be able to open up their heart to feel what the lyric is saying,

MORGAN: Facilitate!

GOLDRICH: Yes! It is more of a *facilitation* rather than a manipulation. Houses of worship still have that live theatrical thing where if you have too many ballads, people are going to get bored. If people are tired or they've been sitting for a long time or whatever, you want to get them on their feet, so you better pick up that tempo. These are all basic things for the pacing of a regular score of a show. I think I've been able to bring my theatrical background to help out, in that regard. The folks at synagogue have given something to me where I have learned about what all these things mean. Now, when I hear these things, I know a little bit more about what they mean. I really enjoy seeing other people being able to experience their spirituality through the music that I was able to create.

MORGAN: Absolutely. It circles all the way back to something you said earlier about what art can do to heal people like how it helped your grandmother. It didn't rid her of cancer, but it made her vitals improve for an amount of time. In this crazy world that we're in, it's

	important to have writers and new work that speak to the current moment or encourage artists to interpret pieces from long ago in ways that are relevant to now.
GOLDRICH:	I feel very lucky that I'm still able to do this, and that I have somewhat of a platform to get my music out. We've been very fortunate to have productions all over the country. We actually did a pandemic musical during the shut-down. Jodi Picoult (a novelist) and Tim McDonald wrote the script. Our cast for our two-person section of this musical was Kelli O'Hara and Brian Stokes Mitchell! That was the joy of my life that made the whole pandemic bearable. I could point to this work of art that came during that time, other than just sitting there.
MORGAN:	What's next for you?
GOLDRICH:	Marcy and I are writing a musical called *Stage Mother*, which is about a Texas choir teacher who inherits her son's drag bar in San Francisco. She's been estranged from him, so it's mixing those two worlds together. There's a movie version. I'm really excited about that. We are also putting together a revue of Marcy and Zina songs.
MORGAN:	Like an official one?! Like *Putting it Together*…[Sondheim revue 1992]?
GOLDRICH:	Yes, exactly. Somebody called it "The World Goes Round Marcy and Zina." All these theatre companies do revues all the time and they often do the same ones, so we want to be out there too.
MORGAN:	Absolutely. I can't wait to see it. Or play it! I wish you the best on these endeavors and thank you so much for your time and generosity.

Georgia Stitt Biography

GEORGIA STITT is an award-winning composer, lyricist, music producer, pianist, and activist. Her original musicals include *Snow Child* (commissioned, Arena Stage), *Big Red Sun* (NAMT 2010), and a children's musical, *Samantha Spade, Ace Detective* ("Outstanding New Musical" from National Youth Theatre). Other shows include *The Danger Year, The Big Boom, The Water*, and *Mosaic*. Georgia has released four albums of her music: *A Quiet Revolution, My Lifelong Love, This Ordinary Thursday*, and *Alphabet City Cycle*. She is currently composing a new album of theatrical art songs and an oratorio called *The Circling Universe*. She teaches Musical Theatre Writing at Princeton University. Georgia is the Founder and President of Maestra, an organization for women and nonbinary theatre musicians, and is in leadership at The Dramatists Guild, The Recording Academy, and MUSE. She has worked extensively as a Music Director and lives in New York with her husband and their two wonderful daughters. www.georgiastitt.com

46   The Writers

Interview with Georgia Stitt and Amanda Wansa Morgan, January 10, 2023 via Zoom[27]

MORGAN: Georgia Stitt! Multi-hyphenate female-identifying musical theatre artist extraordinaire. One of my favorite stories to tell is that, when I was working on a production of *Songs for a New World* (1995) here in Georgia, the producer came up to me and told me that "Jason Robert Brown[28]'s mother-in-law" was coming to see the show. After the show, he introduced me to your mother and he says, "This is Jason's mother-in-law" and I said, "Georgia Stitt's mother!" I told her that I'm a big fan of her daughter's work and we had a lovely conversation, but I think she was a little surprised that I knew about your work. I told her that when I was in college, I was made aware of your composition work. I think *This Ordinary Thursday*[29] came out when I was in graduate school, and it was around that time when I saw Kimberly Grigsby conduct *Spring Awakening*. Those were classic and congruent moments of female representation for me. I grew up performing onstage, but also started to get into accompanying performers; arranging and composing music; and considering music direction in college. It was the representation that I needed to validate my interest in saying yes to requests to music direct, compose, or arrange – seeing a woman do these things. I continued to follow your career and have been so incredibly inspired by the way that you have given back to the community by founding Maestra as an organization, which we'll talk about. You're just such an important figure in our in our industry, especially for female-identifying artists.

STITT: Thank you. It's really nice to hear that about *This Ordinary Thursday* because that album was like food for me. Those are my songs. I wrote them, I released them, and they're out in the world. They don't (or didn't) yield a production. It's not like I can see theatre production royalties come in from that, so it's easy to forget that people listen the music that I put out, or that it has any impact. I don't make albums as vanity projects ... they're ways to put my music out; so to actually be reminded that they have purpose and impact is really significant.

MORGAN: Very much so. For people who want to make musical theatre, they serve as a reminder that there is a middle ground between fully produced and composed "book" shows, and collections of pop songs. There's storytelling that can occur in the middle. Those kinds of projects remind us of that and give us examples of short stories we can tell that have a lot of value to people. They have a lot of value in the educational arena of skill building. They teach a performer how to sing a well-written short story song and connect to it.

Tell me a little bit about your journey from childhood to Broadway.

STITT: I was the piano girl in my little town in West Tennessee. I grew up outside of Memphis, but *way* outside of Memphis, in a really small town. Covington, Tennessee. I moved around a little bit before that, but I settled there in middle school and was the girl who played the piano. That was my thing. I came home from school, I threw down my backpack, and went to the piano and practiced. I read and sang and made things up; and my mom would always make me stop between 4:30 and 5:00 pm because that's when *Jeopardy* was on, and she couldn't hear *Jeopardy* [over my playing]. I was a piano girl, and we went to church, so I started playing the piano in church as early as age fourteen. I played on the hymns, the offering, the prelude… that was my job all through high school. I accompanied the choir, sang in the choir, and then I was a marching band girl. I was so hungry for musical education; in fifth grade, I started playing the clarinet. I was pretty good on the clarinet, and before long, I was sitting first chair and wanted to be challenged more. My band director said the flute is really close to the clarinet and so is the saxophone. So, I learned both!

MORGAN: Wait. You're a reed doubler?[30]

STITT: I was. I mean, the story gets better because I was a reed doubler, but then, when we did marching band in the fall, the clarinet parts in marching band were really boring. I wanted to get a solo and my band director said I could learn the trumpet or the mellophone. So, I learned the mellophone. That felt like the same as a French horn. Then, the French horn had the same mouthpiece as a trumpet. By the time I was a senior, I learned how to play every instrument in the band. I had a semester on trombone, I had a semester on tuba… I had a band director who wanted to keep challenging me, so she gave me a tuba. That band director's name is Trish Doty. Female. How interesting is that…? I went away to a summer music camp in Sewanee, Tennessee: The Sewanee Summer Music Festival [at Sewanee Music Center]. I majored in piano, and I minored in clarinet. For electives, I picked composition. For five weeks, I learned about composing, and at the end of the five weeks, I wrote a piece for my roommate who played the viola and me on piano to accompany her. We performed it at "Parent's Weekend" and my parents came up and they were like, "We didn't know you're a composer!" And I was like, "I didn't either, but apparently I am."

MORGAN: You were, what? 15? 16?

STITT: Yeah, that must be right. After sophomore year, I guess. I came home and I kept that up. My band director helped; I wrote a couple of things for the concert band. I started doing private composition lessons at what is now the University of Memphis. Because of that work, I had compositions for that portfolio and that's what got me into college as a music composition major. I tried to be in the musicals in high school a few times, but I wasn't very good. I'm an "okay" singer, but I wasn't a great singer, and I was never going to be competitive as a musical theatre performer. However, there were times where people asked me to play [piano for a] rehearsal. There was a production of *Little Shop of Horrors* [original: 1982] where they needed a bass player, so I literally played just the left hand on keyboard bass.

MORGAN: Right, right. Been there, done that!

STITT: In a way, that was my relationship to performing in musical theatre. When I got to college – at Vanderbilt… The Blair School of Music – I was a composition major, taking it all very seriously, writing string quartets and art songs and that sort of thing. Midway through college, my conducting teacher, John Morris Russell, said to me that he conducted every summer at a summer stock theatre on Cape Cod and they always needed a rehearsal pianist, and he offered me that job. I said yes, so he brought me to CLOC – College Light Opera Company.[31] It's a summer stock company that does nine shows in eleven weeks.

MORGAN: Some summer theaters still do stuff like that.

STITT: Really?

MORGAN: I mean, at Post Playhouse in 2015, we did five shows in rep and up to eleven performances a *week*.

STITT: Yep. One show during the day and a different show at night.

MORGAN: I was the music director (MD) for three and the assistant music director (AMD), playing keyboard two, for two shows. The other MD and I would switch; so we'd walk into the building, I'd look at the schedule, pick the correct binder off the wall and sit at whichever piano or keyboard I was supposed to be at. We would do changeovers and I was on laundry crew. Also, it was only a four-person band, so we had to do reductions for big shows.

STITT: Oh yeah, I would be in the music office where we're all trying to figure out the reed part because nobody at college was a read doubler, so we break the part up and we would make a flute book for keyboard.

MORGAN: Oh yeah! If it's in concert key, then just put flute onto that keyboard and if it's a clarinet, write "transpose" before you play and go! What a skill set.

STITT: Yes. I remember that summer like being exhausted musically for all of those reasons, but also really intrigued. I remember sitting at the

	piano playing rehearsal for all the shows and some of them were the old handwritten scores. We did *The Merry Widow* [operetta, 1905] and I read off an orchestral score!
MORGAN:	Oh God… turning the page every four measures?!
STITT:	Right. I was intrigued because somebody wrote all of *that*?! I had two years of composition courses under my belt, and I realized somebody *wrote* all those scores. Is that a job? Can you *write* musicals? Can you? I guess I only thought I could write symphonies. I spent a lot of the summer wondering, "How does this work? What do piano parts look like? What do the orchestrations look like?" It was really before the internet. I read a lot of books that came out, I went back to my school, and I told them that I wanted to write a musical. It wasn't a school that had a great musical theatre department, so they suggested that I write an opera. My senior thesis at Vanderbilt was a piece that would now live somewhere between musical theatre and opera. It was a swingy, jazzy piece performed by opera singers. That's what got me into grad school. The NYU Graduate Musical Theatre Writing Program wanted samples of my body of work [for admission]. I had taken a year off [after undergrad] to work at the Goodspeed Opera House as the music intern. I looked on *ArtSearch* (Job board via Theatre Communications Group) and every now and there were music job listings. I applied for anything that I felt like I might be able to do, even jobs on the business side in arts administration or advertising. I definitely sent a resume to the Jujamcyn [Theatres, LLC].[32] I knew wanted to be in the theatre, maybe do music on the side. It is interesting how many things had to line up to get me where I am now. I often remind my kids that there's so much that you just don't know yet.
MORGAN:	Absolutely not. You can plan, but…
STITT:	It has to be the right time… right person… right experience that lead you to where you'll end up.

> The more you can see the *version* of you that you want to be, the more you can stay on the path that gets you there.

Sometimes, taking a turn is okay, and there's a better version of you that you're headed towards.

MORGAN:	Absolutely. You're going to pick up chapters. You might take a diversion into the chapter where you only work at Starbucks and do cabarets or sing for new readings. But you're going to learn so

much in that chapter; or meet your soulmate at Starbucks! Whatever hours you're not doing one thing, you're going to be doing something else. If you could view that as benefiting you in some way, then it will.

STITT: Yeah. That's the whole story of how I got to Goodspeed[33] and graduate school. At Goodspeed, Michael O'Flaherty was the Resident Music Director, and I was the music intern. There were lots of evenings when if he wasn't conducting the show, we would just pull scores off the shelf and play through them. We would spend the evening singing and playing; it was the best singalong party. He'd point out important dance breaks I needed to know and stuff like that. It was an amazing education. I was the intern for a couple of shows and then I got promoted to Resident Assistant Music Director. One of my first professional credits was a show that Jeanine Tesori wrote that was done on their second stage. It was a show called *Starcrossed* that was about Galileo[34] and his daughter. It had this big Catholic mass in the middle of the show, and she had written it out, and so she needed it put it into Finale. That was one of my job responsibilities as Music Assistant, but I didn't know [how to use] Finale. Michael O'Flaherty said I had to learn it! I literally opened the manual and figured out this music notation software that now I use every single day of my life.

MORGAN: That's how I learned SFX[35] which eventually moved over to QLab.[36] Out of necessity. In grad school, I was asked to compose music for a show but was told that I would hand off the tracks to the sound designer for programming in tech. He had to leave unexpectedly, so I was at the computer before tech using the manual and the help menu. Sometimes, we say yes to a job and figure it out.

STITT: The answer is usually "Yes." Not always.

MORGAN: I'll say yes if I know I can do the job by the first day.

STITT: I love that. I get that. I think I operate like that.

MORGAN: Who are those role models coming up, other than that band teacher? Role models for leadership, life, life, survival, whatever…

STITT: Well, certainly all of my composition teachers in college. I was one of two composition majors in my year and both of us were women. I did not know at the time how rare that was.

MORGAN: *And* you had a female band teacher!

STITT: My piano teacher was a woman. I don't think I realized what a dearth of female musical leadership there was among musicians because I didn't experience it, really. Throughout college, I had two composition teachers and I traded off with them both semesters. They were both men, but both of the student majors were women. The faculty brought in artists in residence every semester; composers in

	residence to come for a long weekend and work with us. They were all really prestigious, established composers. They brought in classical composer Joan Tower[37] to work with us. I wasn't aware that it was a big deal that she was a woman; she was just a composer who was coming in.
MORGAN:	You were also graduating into a time where women were being empowered through the Lilith Fair[38] movement and singer–songwriters getting their music played on the radio. We saw a lot of success with Carole King and Joni Mitchell and the singer songwriter movement of the late 1960s and early 1970s; then, we saw a resurrection of popular music written by music in the late 1990s with Joan Osborne, Sarah McLaughlin, Alanis Morissette.
STITT:	I didn't listen to a whole lot of pop music, but I did love Carole King and Joni Mitchell. Then, I hated everything until the Indigo Girls came along. I love the Indigo Girls. That might be why I hadn't really put that together. I lived in Tennessee, so I was more surrounded by country music than pop.
MORGAN:	Right. Dolly and Loretta are timeless and they're representing different class positions in storytelling. Country is kind of timeless and it's probably the closest genre to musical theatre, right?
STITT:	Joni Mitchell's story songs are what always grabbed me. My interest in musical theatre was the storytelling. I was also a girl who wrote poetry in her journal growing up.

I thought a lot about poetry and loved reading it. If I hadn't been a music major, I would have been an English major. I love literature. I read constantly. I was very interested in writing poetry, but I never thought it was something I could do as a profession. Sarah Schlesinger was one of my professors at NYU and she assigned me something where I had to write the lyrics, which was new to me because I had worked exclusively as a composer. She's the first person who told me that my lyrics were good. She said, "You're a lyricist." They didn't accept "composer–lyricists" because they wanted everyone to practice a discipline. However, she said I could be a composer *and* lyricist.

MORGAN:	This is interesting because another subject said she basically needed permission for someone tell her that she writes good lyrics or say, "You're a lyricist," because it's so personal. It's your voice. As composers, we can put our hands on the piano and know what makes sense based on chord structure and music theory. But when it's your words, I think it's harder. I'm the same way. I was a composer who was looking for a lyricist until I was forced to write lyrics, and someone complimented my lyrics. There's some sort of affirmation that needs to go along with that to give us permission to do both.

	Maybe that's imposter syndrome too? We can't self-identify as both of these things until someone says we can. I think *This Ordinary Thursday* is so poetic. It's very emotional... melancholy, even. Do you go back and listen to those songs that you wrote 15 years ago? Do you ever listen to it with your older lens now?
STITT:	Every now and then it comes up or I'll be on a long road trip. I'll listen to the album top to bottom and see what holds up. Or somebody will mention they're doing a song and I'll realize that I hadn't thought about that in a long time. They do sound youthful and very emotional to me. I feel like they hold up.
MORGAN:	How do some of them make you feel now with the perspective of being married with children?
STITT:	*Thursday* itself is so naive, innocent, hopeful, and youthful. It's this idea that you're on the cusp of that time in your life where anything is possible. You're meeting the person that's going to be "your person" for the rest of your life. It's about what it feels like to be loved and seen as a whole person.
MORGAN:	I think our perspective changes, but the core of who we are doesn't.
STITT:	When I was writing all of the songs for *This Ordinary Thursday*, I had them in my back pocket. I was working as a music director, and I knew I was a composer. I identified as a composer, but I had not yet been given a chance to be heard as a composer. I booked the national tour of *Parade* in 2001 and met and worked with Jason Robert Brown – who became my husband. We would play songs that we were writing for each other and that was part of how we fell in love with each other, intellectually and musically. So, for a holiday gift – it was my birthday or Christmas or something – early in the courtship, he asked me to come to the studio where he was recording. He was working on a project with Andréa Burns because she was on the tour with us and he wanted me to hear something. I got to the studio, and they were recording my song, "The Holy Secret." It was a gift for me. That was the beginning of the album. Somebody had to say, "Your song deserves to be recorded and other people need to hear it besides you. Now go finish." That was the beginning of that album. It is interesting to think about that story in the context of somebody having to give you permission to say that your work is valid, you belong here, and you need to keep doing it.
MORGAN:	It's hard to see an identified path on the other side of the table. As writers, how do we have any reflection or feedback process, even with a degree in composition? How do we know how to get from one point to another?
STITT:	I didn't doubt that I knew how to write it, I just didn't know how to produce it. I didn't know how to get it past the sheet music. That

was the beginning of something. I often say I made that record as a business card. I wanted to be able to give it to people and show them what I do. I never expected it to make any money. I think over the lifetime of the album, it's probably paid back what it cost to make it. It wasn't very expensive to make. It's done what it needed to do. But after that album came out, people called me a composer and they hadn't before. I paid for it all myself, self-produced it, with the exception of the gift of the first recording. It legitimized me as a writer. It was really one of the smartest things I ever did, and someone had to give me permission to do it.

MORGAN: Well, this connects to the programs that you've instituted with Maestra. I'm one of the Maestra mentors – I'm mentoring a composer – and while I was in New York, I met up with the gal who's the Maestra mentor to that composer's lyricist partner. We had a conversation about how we're going to do this together. This program alone, in addition to the cabarets and stuff like that, has given platforms for folks to do that, particularly who may be lacking one of the skill sets, but just need the space to do it, which is so important. They need the feedback.

STITT: Yes, the feedback component is related to the permission component. It's lovely to have somebody there to affirm, "You're going to learn how to do this. You can do this, and it doesn't have to be off limits or out of reach for you."

MORGAN: I ended up in some rooms with people who were more theatre-trained than music-trained. Anything that I brought into the room seemed impressive, so it gave me a little bit of momentum to get into the bigger rooms. I would get asked to set something to music and folks liked what I did but I wasn't sure if I was "doing it right."

STITT: I think that's more common than we think. I tended to be a person who thought I needed a degree in this in order to feel like I can do it. I thought I needed to go back and get another degree on how to start a nonprofit. But, at a certain point I realized I just have to figure out how to do this.

MORGAN: I think I ended up falling into writing TYA [Theatre for Young Audiences] musicals because I identified a need in the industry, having performed in a lot of children's shows as an actor in college. I just took some material and started setting it to music. Even poetry. Let's circle back to your relationship to poetry as a writer.

STITT: I always read it, loved it, looked at it. With my background in the church, hymns and anthems are poetry. I was always aware that poetry can be set to music. In my sophomore year of college, my composition teacher wanted me to spend a semester studying and writing art songs and told me to look at poems. There was a real attention to the craft of writing an art song and setting preexisting poetry. There were exercises like reading a poem, underlining the important words, making choices about whether a line needs energy, determining melody going up or down, and deciding where the cadences are. We had to craft it on paper before we ever had any notes or rhythms, to see what this poem needs me to do. It's about being aware when a poem doesn't have room for you, as a composer; the poem is complete…there's already music in it. It's possible that I can't write any music that would make this better. A lot of Edna St. Vincent Millay's[39] poems are so tightly structured and so perfect on the page, that I don't know that I can add anything to make it better.

MORGAN: Like putting makeup on an already beautiful person.

STITT: Right. Putting a "Hat on a Hat" is what we say. So, I look for poems that have space in them or feel like they're getting at something that I know music could enhance. During that college semester, I wrote a couple songs, and it began this lifelong relationship. I love it. I can write an art song pretty quickly, in a few days. Then it's done; as opposed to a musical that you're working on for years. There is something really satisfying about having an idea, writing it, and it's done. I can give it to a singer, and they can perform it and check, its done. It serves my need for accomplishment.

MORGAN: When working with poetry as a composer, it's important to learn the art of scansion and how words are set to melody. In musical theatre, there's some really inconsiderate moments of scansion, like when the unstressed syllable is the sung money note.

STITT: So much of my writing is informed by the fact that I was a music director and a vocal coach for so long. I have spent so much time looking at preexisting songs with singers and examining what the composer's intention was and what the singer has to do; exactly how we are going to solve any problem. What is the composer or lyricist giving you that you haven't identified yet that is actually going to help you? In a good song, all the information is there. If not, then you have to impose things and hope that the song can hold it. When I write, I keep in mind that someday a coach and a singer are going to sit in a room and try to figure this out. Have I given them enough to play with? Have I given them enough to act? Have I given them enough hints and clues in the music so they can do what I intended them to do *and* interpret it in a way that it feels like theirs but doesn't stray too far from what I hoped the meaning would be?

MORGAN: I try to be as open as possible with that, too. I try to put down lyrics that could be interpreted in three different ways.

STITT: When I was younger, I used to be very spare in what I wrote into the musical scores. I wouldn't even write a *ritard*[40] because I thought, *obviously* they need to *ritard* there. That's what it needs. Then, I would hear people sing things of mine and they pointed out that it didn't say *ritard*, so they didn't.

MORGAN: Right, because a lot of people are trained to sing the ink, no matter what. It's enforced in education.

STITT: I've gotten more meticulous as I age. What I put on paper is actually communication to some person in the future who's going to try to figure out what I meant.

MORGAN: Yeah. Dynamic markings are so important when we orchestrate. I learned pretty early on that we have to put staccato markings over *all* of the notes if that's what we want. All the expressions. I learned a lot from doing a copyist gig from time to time for a guy revising old Big Band charts. When you play it all back in Finale, it follows the articulations, so if you don't put all of them in there, it won't play it back properly. Modern technology really helps with that.

STITT: If you don't, the players will all make their own decisions, and it won't sound like a section.

MORGAN: You have served in so many roles: music supervisor, music director, keyboard musician, composer... I mean, recently, you just played keyboards for the Encore's concert version of *Parade* [in 2022]. Just banging on the piano! What position excites you the most? Are there aspects about each position that you get excited to do?

STITT: When I was twenty-four, my business card said: "Georgia Stitt: Composer, Lyricist, Pianist, Music Director, Copyist, Arranger, Orchestrator" It listed all of the things. Now, I think it just says "Composer" or "Musician."

MORGAN: Or just "Bad ass."

STITT: That's it. Bad ass. At a certain point I just had to create an umbrella term. My passport says "Musician." In order to be a functioning musician, especially in the theatre, the more you can do, the more you can work. There's a moment where somebody asks if I can do something, and I say yes. I had studied orchestration for a year in college, so I said I'm an orchestrator. It's not until you actually have done it a few times that you feel like you're able to own the title. I think a lot about how our culture is designed to promote excellence until you get to the point where you've been promoted out of what you do well.

MORGAN: It happens in education. Someone who's really great in the classroom often gets promoted to administration. If I'm in leadership, I'm teaching less... but I'm a really good teacher.

STITT: It's the Peter Principle,[41] where you get promoted out of what you're good at and because the rewards come for leadership. If you happen to be good at leadership, which you are and I am, then you get rewarded for that. But there is something that you were good at before that. For me, that was [playing] piano. If I go too long without playing the piano, I start to feel like I don't do it well and I'm not going be competitive with the other people who do it often. For me, doing *Parade* at Encores![42] was the beginning of my love story with my husband; that show was where we met. I still wanted to be part of it, and I wanted to remind myself that I was a pianist and I like to sit in an orchestra. Also, the book is just piano. It's not keyboard and patch changes.

MORGAN: It's a fun book.

STITT: It is a fun book and a hard book and there's a grand piano in the pit. How often does this come up? There was already team in place of excellent people. Tom Murray is a fantastic music director and Jason [Robert Brown] is very involved. So, my role in that show is The Pianist. I just wanted to do it. I had to go early and warm up, like an athlete.

MORGAN: The end of Act One! Help!

STITT: It's fun, but it's a different muscle. There are times where I like being the head of the music department because I want to be the one that makes the decisions. With a lot of the shows that I've written, I've orchestrated them because by the time I've written a show, I know what I want it to be. It's easier for me than trying to communicate to somebody and then give notes to fix things. It's also a great chance to work with specific players. I just wrote a part for vibes because there was a percussionist that I wanted to work with.

MORGAN: Right. You get to have a more intimate relationship with the music. There are pros and cons, right? You could bring someone in and have another cook in the kitchen – another brilliant genius in the kitchen. Then, there is benefit to realizing you're already knee deep in it; so you go chest deep in it and know it inside and out. Then, you can answer the questions on the back end when you're trying to put it up with the band.

STITT: Sure. Yeah. And then if it's a large orchestration, I sometimes farm it out. Someone else can work on articulation markings and I'll just keep writing.

MORGAN: Right. The middle ground is farming out smaller portions: the copying, a specific chart or part. I'll bring on students to work on the strings and then we'll copy and paste it in. Then, I can double check our work and it can be a steppingstone in mentorship *and* it's taking at least a couple of hours off my plate for sure.

STITT: It's inseparable from the work I do at Maestra,[43] because I think there are times where my administrator brain is so busy. I'm running a not-for-profit organization and managing a family. There are times where

I realize that I don't need to run the music department; maybe I can just be the composer. Maybe I can just be part of the music making. I never want to be too far away from the music making. What I don't find satisfying is when I write it and then hand it off. When I'm creating something, I want to be part of making it in the room, instead of sitting behind the table, watching other people make it.

MORGAN: Have you found yourself as the only woman in the room in leadership?

STITT: Yes.

MORGAN: What does that feel like? And do you have observations about that experience?

STITT: I think a lot of my greatest collaborators and mentors have been men, so I don't want to dismiss any of what the experience of learning or collaborating with has been in those relationships. All that to say, none of that would be what it has been if I didn't have Mary-Mitchell [Campbell, whose interview is later in this book] in my life at the same time. Mary-Mitchell and I have been super close friends since we were in our early twenties. I think we met at CLOC. I had finished my term there but was coming back to visit while she was working there. She was a conductor and a pianist, basically doing the same thing I had done. I remember having a conversation with her and realizing that she was like me. It was a moment of recognition that I didn't know anyone else my age who was like me – not just as a pianist – but also as a leader, a visionary, and an ambitious woman. We both wanted to change the world. Now, here we are at this age, and we've both started not-for-profits that are in partnership with each other. I can't imagine how I would answer this question if I hadn't come through the ranks with Mary-Mitchell. When we were younger, someone would call me with a job offer and if I wasn't available, I would tell them to call Mary-Mitchell. She did the same for me. We were both agents for each other and then we both subbed for each other all the time. We would also consult each other on business questions. They asked me to do this job, and they're paying this. Is that fair? Should I ask for more? Can you recommend someone? Do you have a lawyer? Do you have an agent? She was my person for that. I don't know that I felt the absence of sisterhood in the professional room because I always had her, even if we weren't in the same room. I think a lot of why Maestra began is because I recognized how important it is to have what we're calling sisterhood. You can have a girlfriend to say, "I'm not competing with you. Let's both do this. There's so much room for us both to do this. You be on my side, and I'll be on your side and let's do it better."

MORGAN: I've found a few gals like that in my career, and it is really wonderful if we can vibe together! Sometimes, it takes a little time to get past the initial concern of if that other woman in power is going to vibe with you. Which is weird because I don't deal with that in the same way in rooms with men. I usually come to those rooms simply ready to do the job. I don't know why it's different. I don't know why it occurs that way.

STITT: Yeah, that's how it is. For me, I also happened to meet my equal, my partner, and my challenge in my husband. That's not so much a gender thing, but it's great to be able to go through life with a musician. We challenge each other to raise our game and bring our best. We play things for each other and respond as musicians. I feel like in both of those cases – Mary-Mitchell and Jason – I've had a sparring partner and I know how important that is. It's important to build community so people are more likely to find each other; because we need those people.

MORGAN: You've written a few full-length musicals, but we haven't seen them at the Broadway level. Are there reasons for that?

STITT: I don't know if it's a gender or sexism thing. It might be that they weren't good enough. It might be that I managed to get to the first draft phase of them and then didn't have the either the interest or the opportunity to do the rewrites. Very recently, one of them got all the way to the finish line and then we lost the underlying rights. I have identified in myself that that I am a "big picture thinker" and a big idea person. I have a lot of energy to get something going; but it takes so much muscle for me to finish. So, I tend to get overwhelmed because there are so many things open. To close in and finish it requires you to acknowledge the fear of whether it's not good or not. What if I don't like it? What is it? So, finishing things and getting them out the door is one of my New Year's resolutions. What can I take off my plate just by finishing it? What can I get out the door?

MORGAN: Do you think that's part of being freelance and not having solid deadlines for those kinds of things?

STITT: Absolutely. I also think it's because my writing lives in the space between classical music and theatre music. There's a piece I'm writing right now as an oratorio for choir, three soloists, and orchestra. I don't think anybody knows what to do with me. My publisher and my agent say, "Just keep us posted!"

MORGAN: Many people in the industry say you should stick to your individuality because at some point, that's going to be *the thing*. Your individuality – or that of your work – will be the thing that puts you on the map.

STITT: That's what I have to believe. I also think that's why it's taken me so long to finish. I've been writing this piece for years, and I think the people that were invested in it at the beginning are sitting back, saying, "Just call me when it's done." I can certainly push things to the finish line. I can push other people's projects to the finish line. I can push my children to the finish line. But with my own work, pushing it to the finish line requires me to deal with the insecurity of judgment. Maybe there's some of that, and then maybe I just haven't written the right piece. It hasn't been the right moment. I wonder now how much of the way I'm perceived in the industry is now related to my not-for-profit work. How much of that has shaped the way people perceive me as a writer? How much of it is related to being "Jason's Wife"? How much is still related to my work as a music director? In some ways, there's a curse of being a person who wears many hats. What I don't want is to finally release something and seem like a dilettante because I haven't really been doing it fully. Those are the things I am challenged by.

MORGAN: How do you engage in self-care? What kind of rituals, routines and boundaries have you created for yourself to stay above water?

STITT: Self-care. That's a hard one. I try to be present with my family when family time is happening. In the winter, we light fires in our fireplace and we sit around the fire at night when we are home from the theatre. Both of our kids write music and perform. I read a lot, and while there is there's a part of me that's always reading to find a project, I love disappearing into someone else's world where I can be led. I love a good storyteller. I get really mad when storytelling is bad. Don't waste my time. I go through periods in my life where I exercise a lot and then periods where I don't, but I always feel better when I do. I draw a lot of inspiration from other people's good creative work. I go to museums. I see a lot of plays, classical music, and concert music. When I see other people really working at the top of their game, I'm inspired to go home and work so that I can be like that too, as opposed to being shut down by it.

MORGAN: It reminds us why we're doing it, too. Why am I hustling so hard? Oh, right. Because I love it. Yes.

STITT: You can make things like this.

MORGAN: How do you juggle the parenting thing?

STITT: Now is a tricky time to ask because I have a daughter applying for college and a daughter applying for high school. There's so much right now that is vulnerable and will be different next year. Right now, I'm forcing myself to acknowledge that this is not going to be such a productive time for my work, because I have to be present. When they're really little, we could leave them with a babysitter, but now they need me, specifically me. It doesn't get easier over the years. I wouldn't say it gets harder. It just is hard in a different way.

MORGAN: Life is hard when you're single and it's also hard when you're married; it's just a different kind of hard. Different issues arise.

STITT: That's right. That's how we move through the world. I'm in a post-pandemic moment where I have two teenagers and I'm having to make peace with that. I can't get as much done in a day as I could five or ten years ago. The hustle feels different and when a lot of opportunities come my way, I evaluate them in the context of many questions: How much time away from my family will this require? How many evenings out? How many Saturdays away? What am I going to miss in order to do this? I just wrote a song for my musical called *The Danger Year* and the title of the song is, "You Can't Have It All." It's a callback to this idea that women, can "have it all." You can't; you really can't.

MORGAN: I've read some of your articles (available on the Georgia Stitt website[44]), which were quite brilliant about women in theatre... mothers in theatre... gender parity. Some of the ideas connect to conversations around the wage gap and how some of that is tied to women missing opportunities due to the necessity to care-give. That connects to what events you decide you cannot miss and have to negotiate into your contract.

STITT: Yeah, some miss those events, and I don't judge them for that. I think about what happens to a child, long term, if I miss a particular moment? How does that fuel them? We were talking about the chapters and paths. What is their story if mom was present and what is their story if mom wasn't present? Also, what is their story if mom seemed unfulfilled because she could have been a musician and then she wasn't because she was always making dinner?

MORGAN: Yes. Zina [Goldrich][45] talked a lot about making sure that her kids saw what her art does for her and therefore for them and how important that was to her.

STITT: Yeah, that is the juggle. That is the balancing act now. It's not just an enormous hobby. It actually is your purpose. We are very lucky to be people who have found our purpose.

MORGAN: Sometimes I feel like it's an obligation. If God gave me these talents, do I throw them away? Let's talk about your other baby. Maestra. What have been the highlights of watching Maestra grow? Where are the memorable moments for you or sources of pride, seeing the organization moving forward? You started with some meetings, a directory... and with some resources, grew into this huge network with virtual trainings, a mentorship program, and so many facets to it that now it's become a common thing that we know about in the industry versus this niche thing. I'm wondering about what you're proud of, and what you want to see moving forward.

STITT: I always meant for it to be a network. In fact, the very first incarnation was a cocktail party. I figured we female musicians should know each other, and I invited some of the women that I knew. We were never in the rooms together and we should know each other. The Maestra Directory developed around the same time. We had three cocktail parties and then I worried that people are going to stop coming to these cocktail parties if they're just the same. So how do we grow this event so that people can want to continue to be part of this? Around the fourth cocktail party, I brought in a guest to speak to us about something that we all wanted to hear about. I brought in orchestrators and producers who were women. That turned into what is now our Monthly Meeting program. People change and times change, so how do I keep people invested in this organization? Their investment in the organization is an extension of their investment in the purpose and the cause. We have a lot of passionate people who feel like they're seen, or their needs were met because they came looking for people or resources through us. If that need was met, then they want to continue to show up. Every time Maestra has an idea for something that allows more people to step forward, we go with it. The mentorship program is one of our biggest successes; it keeps growing and I see the evidence of mentees who get a job through their mentor! I am hearing about success stories all the time. The Directory itself is wonderful. We have younger members who moved to New York recently, and they don't know a world before Maestra. Things like that blow my mind. It's only been five years.

MORGAN: You didn't know there was going to be a global pandemic. The virtual workshops have been incredible. I join those Zoom rooms with Jeanine Tesori talking to us in real time, and it's been wonderful. I've watched many, both live and on Maestra Replay. They are so helpful. There's something so special for those of us who aren't in New York to feel connected, in a way, to this. What are your dreams for the organization moving forward? Now what?

STITT: Our mission statement is "providing support, visibility, and community" for our members. I think we've done a great job at creating programs and building little networks. I'm really interested in expanding the regional groups and figuring out how we can be more present outside of New York. I'm going to L.A. in early February, around the Grammy Awards, and I'm gathering a group of people together to meet and to try to build in-person networks there. My mom is in Atlanta, so I'm thinking I can come to Atlanta and do the same thing. How do we empower people to do that on their own? What is the most successful way to make those people feel connected to us now? We all have a bit of Zoom fatigue. Those workshops are not what they were. What's the next step for replacing them? We can consider showing up in more in labor conversations with the unions, contractors, producers, and general managers, and start to have those conversations in the spaces where we might have been seen as merely as a social club for women. We actually have a lot of power here and now.

MORGAN: Right. Fighting for those who need contract clauses around caregiving and resources. Training. Institutions or companies can alleviate that stress through daycare centers, better financial support to afford the daycare closer to the job… all those kinds of things. The industry has changed in the pandemic. There have been pros and cons. What are the aspects of the Broadway-level industry that you would like to continue to see move forward and or what's headed down the wrong path?

STITT: The things I see are changes in conversations around diversity, equity, inclusion and access (DEIA). There has been a big DEIA pendulum swing from the culture pre-George Floyd [May 2020],[46] and in the pandemic things really shifted. It does feel like there are some actions happening that feel performative. I don't think we can go back to where we were. So, when the pendulum swings back, we'll still be better because we're finally having these hard conversations. Maestra has an initiative called "Get to Work" that is really is trying to be at ahead of the fact that the pendulum is going to swing back. How do we ensure that we the important conversations that transpired during the pandemic don't disappear? I don't want producers or anyone to be able to check any kind of box like the work is done and they can go back to doing what they were always doing before [for supplemental reading on the movement spoken about here, please reference the *We See You White American Theatre* manifesto[47] and additional articles from *The New York Times*, provided at the end of this chapter].[48] It's imperative that we keep having these conversations, we keep having them deeper, and we keep having them with the people who challenge us and force us to see the world differently. To me, that feels like a good thing that came out of the pandemic. I would also say the hybrid working model – the combination of having a few days in the office and a few days at home per week – would be great. I can see my kid and make them a snack when they get home from school. That is something I couldn't do if I was in the office until five or six at night or in rehearsal all day. I think that evolution of work–life balance is good.

MORGAN: What's next for you? What's in your next chapter other than getting your kids into schools for next year?

STITT:	I'm going to finish this oratorio and I have an album that's about 70% done, so I'm going to finish that one. I have one that's ready, and one that's kind of an embryo. I hope the one that's closest to being done is done this year. Out the door.
MORGAN:	That's it. You're going to get it out the door. You're going to do it. You've been so generous with your time. Thank you. Good luck on the oratorio, the album, and all of the things!

Kate Anderson & Elyssa Samsel Biography

Elyssa Samsel and Kate Anderson are the Annie Award nominated songwriters behind Disney Animation's *Olaf's Frozen Adventure* and the hit Apple TV+ series *Central Park*. They composed the songs for the Off-Broadway musical, *Between the Lines* (Second Stage) and *The Book Thief* (Octagon, UK tour Fall 2023). Both are members of the acclaimed BMI Lehman Engel workshop. Check out their music on Spotify by searching Elyssa Samsel or Kate Anderson, on IG: @samselanderson, or at samselanderson.com.

Interview with Elyssa Samsel and Kate Anderson, November 10, 2022 on Zoom[49]

MORGAN:	Hello to the wonderful writing team of Anderson & Samsel joining me here today. You're my first duo so far, so this is going to be super exciting to hear both of your takes on some of the things you do individually, but obviously the things that you do together. Can you tell me a little bit about your upbringing and your journey from childhood to where you are now in your career, in a nutshell? Kate is the lyricist and Elyssa is the composer. Two different kinds of keyboards!
ANDERSON:	Yes. I always loved theatre my whole life. I think I fell in love with it because of my older sister, Kristen Anderson-Lopez.[50] She's 15 years older than me. My twin sister and I grew up with her. From the time we could hold our heads up, she would set us up in our little baby seats and perform the entirety of *Les Miz* for us. I remember being little and not wanting to watch anything else on TV except the video of her playing the narrator in *Joseph and the Amazing Technicolor Dreamcoat* at Charlotte Children's Theatre. She split the part of the Narrator with two other girls and she had strep throat. I thought the coolest thing was that at the beginning of Act Two, they came out and sang the top of the act with tea in their hands. Core memory stuff that's imprinted on me.
MORGAN:	I think it's historically appropriate. They had tea in the times of Joseph!

ANDERSON: Absolutely! So, she made me fall in love with musical theatre. I also just worshiped her my whole life. I did all the musicals middle school and high school, and I loved acting. I went to college to study classical voice and graduated with no idea what I was going to do with that. So, I went to New York, and I got an internship at The Public Theater in Development. I had no idea what development even was but that was a cool place to work.

MORGAN: I did an internship in development right after undergrad, too! Planning "Lunch and Learn" sessions and learning how to do a mail merge.

ANDERSON: Mail merge! Exactly. I quickly realized that wasn't scratching my creative edge at all. Kristen, who had been through the BMI workshop, said I needed to go to the BMI workshop. Finally, after a year of convincing, I applied, and that's where I met Elyssa on our very first day. We were paired for our very first assignment. We were some of the only women in the class. There weren't many... maybe 20 to 30% women. It was love at first sight, as we like to say.

MORGAN: Oh, I love that. I call it "falling in artistic love" with someone. I worked locally with a director recently and we're both music directors and directors and we finally got to work together on a production of *Matilda* [Broadway, 2013; our production, 2022]. We both wrote each other these opening night notes that admitted, "I was so intimidated to work with you... I didn't know what you thought of me, but I love you so much..." We fell in artistic love. It's great when you get someone in that way.

ANDERSON: Exactly.

MORGAN: Where did you grow up?

ANDERSON: I grew up in Charlotte, North Carolina. I saw every show. Luckily, my parents were really supportive of the arts, and we got to see every musical that ever came to Charlotte. We would go on Sundays and have lunch and it was like a whole ordeal. I very quickly fell in love with writing lyrics with Elyssa and had a desire to master that. That was my determination. In that first year, I thought, "I have to get really good at this." It was a drive that Elyssa had, too. So, we teamed up. We eventually quit our jobs and nannied [for money] and took every moment we could to write together. That's how it all started.

MORGAN: Oh, I have so many questions about your writing process. I can't wait. Okay, Elyssa, talk about your life.

SAMSEL: My life? I started lessons on piano and violin when I was six. My amazing violin teacher named Sungrai Sohn was my inspiration and he taught me how to memorize long classical pieces by assigning a story to them... adding a story throughout the entire piece as a memorization trick. I think that's where I began to associate storytelling with music. I went on to be a high school musical theatre person. My school did *Les Miz*, which was sort of where I fell in love with being in musicals, and that turned into wanting to be an actress. I still had this love for writing music and playing music. By the time I went AMDA [American Musical and Dramatic Academy] in New York City, I was figuring out how to combine my love for writing songs and acting, and it led me to the BMI workshop because people kept telling me about it. I had gone to see Lynn Ahrens and Stephen Flaherty – who were two of my role models – and they talked about meeting at the BMI workshop. So, I thought it would be a great place to figure out what the heck to do with all the songs that I had been writing. The only advice that I had been given with what to do with all my songs was partner up with a guy and then write more music and I didn't want to do that.

MORGAN: Wow, that's very specific!

SAMSEL: It came from a couple different people; it was their line of thought that if it's a guy and girl duo, you'll be more successful. I didn't love that idea. So I thought I would join the BMI workshop and network there. Lo and behold, it brought me to Kate and that was a partnership that clicked right away. As [Kate] said, we were some of the only women in the class. We had a very similar sense of humor and very similar drive and ambition, and that was where I think both of our lives totally changed. We just merged our paths in life and became business partners as well as best friends. The rest is history.

MORGAN: Can we talk a little more about some of your role models?

ANDERSON: I was very much bitten by the comedy bug pretty early on and I pretty much loved any woman who was on SNL. I first moved to New York around the time that *Bossypants*[51] came out and Amy Poehler's *Yes, Please.*[52] I kept those next to my bed because they were literally my Bibles. Those women inspired me so much. Mindy Kaling's book [*Is Everyone Hanging Out Without Me?*]. I remember thinking: these women went after what they wanted and got themselves into these rooms where they were running the show. I thought that was so cool. When Elyssa and I started off writing, our very first musical was this wacky, comedic musical called *Camp Wish No More,* and we were really channeling what our sense of humor was into this musical. We wanted to push boundaries back then. We were looking at *Book of Mormon* and the way that they pushed boundaries. We were trying to do the same. Mindy Kaling wrote a show that got into the New York

	Fringe Festival and did really well, and then that got her all the way to Hollywood. On the musical theatre side, of course, Jeanine Tesori and Lynn Ahrens [were role models] as well as Marcy and Zina [Marcy Heisler and Zina Goldrich].
MORGAN:	Yeah, I saw a production of *Dear Edwina* when I was a teenager in the early 2000s, and that was the first time like looking at a program and seeing music and lyrics by two women. I thought that was cool.
SAMSEL:	I had been playing and learning music for fourteen years of my life before I noticed two women's names on the top of a piece of sheet music.
MORGAN:	That songbook that's sitting right there on the shelf. That songbook is such an important thing to see.
SAMSEL:	That blew my mind. I think Betty Comden was the first female name that I ever noticed on sheet music; I was probably thirteen years into being a musician, and that blew my mind. Then seeing Marcy and Zina on top of sheet music just further blew my mind because it was two women. They are the ones who paved the road before us and we have always tried to follow in the footsteps of Marcy, Zina, Kristen Anderson-Lopez, Lynn Ahrens, and Jeanine Tesori. Without them being inspiration and representing women in the business, I don't know that we would have had an easy time fitting into it because seeing is believing when it comes to wanting to achieve your dreams. They were there be examples and we have to thank them for that.
MORGAN:	As I've been conducting these interviews, it's interesting to hear responses from many of these women about how they got to where they are and how they felt working their way up. Most of them respond that they were just doing what they had to do, and they don't think much of it. There are certainly writers like Kay Swift and other gals who weren't as popular. Their work is buried in anthologies. For me, it was Lucy Simon, who wrote *The Secret Garden* (1991). I was amazed that a woman wrote that score; it is a complicated, thick-handed score. You need all ten fingers to play that sucker. Also, the work of Mary Rodgers. But those were sort of "one-hit-wonders" … one or two successes. To see Marcy and Zina have repeated successes, and now you two with your work getting production and recognition is a big deal for sure. Tell me a little bit about your working dynamic and process. What happens first? Do you have to do a retreat? Get in one of your living rooms for eight hours with pizza and beer?
SAMSEL:	When we first started writing, we were babies in the BMI workshop, and our moderators were our favorite people on the

planet: Pat Cook and Rick Fryer. The two of them are a songwriting duo and they always talk about the benefits of writing in the same room. We wanted to be like them, so we would sit in the same room. That was partially how we bonded so deeply because we would crack up and we would make each other laugh with dummy lyrics – fake lyrics. We'd go through like 10 to 20, fake versions and crack each other up.

MORGAN: Ah, yes, I call that the "midnight version." Save it for the parody!

ANDERSON: Right. You have to write the wildly inappropriate versions first…

MORGAN: And get it out of your system! Because otherwise you can't unhear the bad word, right?

SAMSEL: We would just have tears streaming down our face laughing, and it was great. After writing together in the same room for so many years, we basically began to just fuse brains. Eventually, we learned how to write apart. We would come up with a hook together and then separate to divide and conquer. A lot of it transpired over emails back and forth because we just got to this point where there was so little explaining that we had to do about our ideas. I would send something to Kate… she'd say "Got it. I exactly what you need "… send it back to me… and back and forth like that. That just has morphed into a 12-year process of honing that craft of collaboration.

ANDERSON: We take a lot of walks. The early creative process starts with walks and talks, and usually that's where we crack the first idea, like a lyrical hook that we both get excited by. Now our process means Elyssa goes home, she tinkers with it, she finds a cool melody or a cool rhythm, and sends me voice memos or rough demos. Then we trade back and forth from there.

MORGAN: I love that. [To Elyssa] Do you layer first in a digital audio workstation like Logic™ or Garageband™ and then go to Finale™? Do you start with chord charts first?

SAMSEL: I will go to Logic and lay down the melody and the accompaniment to make a recording of it. I like to call them blueprints – the architecture of what the song could be. That, to me, captures what I am hoping the subtext is supposed to be doing, so that when Kate puts lyrics on top of it, the subtext is already in the music. The lyrics are their own thing, and that's the action and the motivation of the character. I don't worry about putting it into Sibelius™; not Finale… sorry… I know there's such contention in the world between Sibelius and Finale.

MORGAN: Oh, I'm not judging. I made a face because I *wish* I spoke both languages proficiently.

SAMSEL: I once tried to tinker in Finale…

MORGAN: Same. I get so frustrated because I'm so fast in Finale, and I felt so dumb in Sibelius.

SAMSEL: Generally, I don't put it into sheet music until it needs to be done, so I love Logic Pro.

MORGAN: Do you hook up your keyboard via MIDI [electronic communications hookup device] and then record your voice over it? Or do you just do it all as live audio?

SAMSEL: No, I'll do the MIDI piano, then do the audio for it, then take things to Kate and she'll sing for the demos as well.

MORGAN: So, you do hook first and then music structure and *then* the rest of the lyrics? Fill in the verses?

ANDERSON: Yeah, pretty much. We'll [figure out] the hook first. Once we find the hook, we know how we're going to use it to go from point A to point C. The first verse leads into this… the hook means this here… then second verse… then the hook means this here… then bridge takes us somewhere new. So, we usually know that when we find the hook, then we have a rough idea in our heads of what the lyrics and story need to be. Once I get the music, Elyssa usually provides a *version* of the lyrics, whether it be dummy lyrics or actual lyrics. That's so helpful because then it helps me get the appropriate ones in there. Sometimes they're really good and I say, "Great! Let's keep it!" because she's an amazing lyricist, too. It varies song to song. Sometimes, one of us has a clearer idea of what it is. Sometimes we're both really on the same page. Just depends.

MORGAN: What do you do if those ideas are opposed?

ANDERSON: It almost never happens. We really respect each other's ideas.

> We have this whole mantra: treat everyone you work with like they're genius. Then, you just have this inherent trust in the process, and you never find yourself with a battle of the egos that way. Trust in each other's vision and direction.

Sometimes, one of us has a stronger pull to go a certain direction. Usually, the other just trusts that.

MORGAN: I love this. Treat everyone you work with like a genius. Did you feel that way from the beginning with her or did you have to build that trust? Did you meet this person and immediately think that she's kind of a genius? I'd buy it.

ANDERSON: We wrote our first song together and we knew nothing about each other. That was it. We wrote this very bizarre song. I look back on it and it's funny. Our moderator even said that it was clear there

	were two brilliant minds at work here. But it was a bizarre song. It was very artsy, very "Sondheim at his weirdest" kind of thing.
MORGAN:	You were trying to impress everybody in the workshop.
ANDERSON:	It might have been a little of that. Then, we spent the first year of BMI watching each other work with other people. The more I saw Elyssa's work come in, the more and more blown away I was by her. Every single melody she wrote was such an earworm. I often would sing her songs in class, and I just couldn't get them out of my head. I would listen to her little voice demos over and over while I was at work because I loved her work. I just loved everything she was writing.
MORGAN:	So, a metaphor… you went on a date and then you dated other people in the workshop and then you came back and said, "You're the person I want to be in a working relationship with…"
ANDERSON:	By the end of that year, I had the biggest writing crush on her and was obsessed.
MORGAN:	I love this. It's like meeting someone at summer camp; it's like "Summer Lovin'" from *Grease* [Broadway, 1972]. That's so great. Elyssa, what's your take?
SAMSEL:	Absolutely. She was the lyricist in class who *everybody* wanted to work with because she was so fun. Laugh out loud funny. She had comedic chops that I think everyone was desperate to be close to because it would make them better and funnier and their songs would land better.
MORGAN:	It's also hard to be funny.
SAMSEL:	Yeah, I mean, Kate is naturally laugh-out-loud funny. During that first year [of BMI workshop], no matter who she worked with, the songs were a success because of her lyrics. She's so clever and witty. I was competing for her partnership. Towards the end, I had to take her out to dinner, and I had to cook. Then, I wrote like a long email about the reasons why I think we would make a great team. She was the belle of the ball. I'm lucky because she did end up picking me as her composer.
MORGAN:	I'm just a girl asking another girl to be her writing partner.
SAMSEL:	She was such a standout. I mean, yes, I thought she was a genius, but I was also just so taken with her as a person because she was the social butterfly of the class. She always organized the events and the parties; she was the sorority leader. Any of the misfits in the class – the wallflowers like myself – all gravitated towards Kate because she made us feel comfortable and she was so inclusive, and she was a wonderful human. So, I think if you're looking for someone you want to write with for the rest of your life, you got to pick someone who's the Kate in the room.

MORGAN: Pick the person you vibe with. Your repertoire is quite eclectic. I did find some commonalities in that there are two musicals that are themed around books. Did you all like love *Matilda* as a kid? What kind of material really makes you tick? Have there been a couple of projects that you realize that – when you're on your walks – you realize is your strike zone? I like to talk about strike zone.

ANDERSON: Yeah. I mean, there's definitely things we get so excited about and generally they have to do with like a feisty female protagonist. If it's comedy, all the better. My ultimate dream would be to have a project come across our desk that was starring Kristen Wiig or one of the women who we respect. Maybe it has a fantasy element to it. We're very drawn to fairy tale stuff. Witches have always intrigued us so much. We have never stopped saying that we want to write a female-forward *Book of Mormon*-type show… a dark comedy that is unapologetic with characters that are flawed and complex. We've been a little pegged as princess people.

MORGAN: Ah, yes. *Olaf's Frozen Adventure*.

ANDERSON: We have no shortage of princess projects on our resume. And we love that. We love writing for kids, and we will always love that. I think our dream is to write an adult comedy that's unapologetic.

MORGAN: Have you met Tina Fey yet, since she's in the Broadway sphere now?

ANDERSON: I briefly met her at a Tony party, and I quoted a *30 Rock* episode to her, and I was *so* nervous. I literally was shaking, and I was standing in a circle of people, and nobody was talking to her for some reason. People were sort of introducing each other. I had my moment. I got the courage. I told her I was about to move to L.A. to go work on a comedy series, which was *Central Park*. She said, "Just remember: you know what you know, and that's your strength. You go out there and the other people that you're going to be working with know what they know, but they don't know what *you* know. She gave me a cool pep talk…

MORGAN: Wow. Just sleep with your copy of *Bossypants* under your pillow!

ANDERSON: Seriously.

MORGAN: Elyssa: what is the material that makes you tick? Grown, funny witches?

SAMSEL: Yeah, I think so. I think we gravitate toward whimsy, magic, and irreverent humor; but good natured humor. We have to have a comedy that never makes fun of other people and never punches down, but in part, because we're really drawn to optimism and positive stories. We love when characters change their circumstances through positive thinking and positive acting, and that

	inspires those around them. We both had all the same childhood inspirations… like the Muppets.
MORGAN:	Ah yes! Who are imperfect creatures! Brent Goldstein did a podcast with Brené Brown[53] and talked about how Muppets are so amazing because they're not good at *anything*. My mind was blown. For example: Miss Piggy is not a great singer, Animal cannot play the drums well… but they just find so much joy in it. The point was: couldn't we all just live more like Muppets?
SAMSEL:	It's so great. They're being authentic to who they are. We're really drawn to stories about misfits. We both grew up obsessed with *The Secret Garden* movie and *A Little Princess*. We love stories where there's a magic element, misfits, and humor.
MORGAN:	I love that you said characters that want to better their circumstances because my students can be cynical on social media and on the surface, because they've come up in this generation. Gen Z has grown up and seen a lot of depressing stuff – 9/11, the recession, school shootings – politics and all. I notice that a lot of them say out loud that they I wish there were more musicals that address the issues but show *how* we get out of them. There are a lot of musicals like *Ragtime* that don't have a happy ending. The *Frozen* franchise does do that by showing women who are making their own decisions that affect their journeys. They do something about it.
SAMSEL:	My favorite thing about *Frozen* is that it's a love story between two sisters.
MORGAN:	Right. And we have *Brave*, which is really about mother daughter relationships. How does composing for animation work? Let's talk about *Central Park* and your work with that really adorable show and that super fun music that you put into it. What's the order of operation? How does the product get made? How is it different from theatre?
ANDERSON:	Oh, it's very different. Yeah. Usually with *Central Park*, like we start with some kind of like song prompt and sometimes it's in an outline, sometimes it's the script, but they just sort of set us free. We very quickly said we're probably going to find our own hooks. [The writers] will sometimes suggest a title. Maybe we use it and maybe we don't. It's become a really fun process because just as we finished season three – which is coming out now – we developed a shorthand with everybody and there's a lot of trust in everything. We get these song assignments… we'd get the script and read it. sometimes, we meet with the showrunners… then we'd write the song. There'd be a little bit of back and forth. Sometimes, we don't even see it until it's on TV.

MORGAN:	Are animations last?
ANDERSON:	They [story] *board* it first. It's cool; we've always loved writing for animation because there's a lot you can do in terms of visual stuff. So, we can write lyrics where we can say: "And now I have this Coke"… and then the Coke can just *appear*.
MORGAN:	Oh, right! You're not limited by reality.
ANDERSON:	You're not limited to what a props person can do in a show. You can write a crazy lyric about like a pancake stick ten feet high or whatever, and they literally draw that, and no one questions it because it's animation. It's so much faster than theatre.
MORGAN:	Meaning the compression of writing time because you have deadlines? They tell you to get a song written by Friday and you have to. Do you have to pull any overnights, or have you faced writer's block for real?
SAMSEL:	No. We usually don't have writer's block.
ANDERSON:	Sometimes we have writer's "first-draft-not-so-good."
MORGAN:	Ah, "Writer's Stumble?" One has to get the ideas out… get some of the ingredients out and even if we don't have the recipe or know what the finished product is… we're making a casserole and we know it's going in a casserole dish and it's going to go in the oven. The more we delay and just keep staring at blank things, the more intimidating coming out with a finished casserole looks right. Do you have a mantra with yourself to help you to spit something out?
SAMSEL:	Yeah. It's actually a quote by one of our favorite authors and collaborators, Jodi Picoult. She says: "You can't edit a blank page." We found that pretty early on, and we've used that as a mantra.
MORGAN:	Have you ever felt imposter syndrome? How do you overcome it?
SAMSEL:	I don't know that you do overcome it. I think it's just a work in progress. There are a million negative voices in our head that we could listen to. If you listen to them, then you're just going to sit in that imposter syndrome or you're going to sit in that doubt and it's going to stall you. It's okay that those voices are there, it's okay to think that, and it's okay if that's how you feel. I think that it's important to search for the other feeling on the opposite end of the spectrum – I can do this. I want to do this. I have something to say. No one else is me. I'm me. There's nothing stopping me other than me.
ANDERSON:	I feel like I usually just have to take it out of the context of: I'm trying to write a song that will be on Apple TV. Instead, I think: I'm trying to write a lyric that'll make Elyssa laugh and that's it. That's all it has to be. If she laughs, then maybe everybody else will like it, too. And if they don't, then they're not funny… I'm kidding.

MORGAN: "They can go to Netflix for all I care!" That's so funny. Have there been circumstances where you have to learn a new skill in order to overcome a challenge, whether it's a new musical style or …

SAMSEL: I think we learn new skills on every single job that we take, and they always feel impossible until you just sit down and do it.

MORGAN: I feel like sometimes it's connected to gender. There are men in my life and in our career that seem to have no hesitation of jumping into certain pools. But then, if I don't see myself represented in a certain way, in a certain place, I wonder if they're going to think that I'm a good conductor or director. Are they going to think that this story is cliche? Well screw it. There's like 400 different versions of *Cinderella*. I do always question if [my writing] is original enough.

SAMSEL: I think that's a great time when you're when you're thinking that or feeling that, that's a great time to put on Taylor Swift's "If I was a Man." That'll make you dive in the pool no matter what, because why not? If you are a man, you do.

MORGAN: Have you all been in rooms where you're the only women on the creative team? How has that worked out? How does that feel versus when there are other women in in the sphere?

ANDERSON: Yeah. We've definitely been the only women in a room full of men. There was advice that we got for years: when you go and do a meeting, you should wear a blazer and a plaid button up and jeans. Make sure you're not looking too girly and don't bring cupcakes and be more masculine in the room. At a certain point, we decided that we're going to reject that.

MORGAN: I've heard the cupcake thing. It said: don't bring snacks because it reinforces the caregiver thing. But I thought, Acts of Service is my love language.

ANDERSON: Right. Should we *not* have cupcakes?

MORGAN: What if *I* want cupcakes…?

ANDERSON: Yeah. It's funny. We've heard that from a bunch of different women we've worked with. We've heard stories of times where they are show running, or a female writer's episode came up and they wanted to bring in cupcakes. They had this conundrum of thinking: none of the men have done that, nor would they ever think to do that. So, what does that say or do to your status in the room? At a certain point, Elyssa and I just decided that we're not going to listen to that. We don't care. Our work speaks for itself. We're not going to dress or act masculine. We're going to be ourselves in a room.

SAMSEL: Why not pink and hair ribbons? Why not show up and do the job? The work that speaks for itself.

MORGAN: I really love that. I don't know what *kind* of feminist I am, but I'm the kind that thinks you should dress how you want to dress and live how you want to live and stand in your strength, whether it's heels or combat boots. I have always been that way. I love that, yes, your material has a whimsical feel to it. It has a feminine curve to it, which I really love. I think there's room for all of the material in the canon.

How do you engage in self-care? Have you had to juggle being a caregiver with your career? How do you balance your life? What kind of rituals, routines, and boundaries have you created for yourself while doing all of these things?

SAMSEL: I think we're both natural caregivers to all the people in our lives – our family and our friends. There's definitely been a learning curve on how to balance work and life and how to have both, because work can naturally become the majority of the time. A lot of our relationships, even work relationships, are very demanding. We are usually in situations where there are no boundaries. This job is very much the type of job where you can get a text at 1 am and need to answer it because it's from someone who is up working and that's just how it is. Especially because our collaborators become friends; they become family. There's a lot of caregiving that goes into that. It's really important to have your own methods of self-care and to learn how to create boundaries with the people in your life so that you are allocating your resources and making sure that you're not trying to give to others when you are depleted. So, if you've got any type of drained feeling, share that with others so that you're only showing up to give them your best. The people who love you and care about you will understand if you need time to self-care.

ANDERSON: It's a newer concept for us. For many years, we were *so* about the hustle and so afraid the opportunity would pass us by if we weren't the first people to answer the email within three minutes and be faster than anyone else. We needed to impress. We're just now getting to a point where we're working on having more boundaries and engaging in a little more self-care. I think COVID helped with that in some ways; but, then we have had the craziest year of our lives, putting up two musicals. We've learned that it's okay to have downtime – times where we might not be working in a traditional sense. We're working on replenishing our creativity and replenishing our bodies, our minds, and ourselves so that the next time things do get busy we're ready for it.

MORGAN: Why did you move to L.A.? How has it been?

ANDERSON: We both fell in love with L.A. around the time we were working on *Olaf's Frozen Adventure*. We were coming out here a lot. As that was wrapping up, we were getting some other gigs out here and it was really calling to us. I think Elyssa was in New York for 12 or 13 years, and I was there for 10 by the time I left. That felt like enough. That felt like it was okay to close that chapter and start a new one. We love it. We love the opportunity that's out here in TV and film and the renewed excitement that's happening for musical content. We were really lucky that *Central Park* really was our reason to get out here. We had a job lined up, waiting for us. Now, I realize how special, rare, and spoiling that was for us.

MORGAN: That's the case for either city, right? Both of those cities are different beasts.

ANDERSON: New York will always be there, and we'll always be able to go back and do theatre there and do theatre in London. But L.A. has been really, really great for us as a home base and we've got a lot of ambitions for what we want to do in terms of bringing the craft we've learned from writing theatre pieces out here and seeing that on the screens.

MORGAN: What's the next chapter? Are you doing things one job at a time, one day at a time? Or do you have certain ambitions where you say that you've got a few projects on the back burner? Are there other big, long-term plans?

SAMSEL: It's never one thing at a time. It's always juggling 7 to 10 projects at a time; and five of those might be simmering and the other five are fully boiling, ready to go, ready to plate, because that is the way we've been able to make things happen. We juggle them all because everything is on a different timeline. It's a lot and we've definitely got our hands full, but we love it and we're always hungry for more. We're working a lot now in developing movie musicals. We'll just hope that all of those happen and make it to the big screen so that we've got a new canon of movie musicals to look forward to!

Notes

1 "The BMI Lehman Engel Musical Theatre Workshop" website. See https://www.bmi.com/theatre_workshop.
2 "Kristen Anderson-Lopez" *Maestra Directory*. See https://maestramusic.org/profile/kristen-anderson-lopez/.
3 Kristen-Anderson-Lopez, Interview with Amanda Wansa Morgan via Zoom, December 13, 2022.
4 The Bechdel Test. See https://en.wikipedia.org/wiki/Bechdel_test.

76 The Writers

5 Bartlett Sher directed the 2018 Broadway revival of *My Fair Lady*, known for his staging of the ending, which contrasts traditional productions.
6 The BMI Lehman Engel Musical Theatre Workshop.
7 See https://twusa.org/.
8 Howard Ashman – Playwright and Lyricist of Disney hits such as *The Little Mermaid* and *Beauty and the Beast*.
9 The Disney Renaissance refers to the era of Disney filmmaking in the late 1980s and early 1990s with *The Little Mermaid, Beauty and the Beast, The Lion King, Aladdin*, and more.
10 John Lasseter – director and producer of many Disney and Pixar films – Executive Producer of *Frozen*.
11 Referring to the Arthur Lessac voice methodology, which identifies certain vowels that are easier to belt or yell based on open tongue and jaw positions.
12 "Screlting" is a casual term in the theatre world that combines "screaming" and "belting."
13 Zina Goldrich. Interview with Amanda Wansa Morgan via Zoom, November 11, 2022.
14 See https://en.wikipedia.org/wiki/The_Thad_Jones/Mel_Lewis_Orchestra.
15 See https://villagevanguard.com/.
16 See https://dalcrozeusa.org/about-dalcroze/what-is-dalcroze/#:~:text=Dalcroze%20 Education%20is%20a%20playful,ear%2Dtraining%2C%20and%20improvisation.
17 See https://en.wikipedia.org/wiki/Miracle_Piano_Teaching_System.
18 This is a reference to a lyric from the Goldrich & Heisler song "I Want them Bald."
19 See *Nine* in the show glossary.
20 Conductor. See https://www.mcp.us/michael-kosarin.
21 See *Spring Awakening* in the show glossary.
22 See *Grand Hotel* in the show glossary.
23 See https://en.wikipedia.org/wiki/Larry_Gelbart.
24 See later in this chapter.
25 See *Titanic* in the show glossary.
26 Popular cabaret nightclub in New York City.
27 Georgia Stitt. Interview with Amanda Wansa Morgan via Zoom, January 10, 2023.
28 Stitt is married to Tony-Award-winning musical theatre writer Jason Robert Brown – also a multi-hyphenate artist.
29 2007 album released by Stitt featuring original songs. See https://georgiastitt.com/albums/this-ordinary-thursday/.
30 Reed Doubler – a musician who is trained to play multiple woodwind instruments that share a similar skill set in operation and technique.
31 See http://www.collegelightoperacompany.com/.
32 Jujamcyn Theatres® is a Broadway Production/Producing company. See https://www.jujamcyn.com/.
33 High-quality non-profit theatre in Connecticut that frequently hires Broadway and New York-based artists. See https://www.goodspeed.org/.
34 "Starcrossed: The Trial of Galileo" by Jeanine Tesori. Audio recording via *New York Public Library* online. See https://www.nypl.org/research/research-catalog/bib/b18719010.
35 See Music Glossary in Chapter 3.
36 See Music Glossary in Chapter 3.
37 Joan Tower (b. 1938) – American Composer.
38 Music festival created in the 1990s featuring women in pop, rock, and folk music.
39 Poet (1892-1950). See https://www.poetryfoundation.org/poets/edna-st-vincent-millay.
40 "ritard" – a music term meaning "to slow down."
41 Adam Hayes. "The Peter Principle: What it Is and How to Overcome it." *Investopedia*. Updated March 20, 2021. See https://www.investopedia.com/terms/p/peter-principle.asp.
42 Concert series at New York City Center.

43 Non-profit organization, founded by Stitt, dedicated to providing resources to female-identifying musicians in musical theatre. See additional info in Chapters 1, 3, and 7.
44 "Georgia Stitt" website. https://georgiastitt.com/.
45 See Interview with Zina Goldrich, Chapter 2.
46 In May 2020, police officers in Minneapolis, Minnesota murdered an African-American man, re-igniting the Black Lives Matter movement and national (American) conversations around race, justice, equity, and inclusion. These conversations expanded to problems in various industries, including the theatre industry.
47 "We See You, White American Theater." Accessed January 1, 2023. See https://www.weseeyouwat.com/.
48 Bahr, Sarah. "White Actors and Directors Still Dominate Broadway Stages, Report Finds." *The New York Times*. October 1, 2020. Accessed Online March 31, 2023. See https://www.nytimes.com/2020/10/01/theater/new-york-theater-diversity-report.html.
49 Kate Anderson and Elyssa Samsel, Interview with Amanda Wansa Morgan via Zoom, December 2, 2022.
50 See Interview with Kristen Anderson-Lopez, Chapter 2.
51 Fey, Tina. 2013. *Bossypants*. New York, NY: Little, Brown & Company.
52 Amy, Poehler. 2014. *Yes, Please*. 1st ed. New York: Harper Collins.
53 Brene Brown and Brent Goldstein "Comedy, Creativity, and Roy Kent," *Unlocking Us*, October 20, 2021. See https://brenebrown.com/podcast/comedy-creativity-and-roy-kent/.

3
THE MUSIC TEAM

A Personal Perspective

I saunter down the hallway, past the callboard, past a few actors warming up on the floor... I say hey to the crew member setting props. I pull out my phone to turn on my flashlight as I round the corner and head down the dark stairs to the orchestra pit, under the stage. I am the first one there because I am the Music Director. I've gotten to the theatre early before our dress rehearsal to make a few edits to the programming of the keyboard that I play in the show, as well as make an adjustment to the keyboard programming of the other keyboard rig. I pass out notes that I typed up earlier that morning after taking two hours to listen to last night's dress rehearsal audio recording because I cannot take notes while I'm playing piano and conducting during the show. I have made a short work list for the band to play through during our twenty-minute notes session after sound check with the cast. There is one other female-identifying musician in my band of ten players. This doesn't bother me because I'm accustomed to it. I am also one of the youngest players in the band, and I'm in charge. There is a sense of pride coupled with many moments of self-doubt throughout my evening. My Guitar Two player misses an entrance and I wonder if I should have been clearer with my head nod. My drummer doesn't hit the button on the Act One Finale with me and I wonder if I hit the keys with my right hand out of sync with my left hand giving the cut-off. I sternly hold my ground when the Production Manager asks if we can go over the allotted break time and I tell them no. I wonder if everyone thinks I'm a jerk for that. For the majority of the gigs I play, I'm credited as the Music Director; however, on any given gig, I am also an arranger, a vocal coach, a conductor, a pianist, an orchestrator, a contractor, a manager, a mentor, a therapist, a performer, and a collaborative sound designer. I experience moments of high confidence and control contrasted

DOI: 10.4324/9781003324652-3

with moments of extreme doubt and questions. I am both right- and left-brained. I'm thinking about notes and rhythms alongside phrasing and breath. I will – in one song during a performance – experience the joy of grooving together with the band and cast contrasted with the fear of hitting the beats in sync. There is such joy and such work put into this process.

I've often wondered if my experience was unique. In 2016, I had the great privilege of serving as the Music Assistant to one of Broadway's most notable female-identifying music directors—Mary-Mitchell Campbell—who served as Music Director of the world premiere of *The Prom* during its out-of-town tryout in Atlanta at the Alliance Theater. Additionally, I served Associate Music Director Meg Zervoulis, who would go on to music direct *The Prom* on Broadway. I learned so much from these incredibly graceful, brilliant, kind women during this experience. I asked them questions and we swapped stories. Thus began my interest in documenting these kinds of stories for women like me who hadn't had the experience of working directly in the Broadway arena. I started to research women in music direction, which led to my discovery of an amazing roster of artists, a fascinating history of their work, and the inspiration to document some of their stories.

Notable Figures

In addition to the women interviewed in this chapter…

Trude Rittman (1908–2005) was a composer, music director, and – most importantly – an arranger whose dance arrangements were heard in many Rodgers and Hammerstein hits, including the infamous "The Small House of Uncle Thomas" ballet in *The King and I*; choral arrangements in *The Sound of Music*; and incidental music in *South Pacific*.[1]

Genevieve Pilot (1901–1980) provided dance arrangements for *Kiss Me Kate, Can-Can, Call Me Madam*, and *Candide*.

Karen Gustafson is the first woman on record to play in a Broadway pit orchestra (*The Vamp*, 1955) and would go on to be the first woman to conduct a Broadway orchestra (as a sub for Lehman Engel on *Destry Rides Again* in 1959). She was a dance arranger and served as an associate conductor on the Broadway shows *The Gay Life* (1961), *Wildcat* (1960), and *La Grosse Valise* (1965).

Liza Redfield (1924–2018) was a conductor and composer who is credited as the first "full-time" conductor of a Broadway pit orchestra as the music director of *The Music Man* in 1960.

Kristen Blodgette has worked on over a dozen Broadway shows as a music director and a music supervisor ranging from *Cats* (1982) to *Sunset Boulevard* (2017). She has helped mount the shows of Andrew Lloyd Webber around the world.

Lynne Shankel is a composer, lyricist, orchestrator, arranger, and educator. Her claim to fame is her work as orchestrator/arranger/music supervisor on the original Broadway production of *Allegiance* as Broadway's first woman to solely orchestrate a musical.

Yolanda Segovia was a Broadway music director who began with *Perfectly Frank* (1980) – a tribute to Frank Loesser – and was the Music Director of the original production of *Dreamgirls* as well as a conductor for *Aida* (2000).

Linda Twine served as Music Director on the Broadway productions of *Big River, The Color Purple, Jelly's Last Jam,* and *Caroline, or Change.*

Carmel Dean is a composer/lyricist and music director who arranged music for Broadway hits: *If/Then, Hands on a Hardbody, American Idiot,* and *The 25th Annual Putnum County Spelling Bee.*

Macy Schmidt is a "Forbes 30 Under 30" orchestrator, music director, and producer known for her work on *Ratatouille: The TikTok Musical, Kimberly Akimbo,* and *TINA*. She is the Founder and CEO of *The Broadway Sinfonietta* – an orchestra comprised of all women and a majority of women-of-color.[2]

Julie McBride is a Broadway music director known for her leadership on *Moulin Rouge, The Spongebob Musical* and *Head Over Heels.* She has worked on numerous Broadway shows as an associate conductor and as a music supervisor on many regional productions.

Christie Chiles Twillie is a music director, conductor, composer, sound designer, orchestrator, and arranger.

Sheilah Walker served as the Music Director for the critically acclaimed revival of *Porgy and Bess* starring Audra McDonald in 2012. She has music directed numerous Broadway tours and regional productions.[3]

Wendy Bobbit Cavett is a music director known for her work on the original Broadway production of *Come From Away* (2013). She also worked on the Broadway productions of *Mamma Mia* (2001–2015) and *The Scarlet Pimpernel* (1997–2000).

Haley Bennett is a music director, arranger, and music coordinator, having served as Music Coordinator for the musical TV series *Schmigadoon* as well as on the Broadway music teams for *Diana: The Musical, Come From Away, Once on This Island, Dear Evan Hansen,* and more.

Job Descriptions

Broadway shows – or those under "production contract" (think: National tours, New York level theaters) – typically have an entire music team that can consist of a few or all of the jobs listed in this section. Many of the amazing artist-musicians who serve in these positions on Broadway are capable of, or have experience, doing any of these jobs. However, some of them specialize, given their skills, interests, and life paths. The music team may consist of some or all of the following personnel:

Music Supervisor, Music Director (MD), Associate Music Director (the "Associate"), Assistant Music Director (AMD), Arranger, Orchestrator, Copyist(s), Rehearsal Accompanist, Programmer (typically keyboards but could include percussion or other click track modules), Contractor, and Musician.

Music Director (MD)

The Music Director is responsible for working with the stage director in preparing a theatre production for public performance, including casting, rehearsing the vocalists and orchestra, and working with the orchestra.

Typical responsibilities may include, depending on the budget of the theatre and scope of the project:

- Auditioning the singers and making casting recommendations to the director
  - Auditions often include a general audition where the MD must sightread to accompany, if an accompanist is not provided.
  - Callbacks include sides from the show which the MD chooses with the director. The MD sometimes accompanies the callbacks, or an accompanist is hired; or, tracks are purchased or made and can be used.
- Scheduling music rehearsals in collaboration with the director, choreographer, and stage manager. This process includes creating a music breakdown to determine who is singing when; this doesn't *always* correlate with who is onstage.
- Re-orchestrating in the event the theater cannot afford all of the pre-determined band parts. This can be a long and challenging process if the difference between what the show calls for and what the theater will provide is significant.
  - For example, if a show is written and licensed for twelve (12) musicians and the theatre will pay for five (5), the MD is responsible for re-writing some parts of the orchestration to ensure important sounds aren't lost.
- Programming keyboards
- Working with singers in partnership with the director
- Rehearsing the cast and orchestra
- Serving as a conductor for performances
- Playing piano for performances
- Helping cast members learn their music in advance of and outside rehearsals
- Hiring the band – In consultation with the producer (unless there is a Contractor – this is rare at the regional level)
  - Working with the producer on the budget for the orchestra
  - Working with the musician's union, if applicable
- Working with the production manager and sound designer on pit layout
- Working with the sound designer when microphones will be used
- Attending production meetings and rehearsals, as needed

Piano/Conducting (P/C) is a unique skill in which an MD plays piano for the performance and conducts using her head and/or hand cues, when possible. Often a Piano-Conductor has to come up with creative solutions in rehearsal with the cast and band to ensure cues (entrances and cutoffs) are clean, even if they cannot be given from the conductor every moment.

In some cases (especially with a particularly demanding score), a separate vocal director may be used to aid in this process. An Associate MD or Assistant MD can aide as well. It is essential that the production's director and musical director have an ongoing and mutually supportive collaboration. The director communicates her vision of the show, and the music director uses their understanding of the show's musical demands to help the director (and cast) be successful.

Beyond the expected musical skills, the music director must have strong communication skills and organizational abilities. She must be savvy with online storage "cloud" or hosting sites and be able to navigate sharing groups of files with the cast and/or the band for preparation, rehearsal, and potential changes to the music being used for the show.

Music Supervisor

This term is most often heard at the Broadway level or used in production contracts; very rarely in the regional market, due to budgetary limitations. The Music Supervisor – as Mary-Mitchell Campbell puts it – is the "CEO of The Music Team" when that position is occupied. They serve as a liaison between all of the interested parties, which can mean six to twelve people when a production is a Broadway musical premiere.

Associate Music Director ("Associate")

The next-in-command to the Music Director, the Associate, often carries out the duties of the MD in their stead, which range from accompanying rehearsals to conducting the orchestra; leading the orchestra; swapping places with the MD to take notes for actors and orchestra; and communicating with the other members of the music team as needed. The Associate might delegate tasks to the Assistant MD or the Music Assistant and might carry out communications with the Orchestrator, Programmers, and Copyists. They require the skill set to lead and also to follow, depending on the structure of the music team and if a Music Supervisor is present.

Assistant Music Director (AMD)

An Assistant Music Director (AMD) may undertake some or all of the following tasks:

- Play piano for rehearsals to allow the MD to watch, listen, and take notes
- Rehearse with individuals or small groups to teach music, playing piano and giving notes along the way
- Listen during rehearsals and take notes to give to the MD afterwards
- Aid the MD in the process of working on an orchestral reduction
- Aid the MD in organizing materials, such as band books

Music Assistant

The Music Assistant, different from an Assistant MD, serves the entire music team, not just the Music Director. They may have many of the same duties as an AMD, but their work is typically more geared toward the maintenance of the sheet music through the changes in a new work development process.

Primary duties of a Music Assistant include but are not limited to:

- Attending rehearsals in order to take notes for anyone on the music team
- Making modifications to sheet music files in notation software (either Finale™ or Sibelius™) – this may occur during rehearsal or outside/between rehearsals
- Transcribing changes made in rehearsal not notated by composer
    - To transcribe means to listen to and notate music on paper using aural skills
- Exporting new sheet music to formats for printing, copying, and distributing
- Preparing new/updated music charts for the orchestra if major changes are made during preview performances
- Formatting/re-formatting sheet music upon major changes in notation software
- Required: Working knowledge of Finale™ or Sibelius™
- Recommended: positive attitude, patience

Composer

A musician who creates (composes) original. A composer may do their own arranging, orchestrating, and engraving (sheet music creation) or s/he may not. The composer's music notation skills vary greatly, sometimes requiring additional music team members and sometimes not.

Copyist/Engraver

Primary job is to take handwritten music and create computerized or electronic versions of it with notation software (Finale™ or Sibelius™). This includes formatting the music to be legible by musicians as well as exportable and formatted into various "parts" for the band. This process can range in difficulty depending on the complexity of the music, the number of staves, and the needs of the formatting (lyrics, chords, dynamics, etc.).

The process typically has two parts – the data entry part and the formatting part. Sometimes, the formatting part of the job can require significant fine-tuning and thus be time-consuming.

Worth noting is the prolific work of Emily Grishman, who has served as a copyist, preparing music for 130 Broadway shows and formatting them into the scores we use today. She is one of Broadway's leading experts in score preparation. Her profile on the *Internet Broadway Database* is one of the longest ones, including titles dating back to 1987.[4]

Music Arranger (or "Arranger")

A Music Arranger may work on vocal arrangements, instrumental arrangements, or both. The arranger takes a pre-existing composition and fleshes it out into multiple voicings, perhaps adding phrases that elicit a different feel than the original. Arranging is a process that occurs after composition but perhaps before orchestrating.

Sometimes an arranger takes pre-existing pieces and combines them into a fluid piece (for example, taking multiple songs and cutting them into smaller pieces to put in a medley or montage). This means the arranger wouldn't necessarily *change* pieces of the composition, but rather figure out how those pieces fit together.

Often an arranger will alter the style of a piece. This occurs often in JukeBox musicals where pre-existing songs are re-imagined to fit into a musical. Arrangers tend to have very sharp ears—they can hear the music that someone has played either in audio or MIDI (see glossary) form and turn it into coherent sheet music or a layout that can be translated to a band or a cast of actors.

A Dance Arranger comes up with dance music, underscore, and incidental music that's based on the original ideas of the composer, which is fuller and lusher, perhaps containing various styles and ideas within.

> For example, Elvis Presley's song "Can't Help Falling in Love" was meant to be performed by Elvis himself along with a small rock band. In the jukebox musical *All Shook Up*, which is comprised of Elvis music, the same song is sung by an ensemble of over 20 singers with a band of 8 musicians. The Arranger takes the original song and expands both the instrumental and vocal arrangements with harmonies for depth and a completely different feel.

Orchestrator

The Orchestrator takes the music from the composer and arranger – typically in a piano/vocal score format – and comes up with the full orchestration, keeping in mind what the original orchestration (i.e. which instruments) will be. This process is highly creative, giving the Orchestrator license to flesh out which instruments play what melody or harmony. Some orchestrators do this by hand (necessitating a copyist after this process to computerize their work); however, some work directly into notation software. Some orchestrators also serve as the arranger and sometimes that is a team of people that work together to flesh out a score.

Programmer

This individual might be solely hired to program keyboards or other electronic-based instruments like percussion rigs. Prior to the development of Mainstage™ – a macOS-based software used for MIDI-capable programming – Programmers often created setups within keyboard synthesizers directly to create pre-programmed setups of sounds that a musician could easily toggle through consecutively throughout the live performance of a show. Today, Programmers use software such as Mainstage or Ableton to set up live performance files that allow for the same performance ease. These setups take hours to program as well as years to learn the craft of programming.

Cynthia Meng is a musician and software engineer whose credits include Broadway, Off-Broadway, and regional productions that have benefited from her skills as both musician and programmer.

Cynthiameng.com[5]

Music Glossary

A brief description of terms mentioned throughout this chapter that are commonly known to professionals in musical theatre music making.

Ableton Live™ is a digital audio workstation (DAW) for MacOS and Windows that debuted in 2001 and has gained popularity in Broadway orchestra pits since its usage in *Hamilton* enabled timed, live electronic music moments to be executed in conjunction with live musicians during performances. It is used for contemporary musicals with a pop or hip-hop lean to their style of music based on its capability of timed, live triggers with loops (vs. programs like Logic that focus more on multi-track recording). Commonly referred to as "Ableton."

Click tracks – These are tracks that enable a band to play together to a metronome if they are working with an in-ear-monitoring system. Click tracks can be run by a conductor, a drummer, or another musician or technician. Sometimes, click tracks only play a count-off or a few measures of a sequence to start the musicians at the same time together; sometimes they play throughout the entire song or sequence. Click tracks are often used when a band is playing with partially pre-recorded tracks and the audio engineer can set up the system in a way that the musicians hear both the click track and pre-recorded supplemental band music (along with themselves), but the audience only hears the supplemental track and the live musicians. Click tracks are particularly helpful in circumstances in which choreography relies on a perfectly consistent tempo; or if a sequence of lights or other technical elements (projections, pyrotechnics, etc.) are timed and preprogramed exactly to the music.

Digital Audio Workstation (DAW) – an electronic application software used for recording, editing, and producing music.

Finale™ – Music notation software. Input and editing can be done by hand, using a computer keyboard, or through connection to a keyboard as a MIDI device (see MIDI) for quicker input. Competitor to Sibelius.

Four-Track (tape recorder) – a popular device for recording layered audio (four tracks, to be exact) onto a cassette tape, available prior to digital audio workstations. A musician would record each part at a time, layering parts over one another, to result in a tape that could be played back with four layers/parts on it.

Garageband™ – a MacOS-based digital audio workstation (DAW) built for multi-track recording, capable of capturing both live audio and MIDI data. Often available as a free application to Mac owners.

In-Ear Monitors – Musicians are able to hear each other through an individual system fed to headphones or "in-ear monitors" where they can manage the mix of what they hear in relation to their own instrument, other instruments, the cast, and sound effects. Highly effective for live musicals, since the conductor can talk directly to the band through this system.

LogicPro™ – a MacOS-based digital audio workstation (DAW) built for multi-track recording, capable of capturing both live audio and MIDI data. Similar to Garageband but with many more capabilities, plug-ins, and settings. Only available via purchase. Commonly referred to as "Logic."

Metronome "App"/Tempo – Applications for smartphones or devices that provide a metronome as well as the capability to create set lists of metronome files to use in live performance. This allows a conductor to toggle through the songs and start pre-set tempos in various musical meters for starting musical numbers.

MIDI – A device for electric connection between a computer with recording software and a controlling device for that software; most commonly: a computer with a digital audio workstation and a keyboard (piano) that can be read note-by-note in that program. Similarly, MIDI can connect a electric drum machine module to a drum pad. Once MIDI data is recorded, it can be modified within a DAW to alter the instrument output or quality of sound (reverb, tone, etc).

Noting – The term for giving notes to a cast or band.

Preproduction – **"Pre-pro"** – a process that creatives engage in prior to the start of rehearsal with actors, often with their assistants and in a rehearsal space on their feet, figuring out choreography or physical staging.

Qlab™ – A digital multimedia playback software, designed for MacOS, used in live performances. Capable of triggering audio and video cues along with connections to lights and other technical effects with complicated programming capabilities.

Session singer – a singer hired by a record label or music production studio to sing on multiple albums or demo recordings for only that recording session. Duties can vary based on the needs of a project, but often include backup singing.

SFX™ – A digital multimedia playback software, designed for PCs, used in live performance. Mostly focused on triggering audio cues; was used often in the theatre industry until the development of QLab.

Sibelius™ – Music notation software. Input and editing can be done in Finale by hand, using a computer keyboard, or through connection to a keyboard as a MIDI device (see MIDI) for quicker input. Competitor to Finale.

Stick Conducting – Traditional conducting with a baton (or one's hand) as opposed to conducting while simultaneously playing piano or keyboard (the more common technique with contemporary musicals).

Piano-conducting – Conducting a show (cast and band) while simultaneously playing piano or keyboard. Can be done with a variety of head nods, lifting one's hands for cutoffs when possible, and – more recently – the use of verbal cues to a band through the use of in-ear monitoring and a microphone fed to the musicians' ears only.

Key 2/Keyboard 2 – Many contemporary musicals are orchestrated with a second or even third keyboard, covering (simulating) multiple instrument sounds. One of the keyboards often plays the "piano" part of the musical orchestration. Often, the conductor is playing piano from the "keyboard one" book; however, there are exceptions where the conductor is playing a keyboard book but the part is not the lead piano part, to allow for that conductor to focus more on conducting than playing.

Subbing/Subs – Musicians often hire substitute players – or "subs" due to the length of musical runs. This includes conductors. "Subbing" is known to be challenging because "subs" often don't receive rehearsal time with the full band prior to playing a performance. They must study the music on their own time, practice using a finite number of resources, and often "shadow" the main player during a performance to hear the flow and pace of the show along with audio or visual cues from the conductor not indicated in the score.

INTERVIEWS

Kimberly Grigsby
Mary-Mitchell Campbell
Meg Zervoulis
AnnMarie Milazzo

Kimberly Grigsby – Biography

Kimberly is a music director and conductor based in New York City. Her Broadway career spans 25 years, including collaborations with composers Jeanine Tesori, Adam Guettel, Tom Kitt, Daniel Messe, Duncan Sheik, Michael Friedman, David Byrne, Stephin Merritt and directors George C. Wolfe, Michael Mayer, Bartlett Sher, James Lapine, Alex Timbers, Pam MacKinnon, Kathleen Marshall, Leigh Silverman and Julie Taymor. Her credits include the original productions of *Flying Over Sunset; To Kill A Mockingbird; Caroline, or Change; Spring Awakening; The Light in the Piazza; Head Over Heels; The Full Monty; Amélie; Spider-Man: Turn Off the Dark; Coraline; Songs From an Unmade Bed; The Fortress of Solitude; Here Lies Love*. Other collaborations include *The Light in the Piazza* with Renée Fleming; the premiere of Jeanine Tesori's *The Lion, The Unicorn and Me* for Washington National Opera; Susan Botti's *Telaio: Desdemona*; Barrie Kosky's production of *Fiddler on the Roof* for Lyric Opera of Chicago; and an appearance with The Grant Park Music Festival, conducting the 2022 *Lights On Broadway* performances.

Interview with Kimberly Grigsby, Zoom, October 13, 2022[6]

MORGAN: I've been such a fan of yours since I saw *Spring Awakening* when I was in my first year in grad school. I was really on the cusp of figuring out where I was going. I was aiming to be a performer, and I hit a snag my senior year of college with a vocal injury. I had also started playing [piano] for people and started getting requests to work on little projects and arrangements. I came to see *Spring Awakening* and saw you conduct and run the band. For me, it was a classic moment of representation. It made me say to myself: "You can go down that path. You do not have to keep resisting that path that you think the universe is telling you to do." This was because I saw you on stage running the band, playing piano, and taking part in the action of this rock show. For my generation, that was so important. I came up through the 1990s with *Rent* and it was pivotal for me. So, being able to speak to you is so exciting, knowing the projects that you've worked on and the people that you've worked with on big projects.

GRIGSBY: I have been very fortunate to work with many exceptional artists – actors, directors, choreographers, designers, composers, and musicians. What I learned a long time ago was that, as a musician, I like to tell stories through music; and that's what we do in the theatre. When I was going through school, there was not a degree for music directors. I hear that there are some now.

MORGAN: There's a few… Arizona State… Shenandoah…

GRIGSBY: I was a piano performance major, but I didn't want to be a concert pianist. First of all, I have relatively small hands for a pianist!

MORGAN: Same! I have an octave and a prayer!

GRIGSBY: Yeah, right! Mozart was my guy! When I was a sophomore in high school, the seniors were competing at a thespian conference.

MORGAN: Ahhhh State Thespians…

GRIGSBY: State Thespians…. Right. They were doing *The Apple Tree* and the drama teacher—Rebecca Wilburn—and the choral director—Ms. McAdory—decided I would be the right person for the job of teaching the music to the actors and playing [piano] for the performance. Oh my gosh, that was so much more fun than sitting alone at the piano with my dog napping next to me, while I practiced Mozart… Beethoven… Chopin – which I love, don't get me wrong – but, I was a teenager and I wanted to be a part of something.

MORGAN: Yeah. Part of a team.

GRIGSBY: Yes, being with other people…a part of a community working together toward a common goal.

MORGAN: So, being a military kid, you moved around a bunch. Do you feel like those skills you acquired by moving around helped you out in in this particular Broadway-level market?

GRIGSBY: Absolutely. It helps you with the reality of the theatre business. Shows are going to close. Even if it lasts for a while, it's still going to close.

MORGAN: Even *Phantom*.[7]

GRIGSBY: Yeah. You put your whole soul in… you create a family… you get tight and then… it's over and you're on to the next one. You have to learn how to protect yourself a little bit.

MORGAN: So your heart doesn't break every time…?

GRIGSBY: It does a little bit. You get better at figuring it out. People say I'm non-sentimental, but I'm protecting myself so I can move on. Closing a show involves a degree of mourning and that can take its toll on one's spirit, if you aren't prepared for the shockwaves of that experience.

MORGAN: That's so important to know. I've worked with a couple of folks from the Broadway arena… worked on some Broadway tryouts… And I remember talking to a mutual friend of a high-level Broadway colleague, and they said, "Oh, this person is cold… I never know what they're thinking… they're hard to read…" I had gotten close to that person that they were speaking of, and I said, "Well, think about the rooms that *that person* has to navigate… it's a structure and it's an industry… maybe that's a defense mechanism." You know?

GRIGSBY: Yes. At least now, people will call me on it; people who have known me for a while and care enough to be honest. When I was working with George C. Wolfe on *Caroline, or Change…* we had already done *Radiant Baby* together. George and I were out with some folks from the show and at some point, he said, "You know, Kimberly… some people think you're hostile."

MORGAN: Oh wow.

GRIGSBY: He was being funny, but completely honest. Other people will just ignore you or be silently frustrated, which can then manifest as tension. He knew I wasn't *actually* hostile. He knew that I was in pursuit of perfection, but he wanted me to be aware of the perception of others in the room. I'm efficient in my non-cuddly language when I say, "we've got a job to do." That can be interpreted as hostile by some people.

MORGAN: Well, and here we are circling right into gender. Do you sometimes feel that if you were a man with that behavior, it would even be a question? Jerome Robbins[8] had a crazy strict reputation, but everybody still led with the word "brilliant."

GRIGSBY: Yes. I think the word that got attached to me was "passionate." Passionate. That was the euphemism I often heard when describing me.

MORGAN: I feel like internet culture—or rather social media—has helped us in that regard because of the ability for people to speak their minds. Once we got safety in numbers, it starts to become a question of: "Are you making that assumption because I'm a woman and you expect me to be soft or caregiving or nurturing?"

GRIGSBY: Yes. Right.

MORGAN: Why am I supposed to work harder to hold space for my perfection, which you also expect, and then that's two jobs in one? When I'm working as a conductor or running a band – especially when the band is all men – I have to be your boss and I have to be perfect, and I can't mess up. Otherwise, you're going to throw judgment at me. AND I have to pat you on the back when we're all done, because you expect that from me. That's a lot of work, right?

GRIGSBY: Yeah. If I make a mistake, I'll be the first person to admit it and work to fix it. We're all in this together. When I'm conducting, I often ask the musicians what kind of cues they want.[9]

MORGAN: Ah yes… "You want *three, four*?"

GRIGSBY: What is clear? Do you want two beats here? I prefer to just have one beat because it helps me be tighter on the cue, but if a musician requests two beats, I give it to them. So, I figure out the rhythm of the language beforehand and just hope that the actors are consistent in their delivery of the line. The thing is, sometimes the actors will get to the words that you want [for the cue] and then they pause…

MORGAN: Oh God! And then they don't breathe the same way one night and… they just breathe weird and I'm like "AH! My hands already UP [*in the upswing*]"

GRIGSBY: Yes; you have to help the actors understand the conductor's role as the leader of the music and their partner in the storytelling. We have to empower the actors and the musicians so they are comfortable, confident, feel supported and can excel at their jobs. We're keeping it all together, but the actors and musicians are the ones performing. Unless we're playing the piano [as in: piano conducting] but I'm talking about conducting on our feet.

MORGAN: "Stick" conducting, yeah…

GRIGSBY: They're all playing and performing. We know what that's like. They're the ones getting the sweaty palms, or the dry reed, or having to cough while they play or sing. All we're doing is conducting; not to diminish the importance of what we do. I mean, we are – coordinating many people at one time…

MORGAN: Which is wild when often the music director is left out of the review or off the poster.

GRIGSBY: Well, always off the poster. Always off the poster.

MORGAN: It's a MUSIC-al. It drives me nuts! I had to sub a couple of weeks ago with a few hours' notice as piano-conductor on a show that I had only played once with no rehearsal. And yeah, I was like, "I'm going to go fly a plane and I've only been in the simulator." You know, but it'll be fine.

GRIGSBY: Yes, that's right. It's like flying a plane. *Spiderman* [*Turn off the Dark*] was like working for NASA. That was like Command

	Central because we were nineteen [19] musicians split between two different rooms, communicating via cameras.
MORGAN:	So, are we almost supporting abuse by making those situations work? So, producers go, "Oh, we can put them in different rooms. Kimberly Grigsby pulled that off with Spider-Man…"
GRIGSBY:	Oh, no… They worked so hard to get us all in the same room. No that's not what we're doing. Each situation is unique in how we tell these stories based on the requirements of the tech… requirements of the director's vision… the requirements of the choreographer's vision… the requirements of how big the band is… I mean, Julie [Taymor] originally wanted the band *in* the set on the stage.
MORGAN:	*Next to Normal* style?
GRIGSBY:	No. We were supposed to be on a platform that looked like a cantilever from offstage left with flying happening around us. However, that idea did not make it past the model stage. We looked around the theater for spaces that could accommodate the whole orchestra; and the producers and designers worked hard to make it happen, but it was not possible. Then, we did have two of the musicians onstage, with the rest of us in the basement, but the visual was confusing for the storytelling. So, we all ended up in the basement, in two separate rooms. But my point is: we just make it work. I don't find that supporting abuse. They were using the pit for hydraulics. So, to tell that story, they needed the pit. I get annoyed when they put seats in where there should be a pit because they want to sell more seats. Producers want to make more money by putting more seats in by covering up the pit, and that's when the band has to go elsewhere. If you want music to sound real, then you have to have it in the same space as the people listening to it. You don't get the vibration of a stick hitting a drum or a bow across the strings or the sound of a wind or brass instrument blooming into the space from the pit. You don't get the human… you don't get the soul if it's only coming out of a speaker. No matter how many speakers you have and how fancy and expensive they are, you still don't have humans making music in the same space as the audience, sharing air and exchanging energy. Then we might as well be recorded, and the show can be done to tracks.
MORGAN:	Right?
GRIGSBY:	It sounded recorded. It did not sound live. It sounded more compressed than usual.
MORGAN:	Yeah. In the hole…
GRIGSBY:	It's so important to me to have acoustic information in the space. When I did *Amélie,* there was not going to be enough room in the pit for the eight of us, so we split the band between the two boxes in the house. Some people on the team were worried that the band would

overpower the actors, but we played with dynamics and awareness of balance. The result was successful and some commented that it felt like being inside of a Beatles record with the panning from both sides.

MORGAN: In stereo…

GRIGSBY: Yeah. To me, it's fun to solve the problem. But if somebody asks where my preference is for the band, my answer is in the pit.

MORGAN: Do you like music technology and keyboard programming? Do you participate in that part of the job?

GRIGSBY: When I did summer stock all those years ago, I did all the programming. I traveled around with my Kurzweil PC-88 and Alesis S1.

MORGAN: Yeah, that heavy keyboard.

GRIGSBY: Yeah. I'm not a fan of a keyboard replacing instruments. If the synthesizer is there to produce a particular electronic sound or set of sounds, then great. But, I will ask how we can accomplish something without electronics first because that's my preference, aesthetically.

MORGAN: Do you work with click tracks?

GRIGSBY: We used a click in *Spider-Man* for one of the flights.

MORGAN: You didn't have to use a click for the "Hand Jive" (*Grease*)?! Good Lord. I just know some choreographers will claim that something is too fast or too slow. I'll say, "Really? Because it's on a click." Woof, that hand jive…

GRIGSBY: No, we didn't have click. We didn't click for [*Grease*] at all.

MORGAN: When I pit-sat *Mean Girls*, that thing is clicked within an inch of its life. I know that *Ain't Too Proud* was clicked within an inch of its life because the lights are synched to the click… the tour of *Ain't Too Proud*.

GRIGSBY: Right.

MORGAN: It's all clicked from one end to the other and that is fascinating to me… whether a click is beneficial or not beneficial.

GRIGSBY: Drummers like clicks – particularly sub [substitute] drummers. I get it; it removes some stress. I don't like to have anything in my ear. I want to hear the audience; I want to hear the balance of the vocals and the band in the space. If I have a perfect mix inside my ears, how am I maintaining or controlling what's happening live? Who cares if the sound is good for me inside my head? Part of my job is to make sure that what the audience is hearing is clear and balanced. I never get to hear it the way the audience hears the show; But it's not *for* me.

MORGAN: That is frustrating, yeah.

GRIGSBY: I don't think of it as frustrating. It's my job, along with the sound designer, the mixer, the actors and the musicians to provide the audience with a superb experience. During *Spider-Man*, the guitar players had their fancy mixes, but sometimes they didn't know when their guitar was "on" or not. The guitar could be on in their headphones, but not on in the house. There were nine (9) players down the hall in a different room, which is why I asked for speakers to be in our room – so I could hear them without headphones and hear the cast. Eventually, the guitarist took one ear off [the musicians are wearing in-ear headphones that enable them to hear a customized mix of the cast and instruments]. In fact, everyone benefited from taking one ear off of their perfect mix and listening to what was happening in the room, so we could make music together, listening to each other.

MORGAN: That's what I do! I hate having two ears on. I play a lot of shows onstage because I play mostly rock and pop stuff. I'm always one ear out. I feel the same way. It's a vibration thing. It's a sense thing, almost like I feel like I'm in an airplane if I have both ears in, and I can't do my best. I'm not aware of my surroundings so it's hard to fly the plane like that… here we are again…

GRIGSBY: Yeah…we didn't even use a click for *Head Over Heels*.

MORGAN: Really?! Gosh. And that's a POP show!

GRIGSBY: Yeah, the Go-Go's…

MORGAN: That's wild. Mad respect.

GRIGSBY: Thinking about it now, the drummer – Dena [Tauriello][10] – would check the tempo with a metronome before each song, but there wasn't a click.

MORGAN: Big fan of the "TEMPO" app.

I feel like a lot of people use clicks just so they don't have to argue with the choreographer. It's clicked so it's not faster and it's not slower. In the regions, it's often this passive-aggressive approach. All I know is: we're not robots, but I did click off my metronome and I did count it off correctly … we might have sped up, we might have slowed down…

GRIGSBY: Right. I take the tempo *out* of dialogue.

MORGAN: Right…

GRIGSBY: So, if the actors are talking fast a particular night, then the tempo will be relatively faster… a little bit here, a little bit there… not crazy fast … not crazy slow.

MORGAN: A difference of three BPM [beats per minute]…

GRIGSBY: If we're on a click… I don't like how it feels if the dialogue is slightly different, but the music is not allowed to adapt.

MORGAN: Yes, and then there's audience response; especially in smaller houses. They're like "Oh, the show feels slow." I'm like, "That's because no one's laughing. You're asking for a laugh instead of the cup of tea."

GRIGSBY: That's right. We [should] just stay true to the story. It'll all be fine. Yes, there are all those other factors.

MORGAN: What are some of the personality traits in collaborators that you tend to gravitate towards? When someone asks you to join a project and you say yes right away. What are some of the things that those people do that bring you into a room because it's going to be different? Is it their [pre-production] work? Their collaboration skills?

GRIGSBY: To be valued and treated as a collaborator in the process, musically and dramaturgically.

MORGAN: That connects me to your role models. You mentioned your high school teachers…

GRIGSBY: Rebecca Wilburn and Mary McAdory.

MORGAN: And your band director?

GRIGSBY: Yes, Jim Cooper – the band director. And Roxanne Seftas, who I actually never even had as a teacher. She was a civics teacher who was awesome and so supportive of the drama department. All through the years, they've continued to be my supporters. If I'm questioning something, I'll call them because I know that they always have my best interest in mind and they will be completely honest with me.

MORGAN: Yeah, I still I'm still quite close with my high school teachers. In fact, I saw them this summer and as I was booking some of these interviews, I texted my high school teachers freaking out because during those impressionable years on us… They're like our parents. They're like our idols, our, you know, our, our nurturers and our supporters. I think that's really sweet that you went straight to that demographic of people as opposed to the role models upwards.

GRIGSBY: At SMU [Southern Methodist University], I was a piano performance major, but I was exercising my desire to be in a group by playing in the SMU Symphony and accompanying the choirs. I didn't consider being a conductor. I had taught music; I didn't know that meant you were the "music director." Then, my junior year, the theatre department brought André De Shields[11] in to direct *A Funny Thing Happened on the Way to the Forum* and no faculty member wanted to music direct…

MORGAN: That's how I got into it in grad school! Nobody did it [Well, a really great guy did it well, but he had moved into administration that year].

GRIGSBY: Right. They hired me just to be the pianist and after the first read-through, Andre said, "Well, Kimberly…"

MORGAN: And he's very much famous at that point… This is after *The Wiz*…?

GRIGSBY: And *Ain't Misbehavin'*. This is 1989. He said, "Kimberly, have you ever conducted an orchestra?" I said, "No." He said, "Would you like to? Because I want you to be the music director."

MORGAN: Nice! André De Shields! He actually came to my college when I was there (Florida State University). He's a very generous soul.

GRIGSBY: He's so generous and such a good teacher. I learned so much from him. He would say, "Whatever you're dealing with in the day… you walk through this door, and it all stays out there. We are here to create. You do not bring your troubles into this room. We have this to do. Then you can pick them back up outside the door when you leave." I fell in love with him. Then, the next year – my senior year – André returned to direct *The Threepenny Opera*. The band was on stage, and I was in full costume. That was the first time somebody dressed me up as the music director and put me on stage playing the piano.

MORGAN: Little did you know…

GRIGSBY: Eleven (11) years later, I'd be conducting [André] in *The Full Monty,* where he gets nominated for a Tony playing [the role of] Horse.

MORGAN: So, what do you do to protect your peace? I think this is important for the young artists, especially. You leave that tech rehearsal at the end of the day… I've had plenty of moments where I walk out of tech and I either feel disrespected… I feel stomped on… I feel like I didn't say the right thing… I feel Imposter syndrome…

GRIGSBY: Oh, yeah.

MORGAN: What do you do between walking out of the building and then having to walk back in the next day? What are the ways in which you've learned to cope with leadership?

GRIGSBY: I write in a journal. I write myself a letter.

MORGAN: Atta girl.

GRIGSBY: I've also spent time in therapy because I would get angry at myself… I would go into depression… I would get angry at other people. You learn all about defense mechanisms, like recognizing it in others, but also recognizing it in yourself. One has to understand that often when those people are making you feel that way, *they* are having an issue with themselves and they're taking it out on you. The ego has to somehow stay over here so that you can receive it and go. "Where are they coming from? Why did they say that? They did not *mean* for it to be insulting." That came at me because I'm not giving them something they need. I need to figure it out and not take it as a criticism or as an insult. You are going to get knocked down. You also cannot please all the people in this world. People that you idolize…that you want to work with… you love their work and you finally get in the room with them… and you discover there's a personality conflict. It's not that any either one of you are behaving poorly. The chemistry simply does not work.

MORGAN: Right. Incompatible. You make some great points and sounds like you handle it well.

GRIGSBY: Not always, but hopefully more so these days. I'm lucky to have been celebrated and supported by André DeShields when I was 20 years old; by this "Great" who not once talked down to me or not once told me where my place was... and treated me like an equal in the collaboration. I had teachers who said to me as a teenager, "You're going to be the music director. We're teachers and you're a student, and we're creating this together." I was treated as equal. I've never been treated by my parents or by teachers or anyone with the thought that "You can't do this because you're a woman."

MORGAN: Right. Also, you were young, right? I mean, ageism plays into a lot of this, too.

GRIGSBY: I'm not going to tell the stories of where I was treated unequally. Those exist. I just choose not to talk about them because, to me, that's fueling a fire. I'm going to work and I'm going to do the best job as a music director. I don't want to be known as a "female music director." I don't want to hire somebody just *because* they're a woman. I celebrate everyone and what they bring to the table, but I want the best person for the gig. I find that a generation of people want to get promoted faster, and now we have people in positions that have no experience.

MORGAN: Do you think being told "no" actually helps you learn something?

GRIGSBY: Yes... I learned my craft doing readings and projects at Musical Theater Works[12]... at TheaterWorksUSA[13]... at the NYU grad writing program [for musical theatre][14] teaching scores... sight-reading new scores... helping shape musicals... playing for voice classes and lessons, for little to no money.

MORGAN: I think that's so important with this particular generation. I know that there's a lot of stuff out there about not working for free... for exposure. But I got my first Alliance job by doing a coaching for free. I knew Jody Feldman [Producer, Casting Director] was going to be there.

GRIGSBY: That is my advice to young people. Say yes to everything even if you don't think you have the specific skills for the job. The internships and low-paying music assistant positions are where you make connections and learn your craft through the experience. Look at it as free education and networking, rather than not getting paid a big salary.

MORGAN: Oh, absolutely. Say yes because you'll figure it out.

GRIGSBY: Exactly. You just say yes, and you don't know what door is going to open. You don't know who's going to be listening. If the

	opportunity follows your path, take it; it may not be the exact step you were thinking about, but it might lead to something that you didn't know about it or you thought you were capable of.
MORGAN:	Do you like doing plays with music? Like *Twelfth Night* ... *[To Kill a] Mockingbird*? That kind of stuff. Is it the same? Is it different? Apples and Oranges?
GRIGSBY:	It's easier.
MORGAN:	Yeah, aren't the rooms different? It's a different vibe, too.
GRIGSBY:	Yes; when people are singing, they're vulnerable. Their body is their instrument. They're being judged for how they sound. They have to take care of themselves in a particular way.
MORGAN:	And the expectations... it gets recorded, it gets disseminated... a bar gets set for what people are coming to hear...
GRIGSBY:	It's harder. Singers aren't allowed to make as many mistakes ... in terms of experimentation, you know. I find that doing plays (non-musicals) is a more relaxed vibe.
MORGAN:	I love seeing plays when I come to New York. It's a different vibe than seeing a musical. It's so great.
GRIGSBY:	I prefer a play as an audience member.
MORGAN:	That does tie it all the way back to using story over score, which I hear often from music directors who really know what they're doing. Which is kind of ironic, right? I was raised by a lot of music directors and conductors who were just so focused on the perfectionism of the musicality. As a music director, I'm always going to defer to story over vocal placement or the vocal quality or the tempo or the groove... what's happening on stage right now? How are we facilitating that?
GRIGSBY:	How is it informing how we're going to perform this? What is determining the need for a song here? What is the tone of this? Most of what I've done is work on new things, so those are the questions that come up. It's just something in my body that, if it doesn't feel truthful, then we have to look at the question of why. I will ask either the director or the composer or the book writer: "Why am I starting this? I don't know why I'm starting this song right now."
MORGAN:	Oh, that's it. [Jeanine] Tesori said on a webinar last year via Maestra... It was a "Composer as Dramatist" lecture... she recommended a couple of books about the idea of like finding that moment of: if the scene doesn't go into the song and it doesn't make sense, then what's the point?
GRIGSBY:	I'm telling the story every night. There's a rhythm in the relationship between the dialogue and the music. I don't want to know the music has started. It needs to be seamless. *I'm* doing it because I'm inside of the actor/character's body and I know that you [the actor]

are ready to now go to this place… and I'm going to join you on that dance to support your choices. That's my job. It's not even something that I think about that much, at this point in my life. I cannot start the music… like, my body just won't go if it doesn't have truth in the moment.

MORGAN: AMEN! I say that all the time!

GRIGSBY: I'm going to definitely hire the person who is not considered the strongest singer, but is the most honest storyteller over the astonishing vocalist. It's a bonus if they happen to be the same person.

MORGAN: It's a different medium, right? Then go be a concert singer. Go into a different medium. Go do your thing on TikTok!

GRIGSBY: Correct. Yes. I'm not going to vocalize a person and see how high they can sing. If the director and the writers like somebody, then we'll make that work. We'll transpose the key or change the melody to fit their voice.

MORGAN: I love that. That demonstrates confidence in your abilities, right? We don't have a gate for my university program. We don't have an audition to get in and ends up bringing us all the diamonds-in-the-rough because they're kids who have beautiful gifts. Their high school program didn't have a drama program… or they've been singing karaoke in their basement. It's glorious. It's where I prefer to be because I'm like, I'll help you figure out your laryngeal placement. We got it. I know the anatomy. I love to hear that from the Broadway level. I just think that's the whole point of this book. There's a disconnect between New York and Broadway and everywhere else in the United States.

GRIGSBY: What do you mean by that?

MORGAN: Broadway seems like a mystery. There's an assumption that when you land in New York, all of a sudden you have to change or augment the way you do something because it's like a level up. It's like the next level in a video game. For young people who haven't been there, they just don't know the unknown, right? It's an ignorance thing… and it was an ignorance thing for me. Hence writing the book. Until I got in the room with Mary-Mitchell Campbell and realized that we do things in a similar way… she just does it with a team of seven and I do it with a team of one at a regional theater. I was so nervous. Once I got in the room, I realized that we do things similarly. We play the piano the exact same way. Nothing that those musicians were doing was *so* beyond my level in the game, but I didn't know that. How would I know that?

GRIGSBY: It just costs more. The stakes are higher.

MORGAN: That is the pressure right there… most of it's the emotional abilities.

GRIGSBY: Right.

MORGAN: I watched Mary-Mitchell make a lot of important decisions ... decisions that cost many dollars. At the regional level, you don't get to make those kinds of changes quickly because there isn't the money to pay the people in the event that you want to pivot hard and fast on a hiring decision. So, I think a lot of people take certain liberties because there's no fear of being fired because we can't afford it or then the show can't go on. But at the Broadway level, you *can* because you can afford that high-quality replacement right away. *That's* the pressure that is the difference. Even in this town... working at the Alliance on a pre-Broadway tryout versus literally any other professional theatre or show in town. That feeling of: I could lose my job if I slip up because I could be replaced so quickly because they can afford to do it. That kind of perception.

GRIGSBY: The basic pressure on a commercial show and everyone working on it is that we need to create something that people will want to see and then, tell others to see. For us to succeed means that the producers make their money back and we keep our jobs. The decisions that we are making – not personnel – but decisions as in... does that song work?

MORGAN: Right. I've seen pre-Broadway tryouts with songs in them that are clearly there to serve the purpose of giving a popular actor a song. I mean, "Cooties" in *Hairspray* is there for a costume change! That whole number is a waste of our time because it's cute and a good song for Amber, but it is there so everybody can change, and Edna can get into the can.[15]

GRIGSBY: That's not a reason. You have to make sure that every song and every moment serves the story. What is the story we're telling? What is the core of the story? We must consider what is at the center of the wheel and all the spokes have to be connected to that idea.

MORGAN: That's the dream.

GRIGSBY: Well, it's actually the task.

MORGAN: Yes.

It's really refreshing, though. It's also refreshing to know that there are truth police out there. This is about pulling back the curtain to suggest that when a young person gets to NYC, there are those who really care about the same things that they do.

GRIGSBY: We're here. And hopefully don't forget what you care about. Don't get caught up in the momentary hoopla. Why are you doing it? Why are you going into this very difficult business?

I believe that if everyone was lucky enough to enjoy what they did for a living, the world would just be a happier, better place. People talk about success in terms of wealth… I make enough money to live, but what makes me happy is doing work that I love.

MORGAN: You said in our email exchange "I achieved my goal and didn't know what to do next. Little did I know that maintaining a place in the business is harder than arriving there." For me, that's how getting tenure at age 35 felt.

GRIGSBY: I music directed my first two Broadway shows at age 29. I woke up every day for several months after my 30th birthday, wondering what I was supposed to do next. The journey had been hard, but the path had been clear. It has now been 24 years of ups and downs; but I have never lost the energized feeling of being in a room with colleagues, developing a new show.

MORGAN: Do you like to teach?

GRIGSBY: I love teaching. I go to universities; I go to high schools. I teach a five-year-old the way I teach a thirty-five-year-old. You're going to be a great singer-actor when you realize that your job is to communicate. Not necessarily be the best singer in the room or be the best singer on the planet or have the most beautiful voice. Our job is to communicate. Serving the story, serving the character, communicating to the audience, helping them…. You know, what we're doing is putting life on stage and ideally, creating an opportunity to observe the consequences of one's actions and words. From the outside, a person might realize "that could have happened because I did that, so I can change my behavior because I don't want to be that… I don't want to create that…" We'll go [to the theater] just to learn about things. It's easier sometimes rather than reading a textbook; we get to learn about it in a new way. We, as humans, have been storytellers since the beginning of time. It's just part of who we are. This is the way *we* do it. *We* all have chosen to be storytellers in the arena of music theatre.

MORGAN: Way to tie up with a nice bow. I think that the artist should try to stay true to that, or at least circle back to those nuggets at this level of the work to give us the most hope in the regions as well as in training programs.

GRIGSBY: I enjoy everyone I work with. I feel very fortunate. I like working with new people. Every artist is different and has something unique to bring. We all learn from every new person, even something about ourselves.

Mary-Mitchell Campbell – Biography

Mary-Mitchell Campbell is a conductor, music director, orchestrator, composer, and arranger who crosses genres between classical, pop, and Broadway styles of music. She has been the Music Supervisor or Music Director for many Broadway shows including: *Some Like It Hot, The Prom, Mean Girls, My Love Letter to Broadway, For The Girls, Tuck Everlasting, Finding Neverland, Big Fish, The Addams Family, Company,* and *Sweeney Todd.* She also music directed Stephen Sondheim's last musical *Road Show* at the Public Theater.

She won a Drama Desk for Best Orchestrations for the 2006 revival of *Company* starring Raul Esparza and was nominated for Best Orchestrations for her work on the Off-Broadway productions of *Allegro* and *Hello Again.*

She has a very active concert career and performs frequently with Kristin Chenoweth, Gavin Creel, Jessica Vosk, and Raul Esparza.

In her pop career she has worked with Alicia Keys, Katy Perry, John Legend, Carole King, Amy Grant, Kelly Clarkson, Stevie Wonder, James Taylor, Elvis Costello, and Josh Groban in concerts.

She was the Music Director of HBO's *Homeschool Musical*, and Music Director for *Girls5Eva.* She was the vocal coach for *Better Nate Than Ever* and is currently working on the film version of *Mean Girls.*

She has conducted the Chicago Symphony, the Cincinnati symphony, the Dallas symphony, the Nashville Symphony, The Colorado Symphony, and many other symphonies around the United States.

She is passionate about arts education and access to arts education for marginalized communities. She is the Founder and President of Arts Ignite (www.artsignite.org) which recruits and trains high-level artists to teach young people health education and life skills through the arts. She has been a regular volunteer with Arts Ignite programs in the US, Africa, and India. She is very active in Maestra, an organization empowering female-identifying musicians (www.maestramusic.org) and is on the Founding Membership of MUSE – Musicians United for Social Equity. (www.museonline.org)

She is from North Carolina and has taught on the faculties of Juilliard, NYU, and Boston College. She enjoys spending as much time as possible with her dogs, Maya and Steve.

Interview with Mary-Mitchell Campbell, January 9, 2022 via Zoom[16]

MORGAN: Mary-Mitchell Campbell! You are *the* inspiration for this book.
CAMPBELL: I'm honored.
MORGAN: When we got to work together, it was the most beautiful fulfillment of a request to the universe for me. I saw you play for [Kristin] Chenoweth at a concert and after seeing your name in programs on the internet for years, I finally saw you play in person, and I asked the universe to be able to connect with you through my Broadway friends or conference connections. I thought at the very least, I could meet you and just talk with you. Nine months later, I did a coaching in front of Jody Feldman – the Producer at The Alliance – and she emailed me saying they were looking for a music assistant

for *The Prom* (Broadway, 2019/Alliance production 2016) and asked if I would like to chat with the music director, Mary-Mitchell Campbell. Then, when we worked together, you were so generous to have some conversations with me about your career and life experience. It opened my eyes to how easy it could have been for me to learn these kinds of things, but how I was ignorant about certain aspects of the industry, being outside of New York. I thought about how I would have loved to read some conversations, particularly with women in leadership and behind the table, when I was coming up through the ranks. When I had that idea and started to put the balls in motion, Maestra started, through you and Georgia Stitt. The rest is history. I'm so excited to talk to you and document your experience, so that young people can look back and identify the women who really paved some paths for them.

CAMPBELL: Oh, I love that.

MORGAN: Tell me a little bit about your journey from childhood to Broadway; the CliffsNotes life story.

CAMPBELL: I grew up in eastern North Carolina, on a farm in a small town. My parents were not musical, but my grandfather played piano by ear. I started playing piano in church when I was a child. I asked for a piano when I was three for Christmas, so I gravitated towards the piano very early on. I started playing in church when I was six and started taking formal lessons when I was eight. We didn't have a piano because we couldn't afford one. There was a really interesting turn of events where somebody owed my father money and couldn't pay but offered him a piano. So, we got a piano.

MORGAN: Wow. Was it like a poker game where someone bet their piano instead of their watch or whatever?

CAMPBELL: I wish. That would be a great story, but let's not turn my dad into a gambler. So, I started playing in restaurants when I was ten.

MORGAN: Dinner gigs?

CAMPBELL: Dinner gigs. I played background music. I kept that going through high school.

MORGAN: Would you play jazz?

CAMPBELL: No, I played radio hits; pop songs. Whatever was on the radio and then some "standards." When I was in high school, I remember going to Raleigh and seeing a production of *The Music Man* (1957), which I really enjoyed. Then, in high school, I went away to North Carolina School of the Arts. First, I got into the governor school program [a summer program] as a voice major and in Winston-Salem, I was across the street from North Carolina School of the Arts and there were so many kids that summer that were going there for high school [during the year] that I thought it seemed like a really great idea. So, that summer, I walked across the street and said I would love to apply there. And they said, "Oh, we're actually doing auditions this week. Would you like to audition this week?" I said yes.

MORGAN: At the dinner gigs, were you playing [piano] *and* singing?

CAMPBELL: Just playing. So, I auditioned as a classical pianist, got in, and started school there. It was very fast because it was during the summer, and I applied for the fall. Everyone – my parents and hometown folks – had whiplash because I didn't really have any idea I was going to do that. I was sixteen.

MORGAN: You had to move there?

CAMPBELL: It was a boarding school. While I was there, I saw the college section production of *Baby* and thought, "I want to do this." I didn't love being in a practice room by myself for hours, but I knew I wanted to tell stories through music. I applied to a dinner theatre where I could make money. Money was a very big problem for me growing up. I applied for the dinner theatre, and I got in. They didn't take high school kids and I was incredibly tenacious, but it could have been a lot of other words. Pushy? Bossy?

MORGAN: I don't think anyone would use those words if you were a boy.

CAMPBELL: No, we would say tenacious and entrepreneurial. So, I was tenacious and entrepreneurial, and I insisted that they take me even though I was in high school and they did not take high school students; most were college students. I pushed my way in and it was a dinner theatre with basically a bunch of musical theatre nerds who served as the waiters and waitresses and put on a show at the end of the night. The Farmhouse Inn. That's where I learned so much musical theatre. I didn't know a lot about shows. It was a crash course because everybody would bring me music from all these different shows. I really had only done stuff like the Hal Leonard *Phantom of the Opera* choral medley and …

MORGAN: Oh, we've all done those medleys!

CAMPBELL: I had been exposed to Sondheim, but in a relatively light fashion. I [worked at that dinner theatre] for five summers, so I learned a lot of musical theatre there and I saved a lot of money to pay for college. I went to Furman University and got a piano performance degree. I started my own theatre company while I was there, which coincided with a social problems class I had taken around income inequality. I used all of my shows to raise funds for different causes during college.

MORGAN: So, you were creating space for people to make things and to use your talents to help others as early as college? Exercising leadership skills that early?

CAMPBELL: Yeah, because I realized my towards the end of my freshman year of college that I loved theatre way more than I loved classical performing. I realized that there's really no such thing as a concert pianist career. My professors disagreed because they wanted me to get my doctorate and go on to be a piano professor. I realized in my freshman year that I really wanted to do theatre. I thought about transferring, but that's a lot of work. It seemed easier to start my own theatre company, which I don't think is actually less work, but it's a different kind of work. Sometimes in deep lack of resources, you find opportunity.

For me, the great news was I could pick my own shows. I could be the producer, the director, and learn all of the jobs by just doing it; not really knowing what I was doing. I was very brazen in the sense that I was very willing to fail. I didn't have a deep fear of failure. I figured if it went badly, then oh well. I figured I would throw myself at that. Simultaneously I took that social problems class that changed my worldview and my sort of mission in life. So, my next show was *The Fantasticks* (1960) for Habitat for Humanity. If you were in the show, you built the house. I got the Chaplains of the school involved, and we started doing shows like *Godspell* and *Joseph... Dreamcoat* for United Ministries and we had all of the community organizations come into the school. We did it for "parents weekend" as the Sunday morning service. [This is at Furman University.] I learned a lot and that was a great process. Upon graduation, everyone said I needed to go into a grad program right away. My senior year, I basically had what I would probably call a nervous breakdown...

> Sometimes in deep lack of resources, you find opportunity.

MORGAN: A mental health crisis?
CAMPBELL: Yes. I felt this immense pressure from a lot of professors who were deeply invested in me, which was a beautiful thing. But it had sort of turned into them seeing me as a younger version of themselves. They were overly invested in ways where my decision making was not pleasing to them because I didn't want to be them. I think it felt hurtful to them, which I understand a lot more now that I'm older, but at the time it felt very challenging. So, I told them that I'm not going to go to be a professional professor, nor am I going to become the world's greatest collaborative pianist in the classical realm or an opera director. So, I got a waitress job and sold real estate. They were all deeply disappointed in me and basically said it was really tragic what has happened

to my life. But I needed to save money and move to New York because I was going to go try Broadway! I had a very impactful conversation with one of my favorite professors – who was like my dad – who sat me down and said, "Listen, I'm genuinely concerned about your choices here. You have all of these opportunities that have presented themselves via grad schools that are clamoring for you. We've talked to them about you. You could get in so easily. There are all these opportunities available to you. I know you don't have resources financially and I've watched students move to New York for years. I know you're good, but it seems very difficult. All of them have had just horrible chapters of financial challenges and real disappointment. I don't think you have the kind of backing to pull something like this off and it's going to be really terrible, and I'm scared you're going to miss your window of opportunity that is happening right now. It just feels unwise…" It was really coming out of a place of real genuine love; it wasn't mean spirited. He had watched this happen to other people and they had people to fall back on. He said I didn't have that, so it wasn't a good idea. What was great about that moment for me was it was incredibly clarifying to understand that I believed him. I said, "I know that everything you're telling me is true. It is very likely that this will go very badly. But I still want to go. That means something because I will spend the rest of my life wondering what would have happened if I had not taken this risk. I'm okay with failing."

MORGAN: My therapist calls that "head, heart, gut." If all three things aren't in alignment, then you need more information before you can make a decision.

CAMPBELL: That makes total sense to me. So, I saved up money. I worked like a crazy person for that year and then moved to New York. When I got to New York, I started volunteering at Broadway Cares – doing benefits – and I met Cy Coleman [composer] doing a big benefit. We hit it off and he became my first mentor. He introduced me to Paul Newman [actor, philanthropist], who became another big mentor. So, within my first year in New York City – it was sort of bizarre – I quickly made some very high powerful connections that really opened a lot of doors for me early on. One of my most insane experiences was right after I moved to New York: I found myself sight-reading for Isaac Stern in a concert that I was doing – a camp benefit for Paul Newman's "Hole in the Wall Gang Camps."[17] I had just come out of college, so I was in the best place to try, since I could read a Mozart concerto. I don't think I'd want to do that now, but I was game to try at the time.

MORGAN: Just say yes?

CAMPBELL: Just say yes. Keep saying yes. That was actually so nerve wracking that everything that came after that was sort of less nerve wracking.

MORGAN: I like it! Do the scariest thing first! My new favorite expression nowadays – because everyone is struggling – is: "Well, I have good news for you. You have thus far survived 100% of your bad days."

CAMPBELL: That's good.

MORGAN: Proud of you.

CAMPBELL: Then, I did a lot of new work... I did a lot of theatre workshops and readings. I worked at the O'Neill Theater Center. No one wanted to hire me on to bigger teams, so I was just doing my own little music directing thing... concerts and little workshops... then eventually, John Doyle [director] gave me a Broadway show.

MORGAN: The 2006 *Company* revival, right!?

CAMPBELL: Music supervising and orchestrating *Company*. I sort of started at that level. I never did the common path. I did one associate [music director] job on a regional show, but otherwise I didn't really go the typical Broadway route. I did a little bit of subbing, but I never "had a book." I never did associate [music director] job. I never went through the steps. There is no sort of clear ladder in this industry, but if there were to be a clear ladder, that would be it. So, it was very interesting.

MORGAN: It also probably helped that you had experience and training as a vocalist, because that's part of the skill set. I did that at the regional level – going straight into music directing because people knew I was good with voices. They knew I had a bunch of vocal experience, and I played piano... demonstrated leadership....

CAMPBELL: Yeah, totally! Having a vocal background has proven to be quite helpful.

MORGAN: Tell me about the benefits and the concerts that you were involved in at the earlier career stage.

CAMPBELL: Absolutely. Gavin Creel [actor] and I did a PBS concert during the COVID shutdown that filmed at Westport Country Playhouse in Connecticut. I was downstairs and looked at the wall – they have these unbelievable pictures from shows there. Stephen Sondheim was an intern at the Westport Playhouse! There's unbelievable history on the walls, and there's a whole row of different benefit concerts. There's a ten-year span there where I'm on every poster. I walked through them and noticed all those famous people, but I don't remember any of this. It was such a blur because I was doing so many of them. I remember we honored Angela

	Lansbury and we honored Julia Roberts. That was eye opening. I did a gazillion "Broadway Cares" benefits. I've worked on the *Red Bucket Follies* [formerly known as *"Gypsy of the Year*]. We did an event called *Nothing Like a Dame* that was all about women that was benefiting the Phyllis Newman Women's Health Initiative. I was deeply involved in that for years. It ended up running its course and retiring. Currently, I do Broadway backwards every year, and I still do a ton of benefits for Paul Newman's camps. I'm sort of the in-house music person for all of these organizations and their fundraising efforts.
MORGAN:	Is that because of your unique skill set? What's the skill set that someone has to have to do those kinds of events?
CAMPBELL:	I think one has to have an enormous stage manager brain because it takes so much organization to throw things together. It's sort of like event planning.
MORGAN:	Yeah, it's a combo of stage manager, event planner, music director, and music arranger, right?
CAMPBELL:	You have to hire the band, you have to get support, draw up contracts, all those things. It's a lot of work, so that was a great training ground. It's usually a high-pressure day and everything has to happen very fast, so you think on your feet. There's a lot of problem solving, like being a wedding planner. Sometimes things don't go as planned so you fix them. I remember there was a concert we did – actually at the Westport Country Playhouse – where somebody had to cancel and I had a backup plan within five minutes of a different song with charts that I could find and print.
MORGAN:	Right!? I know that life.
CAMPBELL:	This singer is going to sing this… We're going to do this new song now… That flexible mentality became super helpful for what I ended up doing in the Broadway world. It definitely set me up for understanding how to navigate very stressful situations where there is no time. People are under a lot of pressure; therefore, maybe not in their best mind frame.
MORGAN:	You *still* work on a lot of concert material, yes? I see that you still play for Chenoweth…. You play for Jessica Vosk… Let's talk about that. Why do you do that? What do you love about it? What continues to keep you saying yes to those kinds of events all while you're working on full shows?
CAMPBELL:	I actually love concerts. I love concerts because I get bored easily and I enjoy variety. There's a really great book called *The E-Myth Revisited,*[18] which is about the "entrepreneurial myth." It's really a fantastic book about the realities of being an entrepreneur and how you start being an entrepreneur because you are passionate

about the thing, but ultimately you end up running a business. It could be any business but the example they give in the book is about someone who loves making pies, so they decide to open a pie shop, but they don't actually end up making pies. They run the business. They don't actually ever make pies and interact with customers. Similarly, as you rise in the ranks, you don't actually play the piano as much. It's hard to keep those music skills active. So, what's super helpful to me about concert work is that it forces me to keep my skill set up. I'm not just sitting in the room watching things happen and commenting on other people doing things. I'm actually *in it,* so I really enjoy that.

MORGAN: That speaks to your humility, which is the thing that just radiates from you to everybody. Anybody that I meet that connects over working with Mary-Mitchell Campbell speaks about how great you are, and comments on your humility and authenticity.

CAMPBELL: That's very nice of you.

MORGAN: I remember when we were doing *The Prom* and you were getting ready to play a show in New York after that. You were talking about how nervous you were about that gig, and that you needed to practice. When I came to pit sit *Mean Girls* (2018) you were conducting and playing the *Keyboard 3* book. That was interesting to me that you actively put yourself in those varied positions; whereas some people would take the more comfortable route to stay in one seat or the other. What's it like to bop around between serving as music supervisor versus music director versus orchestrator?

CAMPBELL: I think because I came through a more circuitous route having music directed some smaller projects, I was used to being in charge. I definitely didn't think I'd ever do Broadway. I thought, "That will not be my path." And *that's* the sign. I was totally fine with that because I hit a point where I was realized that Broadway is a genre. Broadway is not a thing that I have to attain. We have this "Holy Grail" where we should move to New York and do Broadway and it took me a minute to realize that Broadway is a more universal, all-encompassing category as opposed to Broadway shows.

MORGAN: Graciela Daniele and Baayork Lee both said to me in their interviews that Broadway is a quality not a specific place.

CAMPBELL: Yes. Once I realized that, I was like, "Oh! I don't need to do 'Broadway shows." I need to do the theatrical work that inspires me and work with people I want to be in a room with. So, that was sort of my mission statement for a long time. I was quite sure I was never going to be asked to do Broadway work because it was … I wouldn't say it was overtly misogynistic, but I would say that there just weren't women in leadership at the time. The only real music directors I knew were Kristen Blodgette, Kimberly Grigsby,[19] and Lynne Schenkel. But I really didn't *know* anybody. I had tried to get on teams, but it was difficult because there's no way to prove yourself. They weren't looking for new people to be on their teams at the time, so I wasn't sure that it was a door that was going to open for me. So, by the time I actually did get into the Broadway scene, I had been working in the city for some time and I came in through the weird route of actor-musician shows like *Sweeney Todd* (2006) and *Company* (2008). They were both Sondheim revivals, both super strange, and required an odd skill set; so, I came in as a Broadway music supervisor. My first Broadway title was Music Supervisor and Orchestrator. Very strange. Beyond that, I would say there was only one time that I ever had anybody above me in the music department, and it was concerning to me. I didn't want to do that again because I got too used to being autonomous and able to run my own department. Music Director and Music Supervisor are just titles that have shifted depending on how big the team is or whether I felt like I needed the Music Supervisor title. With one exception, I've been the sort of "CEO of Music Team" every time. *The Addams Family* (2009), which was my third Broadway show, was quite difficult because I came into that process having done [the aforementioned] two Broadway shows in these very odd ways. It was like I skipped three grades, so when I started doing *Addams Family*, I started to realize I had skipped grades and that I didn't have a lot of information. I had to do a lot of catch-up on a more traditional process very quickly. There are so many union rules around the orchestra and there's all these rules around how many subs that each person can have, depending on the contracting process and the ways that everything has to be handled. There was so much business around it that I didn't fully understand. That was an interesting and critical moment. The other thing I will say is that during this time I started a nonprofit and that honestly served me probably better than anything else I did as music director because I was starting a business. In doing so, I had to crash course myself through my own homemade MBA program in order to learn how to run a business. That changed everything because I was able to have informed conversations with general management, producers, and everyone in the theater. I understood what their jobs were; I understood what they needed; and once I understood what they needed, I knew how to filter and frame what

I needed in a way that would serve both of us, as opposed to being overly artistic and just making demands. Understanding where they were coming from and understanding what they were trying to accomplish made it much easier to have the conversations.

MORGAN: The nonprofit that you're talking about is ASTEP – Artists Striving to End Poverty, now known as Arts Ignite [artsignite.org]. Why did you start that company?

CAMPBELL: I went through a terrible divorce and was feeling very sorry for myself and didn't want to get out of my pajamas and felt like the world was in a very interesting place. This was during the George W. [Bush] years and I moped for a while. I really leaned into my moping. At a certain point, I had to take action, or I had to stop whining. I decided to go spend time serving other people and learning what other people's problems looked like. My problems often paled in comparison once I had that perspective. We have legitimate problems, but they're not life and death in the same way. I decided to go to India and spend four months teaching in orphanages, and that experience was life changing because I could not unsee what I saw. I couldn't unlearn what I learned. I felt that the inequalities of the world were worth taking action around and my best way of combating that was bringing art, music, and other methods that open up the imagination to kids who were in extreme situations where there was no hope. The goal was to provide both temporary relief... fun and hope... but also providing a larger belief and confidence that one could go to college and break those cycles. Those were sort of the things that I became very passionate about. When John Doyle offered me the first Broadway show I did, I actually said, "I don't know if I can take this. I just started this nonprofit, and I've committed myself to these really deep issues." While I love Stephen Sondheim and it sounds like a really fun project, at the end of the day, it would be a show. I don't want to be the kind of person that abandons this project of higher purpose because a really cool opportunity came my way. That's not ideal to who I want to become. He was the one who actually changed everything by saying, "I don't understand why you can't do both." I was like, "Really?" There were several powerful insights about that moment. The first was that he was willing to work with me and help me make that work. He said we could make the rules and set up the system however we want to set it up, which largely has informed by my whole career. The second impact was realizing it took someone else giving me permission to take charge of my life. Why did I have to ask? Why did I need to look for that external permission before

	I felt like it was okay to make those choices? I think that goes back to like a lot of gender programing.
MORGAN:	I think it goes back to capitalist society and capitalism.
CAMPBELL:	There's a thousand reasons.
MORGAN:	I often tell my students, "If someone closes a door on you, build your own door." It doesn't register until they're far graduated. They'll not get cast and I suggest that they put together their own show! They're coming out of high school so programmed to see a singular way of what this looks like. Not only the industry but how we're supposed to live our lives… programing from media and the stories that we see. It's important to hear the stories that don't do that. What's it like to be the only woman in the room of leadership? What's your observation of that experience?
CAMPBELL:	I've definitely grown in that way, and in recent years, I'm usually not the only woman. There was a long span of years where I was the only woman. Initially, I just tried to fit in. I didn't want to rock the boat, so I wouldn't call attention to it. Often, somebody would say something that was questionable in nature about women and suddenly remember I was in the room. They would forget I was female because I was so good at masking that aspect. They would sort of squirm or apologize, and I would brush it off. That was phase one.
MORGAN:	I've been there! Musicians will be on the other side of the pit, not knowing the mics are on, feeding to my ears, and tell a sexist joke.
CAMPBELL:	Still in the room! It's true. Phase two: I started working with a lot more female directors and that actually was interesting, as well.
MORGAN:	Can you tell me about that?
CAMPBELL:	It was interesting because a lot of them were older, and they had really come through at a time when obviously they had been doing the same thing and it had much more effect on them. I felt they were unemotional and very focused. They weren't allowing a lot of their humanity and their personality to be present because they couldn't do that in previous times.
MORGAN:	Like internalized sexism.
CAMPBELL:	Yeah. It was interesting to watch one colleague in particular because she engaged in some behavior that I don't think she was even aware of.
MORGAN:	Sure. I've had a couple of circumstances where I come into the room with a fellow woman in leadership and the vibe is so weird for a while. I'm a Labrador Retriever, so I typically come bounding in like a puppy and it takes a while for some women to warm up because they're threatened, or they think we are in competition. It's sometimes extra labor for me to try to encourage the

	vibe… to make them more comfortable. I have to make men comfortable in one way, but I also have to create comfort for women in a different way.
CAMPBELL:	I think the only solution to that is what we are doing now, which is normalizing teams of women, which I think is happening. It happened on *Prom*, and it's definitely happening on a lot of my shows. I hope that the more that happens, the less all of these things will be issues.
MORGAN:	Who are your favorite collaborators and why? What are the traits and collaborators that attract you to a project?
CAMPBELL:	I have a million favorite collaborators, so I don't want to leave anyone out. Traits? A willingness to get in the room and wrestle ideas without ego – which is very difficult. A willingness to stay curious and open.
MORGAN:	What are the kinds of projects that you now are interested in doing? I know that you said to me when we worked together years ago that you really are just mostly interested in doing new musicals. What are the kinds of projects that interest you in 2023 during the post-pandemic point in your career?
CAMPBELL:	Such a great question; such a hard one to answer. My entire career has been focused on new musicals; or revivals that are done in an odd way. It's almost ironic that I have taken this post at Encores because it is putting up musicals in the form that they were created, which is sort of a new thing for me. That's something I'm in the midst of figuring out right now.
MORGAN:	Why did you say yes to it?
CAMPBELL:	The tradition of it is very meaningful. I took the job because I am excited about celebrating the history of musical theatre. They find ways to keep the past alive in a really specific way and I find that meaningful and important and exciting. It was not lost on me that there were two music directors prior, both named Rob, and so I would be the first music director who is a woman. I don't actually even think there were women on the podium through the thirty years. I think Kristen Blodgette conducted one production. I'm mostly excited about sharing the mic on some level and sharing the podium because it's not my goal to conduct every show. It's my goal to bring new voices to that table through Maestra and Muse; and bringing in women and people of color into positions of leadership in a relatively high-profile New York City situation where the orchestra is the fixture. Music is a primary focus. To me, that is really valuable and really exciting.
MORGAN:	What show projects are you interested in, since you do juggle your nonprofits and concert work, in addition to shows.

CAMPBELL: It's a combination of factors. It typically has to do with team. Also, whether the piece holds a curiosity and whether I think I will learn things about myself and the world through it, which typically I have. I'm curious to see kind of how the industry unfolds post-pandemic. We still haven't really figured that out, as you well know. There's still a lot of learning to do in that realm. I started doing TV film projects and I'm doing a lot more of that and I find that it's very different, but I find it fascinating. I'm mostly interested in learning new things. Whatever comes my way that continues to be opportunities for growth is very exciting.

MORGAN: What are the pieces of advice that you may have not already talked about with me today that you would say to a young person reading this book who maybe looks at someone like you and wants to do what you do.

CAMPBELL: There is no Holy Grail. Don't look for any person, job, award, or achievement to make you feel valid in the world if you don't already feel that in the world already. That will free you up to make better art; if you're not looking for something that proves your worth. Broadway is not the "Holy Grail." Great art happens everywhere. I don't think everybody needs to move to New York. If you don't like living in New York, make great art in other places. I have something I call the "Desire to Fear Ratio." You can do anything in the world you want to do as long as your desire is greater than your fear.

> I have something I call the "Desire to Fear Ratio." You can do anything in the world you want to do as long as your desire is greater than your fear.

I'm a person who *does* get anxious. Some people out there assume accomplished people don't have nerves, but they always have nerves. I've seen lots of Tony winners hyperventilate before walking out on stage and the nerves don't go away. You make friends with the nerves on some level. As a person who has had to deal with fear, focusing on that fear and trying to diminish that fear has never been successful to me. Focusing on the desire of what you're trying to do has. Your fear can be quite high, as long as your desire is higher. It's really about staying focused on what it is that you're trying to accomplish. What is it you want?

MORGAN: What is your "I want..." if you will?

CAMPBELL: Those are the kinds of things I live by. The other thing is power. You're either coming from a place of power over people or power to empower people. That can vacillate back and forth in

	a ten-minute increment of time. I try to stay in the power to empower. It's one of my life philosophies that keeps me learning and helps to create spaces where people can be safe, explore, try things, and do their best work.
MORGAN:	Amazing.

Meg Zervoulis – Biography

Broadway: *West Side Story*, *The Prom*, *Mean Girls*, and *The Great Comet of 1812*. Off-Broadway: *Cagney* and *Rated P*. Selected New Works: Sondheim's *Buñuel* (Public Theater), *Merrily We Roll Along* (Fiasco/Roundabout), Kooman and Dimond's *Dani Girl*, and Andrea Grody's *Strange Faces*. Regional: *Mary Poppins*, *Bandstand*, *Ever After*, and many more at Paper Mill Playhouse. Meg is the resident conductor of Hotel Elefant, a contemporary music ensemble in NYC. She has also served as an adjunct professor/music director at Montclair State University for several years. Education: Carnegie Mellon University. Meg is also a member of the Lilly Awards Power Network. www.megzmusic.com[20]

Interview with Meg Zervoulis, November 5, 2022 via Zoom[21]

MORGAN:	Tell me your story! Tell me about your journey from childhood to Broadway, in a nutshell.
ZERVOULIS:	I started piano lessons very young, around the age of five. I studied privately at that time. From age 8 to 18, I took lessons in New York City at Juilliard Prep School and was heading more in the direction of being a concerto soloist… a classical solo career. Then, in high school, my choir teacher took a maternity leave, and they had a regular sub filling her place. In order to kind of keep the program going, I started accompanying the shows, and accompanying the choirs. From then on, I just kept myself on more of a collaborative piano and musical theatre piano-playing journey. I went to Carnegie Mellon in Pittsburgh for piano performance, with a minor in theatrical conducting and teaching certificate. I started apprenticing at Paper Mill Playhouse, and I've worked there since then. Papermill continues to be my home base. After Carnegie Mellon, I moved back to New York. I was playing audition piano for a while and was teaching as a music educator and music therapist for students with autism for thirteen years. I did an Off-Broadway show called *Rated P for Parenthood*,[22] which was very exciting. That was my first New York commercial music directing credit. Some friends of mine and I had developed the piece at SOPAC [South Orange Performing

	Arts Center] in NJ and then it got picked up. Ever since then, I've just been trying to expand my work and learn new things, meet new people, and continue music directing while also keeping a foot in either mentorship, teaching, or music education.
MORGAN:	Do you have educators in your family?
ZERVOULIS:	Yes. Most of the people in my family are either firemen or educators.
MORGAN:	So, they're always putting out fires either way, right?
ZERVOULIS:	Right. Exactly.
MORGAN:	Public service!
ZERVOULIS:	Yes, pretty much. It's an inherited interest of mine. I also worked with so many solid teachers and mentors along the way, I feel a drive to continue to pay it forward.
MORGAN:	Love that. Can I ask you a question about your transition in high school between the concerto-minded path and musical theatre? Perhaps this is relevant to college time. If you majored in piano performance, I assume you had a senior recital full of classical stuff, right?
ZERVOULIS:	Yes; I'm old enough that there were still little-to-no options in college training to be a musical theatre music director…
MORGAN:	What turned you on about the collaborative piano experience? What turned you on about that theatrical world versus playing concertos and classical repertoire?
ZERVOULIS:	I enjoyed making music with other people and I enjoyed the excitement and detail of the responsibilities of a music director. In a solo career, I wasn't really playing in the orchestra. I had some chamber group experience, but I enjoyed playing in bands… the social aspect of it… the humanity of working with other people and collaborating was interesting to me.
MORGAN:	I love that. Who were your role models coming up? Either *in* the industry or people in your regular life or family, etc.
ZERVOULIS:	Well, I definitely remember my mom clipping a newspaper article about Kim Grigsby regarding her *Full Monty* experience. I thought that was so exciting. I was also aware of Cherie Rosen[23] from a young age and admired her.
MORGAN:	How about outside the industry? Like even in leadership?
ZERVOULIS:	I mean, my mom. She is always helping others and she has a shining light about her. She gathers people and is incredibly strong. She continues to be a driving force.
MORGAN:	Yeah, she seems like the *nicest* person. Like really jovial. She's always smiling and everybody around her just seems to really love her. That's the vibe I get being peripherally connected to you on social media.

ZERVOULIS: Later in life, it would be Mary-Mitchell Campbell, who I'm so lucky to have been mentored by once I was coming closer to accessing Broadway.

MORGAN: Regarding that mentorship from Mary-Mitchell: Do you feel like the actions were direct through advice? Or just by you having proximity to her and watching and observing her and thinking about how you want to do the job?

ZERVOULIS: We were working together on a production at Paper Mill Playhouse and she was gently and excitedly encouraging me to consider stepping out a bit. She was offering to introduce me to people in New York. She was aware of a need at *Matilda* to have some more keyboard subs who had classical background. She was mentoring me in how to become a part of the industry and community. Whereas with Cherie Rosen... I was working with her on conducting technique in the inaugural Marvin Hamlisch Broadway Conductor's Workshop.[24] I was able to actually conduct with her and gave specific technique notes and advice so that that's another example of mentoring I was lucky to experience. I also want to go back and acknowledge my high school band and choir teachers. They were extremely involved in that period of time in my life with teaching me music theory, how to play in an ensemble, the appreciation of music, etc. In college, Dr. Robert Paige, who is the father-in-law of Paul Gemignani,[25] (and thus the grandfather of my dear colleague from the 2020 *West Side Story* Revival Alexander Gemignani) was my inspirational mentor. He introduced me to conducting via the scores of Leonard Bernstein and the like.

MORGAN: I know you've done a lot of subbing in Broadway pits, as both a keyboardist and as a conductor – on *Great Comet*, right – before you got the title Music Director. Can you talk a little bit about how you got into that and like what that process is like?

ZERVOULIS: Sure. The first sub-conducting job that I landed was at *Natasha, Pierre and the Great Comet of 1812*. I had worked previously with Matt Doebler, who was the Key 2 [keyboard two player] and Associate [Music Director] on that production. I played accordion, which is an essential part of that production.

MORGAN: Wait. That was so casual... hold on... you *played* accordion?

ZERVOULIS: Yeah. I was a keyboard sub at *Finding Neverland* (musical, 2014) on Broadway and that involved accordion, so I learned accordion for that position. Since then, I've taken other roles in shows [pits] that involve accordion.

MORGAN: How long did it take you to learn?

ZERVOULIS: I can't even remember. It was not quick. I think it was, like, two months.

MORGAN:	That *is* quick.
ZERVOULIS:	Okay; that's quick… yeah.
MORGAN:	So, Mary-Mitchell gets you this gig with *Finding Neverland*… you learn the accordion… you work with your *Great Comet* buddy… And then he's like, "Hey, you can handle flying the plane…"?
ZERVOULIS:	Yes. They were looking to add a conductor at a certain point in their run with *Great Comet*. They actually had Matt conducting a fair bit during previews, so I was in [the pit] during previews… So, it just kind of made sense because then I had like the historic knowledge of the piece that had occurred over those months.
MORGAN:	And you're on stage for that, right?
ZERVOULIS:	Yeah. On stage… in costume… highly complicated… running Ableton… playing accordion… playing piano… and dancing.
MORGAN:	Does that kind of pressure excite you, scare you, or both?
ZEROULIS:	Both. I would not recommend that level – that number of responsibilities – to be part of one's Broadway conducting debut. It's how it worked out and it was ultimately great. Then, that led to other sub-conducting gigs.
MORGAN:	What are the skills or personality traits that you think a music director at the Broadway level has to have, outside of excellent musicianship? Have there been any moments where maybe there was a specific lesson you learned, in terms of like leadership, running the room, or getting something to happen where you needed to adjust on a major level?
ZERVOULIS:	Yeah. Managing the instrumentalists is an important skill to have. Learning the nuance of a "noting" process, which becomes a central administrative responsibility that music directors have. I think that was something that definitely has a learning curve for everyone because you're really managing the human aspect of it, considering these are people that you're going to continue to play with; however, you're also needing to uphold the standard of what the score and the production itself requires. Working with principal actors is another thing that has such nuance to it and is so exciting and special; it's also important to maintain those relationships. It's important to be fluid and reflective of one another. Then, of course, basic life things like time management, physical health, and stamina. Those are all important elements thriving as a music director on Broadway.
MORGAN:	Let's talk self-care! Have you had to be a caregiver to anyone? I know you have a little girl. And you live – what – an hour commute into the city?
ZERVOULIS:	It can be as little as thirty minutes and it can be as much as an hour and a half. On average, it's more like forty-five minutes.

MORGAN: How do you juggle having a house, a family, and a commute with this Broadway career?

ZERVOULIS: Well, a lot of people say like it's the same commute to Brooklyn. So, I just appreciate having a little buffer on the beginning and end of the day to decompress or to take meetings so that I'm not taking meetings in my home (as little as I can). Juggling this career with being a caretaker is very complicated, but so special and exciting. It requires a lot of help, obviously, and a lot of advance planning and a lot of saying no to other opportunities.

MORGAN: Do you have certain routines, rituals, or boundaries that you've created? It's good that you've learned to say "no." Do you have other things that you engage in for self-care?

ZERVOULIS: I mean, simple things like bubble bath and long walks.

MORGAN: A classic Millennial[26] answer! [Author's Note: Meg and I are the same age.]

ZERVOULIS: Yeah. Another thing is: I can arrange and orchestrate and all that stuff, but I kind of have remained committed to trying to focus on work that happens in live time in a rehearsal room and in a show. Obviously, there's always going to be outside hours work, but I tend to try and really kind of keep the separation between work and life, if possible.

MORGAN: I think about that a lot. When you reach a certain level and a certain age and you start thinking about the trajectory of the whole career, it's important to say, "I might do some of that other stuff in this other phase of my life when I might be at home more." Maybe focus on the gigs while I've got certain connections; but also thinking about, while my kid is a certain age, then I'm going to spend this much time at home and therefore I'm going to compartmentalize my work in this way. Then, maybe I'll spend more time doing this other thing when [the kids are] in a different phase of their life or I'm in a different phase of my life. I think about "people, project, pay". How a gig is going to affect my overall health, overall year, and overall bank account; all of those layers before saying yes? Whereas, when I was younger – in my twenties – I was just saying yes to a lot of things.

ZERVOULIS: Yes.

MORGAN: What kinds of shows really make you tick? Are there certain kinds of projects that you want to say yes to when they come to your doorstep because it's a particular kind of story or group of people? Let's talk about projects and material first.

ZERVOULIS: I like pieces that feel like they're going to make a difference in some way or have some sort of twist... something with a really strong plot that is kind of aimed towards the greater good, if

	possible. Generally speaking, I love to work on new musicals, but as of late, I've also been working on revivals that have a twist or an update to them. Musically speaking, I am attracted to the involvement of the book that I will be playing. I like to be busy and challenged in terms of material. That is another thing that I have found to be important to me in order to keep the momentum going from day to day.
MORGAN:	What [genre] is a challenge to you? My strike zone is pop-rock, even though I'd say I can handle any; therefore, there are some genres that are more of a challenge. What's a challenging genre to you?
ZERVOULIS:	It can vary. It can be either of the things you mentioned – like the improvisation aspect – or it can be something like the conducting if it's a sophisticated score like *An American in Paris* (2014). I subbed at that show over a long time and that was highly sophisticated. It felt so natural and exciting and featured such beautiful ensemble-playing within the orchestra. It was such a delight. They're not prerequisites, but they are things that make a "yes" feel easier.
MORGAN:	Are there particular individuals that you're always excited to work with? Even people you haven't worked with?
ZERVOULIS:	It's exciting to work with people who are focused on being excellent musicians but also being kind people.
MORGAN:	That's great. Absolutely. People who do great work, but they don't let that get in the way of their ability to be human and compassionate and empathetic. Discipline and excellence are connected, but discipline doesn't always have to look like being rude, cold, or callous. We don't have to sacrifice warmth for that excellence.
ZERVOULIS:	Right. Yes.
MORGAN:	Have you found yourself as the only woman in the room in leadership? Do you feel like rooms in which there are other women by your side make a difference for you or no?
ZERVOULIS:	Yes, to both questions. I have found myself in rooms where I am the only female in leadership. However, if there are other women who are in leadership positions on the production there is always an added level of comfort. There's encouragement and recognition of whatever it might mean to be a woman in leadership in that particular room.
MORGAN:	Let's talk about Maestra [Inc.] You've taken on a significant leadership role in the mentorship program. Why did you feel motivated to get involved and stay involved?
ZERVOULIS:	That comes back to the pay-it-forward energy I carry. It's a way to provide colleagues with a forum to employ to their teaching

interests while also pursuing positions in the industry. It is a way to continue to enhance the pipeline and increase gender parity in the industry; also, as a way to continue to expand the web [of connections] and provide a welcoming atmosphere to other Maestras who are seeking involvement in in the community.

MORGAN: Do you think the industry has changed from the pandemic? Have there been pros vs. cons? We all know theatre is still struggling in terms of getting patronage back. Obviously, the shutdown was difficult for theatre artists everywhere, because our art is an in-person art and trying to do Zoom theatre is hilarious. How do you think the industry has changed and what are some of the things that can stay versus go?

ZERVOULIS: I have been in direct involvement with the shift in mindset and goals with regard to contracting orchestras; which has been really nice to see that there is more equity and perspective in the process of hiring bands, which I think is so important in order to make some positive improvement in the industry. That is definitely happening and is definitely a result of the pandemic and social justice movement.

MORGAN: Weren't you working on *Funny Girl* (revival, 2022) when there was a weekend where there were nine people out and some gal got the call to come learn the show and go in?

ZERVOULIS: Yeah, we had just hired a vacation swing for the "poker ladies" on a Friday. That Saturday, she was asked to come into town and go on stage with pages [in hand] to play one of the roles.

MORGAN: Have the conversations around understudies and covers changed? I know Broadway has always had understudies and covers. It's a little different in the regional markets where theaters are now putting up the dollars to hire understudies or at least bring in interns or college students as interns for a small stipend, which wasn't happening before. "The show must go on" is the theme of the regions and communities outside of New York. Do you feel like it has changed at the Broadway level ... or just the severity of it?

ZERVOULIS: I think that we're hiring more people. For example, hiring that vacation swing was not to cover vacation; it was to protect us against further COVID outages. So, that's definitely happening. I feel like we're rehearsing the same amount of frequency to just always be protected with understudies. I guess the biggest change is that understudies are going on *more*.

MORGAN: There's simply an awareness, too, of understudies and like swings being the heroes. There's just more visibility to it in the national conversation, yeah?

ZERVOULIS: Yes, definitely.

MORGAN:	Are there aspects of Broadway that you want to see change? Let's look forward 5…10…20 years… are there things that you would hope you would wake up and see?
ZERVOULIS:	Yes. More women in [orchestra] pits.
MORGAN:	I love it.
ZERVOULIS:	More new musicals being produced.
MORGAN:	I love that. The answer has been to do the mentorship. At the end of the day, I think we all want to be hired based on the merit of what we're doing. That means that we have to get the same amount of opportunities early on to bring us to the same level. So, I think the mentorship program and the Student Maestra program that you all have is really fantastic. What's it like to bop between being the Music Director versus the Associate MD versus a Sub-Conductor? Do you like that? Sometimes, I feel like folks won't offer me a job to play keyboards because they think I wouldn't take it. Do you have feelings about that, or do you like it… switching chairs?
ZERVOULIS:	Yeah, I really like it. Realistically speaking, I would not have been able to fully serve as a music director this year as a new mom. I have heard many people assume I'd probably not take any gig that's not a music direction gig right now. That's just a concept that I've never understood. In New York theatre, a lot is about perception of what you do in the industry. There are organized trajectories, so that's a tricky question.
MORGAN:	Have you had to step into a music supervisor role yet?
ZERVOULIS:	Yes, I'm doing that right now. I'm music supervising *Only Gold*, which is a musical with a score by Kate Nash – famous rocker chick. It is conceived by Andy Blankenbuehler – of *Hamilton* fame – and he is the director and choreographer. Ted Mellower is the book writer. That has been an exciting experience over there. I am Music Supervisor and Cynthia Meng – who is another Maestra – is the Music Director and it's been really exciting to curate that relationship and learn a bit more about how to effectively supervise in a new musical setting.
MORGAN:	Can you tell me the bullet points of what a Music Supervisor does?
ZERVOULIS:	The Music Supervisor in this particular setup is like a [music] team manager.
MORGAN:	Are you contacting the band?
ZERVOULIS:	No, there is a Contractor for that. It's more about coordinating everyone on the team: Music Director, Associate Music Director, [Synthesizer] Programmer, Ableton Programmer, Music Assistant, Contractor; and also, the sound team as well.

MORGAN:	So, during rehearsals, you're not playing [piano] at all?
ZERVOULIS:	I subbed one day because of a conflict, but other than that, I haven't touched the piano much, which is new for me.
MORGAN:	Right, right. You're just taking notes and taking names! That's awesome. I think the job of Music Supervisor, outside of New York, is a fairly misunderstood job.
ZERVOULIS:	I think it's loosely defined on purpose.
MORGAN:	Right. For flexibility.
ZERVOULIS:	It can be. Sometimes, it's a full-time thing and sometimes, it can be a range of responsibilities.
MORGAN:	I love that. Awesome. I really am very excited to see where your career continues to take you and where you continue to take *it* because you are the *driver* of all the cool things that you've been working on!

AnnMarie Milazzo – Biography

Broadway (Vocal Designer): *Spring Awakening, Next to Normal, If/Then, Finding Neverland.* Off-Broadway: *Carrie, Bright Lights Big City, Superhero*; (Orchestrator, with Michael Starobin): *Once on this Island* (Tony, Drama Desk, Outer Critics Circle nominations). Regional: *Dangerous Beauty, Some Lovers, Dave, A Walk on the Moon, Almost Famous.* Other credits include The Radio City Rockettes' *Summer Spectacular 2016* (co-arranger/lyricist, co-composer); Cirque du Soleil's *Le Rêve* and *La Perle.* Film: *Pretty Dead Girl* (Composer and Lyricist; Special Jury Award, Sundance Film Festival). A.R.T.: JOY, *Finding Neverland, Prometheus Bound.* Milazzo is the Grammy-nominated female vocalist for East Village Opera Company on Decca/Universal Records.

Interview with AnnMarie Milazzo, October 25, 2022 via Phone[27]

MORGAN:	Let's talk about you! AnnMarie Milazzo! I loved your podcast episode with *Page to Stage*[28] that came out a few weeks ago. I was listening to it yesterday and it gave me so much contextual information about stuff I was already wondering about. Where did the term Vocal Designer come from? What's the difference between a Designer and Arranger? What's the story with that?
MILAZZO:	For me, there's nothing deep there; it's just what I feel the job is. I make decisions about the vocal sound that the show needs, so it's the vocal design of the song. We have to ask questions like: "Are the songs narrative? Are they plot-pushing? Are they inner monologue? Are we designing the sonic world? When is it breathy? When do we poke holes in the sound? When is it straight tone? When do we bend notes?

MORGAN: Yeah… thinking about unity versus harmony.
MILAZZO: We deal with texture and color, so it's much like costume and lighting design. There's so much of the same sonic dramaturgy in vocal design. I just think the job definition should change because in [music] arranging, it's like "I'm going to put a chorus here… maybe I'll double the chorus…" The arranging is just like arranging a room; you arrange what's *in* the room…
MORGAN: That's so funny you say that because I was just going to say if it was furniture, you'd already have the furniture in the room. You're just placing it in different places, but you're *building* a piece of furniture as a part of vocal design?
MILAZZO: You're designing it. "This would go great with a red rug…" or "The wall would be green…"
MORGAN: Because you're, you're making additions and subtractions versus just moving the pieces that are already there?
MILAZZO: I've always seen it that way. I never thought it would be such drama to change the [job] title.
MORGAN: I love it. I just had a meeting this morning, mentoring someone who's writing a musical and I recommended that they lean into the style of the story, which means they're going to have to go away for a couple of weeks and go listen to certain genres of music as influence. So, if you're arranging, you're moving around the pieces that are there versus bringing in other influences, which is design. That is part of a visual designer's process… when they bring in their pictures and their references, right?
MILAZZO: It's texture. Music has texture. Music looks like something *new*. It makes you feel something. I feel like all those decisions are made with people's voices.
MORGAN: Let's nerd out for a second. Do you like contemporary a cappella music? Are you in that world?
MILAZZO: No, I'm not in that world at all. It's not where my ear goes; maybe because I just didn't grow up with it.
MORGAN: What did you grow up with?
MILAZZO: Oh my God… I grew up with Journey… Infinity… Stop Making Sense… Fleetwood Mac… Rumors. My dad's a fan of jazz, so I grew up with Charlie Parker and John Coltrane. My mother listened to opera. I grew up with a very eclectic musical taste that didn't include musical theatre. I'm from nowhere. I was from "Nowhere Land."
MORGAN: Where are you from?
MILAZZO: I was from originally from Barton, Vermont. I grew up in a log cabin and a converted funeral parlor.
MORGAN: Oh! Do you like *Six Feet Under*?

MILAZZO: I never watched it. I loved *The Wiz*... my dad had that record, so I loved listening to *The Wiz*... they used to put musicals on in the town, so I would sit in the back of the theater and watch them.

MORGAN: So, what's interesting is you didn't name any R&B groups. I grew up listening to Boyz II Men and a lot of hip-hop and R&B. I hear a lot of those influences in your work. I'm talking about the girl and guy groups that do harmony exquisitely well. I think you have a really keen sense of when to put voices in unison, when to break them into harmony, when to do a "stack" like in the music of Janet Jackson and Brandy.

MILAZZO: Right. Right.

MORGAN: The Motown groups gave us triads and four-part harmony. But Brandy and Janet gave us 13-part harmony, because they're just in the studio, adding and stacking. I feel like that's present in some of your arrangements. I just directed *Next to Normal* (2009)... I've been in *Spring Awakening*... I've worked on material from *Once on this Island* (1991)[29] ... So, where do you think those influences for those decisions came from? Can we unpack your genius for a second?

MILAZZO: Genius is in all of us. I don't know... I live in the world. I absorb music in cars and planes and homes and parties and people and streaming. I just *love* music and I think that it doesn't have any boundaries.

Genius is in all of us.

MORGAN: Right.

MILAZZO: It has laws in which it needs to function in theatre. But the good thing about theatre is: if you're going in someone's head, or if you're trying to make a point with a modern-day audience looking back at something that's a revival, there's so much you can do... there's so many colors you can play with.

MORGAN: The only guideline is the story.

MILAZZO: Right. The only guideline is the story. So, I think that if you live in the world, you can draw from your experience as a human being in the world.

MORGAN: Jacob Collier talks about that, too. He unpacks a lot of thinking outside of the boundaries.

MILAZZO: You know... I don't read music. I don't *write* music. If you don't know the rules, you don't know you're breaking them. I'll just say that.

MORGAN: Let's talk about that for a second. You don't read music. You don't write [notate] music. That is so refreshing to hear because musical theatre as an industry is borne out of elitist art forms, rooted in exclusivity for "Western" structure as being right. There's such a perception, coming through training programs, that a "good musician" performs a particular way and has a defined skill set. What I really love about some of the things you've said or that I've read about you is that your way in sets the example that there are so many ways in. Let's talk about your way in.

MILAZZO: I am jealous of people who read music, to be honest. I wish I could have a total understanding of it, and it's completely helpful. But I think [that kind of training] sets something for life, and I love movable things.

MORGAN: Hmm. That's a good point.

MILAZZO: When I go in – like with the Deaf West *Spring Awakening*[30] – I'll just think about arranging things – I love to move a part. The permanent thing on the page freaks me out a little bit, so there's a lot that I don't have to deal with because I don't know what is on the page. I'm just living in the air! But I do wish I could read it.

MORGAN: It sounds like you speak the language in a different way, which actually helps us dismantle some of the elitist and racist aspects of training in music in America. I live in Atlanta, and I'm surrounded by artists who are amazing musicians. Some of them don't read score. They were trained in church, and they can out-sing or out-play anyone. They just they think of it visually… in their brains differently. I speak all of those angles because I was originally self-taught by ear and then I learned to read music in college. I practiced so dang hard that I refined my skills over the past twenty years. I talk a lot to students about that and I mentor young people who are trying to write musicals and scared because they don't know how to write music. I try to say to them that we'll figure it out. There are so many different ways.

MILAZZO: Yeah, because there's so many tools.

MORGAN: Tell me about the tools that you use. Do you hire really great music transcriptionists and assistants? How do you get your ideas from your brain to the page to the actors to the score?

MILAZZO: Well, it depends. I love to design on my feet. I like to have the human beings in front of me and I love to say, "What does this song need?" And we just start. You know, things will just come… "Hey, you sing this…" It's kind of like… improv…

MORGAN: Then, does your music assistant or does the associate or composer record that?

MILAZZO: Yeah, they record it and get it written down…

MORGAN: They do the book work later in Finale™?

MILAZZO: Yes, when it's set. There's also Garageband™.

MORGAN: Yep. Good ole Garageband, baby!
MILAZZO: There's just so many ways in which you can do it.
MORGAN: So, you multi-track it? You record track by track, layer by layer, in GarageBand?
MILAZZO: I could do that too. Yeah, I do it many ways.
MORGAN: Do you ever sense that some actors are frustrated by that or struggle to adapt to that if they've been trained the old school ways?
MILAZZO: No. Maybe the first hour. People's brains are amazing. They connect with each other's brains.
MORGAN: That's great.
MILAZZO: The minute they pick up what I'm doing and how we're doing this, they get on board.
MORGAN: Yeah, they rewire their thinking about how it should be done.
MILAZZO: You rewire. You think you need this thing… Actors will say "oh I'm not good at this; I don't have a good ear." I'll tell them to close their eyes and listen, and repeat… then it sets people free. I have never had a problem. I've worked with many, many casts. I've never gotten pushback like "I can't do this." In fact, I've gotten smiles, like, "I *can* do this. This is awesome."
MORGAN: Right. It's the side of the spectrum of actors who are skilled in different ways. I've seen so many interviews with Broadway actors admit that they never really learned to read music. Their program didn't teach them, or they didn't go to college or whatever. It's such a middle ground of folks to want just to sing what you want them to sing… just find the "third" and go!
MILAZZO: Yes, and a lot of people have great ideas, so it can be very collaborative. I'm real particular, though, at the very end. I love to then carve it all down and say, *this is it.*
MORGAN: Wow. I love that. It's interesting to have to approach process sometimes from the front end knowing you gotta get some amount of the work done, so you got to do it by layering yourself in GarageBand and singing with yourself. It's different to be able to be in a room, in a workshop style, and collaborate. Which kind of relates to how vocal arrangements are created in the studio for an album, right? Back to developing stacks on the fly with a vocal producer on a pop or R&B album versus getting arrangements done in advance. Nowadays, especially with Tik-Tok™ culture, there are some wonderful music producers who livestream or record themselves on the other side of the glass in a studio session, going back and forth with the backup singers or even that lead singer. They're giving them corrections on the fly and it's so fast and really cool to watch. Was that some of the experience that you got coming up? Do you work in that studio world, where you build that way?

MILAZZO: I've been a session singer before, so harmony comes naturally for me. I think music is very natural. It's like drawing is very natural. It's so primal. I feel like I've never met anyone who didn't like music of *some* kind. It's a language that we all need and speak. I just think people should just try it. In theatre, you have to tell the story; you have to have a purpose to [the harmonies]. I guess the difference is that studio harmony can do a lot of things, but it doesn't have to tell a story Sure, there's the story of the song, but there's no there's no deep one act... two act arc... there's no character...

MORGAN: It's more about feeling.

MILAZZO: And what sounds good. In theatre, it's important to sound good; however, there's an actual plot. There's a storyline and characters... maybe they sound different.

MORGAN: Let's talk about when you were first starting out, hopping into that industry... I read somewhere that you started in New York doing band work, right? Live music work... as a performer?

MILAZZO: I've been in bands my whole life. The very first thing I arranged... designed... I was in a musical called *Bright Lights, Big City* at New York Theatre Workshop[31] and they didn't have any kind of anything going on there [harmonies]. So I said, "Hey, I'm hearing some stuff." Michael Grief[32] said, "cool," so I would just teach them on the fly. There wasn't any sheet music; no one ever transcribed it. Even though we did it at New York Theatre Workshop, it was all done live in the room. I just did it in the room. [The actors] had their tape recorders. It was 1999, I think. It was just a natural thing. I said, "Hey, there's some stuff I'm hearing. Is there a way we can end it like this?" And that was my first experience.

MORGAN: Who were your role models coming up? It could be in the music world or it could be people in your life who were your role models?

MILAZZO: If I can truly be honest, my true connections are my parents. Also, since I was in the middle of the woods, my musical, sonic role model... my true connection... is with nature. My backyard was an apple orchard with no one there... the sound of the falling snow and the cracking of the leaves hitting a branch... the deer that used to grab the apples that used to crash ... There's so much natural sound and rhythm in everything outside.

MORGAN: Oh. Have you ever heard India. Arie's song "Always in My Head"?

MILAZZO: No.

MORGAN: Oh, you should listen to that song. The song starts off and you think it's about a person. Then, if you listen to the lyrics, it's about music being *in* everything. "Like a cool breeze on a summer day... an airplane in the distance plays a beautiful cello line..." all that kind of stuff. It's a great song.

MILAZZO: I mean, that's an honest truth. My inspirations are my parents and nature.

MORGAN: Why did you move to New York?

MILAZZO: I had to.

MORGAN: Tell me more!

MILAZZO: It was my Friday night meeting! Saying, "Hey, everyone. I'm going to New York." I was four [years old].

MORGAN: [laughs] Well, here I am, thinking you're 18 [years old].

MILAZZO: No, I remember thinking: I'm not supposed to be here. I used to say that all the time. This is not the right [place for me]. I don't know what's happening. I would say, "I need to go to New York," and they're like, "You don't even know what you're talking about." I just knew I had to go there. It was just one of the things. Then, when I could, I took the bus with my sister, Florence. My parents said she had to go with me. They were fully expecting us to come home… but we didn't.

MORGAN: Do you have a particular gig, opportunity, or encounter that you would consider your "big break" moment into the Broadway market? Or was it incremental….

MILAZZO: Oh. *Spring Awakening*. New York Theatre Workshop used to have these things called ten-minute musicals. It was like a class; and I wrote a ten-minute musical. I figured I'd try it out. I love musicals and I love stories. There was this guy in the audience named Shawn Ku who was going to USC at the time, and he's like, "Hey, do you want to do a movie with me?" It was a short film about a mortician in love with a dead body and I said yes. So, we did this thing called *Pretty Dead Girl*. I was 24. Everyone who asked me what I was doing thought that was ridiculous. I said, "I think it's going to be fun and it's going to be an opera and it's going to be a movie at the Sundance Film Festival." I was making sandwiches for everyone to beg them to sing and we were building our own sets. It got into the Sundance Film Festival and it won the "Special Jury Award" and it was crazy and amazing. When I got back [to New York], I wanted to turn it into a full-length musical… which was a failure. So, Kimberly [Grigsby] was the Music Director. Then she said she was doing a show called *Spring Awakening* and they're looking for a vocal arranger. She asked if I wouldn't mind auditioning? I auditioned. I did "Touch me" and "Mama Who Bore me" for my audition (as an arranger). Duncan [Shiek, composer] had this other guy in mind, and Kim said she'd like to throw my name in the hat. Kim said I'd be right for that, but I had to audition. I didn't really know what that meant. So, I [arranged] two songs and I won.

MORGAN: Did you do them in the room, like we talked about before, or did you come in with like an arrangement of "Touch Me" …

MILAZZO: I did it on my Four Track.
MORGAN: Nice. Oh, my gosh. You arranged "Touch Me" on a Four Track. The best vocal arrangement in the show, arguably other than "Left Behind", in my humble opinion. That vocal arrangement will cause me to stop the car and pull over to listen.
MILAZZO: Thank you. I would record one track at a time.
MORGAN: Oh my God, do you still have it? Do you have it somewhere?
MILAZZO: I do not. You know what's so funny? I don't have anything. I didn't know.
MORGAN: How were you to know it was going to be one of the best ones? I think it's one of my top-ten favorite vocal arrangements in a musical, for sure. It's up there with "Can't Help Falling in love" in *All Shook Up*... that adaptation is dope... the Quartet from *The Secret Garden*... and then your stuff from *Next to Normal*! "Make Up Your Mind"... "Catch Me I'm Falling"...
MILAZZO: Oh, I did that at Tom's house. [Tom Kitt, American musical theatre composer and arranger]
MORGAN: Gosh... that tenor part... the movement away from the melody? Oh, I get goosebumps just thinking about it. It's beautiful.
MILAZZO: I remember Tom called me and said, "Hey, I was wondering if you could arrange my show called *Feeling Electric*." I wasn't doing anything; I went back to my band because at that point, I didn't know [arranging] was a job. I honestly, I didn't.
MORGAN: I wouldn't have known either. This is the same exact time period where I was doing some vocal stuff, but I looked at the industry and I thought that if I can't play piano, there's not a space for me because everyone's piano-conducting. I kept getting asked to do little arrangements here and there. It wasn't a full-time thing you could do because stick conductors were on their way out. The only conductor you saw was on *Light in the Piazza* [2003] or the big Lincoln Center revivals that were coming out. It was the only time you saw a stick conductor. So, I beefed up my piano skills. Who knew that composers could bring in a vocal designer or arranger to do that part?
MILAZZO: As one who doesn't read or write music, I wasn't telling anyone that I *didn't*. I got away with it. So, with *Spring Awakening,* I was thinking that it was "just kids."
MORGAN: Sure. Oh, wow. *And* it's a pop guy. It's Duncan Sheik. He's from the outside, too.
MILAZZO: Yeah! So, then this real [Broadway composer] calls me – Tom Kitt – and I'm like, "I'm not your girl."
MORGAN: Yes, you were! Oh my God.
MILAZZO: So, I met him, and we had lunch... and then I met his mom and I met his son. I said to him: "Here's the deal, Tom. I have to be

willing to fail. So, if you're willing to just let me come over and do what I do and know that it might not work…" At that point, I'd only done a few shows. He said yes. So, I would go to his house, and he would get these honey pretzels and we would laugh. We had the best time and the start of a great friendship. It was the beginning of our collaboration, although I didn't know it and I don't even think he knew it.

MORGAN: When you're building it in the moment, you're not thinking about how, in twelve years, someone's going to sit there and analyze it in order to produce it on their own. When artists produce a pre-existing show, we get a score, and we analyze it for character and content. The amount of times that I talked with the actors in my production of *Next to Normal* about the way that the vocal lines move together and apart in metaphor with how these characters are moving together or apart in their relationships… or how Diana's psyche is stable then unstable… how the vocal lines represent some elements of her Bipolar disorder… it really works.

MILAZZO: Of course. That's kind of cool.

MORGAN: It's what we talk about! If I'm over here as a music director or director, I'm going to look at the score and interpret that. It's what I lead with: story.

MILAZZO: Yeah, but when you're [arranging] you're focused on: What's the story? Can I read the play? I have this idea. You're still finding your sea legs, too. You know, there's not a lot of money. I mean, that's just reality.

MORGAN: This is important for those who are trying to come up through this angle. Do you get a flat fee, or do you get some of the royalties or does it depend?

MILAZZO: I'll just be honest. I remember for "Bitch of Living," I got a check for $56.

MORGAN: Oh, my God. I'm going to I'm going to lay down and cry.

MILAZZO: I didn't get a lot of money at all for the early stuff.

MORGAN: Oh, I've definitely done some arrangements as a part of another job or in circumstances where I was doing a favor and didn't think anything of it. Then, the show *goes* somewhere, and I realize what I didn't end up getting paid for.

MILAZZO: Right. Because you don't know. There's not a lot of money. I didn't do it for the money. If you want to make a living at it, you'd have to arrange or design *many* shows. We don't have a union for arranging or designing [exclusively. There is a musicians' union. Often, the language in the union handbook applies to musicians who *also* arrange.]

MORGAN: How do you negotiate, now? I've learned to negotiate at least having my name travel with the piece in credits. I just recently helped orchestrate a show for a world premiere, but it was it was a hybrid job of part-copyist – because the composer had done some of the work in Logic; part-arranging, because I was coming up with additional string parts; and part-transcribing, for the material not notated but in the demos. It was a little bit of everything. I made sure the contract said: "Additional arrangements by Amanda Wansa Morgan" always goes with it, unless they completely delete that work and start from scratch. I took a flat fee for the work, but they have to keep that language with the project. I learned my lesson. You know, in case the show becomes a Netflix movie or something.

MILAZZO: I'm not part of the royalty pool at all. They just don't do it.
MORGAN: With *Next to Normal*? HOW?!
MILAZZO: Well, they give you a fee and then you get a weekly cut, no matter if the box office is up or down...
MORGAN: Right. On the original.
MILAZZO: I'll never say no. Then you get bought out.
MORGAN: It's important to know. I can't tell you how many people come to me trying to figure out what to ask for or what to say yes to or what to sign. Young arrangers, designers, composers.... A friend wants you to help write a song for a thing. What do I do? It's really tough because it's a "no man's land," right? Who does this?
MILAZZO: The reality is: even the at the top, [West End or Broadway], you'd have to be designing many shows to be able to pay your rent.
MORGAN: So how do you pay rent?
MILAZZO: I design many shows.
MORGAN: That's why this IBDB [Internet Broadway Database] website that I'm staring at has a lot of credits!
MILAZZO: I am also a session singer. I do many things. I'm a writer... singer.... All of us have to [hustle]. If you want to write musicals for a living, it's like winning the lottery if you want to make a *living*. If you want to live the life of a person that doesn't have a steady job, it's built in... that your job will end. So you have to have that like spirit of: I am really going to trust the universe here.
MORGAN: That's important for the young generation coming up to understand. Many of the conversations in this book center around finding the balance of speaking up for yourself *and* understanding we're in the arts. So, you've got to do some things for the love of the art or for desire to contribute.
MILAZZO: Yes, and to meet people.
MORGAN: Great segue. Who are your favorite collaborators? Is there a difference for you in working with humans who share some of your identity traits? For example, a creative team of women versus not? Is there a different vibe when it's all women?

132 The Music Team

MILAZZO: When I first started, I was mostly dealing with men. There were tons of men in the room. I was lucky enough to have Kimberly [Grigsby] there…

MORGAN: Yeah. You got *the* role model. Yeah.

MILAZZO: I was kind of dropped in at the beginning of the time that it was shifting. Make no mistake: we have a long way to go. Then, Mary-Mitchell [Campbell]… Diane Paulus, I love collaborating with. I love Tom Kitt; I love collaborating with him. Stephen Schwartz. I love collaborating with Andy Einhorn; he's one of my favorites. David Chase. Tina Landau. Julie McBride. I worked with Jeanine Tesori on something we a long time ago and just got to know her. I've never met anyone in the industry that I've been asked to do something with that I haven't had a good experience with and that's just an honest truth. I have a soft spot for Andy Einhorn and David Chase; those are my soft spots. And Kimberly, because, if it wasn't for Kimberly, I wouldn't be here. It's really true. I mean, I'd like to think I'd be doing it, but I don't know.

MORGAN: Let's talk about *Joy*.[33]

MILAZZO: *Joy* is the joy of my life. I think as designers, we come at things *as* writers. I don't know how it can be separated. I think it is a natural thing. Storytelling is something that I've loved ever since I was little. My mom would always talk with me every night before bed, and she would sing these songs attached to the stories.

MORGAN: Like, songs that existed? Or, she would make them up on the fly?

MILAZZO: We'd just make them up! Here we go! I found that it made instant connection to a story that you didn't need; you could just imagine it in your head. Had a full soundtrack. It's an exciting thing to think. Then, I learn there's something called musical theatre and it exists on stage and then, when I used to watch my dad direct the musicals, I would just absorb the way music works and the way it's helping tell the story. I, as a singer–songwriter myself, used to write songs. I taught myself guitar. When I was doing *Once on this Island*, Ken Davenport[34] asked me one night if I write. I said, "Yes, I'm actually a composer & lyricist who is arranging and designing for her supper." He said, "I have the rights to Joy Mangano's [story]." She'd been at the center of this Miracle Mop on the QVC thing… it's all about women in business. It's a story about a family and it's really a story that I could relate to. I could relate to this woman and this story; from having no money and no resources… kind of figuring out things yourself to help the universe. So, I auditioned to write music and he asked me to go on this journey with him? I said, "absolutely."[35]

MORGAN: That's a movie, right? It was the Jennifer Lawrence movie, right?

MILAZZO: Yes. It is based on the real-life story.

MORGAN: So how did you option those rights, knowing that it's already been a movie?
MILAZZO: Well, it's still her life and she has the rights to that. I can't remember who brought it to Ken, but [Joy] met with Ken.
MORGAN: It's important to talk about optioning and all that kind of stuff regarding collaborators, agreements, optioning agreements, all that kind of stuff. It's interesting to hear about how when people have ideas for shows based on real life events but there's another telling of those events. I'm thinking about how Lin-Manuel [Manuel] wrote this musical based Hamilton's life but he heavily referenced the book by Ron Chernow; you know what I mean? He admitted that he based a lot of it on Chernow's book, so Chernow deserves some of the cut.
MILAZZO: I urge everyone who – unless you're going down a journey as an exercise – if you're serious about something, get the rights. I mean, that's a hard lesson. Unless you're doing it as an exercise, you better get the rights. It's years of your life. It's years of dedication, not knowing if it's actually going to go to a stage. Some of them are not easy to get. It's your time and your creativity.
MORGAN: You are going into rehearsal soon for *Joy*, yes?
MILAZZO: I am so excited. We start rehearsal in November [2022].
MORGAN: Right. And Casey Hushion[36] is directing, yes? We worked together on *The Prom*.
MILAZZO: Casey is everything. She's just so expansive and so wonderful and has the most generous of ideas, open heart, always in a good mood. She comes out with positivity and the show goes away. It's a good fit. She's tough and she's brilliant. I'm so honored to be working with Ken writing the book and producing, Casey directing, and Andy music supervising that. I'm really excited and it goes to George Street [Playhouse], opening December 16th. I'm really proud. Last year, I did *Walk on the Moon* because the original writer–composer wasn't able to continue with the project and so I had to step in and it was awesome. Sheryl Kaller directed it.
MORGAN: This is *also* based on a movie, right?
MILAZZO: Yeah. Pamela Gray wrote the book and some of the lyrics… I took it home and it's so moving. It's really cool to see it come to life on stage when it's lived in my guitar for so long.
MORGAN: I love that you say that it lives in your guitar for so long because again, to everyone reading, you can write a musical on a guitar! It's fine!
MILAZZO: Oh, please do! I'm writing a piano score on the guitar.
MORGAN: Do you have a great music assistant? Who's notating it for you?
MILAZZO: Yes. Andy Einhorn is bringing it to life as Music Supervisor.
MORGAN: Rick Edinger is music directing, yes…
MILAZZO: And John Clancy is orchestrating.

134 The Music Team

MORGAN: Oh, yeah! Who did the hip hop stuff for *The Prom*? He's great. So, you really have a great team.

MILAZZO: I have the greatest people around me holding me up my entire life and I'm really lucky that way, thank God.

MORGAN: Well, maybe it's because you're fun to work with and they want to be around you. Maybe that's the thing. Maybe because you're cool.

MILAZZO: Well, none of us are doing it for the money!

MORGAN: Apparently not. $56 for "The Bitch of Living." That's going to be imprinted on my brain. I can't believe that. It seems like the Broadway industry is still growing in a way that hopefully we can look back on and identify this time period as a phase of figuring it out. Maybe we'll end up with a result, like a particular kind of contract that really works. It's going to take a certain number of years for us to get to there because of the hard work of AnnMarie and her friends… her vocal design friends!

MILAZZO: It's ever evolving, but let's just be honest. Theaters are where people who have the money to afford it can go. I wish theatre was for everybody, but you can't afford to go to every show.

MORGAN: I feel that; and I agree. Do you think the industry changed from the pandemic? Have there been pros and cons? I think access has been glorious… meaning: the expansion of access to those not in New York has been significant.

MILAZZO: Yeah, I think it has changed and I think it's continuing to change. The bottom line is that it's expensive it is to produce a show. How much can it change financially for everyone? Not that much if a show costs 15 million dollars to produce.

MORGAN: Right but real talk… Sometimes, shows are paying celebrities thousands and thousands of dollars per week to perform in the show. I remember hearing somewhere that Chenoweth and Menzel made upwards of ten grand a week at some point for *Wicked*. I get that an actor could be a marketing tool for a show to succeed and stay open; whatever. But then we turn around and AnnMarie – who arranged the vocal arrangements and was a part of creating the literal magic that makes the show work – was paid a couple of thousand total as a flat fee?

MILAZZO: Well, they'll say "you didn't sell any tickets."

MORGAN: Yeah, but you *did* with your arrangement of "Touch Me." People hear that on the cast album and go "I want to see that live."

MILAZZO: What's quantifiable? I really don't know. We do need people to *want* to go. We lost 25% of the workforce, so they don't come into the city anymore because they work from home. That means they're not here for work where they would stay and catch shows. Theatre tickets are not cheaper. I literally cannot afford everything, and I'm

	in the industry. I love when someone has a free ticket for me. I understand that producers have to pay for real estate. it's still just….
MORGAN:	All up to capitalism.
MILAZZO:	It is; and that's not going to change. I think the thinking has to change. Broadway can't be the end-all, be-all. If you painted something and it's hanging in a coffee shop in Seattle or the same painting is hanging in the Met… it's of equal value. People have this thing – and I had it when I was young – of going to go to New York because of theatre in New York but… there's theatre everywhere.
MORGAN:	You're talking to a music director of Atlanta, who works with some of the most exquisite performers, voices, and musicians. Yet, we know that if a local theater brings in someone that they can put on the poster is "from New York" or "from Broadway," our local patrons see more value in that and go to that. It's wild.
MILAZZO:	That's what's not talked about, and I feel like that's what fundamentally has to change.
MORGAN:	When the pandemic hit, so many performers and artists left New York City to go to other homes or stay with family in different states. While it was terrible and heartbreaking… is it such a bad thing to disseminate the talent in our industry to other cities? Baayork Lee was telling me that Broadway is not a *place*; it's a level of excellence.
MILAZZO:	Right.
MORGAN:	Disseminate the talent to different cities around this country and around the world, so musical theatre becomes owned by America, not just New York, especially if some of the work (prep and rehearsal) can be done virtually. We're in a cycle where people are going to go to New York because that's where all the opportunity is and that's where the connections are, and then the patrons in the region still value "New York people" as the valuable artists over their local talent. So then, the cycle continues, and it is really hard to break. I'm so keenly aware of this because Atlanta is a stepping stone for many artists… a lot of the kids in the South or Florida coming out of these training programs who are very talented come to Atlanta to cut their teeth. It's a little cheaper – not a lot, now – but a little cheaper. They come here for a couple of years, and they do some shows here and then they go to New York. Great. I support that. However, you're always welcome back here. We're still doing good work and making new things.
MILAZZO:	You know, it's the truth. Wonderful things happen in New York, but wonderful theatre happens everywhere.
MORGAN:	Well, there's space for both, right? I heard you say in that podcast episode that you're a "downtown girl." You like La Mama?[37]

MILAZZO: Yeah. Give me a rope and a box! Talk about [money challenges]… You're charging $3, you're going to make ten cents. It's so hard. Art doesn't need New York. If you're happy and you have a great community and you're affecting lives and you're changing lives, you are already there. I was coming here no matter what; if you would have told me otherwise, I would have never listened.

MORGAN: These are the small ripples that you are making throughout the industry. Even for someone else to call themselves "Vocal Designer" and shift the job title because that's what feels right to you.

MILAZZO: I mean, that's how I feel.

MORGAN: Look at where theatrical intimacy practice was five years ago. Now, it's almost standard in every room, because a couple people dug their heels in and said we really have to change this.

MILAZZO: Right.

MORGAN: We've seen a lot of progress in the language around conscious casting.

So, it should be the same with the title Vocal Designer and the job. Can we arrange without someone that knows how to notate fully? Yes. Can we just let you build it on a four track? Yes, we can.

MILAZZO: Yes. We're artists. We're very pliable.

MORGAN: I mean, you were able to come in with the revival of *Once on this Island* and take a show that already like blew the roof off – a *great* show – and dig a little deeper with those vocal arrangements.

MILAZZO: It's an interesting story because it started out with this devastation. What does that look like? We already know. We watched it on TV with Hurricane Katrina and all of the storms that have hit everywhere. It's not just happy people a second later. So, we wanted to know what that sounded like, what that looked like, and what that meant.

MORGAN: I read that you wanted to do it as a "happening" in the park [Central Park].

MILAZZO: Yeah, originally it was going to be voice and drums. No piano. It doesn't need a thing; it's all there. The only thing that I realized was that you need a bass [for a foundation]. But it's all there. You have to listen differently.

MORGAN: I have to look to see if they're licensing your new(er) vocal arrangements. I hope so, because they're delicious. Same thing with your *Spring Awakening* revival. That was also groundbreaking because it was so soon after the original, but it was because of the new twist, the message, of doing it with deaf actors.

MILAZZO: Imagine working with the deaf community as a music person.
MORGAN: How was that?
MILAZZO: It was dope. It was *amazing*. Huge learning experience. It was going to school real quick. Michael Arden[38] is another one of my favorite people on the planet to collaborate with. It was awesome, learning about that interaction. I don't know what they're hearing. I don't know if they're not hearing [certain individuals]. I will never know. They'll never know what I'm hearing. There were some people from Deaf West who heard a little and some who were completely deaf.
MORGAN: It sounds like that experience in itself helped you grow as an artist and helped you learn how to communicate in different ways.
MILAZZO: Yeah. It helped me open my book in terms of even being human.
MORGAN: Our industry is seriously behind the ball on theatre for varied abilities or the disabled. You could discover something even more magical by the inclusion and acknowledgment of folks with different abilities or disabilities.
MILAZZO: Yeah, it'll happen. It's guaranteed. If you dropped yourself into a situation where it just might not be your comfort zone... where perhaps you have experienced something *like* that before at least, not exactly... I was just blown away. I would skip to work, you know, I really would. I loved all of that cast. I learned so much from everybody.
MORGAN: Well, I have to talk about Neil Diamond.
MILAZZO: Oh, it's a good musical. It's a good story [*A Beautiful Noise*].
MORGAN: I have been personally dragged to three Neil Diamond concerts before the age of 22 by my uncle. Yes. It's a really special feeling to have three teenagers in a concert arena full of mostly middle-aged people, stomping around to "Sweet Caroline" with T-shirts with the man's face on them. It's really something.
MILAZZO: It's very moving. When we were in Boston, I would go to the theater and see people – maybe I'm making a general assumption here – that maybe wouldn't go to see *Into the Woods*. They were having a grand old time.
MORGAN: Yeah, my family is not a "theater" family, but they love *Forever Plaid... Million Dollar Quartet...* I texted my uncle when I found out about *A Beautiful Noise*. He's a retired physician who *loves* Neil Diamond.
MILAZZO: I got to work with Bob Gaudio on [*A Beautiful Noise*].
MORGAN: Oh, man. An original "Jersey Boy." The Four Seasons.
MILAZZO: It was amazing. He's got so much to give.
MORGAN: Well, some of these guys are like walking history. It's like when you watch Liza Minnelli perform, you look at her and see literal history, like a time capsule.

MILAZZO: Yeah, kind of! Sometimes, I just go in rooms and stop breathing… I'm like "I'm from a log cabin…" I have to take a breath and say to myself, "I deserve to be here."

MORGAN: That's it, though. That's the thing, right? You can be from a log cabin. You can be from Argentina. [Graciela Daniele] told me this lovely story about how she got ballet training because Eva Peron instituted an education program.

MILAZZO: I mean, that's insane.

MORGAN: Baayork Lee told me a wonderful story about her parents taking her to this audition call for the original *King and I*.

MILAZZO: She's making history, but she's just living her life. You don't know the thing that you're going to do because you just did it because it was your life.

MORGAN: I'm excited about seeing this musical that lives at the intersection of my interests. I hope I can see it with my uncle.

MILAZZO: Yes! You get to go to theater, and he gets to go to the theater and have a different experience.

MORGAN: Right! I'm going to be listening to how you rearranged or designed the music! I'm curious about what are you going to do with "Sweet Caroline," in terms of harmony?

MILAZZO: It's so much fun. There's this whole thing! So, a book of his lyrics opens, and I designed an a cappella thing where all his songs come flying out of the book. I was geeking out on how cool it could be.

MORGAN: I love jukebox musicals. One of my favorite Broadway experiences ever was going to see *Rock of Ages* (2005).

MILAZZO: Oh, I loved *Rock of Ages*.

MORGAN: I went with my friend Dana – an actor in the city – and we were in our twenties. We got standing room only tickets for $25. We were drinking and they handed out those fake LED-lighters that we got to wave around, and it was everything.

MILAZZO: I go to the theater for tech and previews to see it and check in with my little pass. I'm like a kid. I have my *Almost Famous* (2022) pass. It has my little picture on it. I get to go through the door and say, "Oh, I'm working on the show."

MORGAN: Well, I have these questions that we haven't hit about self-care and caregiving and stuff, but you just sound like you're having a great time.

MILAZZO: Are you kidding? I love my life. I have a great life. I really have a great community of friends who live in New York. It's because theatre is not my entire life. I have a life and theatre is a part of my life. I guess that's how I self-care. I love astronomy. I have other hobbies. I have a partner who's an artist; she's a painter. I have a whole big life that incorporates theatre. I cook.

MORGAN: It makes sense that you cook because there are so many food metaphors when talking about music. I talk about how the ingredients collide to make a meal. I often talk about a casserole. Sometimes the metaphor is we are sounding like a TV dinner right now, with everything separated. How are we going to put this thing together to make more of a casserole?

MILAZZO: That's amazing. Yeah, it's whatever works.

MORGAN: I love cooking, but I don't like baking as much because it's so precise. If we mis-measure an ingredient, the cookie is going to bounce off the floor.

MILAZZO: Oh, I like baking, too. Like, what if I added a half a cup more butter? Oh, my God, the cookie is going to be flat and crunchy.

MORGAN: Nope, I'm not good at that. I'm an Aries. That's an area where reading music does come into play.

MILAZZO: I'm a Sag [Sagittarius].

MORGAN: Oh, I'm married to a Sag.

MILAZZO: Aries… Sag… that's a good combination, actually.

MORGAN: Well, here we are, and I've taken up too much of your time!

MILAZZO: Oh, it's been wonderful. What a joy.

Notes

1 Jennifer Jones Cavenaugh, "A Composer in Her Own Right." *Women in Musical Theatre* (North Carolina: McFarland & Company Inc. Publishers, 2008), 86.
2 "Macy Schmidt: About" *macyschmidtmusic.com*. Accessed January 20, 2023. See https://www.macyschmidtmusic.com/about.
3 "Sheilah Vaughn Walker" *Maestra Inc.* Accessed January 20, 2023. See https://maestramusic.org/profile/sheilah-walker/.
4 "Emily Grishman" *Internet Broadway Database*. Accessed January 10, 2023. See https://www.ibdb.com/broadway-cast-staff/emily-grishman-106345.
5 "Cynthia Meng" *Maestra Inc.* Accessed January 18, 2023. See https://maestramusic.org/profile/cynthia-meng/.
6 Kimberly Grigsby, Interview with Amanda Wansa Morgan via Zoom, October 13, 2022.
7 After running on Broadway for 35 years, *Phantom* has been set to close in 2023.
8 Jerome Robbins (1918–1988), An American theatre director and choreographer with a prolific career, best known for his direction of *West Side Story* and choreography of many American musical theatre classics.
9 Conductors give their musicians indication of when to start as well as the tempo at which the band or orchestra should play through beats prior to the downbeat of playing together. This can sometimes be one beat (an "upswing") or more, based on what might help keep players in sync.
10 Dena Tauriello is a Broadway musician – drummer/percussionist. See https://www.ibdb.com/broadway-cast-staff/dena-tauriello-518824.
11 André De Shields is an American performer, director, and choreographer.
12 Musical Theatre Works was a non-profit company based in New York City dedicated to creating and developing new musicals that closed in 2004 after 21 years of operation.
13 TheatreWorksUSA is a professional theatre company based in New York City dedicated to the development and production of Theatre for Young Audiences (TYA).

14 See info in Chapter 7 about the NYU Graduate Writing program.
15 In the musical *Hairspray*, the script indicates that the character Edna pops out of a giant hairspray can during the Finale and the gimmick is that the actor is preset inside the set piece before the beginning of the number.
16 Mary-Mitchell Campbell, 2023. "Interview with Amanda Wansa Morgan" *Via Zoom*, January 9, 2023.
17 Hole in the Wall Gang Campus serves seriously ill children and their families, giving those children an opportunity to have fun, just be a kid, and "raise a little hell." Founded in 1988 by Paul Newman.
18 Gerber, Michael E. *The E-Myth Revisited: Why Most Small Businesses Don't Work and What to do about it.* Harper Business: 2004.
19 See Interview with Kimberly Grigsby.
20 "Meg Zervoulis" *Maestra Inc.* Accessed January 29, 2023. See https://maestramusic.org/profile/meg-zervoulis/.
21 Zervoulis, Meg. 2022. "Interview with Amanda Wansa Morgan" *Via Zoom*, November 5, 2023.
22 See https://broadwaylicensing.com/shows/rated-p-for-parenthood/#:~:text=Rated%20P%20for%20Parenthood%20chronicles,of%20comic%20and%20musical%20vignettes.
23 Cherie Rosen. Broadway Music Director. See https://maestramusic.org/profile/cherie-rosen/.
24 A four-day intensive workshop in 2013 during which ten aspiring musical theater conductors were given hands-on experience with Broadway professionals.
25 Paul Gemignani – American music director with a 40-year career on Broadway and the West End. 2001 Tony Award for Special Lifetime Achievement.
26 Generation of Americans presumably born between 1981 and 1996.
27 AnnMarie Milazzo, Interview with Amanda Wansa Morgan via Zoom, October 25, 2022.
28 "Page to Stage: A Conversation with Theatre Makers" *The Broadway Podcast Network*. See https://broadwaypodcastnetwork.com/podcast/page-to-stage/.
29 These are three shows that Milazzo is known for providing vocal arrangements/design.
30 The Deaf West Theatre Company – based in Los Angeles – mounted a production of *Spring Awakening* featuring a cast that re-imagined and performed the show simultaneously in English and American Sign Language, which transferred to Broadway as a revival in 2015.
31 "Bright Lights, Big City (musical)" *Wikipedia*. Last modified November 1, 2020. See https://en.wikipedia.org/wiki/Bright_Lights,_Big_City_(musical).
32 American theatre director (b. 1959).
33 2022 musical that Milazzo wrote. World premiere at the George Street Playhouse in December 2022.
34 Ken Davenport – American theatrical producer and writer (b. 1970). See https://kendavenport.com/project_category/shows-written-by-ken/.
35 *Joy* – a 2015 film starring Jennifer Lawrence based on Joy Mangano's life and career. See https://en.wikipedia.org/wiki/Joy_(2015_film).
36 Casey Hushion – American director and Associate Broadway Director. See https://www.caseyhushion.com/home.
37 Experimental theatre club in New York City, open since 1961. See https://www.lamama.org/.
38 Michael Arden (b. 1982) American theatre director.

4
DIRECTOR/CHOREOGRAPHERS

Introduction

"Directors tell stories. While others usually write those stories, the director guides their telling. She decides what's important to highlight […] and then takes the audience on a journey into and through that world." – from Joe Deer's *Directing in Musical Theatre: An Essential Guide*.[1] This quote from Deer really boils down to the directing experience through a holistic lens that moves me as a director. Similarly, Susan Stroman said in our interview, "You feel very protective of a cast, and you want them to feel comfortable enough to take a chance. You want them to feel like they could run into your arms and that you would catch them." I sat with that for a number of days. It was such a nurturing thing to say and she said it so matter-of-fact.

I grew up performing in musicals, but I didn't get the urge to direct until college because I didn't see myself able to do what my directors from high school and even elementary school could do. They seemed to come in and know *everything*. I doubted my capacity to think so deeply and thoroughly about a piece and know every detail of it in order to come in and tell everybody what to do. My assumptions were wrong because I didn't know what was behind their process and purpose. When I came to college, I walked into some rooms where directors – sometimes professors and sometimes student directors – simply asked us to try anything. I thought, "Well, I can do *that!*" But, that wasn't it either.

I heard Kenny Leon [American director of stage and screen] say in a live masterclass once (and I'm paraphrasing) "As a director, I simply answer a lot of questions. If I don't know the answer to that question, I'll admit it, and then go find out the answer."

I've watched directors sit back and let a music director and choreographer set most of a show while I've watched others micromanage each decision right down

DOI: 10.4324/9781003324652-4

to the location of snaps on a costume in a quick change. There is no formula, but there are certain steps to the preparation and rehearsal process that can set one up for success, as well as some character traits and leadership skills that create spaces in which artists are ready and willing to make art because they feel safe, heard, empowered, and supported.

Much of my development as a director has been in the area of interpersonal communication – navigating the personalities of my creative and design team as well as hearing the needs of my actors and what the show needs in order for the room to have a good vibe. There is, of course, the process of learning how to create thorough paperwork, dramaturgy, and play analysis; how to communicate with actors in a way that is not prescriptive but guiding; and how to communicate with designers and production team in a way that demonstrates vision *and* grace. Some of this can be learned through training and excellent books; however, most directing skills are learned through doing it. Directing is an experiential art. Almost every director or choreographer that I've spoken with confirmed that they started directing on a small or DIY ("Do It Yourself") scale, by assisting who someone who knows what they're doing, or both. If collaboration and communication are the keys to success in directing, then experience is the only way to sharpen those skills. Leigh Silverman says, "You have to stay completely in control and yet be utterly flexible. [....] You can't leave people behind. I think that's hard because you're all the time managing personalities, managing other people's anxieties, managing your own anxiety, managing expectations, managing the noise of the world [....] everything passes through the director so you can get everybody in the same car, going to the same destination."[2]

Directing and choreographing *can* be handled by two different people. I happened to connect with the crown jewels of the hybrid position at the Broadway level: Susan Stroman, Graciela Daniele, and Baayork Lee.

Choreographing is its own art form, but the two jobs are inextricably tied together in storytelling, and if they can be completed by the same person – perhaps with a solid team of associates or assistants – the potential for misunderstanding in rehearsal is significantly diminished.

Additional Directing Team Members

Associate Directors serve as an extension of the director. They are often on their feet, staging scenes, cleaning scenes, and fixing material when the director is perhaps in another room working with other actors or the creative team on solving a conundrum. "Associates" have typically served as a sounding board for the director throughout the preproduction process and have been included in essential conversations with design team members and other members of the creative team.

Assistant Directors are presumably in an apprenticing position, often aiding the director and associating with tasks related to research, dramaturgy, actor management, communication, and miscellaneous duties that support the assistant's learning experience, and benefit the director by relieving them of that time commitment.

Choreographers create choreography – dance and/or movement – for musical numbers and possibly incidental movement (e.g., scene changes). One of the cornerstones of musical theatre is that the choreography *continues* the storytelling – it augments it, rather than detracts from it. In the days prior to the Rodgers & Hammerstein musicals, namely *Oklahoma*, choreographed by the incredible Agnes DeMille, choreography often occurred as a diversion from the story being told, or a performance within a play. DeMille and subsequent choreographers Robbins, Cole, Tune, Genarro, Fosse, and Stroman ensured that character would be at the *center* of choreography in musical theatre.

Associate Choreographers – Similar to the associate director or associate music director, this "associate" works *with* the choreographer to solidify ideas, perhaps as a partner in preproduction to physically help figure out staging that makes sense. Some choreographers use their associates to teach the choreography to the actors in rehearsal or as additional demonstrators.

Assistant Choreographers – Duties may include, but are not limited to, partnering with the Associate in demonstration, working with the Dance Captain to clarify or clean dances, and pay attention to choreography conversations in an apprenticeship-style role.

Dance Captains are typically members of the cast who have been assigned the duty to maintain the choreography as the run of the show continues, even beyond the dances they are performing in as a cast member. Dance captains help rehearse understudies alongside stage management and help run any "brush-up" dance rehearsals with the cast after opening. Furthermore, they serve as a liaison between cast and creative teams in the area of choreography.

Important Figures

Agnes DeMille (1903–1993) was a choreographer (and dancer) whose work influenced the rest of musical theatre history with her iconic choreography for the original productions of *Oklahoma* (1943), *Carousel* (1945), and *Brigadoon* (1947). Her career spanned 40 years through ballet, musical theatre, film, and education. She mentored many dancers and choreographers and became an advocate for dance education in America.

Dame Gillian Lynne (1926–2018) was a British choreographer most famous for her choreography of the Webber hit musicals *Cats*, *Phantom of the Opera*, and *Aspects of Love*.

Patricia Birch is a two-time Drama Desk winner and choreographer of over a dozen Broadway musicals including the original productions of *You're a Good Man Charlie Brown* (1971), *Grease* (1971), *A Little Night Music*, and *Parade* (1998). She also enjoyed a significant career as a Broadway performer and choreographer for film.

144 Director/Choreographers

Lynne Taylor Corbett created the classic choreography for the 1984 film *Footloose* as well as directed and choreographed *Swing!* (2000) on Broadway in addition to an illustrious career as a dancer.

Mary Hunter (1904–2000) was a director of works on Broadway and regionally and also helped originate the Society of Stage Directors and Choreographers and was the associate producer for the TheatreGuild.[3]

Vinnette Carol (1922–2002) holds the distinction of being the first African-American woman to direct for Broadway with the 1972 production of *Don't Bother Me, I Can't Cope,* which she also helped write. Her resume included credits directing Off-Broadway, regionally, and internationally.[4]

Julie Taymor is a Tony-award-winning director of stage and screen, noted most for her direction, puppet, and costume design of Broadway's *The Lion King* (1997), her direction of feature films *Titus* (1999) and *Across the Universe* (2008), and a slew of other visually stunning operas and Shakespeare plays. Taymor's work is marked by intricate use of puppetry, design, and bold spectacle. She, alongside Graciela Daniele and Susan Schulman were the dominant, visible women in direction on Broadway in the 1990s.

Susan Schulman is a Broadway director and educator most famous for her direction of the Tony-award-winning original Broadway production of *The Secret Garden* (1990). She has directed many other Broadway hits, often centering on strong women, like *Little Women* (2005) and the 1998 revival of *The Sound of Music.* She teaches in the graduate directing program at Penn State University.[5]

Diane Paulus won the Tony Award for Direction of a Musical with her 2013 revival of *Pippin* and is also noted for direction of *Finding Neverland* (Broadway, 2015), *Porgy and Bess* (revival, 2012), *Waitress* (2015), and *Jagged Little Pill* (2018).

Rachel Chavkin is a Broadway stage director best known for directing *Natasha, Pierre, and the Great Comet of 1812* (Broadway, 2016) and *Hadestown* (2019) for which she won the Tony Award for Best Direction of a Musical.

Tina Landau is a theatre director and playwright, known in the Broadway community for her direction and conception of *The Spongebob Musical* (Broadway, 2017) along with her direction of the 2001 revival of *Bells are Ringing* and her prolific resume of directing plays. She penned the book to the Adam Guettel musical *Floyd Collins* and has been a member of the Steppenwolf Theatre Company since 1997.

Leigh Silverman has directed Broadway shows and Off-Broadway shows, garnering a Tony nomination for Best Direction of the 2014 Broadway revival of *Violet*. She is a two-time Obie Award winner. Her resume contains plays, musicals, and special events around the country.

Marcia Milgrom Dodge is a director-choreographer best known for her direction of the 2009 Broadway revival of *Ragtime*. She is also a dramaturg and writer.

Kristin Hanggi directed the 2009 original Broadway production of *Rock of Ages* and boasts a resume of additional theatrical direction credits and film work.

Camille A. Brown is a lauded choreographer, director, and dance educator, most known for her choreography of *Once on this Island* (2017 Broadway Revival),

Choir Boy (2019, Tony nomination), and *Jesus Christ Superstar Live in Concert* (2018). She is the Founder & Artistic Director of Camile A. Brown & Dancers.

Hope Clark choreographed the original Broadway productions of *Jelly's Last Jam* (1992) and *Caroline or Change* (2004). She is also known for her direction of a 1995 production of *Porgy and Bess* that ended up touring both in the US and Internationally.

Debbie Allen is one of America's premier multi-hyphenate artists as a director of both stage and screen, choreographer, songwriter, performer, and producer. She is a 20-time Emmy nominee, Golden Globe winner, and has a star on the Hollywood Walk of Fame. In the Broadway world, she choreographed the original production of *Carrie* (1988), directed the 2008 production of *Cat on a Hot Tin Roof*, and starred in numerous productions. Her contributions to choreography on film are prolific, including the TV series rendition of *Fame*.

Kathleen Marshall is a three-time Tony Award-winning director and choreographer, noted for her work on the 2011 Broadway Revival of *Anything Goes*, the 2006 Broadway Revival of *The Pajama Game* and the 2004 Broadway Revival of *Wonderful Town*. She also choreographed the 1999 Broadway Revival of *Kiss Me Kate* with Marin Mazzie and Brian Stokes Mitchell.

Ann Reinking (1949–2020) was predominantly known for her work as a performer in the works of Bob Fosse; however, she earned a Tony Award for Best Choreography for her work on the 1996 revival of *Chicago* and was known for her co-direction and creation of *Fosse* (1998) and her contributions to musical theatre dance education.

Lorin Latarro has choreographed Broadway productions of *Into the Woods* (2022 revival), *Mrs. Doubtfire* (2022), and *Waitress* (2016/2021). She has worked on numerous Broadway shows as an Associate Choreographer and performer, and works as a director-choreographer around the country and off-Broadway.

Carrie-Anne Ingrouille choreographed the original Broadway production of *Six* (2021).

Ann Yee choreographed the 2021 revival of *Caroline, or Change* and provided musical staging for the 2017 revival of *Sunday in the Park with George*.

Katie Spelman has served as Associate Choreographer on Broadway productions of *Moulin Rouge! The Musical* (2019), *Amélie* (2017), and *American Psycho* (2016).

Kelly Devine choreographed *Diana The Musical* (2021), *Escape to Margaritaville* (2018), *Rocky* (2014), and *Rock of Ages* (2009), among many other credits.

Casey Hushion has served as an associate director on seven Broadway shows including *The Prom, Mean Girls,* and *Aladdin* while building a resume as director of world premieres including *Mystic Pizza* (2021) and *Joy* (2022).

INTERVIEWS

Graciela Daniele
Susan Stroman
Baayork Lee

Graciela Daniele Biography

Graciela Daniele has earned 10 Tony Award nominations and six Drama Desk nominations. Her Broadway Director/Choreographic credits include Chita Rivera: *The Dancer's Life, Annie Get Your Gun, Marie Christine, Once on This Island, Chronicle of a Death Foretold* and *Dangerous Game*. She directed and choreographed Michael John LaChiusa's *Hello Again* and *Marie Christine;* and Lynn Ahrens and Stephen Flaherty's *Dessa Rose* and *The Glorious Ones* (Lincoln Center). She has musically staged and choreographed *Ragtime* (Astaire, Ovation [L.A.], NAACP, and Callaway Award), *The Goodbye Girl, Zorba* with Anthony Quinn, *The Rink* starring Liza Minnelli and Chita Rivera, and *The Mystery of Edwin Drood*. She choreographed the New York Shakespeare Festival's *The Pirates of Penzance* on Broadway, Los Angeles and London, the motion picture of *Pirates*, and three Woody Allen films including *Mighty Aphrodite* (1996 Fosse Award), and *Everyone Says I Love You* (1997 Fosse Award). Ms. Daniele directed and choreographed *A New Brain* at Lincoln Center Theatre. She is recipient of the 1998 "Mr. Abbott" Award for Outstanding Achievement by a Director/Choreographer. Ms. Daniele directed and choreographed Michael John LaChuisa's *Little Fish* (Second Stage) and *Bernarda Alba* (Lincoln Center Theatre) along with the Lincoln Center Theatre production of William Finn's *Elegies, A Song Cycle*. Most recently, she has choreographed *The Visit* on Broadway. Recent: *The Gardens of Anuncia* (Old Globe). She is a member of the Theater Hall of Fame.

Interview with Graciela Daniele, October 17, 2022, via Phone, 10/17/22

MORGAN: In your words, tell me about your journey from Argentina to Broadway. I can read the basics on the Internet, but I'd love to hear it from you.

DANIELE: There was a big slice of life between learning ballet in Argentina and Broadway. When I started [dancing] in Argentina, I was 7 years old and I went to the Theatre Colón[6] to learn ballet and that was the beginning of it all. The Theatre Colón ran in the times of Juan Perón, under his dictatorship. His wife[7] did good things helping children without much money and we [my family] were only four women: my grandmother, my mother, my aunt, and myself, a child. And so, whoever couldn't afford education for something like The Theatre Colón, which was an extraordinary school for ballet and opera… It was free! So, I started at seven and I graduated at [age] fourteen. I went to elementary school in the afternoon. Our first class – ballet class – was at 7:00 in the morning. So, I went to elementary school and I skipped [grades] – we had six or seven [grades] for elementary school – and I did them in five because they would use us, for – which was tremendous, really – extras in the operas, during school hours. They didn't pay, of course, but I was 7 years old and I was on the stage! We played all of the little slaves in *Aida*, and the gods flying fifteen feet up in the air in *The Magic Flute* and all this – for a kid, you know – was just extraordinary. People would ask me, "Didn't you miss your childhood?" I said, "Are you kidding?" I lived a fairy tale for 6 or 7 years! It was extraordinary! It was hard work, but wonderful. They were very selective. I mean, in the first year that I started, there were thirty or forty kids and, eventually, only three girls and two boys graduated in the last year. It was extremely tough, but I loved every moment of it. In the last years of the school, they would use us to reinforce the Corps de ballet[8] in The Theatre Colón. It was fortune for us; unfortunate for the dancers. Since it was government-funded, they had a certain age that they could retire. There were 55-year-old women who couldn't dance anymore. So, they took us from the upper grades of school and *I* would go to work with some of these extraordinary ballet choreographers. I mean, Balanchine[9]... Massine[10]...

MORGAN: Wow.

DANIELE: No pay and hard work! But that was the beginning, and I was totally convinced that that's what I wanted to do. To be a ballerina and I became a ballerina!

MORGAN: Right. You went to Paris?

DANIELE: Yes, of course.

DANIELE: When I graduated, there were people waiting to retire, but there was no place for the three girls and the two boys to dance at The Theatre Colón, so there was *another* theater in the city La Plata – very close to Buenos Aires – this *wonderful* theater – Teatro Argentino [de la Plata]. So, they hired me as a soloist there. I was 15 years old, for Christ's sake. It was ridiculous! It was a wonderful ... again, *great training* there. I got a small payment but enormous experience. Then, somebody who was a great ex ballerina from The Ballets Russes[11] was forming a ballet company in Brazil to tour through Brazil and South America. She came to see us, and she offered me (and my partner) to be the prima ballerina of this company. And I said, "Okay!" My mother had to travel with me because I was only 15 years old. We traveled and went to Rio De Janeiro and did the whole tour of the East Coast [Brazil]... all these magnificent theaters that they have in the middle of the jungle in those days...we did that for a year or so. Then, we got to Bogotón, Columbia and the company closed. So we said, "Okay, we have to get back to Argentina." At that time – I guess that was 1956 or so – they had a huge national television program in Bogotón called The PanAmericana[12] and it was really educational. They came to my partner and I to see

	if we were interested in doing a weekly program based on the history of ballet. I said, "Okay!"
MORGAN:	You are really good at saying okay!
DANIELE:	Oh, that is my favorite word! Well, sometimes I think it gets me into trouble, but it works for me most of the time! So, we stayed there and made some money. This is a marvelous little, internal story: My father had abandoned us when I was 6 or 7 years old. The director of this weekly educational program was a Spaniard and great man. He and my mother fell in love, and I was *so* happy. It was a double thing: I was happy for them because they were both lovely people, but it was also my chance of going to study in Paris. The best ballet teachers in in the world in that time – in the 1950s and early-1960s – were in Paris. So, I went to Paris by myself with a little money and said, "Okay!" I figured I'd go there for a month or two. I went to the best school with all these wonderful teachers of ballet of all different styles. I didn't know the way they hired people for the ballet company was by going to their school and seeing a class and then picking up somebody. So, the second week I was there, somebody who was the assistant of Roland Petit[13] [a renowned French choreographer] picked me to become a soloist at the Opera of Nice which is in the South [of France]. So, I went to Nice! I was actually living in Paris, but every summer and winter, we would go to Nice, and it was just extraordinary. I got to work with a lot of extraordinary choreographers who go over there. Finally, it was maybe 1960… 1961… something like that… and I finished the season in Nice and go back Paris… and a friend of mine, she says, "Oh, Graciela, you *have* to see this marvelous musical!" And I said – in my fifth position, you know – "Oh I *hate* musicals." I had never seen a musical in my life! She said, "No, no, no, but you have to see it because it's been directed and choreographed by a choreographer you *know*… you have seen his work and you love it." I say, "WHO?" Jerome Robbins. I agreed to go see it. It was closing night. So, I went… standing room only. I went and I stood at the back, and I didn't expect too much, you know, because this is a "musical." On top of the proscenium, they had the translation to French [from English]. I think I looked up once and never looked at it again. The *moment* the lights came down in that theater and I heard… (*sings the first phrase of…*)
MORGAN & DANIELE at the same time:	West. Side. Story.
DANIELE:	Yes. And I didn't move… even at intermission, I just stood there… I couldn't move. The theater was right by the river. So, when the show ended, I sat by The Seine and I said… I must go to America and I must go to New York and learn how to do that. And that's what I did. I came over here in 1963 and I immediately asked for the best

Director/Choreographers 149

teacher. Of course, Jack Cole[14] was the creator of Jazz (in American theatre dance) … but the best teacher who was still around at that time was Matt Mattox.[15] I went to [Mattox's] school and I continued my ballet classes; I would take three classes day. I tried modern dance… I went to Martha Graham[16]… I loved her work… but… it wasn't me. It was too many contractions, too much suffering.

MORGAN: *(laughing)* Did you say *too much suffering?!*

DANIELE: Max Mattox told me that he thought I should go to Merce Cunningham.[17] I said "Okay!" Imagine: the first thing that happens in the studio… he says, "Everybody in the corner! Everybody just run across!" We are doing whatever we are doing on the diagonal, so liberated. And I thought, "*This* is it. I really like this."

MORGAN: Right. Let's feel some feelings.

DANIELE: Yeah, he had a charismatic personality.

MORGAN: Right. In ballet, it's all upright and about lines, yes? Then, you have to release it.

DANIELE: Exactly, oh, it's very confined … restricted; although; it changed throughout the years.

MORGAN: What did that feel like? To be able to just run across the room like that and feel feelings?

DANIELE: I loved it! It expressed something that I was missing, I think. Although I could do a role and be very expressive – it didn't have that level of freedom or expression.

MORGAN: Did you talk about that with Agnes de Mille? She really changed the game for us in musical theatre. A lot of people think she changed the game.

DANIELE: Yes, actually, she did. I did work with her years later… I played one of the three cowgirls…

MORGAN: … in *Oklahoma?*

DANIELE: Yes, the cowgirls! She was amazing. She was sitting in a wheelchair already, but she was amazing. Again, it was about this spirit… that power… *and* style… and *acting*! That's what I was missing. I was so lucky, Amanda, and it's all because I would say OKAY.

MORGAN: You said okay!

DANIELE: You call me, and I said okay! So, I started working with Matt [Mattox] and I went to the beginner's class, which was taught by his wife. The second class, I see this beautiful man standing on the side looking at the class and I didn't know who he was. I continued trying to close my feet [this is a reference to "turning in" to parallel foot position] as opposed to being always in fifth position. I tried really hard. He called me over and asked, "why are you in here with the beginners?" and, with my poor English I said, "No, no, I have to learn…" He said, "Oh no, you have to come to a professional class." Well, it was hard, but I did that. I worked with him for about two weeks, taking classes every day with him. One day he calls me and says, "You know... I'm choreographing a Broadway show with Steve Lawrence[18] and it's called *What Makes Sammy Run?*

MORGAN: 1964, yes?

DANIELE: That's right. In the middle of this show, there is this long ballet – 9 minutes long. He says, "And I would love for you to audition for it." So, I said...

MORGAN and DANIELE together: Okay!

DANIELE: I said, "When is the audition?" and he said "No, you don't have to dance. They know that you're great. You just have to talk to the producer and the director."

MORGAN: Okay...

DANIELE: So, I dressed up. I sat there and smiled. I might not have known what they were saying but I smiled and was saying "okay" to everything. That raised everything for me... the permission to work... it was just amazing.

MORGAN: Amazing. Do you remember that opening night for *What Makes Sammy Run* on Broadway? Your Broadway debut?

DANIELE: I don't. See, I'm a peculiar person, Amanda. I love to work. I don't like show *business* at all. I never did.

MORGAN: Wow. That seems to be a common theme among the couple of women I've talked to thus far...

DANIELE: You know, it's a chore for me. I'm sure I went [to the opening party], but I don't remember. I don't remember anything about it. I can't say. What can I tell you?

MORGAN: So, you assisted Michael Bennett with *Follies* (1971)?

DANIELE: I first started working with Michael on *Promises, Promises* (1968), which was very difficult because his style was not entirely the Jack Cole style. It had the "Hullabaloo"[19] dances, and all of that... so I had to really loosen myself up. I had a wonderful woman – Margo Sappington who helped me enormously. She was a wonderful choreographer. On the [rehearsal] breaks, she would say "No, no, no! Move those hips!" I understood that as a Latina! From there, Michael brought me to work on *Coco*; for that one I was his "girl assistant."[20] And then from there he took me out of there and we did *Follies* (1971), which was my favorite show, of course.

MORGAN: You got to work with Stephen Sondheim, yes?

DANIELE: *Great* people! Great actors, wonderful director... Hal Prince ... and Michael.

MORGAN: Were you thinking about choreographing at that point? By that level?

DANIELE: I was assisting Michael, and those were the times where I was learning. There was a huge industrial show called The Milliken Show[21]

Director/Choreographers **151**

here in New York. Milliken was a fabric and textile company. Every Spring, they would [recruit] these fantastic stars because they were paid so well. So, we would rehearse and do the fashion show at 6:00 or 7:00 in the morning. This was a breakfast show at the Waldorf Astoria.[22] I started by dancing *in* the show. [Bennett] always had his right-hand man Bob Avian,[23] of course, but I was his girl assistant… and I kept on doing that. Then, when Michael didn't do it anymore, somebody else came in and he said to the producers of Milliken, "You have to keep Graciela as an assistant to the new choreographer because she knows how this works." It wasn't only the choreography; it was the costume changes and the [tracking]. In the same musical number you had twenty seconds to change within… it was incredible… very difficult to organize. So, they said "Yes" and I said "Okay!" Eventually, Michael said, "It's time for Graciela to choreograph it." So, I started choreographing the Milliken show. During the process for *Coco*, we would be in pre-production[24] and he would say, "Improvise something for me…" and I would do it; and there would be something he liked, like a change or a touch or something else. So, he was allowing my invention in the work to come through, as opposed to "5-6-7-8… do this… do that." Michael Bennett was amazing and I owe him so much. I started choreographing The Milliken Show *plus* dancing in shows on Broadway. Milliken paid so much money – it was the first time in my life that I had money. I got to work with the most extraordinary stars in the world! Ann Miller! Van Johnson! Gloria Swanson! I mean, every single *year* we had seven or eight extraordinary stars. I met Gloria Swanson in a kick line! Ginger Rogers! Do you know how difficult it was for me to tell Ms. Rogers what to do?!

MORGAN: Right! "Excuse me, *Ms.* Rogers…" *And* you're learning English and speaking three languages, yes? You moved to Paris and learned French… you came to America and learned English…. tried to figure it out?

DANIELE: That's right, that's right! One of the stars was Elaine Stritch. Brilliant, brilliant actress… but tough lady.

MORGAN: You did her movement for her one-woman show, *Live at Liberty* (2002). Right?

DANIELE: Right; but, long before that – at Milliken – we were in rehearsal. I said something and she looks at me and says, "*Why don't you speak English?*"

MORGAN: Oh no….

DANIELE: The dancers – my dears – were *so* supportive… they went "Ohh-hhhhhh" and I turned to her smiled, and said, "Elaine… it has not stopped me, has it?" That was it. She didn't say anything after that.

	Then, I worked with her in other things, and she was fine. I was always very strong. Nice, but very strong.
MORGAN:	Would you say is there a difference between the processes where you got to work with either fellow women or fellow Latinas like Chita [Rivera] and the rooms where you were the only one representing either of those identities?
DANIELE:	Oh yes. In the 1960s and 1970s – there were not too many women choreographers in the commercial theatre. There were the greats… Martha Graham and Agnes De Mille…. but in the commercial theatre, there were not too many. So, that was unusual. On top of that… a Latina? I didn't know *any* Latinas in the room. I mean, once there were, there would be one person… No. I was very, very closed off. I just so glad that it's changing. Not fast enough, but it's changing.
MORGAN:	How did that feel? To be the only person in the room in that way? Did you feel powerful and strong or was there insecurity or both?
DANIELE:	I was never insecure because I believed that all I had to do was to be the best of myself. To tell you the truth, I was so busy that I didn't have time to feel hurt or put aside. I was always working. When you're always working and doing the best you know that you can do – which is not to say the best of the world, but the best of yourself – you're focused. It totally inundated my brain, my body, and everything. When I was doing my first show on Broadway… *What Makes Sammy Run?*… I had a developed wonderful friendship with Diaan Ainslee… we shared a dressing room… and she helped me enormously with my English. One day, she says, "I have to tell you something, I hope you don't mind…" I said, "Go ahead with whatever it is." She said, "You know, when the boys smile at you and say 'Hi, S**c,[25]' you don't have to smile back."
MORGAN:	(*gasps*) Oh no…
DANIELE:	I said, "Why…?" She says, "It's an insult."
MORGAN:	Wow. You had no idea.
DANIELE:	I had no idea it was different.
MORGAN:	Oh, wow. How would you?
DANIELE:	I thought they were saying, "Hey! Nice to meet you!"
MORGAN:	Right. Gosh. When you moved to New York, did you have community with anyone?
DANIELE:	Not really, no.
MORGAN:	Just… alone?
DANIELE:	I had more in Paris, actually. I had some Argentinian friends in Paris, but I didn't here. Maybe it was better because that made me try to learn English faster… which was the hardest thing we've ever… learning French from Spanish… that was easy… but… ¡Dios Mío![26]
MORGAN:	Did some of that lead you to your work with Ballet Hispanico?[27]

DANIELE:	Yes, even though that was much later. You know, Tina Ramirez and I became the closest of friends. I agreed to do some ballets for her and I loved doing that. I really, *really* loved it. Then, I got into directing. It was very weird because I had been choreographing for a while already on Broadway and in regional theater. There was this place called INTAR [International Arts Relations][28] and it was run by a Cuban man named Max Ferrá.[29] Max called me, and he said, "We were just talking a little bit about doing some workshops of musicals with Latino actors… I said "Absolutely…."
MORGAN:	You said, "okay"?
DANIELE:	Yes! So, I would go twice a week and talk about musicals with Max. God bless him. I miss him. He was really poor and there was no money there so I worked there for nothing because I wanted to help. Max said to me, "Did you want to create something? We can help you here." And I said, "What do you mean?" He said, "A little something that you would like to do… either direct … or do your own show?" I said, "Well, let me think about it…" and so he put me together with Jim Lewis, who was wonderful… still is my best friend. He was a writer, and he knew about running the programs. He sat me down and he says, "Okay, do you have any ideas about who you would like to work with? The only thing that you have to understand is that the composers had to be Latinos… Who would we want? Who would you want?" Well, as a writer? Jorge Luis Borges.[30] I grew up with him and I loved everything he did. And a composer? Of course, Astor Piazzolla.[31]
MORGAN:	Oh! He's my favorite [Piazzolla is really one of my favorite composers outside of the musical theatre and pop canon]!
DANIELE:	Jimmy said, "Well, you just told me *where* this story is going to happen. It has to happen in Buenos Aires!" I chose these two brilliant geniuses. So, we started on the project and I did *not* think we were going to get them. Unfortunately, Borges had passed away. But then Max comes in like Superman… and I say "You're not going to get Piazzolla …" He said, "Wait!" He gets on the phone, and he gets Astor Piazzolla on the phone. He said "Señora Daniele would like to do a show…" and he said, "Do you know the work…" and Astor said, "Yes, I saw a couple of shows that she choreographed on Broadway." Three days later, Astor was here, *in my house*.
MORGAN:	Wow.
DANIELE:	I was adoring him, sitting at his feet.
MORGAN:	Never move or wash that chair again!
DANIELE:	It was the greatest moment. Jim Lewis, who helped me enormously worked with me to choose three short stories by Borges and we did a show called *Tango Apassionado*[32] that was played at the Westbeth [Theatre Center, 1987][33] here. We co-wrote it; we adapted from the

154 Director/Choreographers

	originals and I choreographed it *and* directed it. It was very successful. It ran for a very short time; but it was so successful, that I was immediately getting offers to direct.
MORGAN:	That's it.
DANIELE:	I didn't do anything!
MORGAN:	You said, "Okay!"
DANIELE:	Well, that's the story of my life. It keeps being like that all the time.
MORGAN:	Wow, that's incredible. You just kept saying, "Okay" and being strong in those spaces and holding to your ground. How do you balance storytelling with staging? I'm thinking about the storytelling through movement within your choreography. I think about musicals like *Once on This Island* (1991), *Ragtime* (1998), and *The Visit* (2015). How do you balance that? How do you make decisions?
DANIELE:	My first thing is: always tell the story. That's what it's about. It's not about how to choreograph or even *how* to direct. What is the story about? What is in the music that gives that story spirit and soul? What makes you crazy about it? It's really about the writers. To me, everything I've done that I liked or connected to was because of the writers. I am in awe of that. Tomorrow, I am seeing Lynn Ahrens for coffee. She is so brilliant and an awesome writer. This beautiful woman is a wonderful *human being*. You know?! I have worked with many extraordinary writers, and I adore and worship them. But there are a couple of them like her and Michael-John LaChuisa [composer], who I do most of my work with. They have a divine touch when we're working on something and we're in rehearsals. I'll think, "Okay, I have to talk to Michael about this moment" or "I have to ask Lynn permission to add this part over here." We go to a [rehearsal] break and either Lynn [or Michael-John] will come to me and say, "You know, I was thinking we don't need that. Let's cut it!" Those two are extraordinary. There are other brilliant writers… Bill Finn[34]! I *adore* Bill, but he's going to want a *good reason* to cut a line or do something and defend his own work. In musicals, it's a combination of art and being present in the room. But the two of them – Lynn [Ahrens] and Michael-John [LaChuisa]… I never have to open my mouth. I would look and say, "I think you're right. Yes. "I would be preparing a speech the night before, ready to be *very* respectful in asking to make a cut and they get ahead of me; it's brilliant.

My first thing is: always tell the story. That's what it's about. It's not about how to choreograph or even *how* to direct. What is the story about? What is in the music that gives that story spirit and soul? What makes you crazy about it?

MORGAN: Can you think of a specific example – like in *Ragtime* or *Once on This Island*, working with Lynn – where something changed because you gave that look?

DANIELE: *Ragtime*. Many examples. Oh God, that was a tough one. Every time I start a new show, I study what the dances are… what the history was… believe me, the theatre has taught me a lot about history, politics, and everything.

MORGAN: How did you deal with the pressures of the Broadway industry? Meaning: what we call self-care nowadays? How did you take care of yourself through this whole, 70-year career? I'm talking about survival, stamina, and staying healthy.

DANIELE: I didn't have time to think about it. I didn't have time to say "Oh, I'm tired." I had to get up and move! I've had a long life already. My God, I'm going to be 83 in December (2022) and I've been doing this since I was 7 years old. But it's always good. That's my nature. I'm even like that with my gardening, cleaning the house, or cooking. You know, it has to be done. I have to be in control… like, *who is doing this?* I think it's something that my three goddesses – my grandmother, my mother, and my aunt – put into me. They were three women – working class – sustaining this little girl; they had to do it. I think they gave me that gift. When I talk to students, I always say: don't ever feel sorry for yourself. Get up and shake those buns. Think! Move! The moment that you do that, the blood flows and ideas and choices come in. Physically, mentally, and spiritually.

MORGAN: That's so beautiful. Absolutely. Get up… move… think… That leads to the final question. What do you tell an aspiring choreographer or director? It's a different experience in leadership… versus just performing. What do you tell them as they're coming up in terms of how to deal with whatever barriers they face either as a woman… as an immigrant… as a person of color? What if they feel intimidated by leadership or not seeing themselves?

DANIELE: "You have to Get over it!" It's so better now. I look around and it's because of…

MORGAN: Because of *you*.

DANIELE: Well, it's not perfect yet, but it's getting better. Women are starting to open their mouth(s) and be heard and that's what is important.

MORGAN: Do you have women confess to you that you were their example? That you were the role model for them?

DANIELE: Oh, yes, but I don't pay too much attention to that. You know, my examples were – as I said before – my grandmother, my mother, and my aunt. They gave me that love and passion for getting up and doing something. If I'm not working, I'm doing something when I can have fun. I think – as a director – that is how I function… because

I've been directing and choreographing so much that it's hard for me to separate the two now. I think it is best for a choreographer to have a very good relationship with the director. I never had that problem. There can (sometimes) be friction and you can't have friction. It's a marriage to somebody and you *have* to respect each other. You can be humble. You don't have to say yes to *everything*. I've had good discussions with great directors... not screaming or yelling... but I say, "Let me try *my* way and if you don't like it, I change it." You know, those things are things that a good marriage should have. But frankly, I like doing both [directing and choreographing] because there's only one brain... one mind... one soul doing it, as opposed to trying to understand the other person. I never directed with somebody choreographing.

MORGAN: You didn't need to.

DANIELE: I had fantastic assistants that helped me enormously. I love the combination of directing and choreographing because I was taught by those great director-choreographers like Robbins... Bennett... Tommy Tune... they did both things. You don't have to ask anyone permission to change the blocking or choreography.

MORGAN: Well, in collaboration, there's a saying I love: Love without honesty is meaningless. Honesty without love is mean.[35]

DANIELE: Oh, that's wonderful.

MORGAN: We want honesty, but it *must* come with love. Sometimes the people in our industry are missing one or the other in their communication.

DANIELE: I love the theatre, but I don't like show business. There is something about show business that makes me a little nervous; to make it about awards, popularity, and authority. Who is trying to do all *that*?

MORGAN: I do not know.

DANIELE: There's something kind of phony to me. I'm not saying everybody [is like this]. There are great directors and choreographers who have done extraordinary work on Broadway. In the theatre, we are here to make it happen. This is the reason why I love regional theatre... because they don't have too much money, so they have to do the work.

MORGAN: Yes, we do. I work in regional theatre. Awards aren't even a part of the consideration and money is a challenge. The focus is what we can do with the money in order to tell a story and to reach those audiences in that location. Theatre should belong to everyone, not just New Yorkers.

DANIELE: Yes, exactly.

MORGAN: We work hard to tell those stories out here in the regions. I'm in Atlanta, Georgia. We have amazing artists and collaborators here. Sometimes we get friends from New York to come in, but it's really about the audiences here and their experience.

DANIELE: How do you tell a story? I think it's reason why I love the theatre. I've always loved stories.

MORGAN: You are the "real deal." If no one's ever used that term with you before.

DANIELE: The real deal? I've never been called that.

MORGAN: Now you have been! At eighty-three; you're the real deal.

DANIELE: Yes. I like that.

MORGAN: The way you speak about theatre is as eloquent as the way you've danced throughout the years. You've brought that grace and warmth into the work, which is so inspiring. It is inspiring to all of the young artists who want to take that path.

DANIELE: I'm open to all of them! Whenever a college calls and asks me to visit, I say, "Okay! I'm going!" It's very important. I've had the fortune of working with such extraordinary people. It's important that they get the message from someone who went through it. It's kind of lonely when you're alone, starting out. But… you get up and you shake your buns!

MORGAN: That is a wonderful way to conclude all of what we've talked about. Thank you so much!

Susan Stroman Biography

SUSAN STROMAN *(Director/Choreographer)* A five-time Tony Award winning director and choreographer known for *Crazy for You, Contact, The Scottsboro Boys*, and *The Producers*. Her work has been honored with Olivier, Drama Desk, Outer Critics Circle, Lucille Lortel, and a record five Astaire Awards.

She directed and choreographed *The Producers,* winner of a record-making 12 Tony Awards including Best Direction and Best Choreography. She co-created, directed and choreographed the Tony Award winning musical *Contact* for Lincoln Center Theater, which was honored with a 2003 Emmy Award for "Live from Lincoln Center." She directed and choreographed the critically acclaimed musical *The Scottsboro Boys* on Broadway and in the West End, where it was honored with the Evening Standard Award for Best Musical.

She directed the Broadway play *POTUS: Or, Behind Every Great Dumbass Are Seven Women Keeping Him Alive.* Other Broadway credits include *Oklahoma!, Show Boat, Prince of Broadway, Bullets Over Broadway, Big Fish, Young Frankenstein, Thou Shalt Not, The Music Man, The Frogs, Big, Steel Pier,* and *Picnic*.

West End productions include *Crazy For You, Oklahoma!, Show Boat, Contact, The Producers*, and *Young Frankenstein*.

Off-Broadway credits include *The Beast in the Jungle, Dot, Flora the Red Menace, And the World Goes 'Round, Happiness,* and *The Last Two People on Earth: An Apocalyptic Vaudeville.* For 10 years she choreographed Madison Square Garden's annual *A Christmas Carol.*

Other theater includes direction and choreography for the Broadway-bound Ahrens/Flaherty musical *Little Dancer* (5th Avenue Theatre, Seattle); and, in collaboration with Williamstown Theatre Festival, she directed *Photograph 51* for Audible.

Ballet and opera include *The Merry Widow* (Metropolitan Opera); *Double Feature* and *For the Love of Duke* (New York City Ballet); *But Not for Me* (Martha Graham Company); *Take Five... More or Less* (Pacific Northwest Ballet).

Television and Films include choreography for *Liza – Live from Radio City Music Hall* (Emmy Award nomination) and *Center Stage*(American Choreography Award); and direction and choreography for *The Producers: The Movie Musical* (four Golden Globe nominations).

She is an Associate Director for Lincoln Center Theater and a member of the Board of Directors for the Ronald O. Perelman Center for the Performing Arts at the World Trade Center.

She is the recipient of the George Abbott Award for Lifetime Achievement in the American Theater and an inductee of the Theater Hall of Fame in New York City. For more information visit www.susanstroman.com

Interview with Susan Stroman, October 25, 2022, via Zoom[36]

MORGAN: Woo! Susan Stroman. The woman who we all aspire to be. I grew up in San Diego, California and family moved to Florida when I was in high school; I've been doing musical theatre since I was 6 years old. Gosh, you were – at the time – the only *visible* woman to little girls like me across the country. I was a performer like everybody else. But I knew I wanted to be a teacher, or a leader, or *something*. Women like you; Kimberly Grigsby, as a music director; and Graciela Daniele were very important to us. You were the most visible and the most graceful. Every photo, every video clip, with your beautiful, big smile, and the *hat*... the black baseball cap! At every high school thespian conference... we were all in our black caps if you were a serious choreographer or director on the rise. Such grace and graciousness. I've been able to dig into what's already out there... the facts are all online. But... tell me about your journey to Broadway, in your own words. You didn't major in theatre... you went to [The University of] Delaware and majored in English, yes? Who were the role models for you growing up? What was the journey? Give me the story.

STROMAN: Well, yes, I am from Wilmington, Delaware, and I had been in dancing school since I was about 5 years old. My dad was a wonderful piano player, so the house was always filled with music. My parents loved movie musicals and variety shows. It was always a big deal if there was singing and dancing on the television. Everything would

Director/Choreographers **159**

	stop, and as a family, we would sit around the television and watch. I have to say, even at a young age, I could watch some of those movies and connect the dance and the music and the orchestration together as one. Even at an early age, I was able to see how things worked or analyze them clearly. I would say that kind of inspiration came from my father playing the piano. My father also told big fish stories. I don't know if any of them are true today.
MORGAN:	Awwww, I bet that was special when you directed *Big Fish*.
STROMAN:	Yes! Our house was always filled with stories and music. Both were very much part of my journey growing up. At an early age, I discovered I could visualize music. Whether it was classical or rock-and-roll or old standards, I would imagine all sorts of stories in my head and I could see them onstage. I still do that with music. So I think those old black-and-white Fred Astaire and Ginger Rogers movies were my first real influences, watching them with my family and understanding how music and storytelling came together. Ultimately, my biggest influences were Jerome Robbins and [George] Balanchine. The combination of those two choreographers – the romance and partnering of Balanchine, the character-driven storytelling of Robbins – was just inspiring.
MORGAN:	I've certainly been in many shows where the choreographer is telling us to do this step, and then the next step, and the throughline wasn't being talked about. Why do a jazz square? How does the jazz square further the story? Were you questioning that actively at a young age? Wondering, "*Why* am I doing this?" Or were you inventing it, yourself?
STROMAN:	I have to say I was inventing it myself because I know I combined that idea of storytelling and dance together and knew that you can only move for a reason. You can only move because your character is *meant* to move that way. Characters move differently. Max Bialystock moves differently than Leo Bloom.[37] You know, The Girl in the Yellow Dress moves very differently from the male character, Michael Wiley.[38] So, it's finding those moments in dance that help tell the story. People move differently from the North than they do the South; and they move differently from the East and the West. It's the decade and the geographical area that informs you about choreography and about the story.
MORGAN:	Mm-hmm. Were there people growing up that you think were role models in terms of leadership? Modeling behavior… good room management… teaching skills?
STROMAN:	That is a good point. I emulated those people I loved as choreographers – but not so much their personalities, just their talent. I think I was able to apply just what I learned from growing up about

160 Director/Choreographers

how to run a room. In the end, it's about respect, isn't it? It's about respecting people in the room and listening to them and being respectful of how fast they learn or how slow they learn and making sure everyone feels comfortable. If you can get that kind of trust going in a room… a room of respect… I think you get the best out of people. You feel very protective of a cast, and you want them to feel comfortable enough to take a chance. You want them to feel like they could run into your arms and that you would catch them.

You want them to feel like they could run into your arms and that you would catch them.

MORGAN: That's such a beautiful visual. I love that. Who do you think really helped you on your journey to become a director and or choreographer, directly inspired you, impacted you, you know, took your hand and said, "Come over here and do this thing"?

STROMAN: When I first came to New York, I really wanted to create. I didn't love performing as much as I loved creating, but I could make a living at it because I could sing and dance. I was kind of a big fish in a little pond in Delaware working at the community theaters and colleges and such… and I came to New York to sort of assess the situation, if you will. I was quite lucky that when I crossed over into choreographing, I worked with some of the best directors right away. I worked with Hal Prince[39] and I worked with Nick Hytner.[40] I worked with Mike Ockrent.[41] I worked with Trevor Nunn.[42] They're who I learned a great deal from. I was very fortunate, though. The very first show that I choreographed professionally was an Off-Broadway show called *Flora the Red Menace* [Original, 1965/off-Broadway, 1987]. My relationship with Kander and Ebb really changed my life… learning about collaboration… learning about what it takes to create a musical really came from Kander and Ebb.[43]

MORGAN: Wow. Can you tell me more? Can you give me an example?

STROMAN: They're very much a part of sitting around a table and telling the story and then saying, "Well, what if the story went *that* way? What if that story went the other way? What if this character did this?" So, they play a sort of What-if game. That's very, very important when you're fleshing out characters and fleshing out a story. Also, there was no ego in the room. You'd have to check your ego at the door and really talk with one another. Fred always said, "there's no bad idea," because someone could take an idea that doesn't seem

	quite right… throw it on the table… and someone else will pick it up and turn it into gold. You should never be afraid to say what your ideas are.
MORGAN:	Said the guy who wrote three different songs for the same scene in *Cabaret* (1965)!
STROMAN:	Right!
MORGAN:	"Don't Go"… "Why Should I Wake Up?"… "Maybe This Time."… just keep messing with that scene!
STROMAN:	Yes! Just keep going.
MORGAN:	"What's the song here?" I think it's interesting that for two iterations of that show, 20 years apart, it's Cliff's song and then, eventually, it's Sally's song.
STROMAN:	Yeah, absolutely. This is how I understand collaboration and its importance and try to pass that on when I'm in another room with new collaborators. I really attribute that to [Kander and Ebb].
MORGAN:	Have there been times when you're the only woman in the room in the leadership position?
STROMAN:	Yes. That is the situation most of the time.
MORGAN:	What does that feel like to you?
STROMAN:	It is different now, but when I started, I was in a male-dominated field. However, I *so* believed in what I was doing. I *so loved* what I was doing. I love collaboration. I love creating. I love music, dance, *and* story. I loved it so much that, somehow, I had blinders on and just kept hoping that it would all go well, and not thinking they wouldn't accept me because I was a woman. I mean, of course, I was aware of it, but I couldn't dwell on it. It has changed. I have to say, it's only changed in the last fifteen [15] years, which is crazy to me… to have women in charge… women directors… and women choreographers. It's taken a long time.
MORGAN:	What has it been like when you're in the rooms that have other women in leadership positions with you? For example, getting in the room with Mary-Mitchell [Campbell][44] on *Big Fish* and numerous other female-identifying composers. Is that different to you to be in a room of collaborators that are also women? Have you identified those moments in your career?
STROMAN:	Sure! I love it! Very recently, I was very lucky to do *POTUS: Or, Behind Every Great Dumbass are Seven Women Trying to Keep Him Alive* (2022) on Broadway, which was a cast of seven women… female designers… female associates… and it was great! That show was a real gift… I loved working with those comediennes.
MORGAN:	What about in relationship to collaboration on the creative team? I'm thinking about *The Producers,* and I think it's interesting that you worked with Mel Brooks, who is this comedic genius but who

has a distinctively old-school male point of view in his comedy. A lot of the jokes are at the expense of women like Ulla. I teach whole lectures on the Ziegfeld Follies and what Florenz Ziegfeld[45] did to glorify women, but also objectify them and those kinds of things. Those concepts are rampant in Mel Brooks' work. How did you approach those conversations regarding staging? Or… was it just second nature because you're trying to stay true to the punchline?

STROMAN: I have to say: Mel was unbelievably respectful. I know because this material *is* old school – as old as it gets. Every single minute, he was respectful. He *so* believed in me. Even our Ulla[46] in the musical was very different from the Ulla in his screenplay.

MORGAN: Right.

STROMAN: You know, Ulla in the musical is very smart. She knows exactly what she's doing. She knows exactly who she wants. She knows she is smarter than Max Bialystock. She's the smartest one on the stage. That was very different [from the movie]… Mel went with it and Mel *loved* it. I feel like I was able to add that perspective to a lot of things that might have been old school at one time.

MORGAN: I'm always interested in how a director can make a decision that has nothing to do with changing the ink. Have you felt like you've done that a lot as a director? Have you just sat there and wondered: "How are we going to do this without changing the script…?"

STROMAN: Yes; but, since I work on new stuff all the time, I *can* change the ink. I can collaborate with my writers to change the ink. I'm very much a part of that with the writing team. In doing revivals… *The Music Man* that I did with Craig Bierko [Harold Hill] and Rebecca Luker… [Marian] was a strong woman. It was very much about that relationship and what they brought together, and the journey of the movement through the show. The same thing goes for *Oklahoma*. The women were pioneer women! They were very different from the movie that we know of *Oklahoma* and the original *Oklahoma* with the daffodil dresses and such. They were real pioneer women, and the choreography was fight-oriented and based on things like, "can you top *this*?" So yes, I'm able to infuse real women into the things that I do.

MORGAN: That's a good segue! As a director and a music director, I'm often thinking about my actors and collaborators and their experience on making the art. I care, especially because I work in education and regional professional theatre, about how the room is and the actors' experience. I believe that if we treat the artists with love and respect and honesty, then the product will be good because they'll work hard to make it better every day. You really paid your dues as a performer in all the venues. From dancing on the steel pier of Atlantic City and then directing *Steel Pier* (1997)… performing in the National Tour of *Chicago* with Gwen Verdon and Jerry Orbach…How do you think that informs your work as a director and choreographer outside of the obvious understanding how to put on a play? How did that perspective help you create working environments in these rooms that you run?

STROMAN: Well, I was able to work with Bob Fosse on that tour and just admired how a lot of the movement was all motivated to achieve some sort of visual. I don't know if it made sense when we strung those visuals together.

MORGAN: [Fosse] was a complicated guy!

STROMAN: When we were dancing, Fosse would always put some sort of visual [imagery] on it… whether it was a palm tree blowing in the breeze or Manson [Charles] wiping blood off his hands on the wall. These things stick with you. There's a way to take that and motivate an actor to help tell the story visually through dance. You learn these things and try them and apply it to your own process. I've been very lucky to learn from these great artists and I'm able to pass it on as well as apply it to my own process. That's how you get the best work; to stand on the shoulders of these greats and then apply it to your own work and change the work according to your own spirit specifically in the storytelling.

MORGAN: As a director, I struggle to find balance with the following ideas regarding pre-production & design process. I want to come into the room prepared with ideas to drive the concept; to demonstrate I know what I'm talking about to my team. That might be the Aries in me or "Imposter Syndrome" or whatever. However, I want to leave room for magic for my creative team. I question how much information I bring into the room to demonstrate my concept and my ideas, but leave room to really *hear* what the designers have to say and see what images they bring in. Hopefully, their work sparks a new idea or a better solution to a challenge. Where do you feel like you lie on the spectrum at this point in your career? How has that grown? How much of your vision do you feel like you need to map out in advance and then, how do you like marry that with the requests or demands of the producers? You've got producers and then you've designers and then you're in the middle trying to drive the boat…

STROMAN: Going into a project, you need to have some sort of vision that you share with your designers; and you share a lot of your research. And each department does a *lot* of their own research. Collaboration is key to musical theater. Working together and listening to your designers' contributions is how your vision ends up realized onstage. The process is very similar with actors. When I go into a room, I have it mapped out in my head. I don't necessarily share that information because they need to be part of the process, they need to bring their character into the work. Of course, they could be heading down the wrong path. I'm like a parent because I can guide them back, but they have to be part of it. Even in dance, I'll have a whole combination ready, but when I go into rehearsal a dancer might say, "I would do that better if I could turn to the left…[instead of the right]" and then you make it happen. Then, there's a domino effect and that's just part of the life force that comes from creating theatre. I think you get your best result if you start with a plan of action and then allow yourself to be inspired by actors and designers. That doesn't mean that you shouldn't do the homework. You do the work, and you have the vision, but you have to be open to be inspired.

MORGAN: I love that… holding that back. I have an assistant director on our upcoming production of *Rent* (that I'm going to direct in the spring) and we're in design process right now. She asked me early on if we are using scaffolding or not. I said, "Look, I think that, in the back of my mind, I know where we can get some and it's a total possibility; however, I'm not going to talk about it yet, until our designers respond and that's indeed where we are headed. If we settle on actual scaffolding, then we'll get the rental."

STROMAN: Yeah, you have to hold back a little bit.

MORGAN: Let's talk real quick about working with dance arrangers. I've actually worked with Glen Kelly. I know you've worked with him a bunch.

STROMAN: Oh, he's a genius.

MORGAN: He *is* a genius! He's a worker bee, right? I feel like there isn't as much visibility for dance arrangers… you see the composers. I mean, he'll come in with 32 new bars [measures] of something overnight, between calls, and they…

STROMAN: They are the unsung heroes really. Sam Davis just left my office here, and he's wonderful dance arranger. He did the Lynn Ahrens and Stephen Flaherty musical *Little Dancer* [2014] with me. Now he's doing the dance arrangements for *New York, New York* and he's done a beautiful job. I was very lucky to work with the father of all dance arrangers, Peter Howard. He did the famous "Waiters Gallop" in *Hello, Dolly*… "Hot Honey Rag" in *Chicago*. He did the dance arrangements for *Crazy for You* (1992), and it was a joy to work with him. He would support the choreography with his music. He actually taught me a lot about dance arranging because

	very much of what I do when I'm developing choreography is: I sit with my dance arranger, and I work it out musically, so the music tells the story as well. I work it all out in preproduction and then it just develops more in rehearsal.
MORGAN:	Yeah, those dance breaks in *Crazy for You* are something *else*.
STROMAN:	They're beautiful; they really tell the story. If I wanted Bobby and Polly to be coy and shy with each other, we'd play "Shall We Dance" in a "soft shoe"… if I wanted them to chase each other, we'd put it in a "fast two"… and if we wanted them to fall in love, we play it in "three quarter time." That manipulation of the time signature helps the audience know what the emotion is on-stage, whether they know that or not.
MORGAN:	This is the good stuff right here. I could for hours about changing meter to manipulate storytelling… changing key and changing grooves… cuts… fermatas versus a cut-out. I've had to play that score version of "I've Got Rhythm" cover to cover on the piano… I'm pretty sure it's about 30 pages long in the piano-vocal [score]. I'm going through it, and as I'm turning pages, I felt like it would never end!
STROMAN:	I know!
MORGAN:	It's incredible. Do you do you have a visual map? Do you put post-its up to map the journey? Or just go chronologically?
STROMAN:	There was a strong collaboration with Robin Wagner,[47] the set designer, about what would be in the Feed Store on stage that I could use. [The song] is all about how everybody's depressed because the show [within the show] didn't happen … then Polly says to Bobby, "No, you brought this town back to life. Although the show didn't work, you brought the town back to life, and you've given us rhythm and life." Then, they *show* him how he brought the town back to life… how he did that. So, they grab what's in the Feed Store – pickaxes and mining pans and…
MORGAN:	…a washboard…
STROMAN:	… poles and washboards and everything that you'd find in a 1930s Feed Store in an abandoned mining town! It was like a toy store of props for me to use. Then, the Dance Arranger, Peter Howard, would help us build on what would be good musically with percussive sounds. So it all happened together rather than a chicken-and-the-egg situation.
MORGAN:	Which is amazing! I'm thinking chronologically because I know the "mug dance" [in the song "Gaston"] in *Beauty and the Beast* was 1994. The I'm thinking about usage of props as intentional choreography when building a dance break. In *Newsies*, we have the newspapers – that's about 10 years later… So,

what inspired you to do that? Something earlier in the canon or from movie musicals?

STROMAN: Absolutely. If Fred Astaire's sister didn't show up, he would dance with the coat rack. It was very much a part of watching those old movies and seeing how a prop could strengthen a character and make that character stronger... to demonstrate what a character does for a living or whatever the detail is. There's never a prop that's extraneous; it's always something that will strengthen the character or the storytelling.

MORGAN: Mm hmm. I love that. Regarding your use and love of percussion... I'm thinking about "Hop Clop" ["Der Guten Tag Hop-Clop" from *The Producers*]... Oh yeah... and *The Frogs*... that whole thing! It's all based on character sounds and Sondheim's use of that as well. There's a lot of stuff in *Big Fish* (2013) that has to do with that because of the different vignettes of locations and character, right?

STROMAN: Right...

MORGAN: I'm thinking about the marriage between style and story. *Chicago* is a perfect example of that, right? It's less about posturing that we're dancing "sexy" and more that it's a part of the story of these women who have actual trauma that they're trying to slink through life. Your work reflects [those ideals]. So, I believe *Crazy for You* is the one that comes with "the book," right? Your choreography notes can be rented?

STROMAN: Most all of them [Stroman shows] do [allow the rental].

MORGAN: What led to that? What led you to agreeing to allow the licensing company to take the notes and rent them out?

STROMAN: Well, it makes choreography tangible. Listen, there are people, even in my own business, that don't understand what choreographers do, and they don't get it. So, it's a way to make choreography tangible and real and that it means something. So, if somebody in the middle of the country wants to try to do any of my shows, they have a chance to try to understand the intention of *how* that dance arrangement happened. I love that there's an intention, which is very important when you pass these shows on. We have all seen some shows that get passed on and it doesn't work out well.

MORGAN: We have a history in in American contemporary theatre of producing Shakespeare and trying to mine what he meant by the punctuation, all that kind of stuff. I like that. We have those Sondheim books [*Finishing the Hat* and *Look, I Made a Hat*[48]] where, after the fact, Sondheim sat down and wrote down what he meant. Conversely, I love when Hal Prince was interviewed for the *Broadway: The American Musical* series[49] that you all got interviewed for...

	and there's this great quote where Hal Prince said he tried asking Andrew Lloyd Webber[50] what *Cats* is "really about." Is it a representation of Queen Victoria? Is it a metaphor? And Webber supposedly, dryly answers, "No, it's just about cats." He just wanted to write a fun show about cats, and everybody liked it.
STROMAN:	*(laughing)* I know!
MORGAN:	In short, it's great to have your notes.
STROMAN:	That's a great story. Hal was wonderful. I miss Hal.
MORGAN:	Ah, yes, you co-directed *Prince of Broadway* (2017) with Hal. You brought his story to life. The true "concept musical" guru… the guy who helped deconstruct it from the formula created by Rodgers & Hammerstein. He deconstructed everything again and it'll be reconstructed later. It sounds like his legacy really influenced yours.
STROMAN:	Yes!
MORGAN:	How is your process different when you are *only* directing versus *only* choreographing … versus directing *and* choreographing? Are the lines so blurred? Was your first show doing both *Contact*? Is your process different or do they just really meld together?
STROMAN:	The first show that I directed *and* choreographed on Broadway was *The Music Man* [2000 revival]. But *Contact* was the first one where I was really a part of writing, directing, choreographing, and creating. That was a very unique situation. Andre Bishop[51] asked me if I had an idea and I happened to be in a club about two weeks before and saw this girl in a yellow dress; and I knew that she would change some man's life that night. When Andre asked me if I had an idea, I said, "Yes, I do." I called my good friend John Weidman (librettist), and we created *Contact*. I still think it might be the longest running show up there with the combination of the Mitzi Newhouse [Theater] and the Vivian Beaumont [Theater].[52]
MORGAN:	It's also a show that required a new Tony category. People lost their *minds* over that. I like the break of form.
STROMAN:	Some people hate change.
MORGAN:	Let's talk about [your work in] film. Allow me to gush on the impact of *Center Stage*[53] on my generation.
STROMAN:	You know, they have now started a "Rocky Horror Picture Show" type of experience… they do a "Center Stage" evening.
MORGAN:	Do they throw things?! Are there things you can do [along with the movie]?!
STROMAN:	There's things you can do…. Everybody screams out the lines and then they rate the dancers… who has the biggest leap or…
MORGAN:	Oh, who can forget Donna Murphy at the [ballet] barre, with the hand on the barre… "It's *here…*"
STROMAN:	I know, it's very funny. I love that.

MORGAN: Well, not since *Fame* had shown people had a movie for *us*, you know, that talked about industry or training… then *Center Stage* happened and then 10 years later was *Glee*. But, Center Stage, I mean, that Michael Jackson ballet! Do you like choreographing for film? How is it different than working in theatre?

STROMAN: Oh, it's very different. I'm a theatre animal and so it's very different. It's not quite as fulfilling [for me] although I admire it. I admire filmmakers a great deal and I love to go to the movies. But for me, personally, there's nothing like live theatre.

MORGAN: When you were asked to work on *The Producers* movie, did you eagerly say yes? Were you hesitant? Did you feel obligated? Were you excited?

STROMAN: I was very excited! Mel was having such a good time with that. The show was such a hit, and he wanted to [do the movie]. He just kept saying, "Stro, just do the musical. Just do what we did!"

MORGAN: Yeah, *Chicago* in 2002 just broke it wide open… it came out and musicals were cool again on the big screen.

STROMAN: [*Chicago*] is a beautiful film.

MORGAN: *Chicago* had a strong concept with the sequences in the mind of Roxie Hart …. And then the *Phantom* [*of the Opera*] movie was kind of in between… I felt like with *The Producers*, you all really tried to put the show on film, for better or for worse.

STROMAN: Yeah, right. That's what Mel loved. A concept of that would have been hard to do. "We've got to do this in the mind of Max Bialystock?" No.

MORGAN: Yeah. Save it for *Nine*.[54]

STROMAN: Exactly.

MORGAN: What are what are some of the difficult decisions you've had to make from the director's chair? You're such a joyous, gracious person. What are some of the things you struggle with?

STROMAN: Wow. Well, as time goes on, budgets are more difficult to deal with. It's just harder. The price of tickets… what producers have to go through… I do feel for them, you know, because times are changing. The most difficult thing now is trying to do everything within a budget. That's why I really love working Off-Broadway in a very small venue. There's something quite focused about the art of it there. It's quite the thing now to put a show on Broadway… it's very difficult… everything is very expensive. Coming out of this pandemic, it's even *more* expensive.

MORGAN: I think that there's something to be said about the magic of live theatre. Sometimes that can get lost with the big budget stuff. The live, breathing, living thing is what separates live theatre from the ability to watch a clip on TikTok.

STROMAN: So true. It was hard during the pandemic listening to people sing on Zoom. It's not the same.

MORGAN: I'm sure all of you felt the same way up in New York. Where were you? Was it tough?

STROMAN: It was tough. New York was tough during the pandemic.

MORGAN: Do you think anything good came out of the learning experience out of the pandemic, for the Broadway industry? Other than me being able to talk to you on Zoom, which is a miracle in itself.

STROMAN: Well, that is a miracle because no one even heard the word "zoom" till like a week after. There was something called Zoom by Friday. Amazing.

MORGAN: I mean, it's enabled me to talk to my idols! I mean, it's wonderful, but other than that…

STROMAN: Yes, absolutely. I think there's a lot of good things came out of it. I think we're learning that theatre industry is changing, and new plays are being written. New stories are being told as they should be. I think it's quite wonderful, what has happened. We're being challenged in a way to take different courses and different classes on all sorts of situations, whether it be about "Me Too" or race, or whatever.[55] Now, we all are more educated because of what went down during the pandemic, and that is a good thing. That only makes the rehearsal room stronger.

MORGAN: 100%. I mean, theatrical intimacy![56] I was just talking about some of the vocabulary with another artist about terms that only a couple of people were using, but now have become more commonplace, like "theatrical intimacy," "conscious casting," etc. Thanks to stronger movement amongst artists, we know the way to do it better.

Have you had to be a caregiver to anyone whilst juggling this career? Let's talk about work-life balance, and self-care, and all that juicy stuff.

STROMAN: You mean personally? Children… parents… All of it. Everybody. I've taken care of everybody. Yes, sure!

MORGAN: How did you manage?

STROMAN: They say that theatre really saves you. You know, you're going to lose a parent… you lose a husband… you go through the AIDS epidemic and lose dance partners and roommates… Yes, I've had a great deal of loss and a great deal of grief. I have to say that the theatre has saved me every time. I actually don't know how people who are working in a respectable 9-to-5 job go through such grief. How can they go back to that cubicle the next day? At least what we do in the theatre is life-affirming. I think it really has saved me every time. I don't think I would have been saved had I not been in there. I'm a lucky gal that I'm in the theatre.

MORGAN: I agree. There are many times where I've had to rush to the theater after getting sad test results or bad news to get to rehearsal. I thought, I can either go home to my empty living room, or I can go to rehearsal and I can be a part of this art, which might be comforting… cathartic… etc.

What's the thing that you tell the aspiring choreographer-director, who is a woman who has expressed to you that she feels like sometimes, she's the only one in the room? Perhaps she is facing obstacles… feeling talked down to… whatever barriers those are. What's your nugget of advice?

STROMAN: Even if you are the only person in the room with your identity, you are equal to everyone. Just because you're a woman and you're the only one in the room doesn't matter. Believing in your own talent is what matters. Also, making a point… making a statement… allowing people to see you for who you are and allow yourself to be heard for them to understand. Communication is key. If you really believe in what you do, you're only going to enhance the work. The best advice I got was not to be afraid to ask the question, because the worst thing that could happen is somebody could say, "No." And if the answer is "no," then you move on. Don't be afraid to knock on someone's door; don't be afraid to ask the question. Nine times out of ten, the answer will be "yes," but you can't be afraid of it. You can't be too afraid to even try it.

MORGAN: Sounds like you have a good relationship with vulnerability.

STROMAN: Yes. Maybe.

MORGAN: Which is, again, kind of shocking, considering the kind of history of dance training in this country. You seem to have tapped into vulnerability. Do you know why and how you were able to do that? So early? [in your career]

STROMAN: I don't know. I guess I was very lucky to be raised by a very strong father and a very loving mother. I feel like I was lucky to get the combo platter. Some people get too much of the one parent and too little of the other, you know? But I got the good combo platter, so I think that's how it all happened.

MORGAN: That's so sweet. What's next for you? What's the next chapter look like for you? My gosh.

STROMAN: Since *POTUS*, I went and did a big revival of *Crazy for You* in Chichester and it's coming to the West End, in Summer 2023. I've done two play readings which I hope will both end up becoming full productions at some point. I'm going into rehearsal in January

	for a new show called *New York, New York*. And it's written by David Thompson and Sharon Washington. It's Kander and Ebb music with additional lyrics by Lin-Manuel Miranda. We go into rehearsal in January 2023, and we open in April. Very exciting. This fall I'm dealing with all the preproduction [for *New York New York*], which means working with the set designer Beowulf Boritt, the costume designer Donna Zakowska, and the lighting designer Ken Billington. That's what I'm doing along with dealing with casting and dance arrangements.
MORGAN:	It's like cooking in the kitchen. Do you like to cook?
STROMAN:	What's funny is that I couldn't boil an egg before the pandemic, but during the pandemic, I became a gourmet chef. Now that New York has opened up again, I kind of went back to what we New Yorkers would do… eat out and order in.
MORGAN:	I love that you're in preproduction now and you're cooking. It's come up in these interviews… cooking and gardening… these powerhouse ladies … and it seems like there are some common activities like gardening, cooking, or activities that get us in nature and out of our heads and out of the studio…. Many have said that theater is as nourishing to our soul as it is draining.
STROMAN:	Yes, that's true.
MORGAN:	Well, Susan Stroman. You've given me so much time and I can die a happy woman! You're glorious. Thank you for chatting with me today.

Baayork Lee Biography

Baayork Lee has performed in dozens of Broadway shows and created the role of Connie in *A Chorus Line*, also serving as Michael Bennett's Assistant Choreographer on *A Chorus Line*, which she has directed and choreographed many times for national and international companies.

Her directing and choreography credits also include *The King and I* and *Bombay Dreams* (national tours); *Rodgers and Hammerstein's Cinderella* (NYC Opera); *Barnum* (Australia); *Carmen Jones* (Kennedy Center); *Porgy and Bess* and *Jesus Christ Superstar* (European tours); *Gypsy*; and *A New Brain*. She has also choreographed *Miss Saigon* (Kansas City Starlight), *Mack and Mabel* (Shaw Festival), *Animal Crackers*, *South Pacific* (Helen Hayes nominations) *Coconuts, Camelot, Damn Yankees*, all at Arena Stage in Washington, D.C., *South Pacific* at City Springs Theatre Company, GA., and most recently, *A Chorus Line* Spanish Production with Antonio Banderas (Malaga, Spain).

Through her nonprofit National Asian Artists Project (NAAP), Lee's vision includes educating, cultivating, and stimulating audiences and artists of Asian descent through the many outreach programs the company offers. The organization has produced *Oklahoma!, Carousel, Hello Dolly!, Oliver!*, and *Into the Woods* and *Honor* (collaboration with Prospect Theater Company) with all Asian American casts. With these classic shows, NAAP has demonstrated that famous works can speak to all audiences and ethnicity is no longer a barrier.

Lee has been the recipient of numerous awards for her work, including the Isabelle Stevens Tony Award, the Paul Robeson Award from Actors Equity Association, the Asian Woman Warrior Award for Lifetime Achievement from Columbia College, the Asian Pacific American Heritage Association Achievement In Arts Award, the Dynamic Achiever Award from OCA Westchester, the Chen Dance Center Artist Award, the Arena Stage American Artist Award, and the Actors Fund for Outstanding Contribution to the World of Dance.

Interview with Baayork Lee, November 21, 2022 via Zoom[57]

MORGAN:	I watched your interview on American Masters,[58] and I learned so much about your childhood performances like *The King and I* (1951). You started working so young and at such a high level of performance quality. Can you tell me about your training at that time in the areas of discipline?
LEE:	Casting agents came down to Chinatown looking for kids for *The King and I*. A lot of us from my school went up to the Majestic Theater[59] and had to stand on the stage. My brother tells me now that we had to sing "Happy Birthday," but I don't remember that. I was one of the tiniest, so I was hired. 14th Street was the barrier. There was no need for us to go uptown, so this was an incredible experience. We didn't know anything about Broadway.
MORGAN:	Do you have perspective on what that was like for your parents? When you got older, did you ask them what it was like to take their kids up to that area of town?
LEE:	My father had a restaurant, so he was working all of the time. My mother had three other children, so my brothers sometimes had to take me uptown. How exciting for all of us to walk into this ornate theater with red velvet seats and chandeliers. I mean, at 5 years old… Wow!
MORGAN:	Good God. Right.
LEE:	Seeing people warming up… vocally and physically… I said to my mother, "This is what I want to do." You know, most kids want to be firemen, nurses, and all of that. I wanted to be in the theatre! My mother would take me to the theater right after school, which was around 4:00pm. I wanted to be there first. She had to lift me up to sign in![60] I loved that process. I became friends with Wilbur and Marian – the doorman and his wife – so my mother would leave me with them so she could head back home. It was so early; the

	show didn't start until 8:30pm in those days, but I would get there around 4:00pm and Gertrude Lawrence[61] would get there early as well. I would sit on the stairs up to her dressing room and listen to her vocalize. Finally, her maid, Hazel, would let me come and sit in the doorway. Then, she would go to the ante[62] room where she had a ballet bar, and she would do her barre routine.[63] Then Wilbur, who would have to check on different things in the theater, would take me along. I loved the ghost light onstage… and he had to check all the things… and I just *loved it*. I loved exploring the theater. They kept all of the kids on the eighth floor because we all made a lot of noise. The bigger kids would open up the door to the catwalk. We would look down below and watch the ballet!
MORGAN:	"The Small House of Uncle Thomas."
LEE:	Yuriko[64] became my idol. She recently passed away at the age of 102. I spoke at her memorial at the 92nd Street Y[65] and talked about the Jerome Robbins dancers who came from New York City Ballet. Then, was the Martha Graham group. I didn't know anything about dance technique, Balinese, or Cambodian dancing, so it fascinated me. Of course, I was in early watching them do something on the floor. I said to my mother, "Ask them what they're doing"… they said, "Warming up." I said, "That's what I want to do!"
MORGAN:	So, you continued to work on Broadway as you grew up… right? *Flower Drum Song* (1958). *Bravo, Giovanni* (1962). *Mr. President* (1962). Did you then pursue formal dance training or did you keep learning through doing?
LEE:	I was fired at the age of eight because I outgrew my costumes. There were three of us that were let go. The R&H Office[66] asked us what we wanted to do. One girl wanted piano lessons, one girl wanted to be an actress, and I wanted to dance. Jerome Robbins was with New York City Ballet, so those connections helped me get into The School of American Ballet. That's my training.
MORGAN:	Wow. Jerome Robbins. "Here you go. Have some classes."
LEE:	I stayed there for many years. Balanchine[67] was creating his first *Nutcracker*, and he used the kids! So, I was in the first *Nutcracker* that he created.
MORGAN:	That is so incredible.
LEE:	Years later came *Flower Drum Song*. I heard that Rodgers & Hammerstein were doing another show. So, I went to the audition, and they walked us across the stage, type casting us, and they let me go. I was devastated. Then I saw Richard Rodgers and Oscar Hammerstein walking into the theater through the alley. I ran after them, and the monitors weren't going to let me back in. I don't know how I got back in, but I did. Then, Richard Rodgers recognized me in

MORGAN:

LEE:

MORGAN:
LEE:

MORGAN:
LEE:

MORGAN:

LEE:

the line-up. Carol Haney was the choreographer.[68] She saw that I had ballet training and put me in the flower boat to dance with the adults… I was only 11 or 12 years old!

Who would you say your role models were, coming up through those ranks? I know you had like a bevy to choose from, but I'm interested in learning about those in the industry and people in your in your daily life who influenced you as a director and a choreographer. Who demonstrated leadership for you that you may have not known at that time? Who demonstrated the kind of leader that you wanted to be in a room or the kind of creator that you turned out to be?

It's so difficult for me to answer this because… I could talk forever about Michael Bennett, Bob Avian, Tommy Tune, and Graciela Daniele's influence in molding me. Another is definitely Syvilla Fort.[69] She danced with the Katherine Dunham Company[70] and she ran that school. So, on Saturdays, I was running across the room. By the time I was five, when they had this audition, I went, but I didn't have any *training*. When I left *The King and I*, I was at The School of American Ballet *and* I continued to train with Syvilla Fort. She left the Dunham School and she opened her own school, so I continued to train there. It was interesting because I didn't know she was training Chita Rivera, Peter Gennaro, James Dean, Jane Fonda… and I was this kid watching them! Ms. Fort had the base for Afro Cuban dancing and Jack Cole had the base for East Indian dancing. Combined, I believe this became the root for theatre jazz dancing. On Saturdays I would clean the mirrors and dressing rooms then spent my whole day taking class as a scholarship student. Harry Belafonte and Sydney Poitier would bring their kids…

What!? Wow.

And, you know, we were just *dancing*. We loved it. Then, during the week I was at The School of American Ballet.

What a contrast! In styles, etc.

To have that kind of background was unbelievable. Never thinking that I would do anything *with* it because I wanted to be like another role model of mine, Maria Tallchief.[71] When I was in *The Nutcracker* with New York City Ballet, she was the Sugar Plum Fairy and an "American Indian."[72] She was tall and that's what I wanted to be. She was my idol. That's who I sing about in *A Chorus Line*. I wanted to be Maria Tallchief.

Oh, man, that's it. Gosh, what a cycle. I grew up listening to *A Chorus Line* and, you know, singing all three parts about the ballet in my bedroom, like most little girls in the 1980s and 1990s who loved musical theatre.

Right.

MORGAN:	It's just so cyclical. You then *became* the person. The role model.
LEE:	Well… you're never thinking about that [when you're doing it].
MORGAN:	It's the reality, though!
LEE:	Yul Brynner was very close to the kids in *The King and I* and he would take us to the circus and anything having to do with advertising the show. When I was fired because I outgrew my costume, he gave me a pin with a white elephant. In the show, the white elephants are sacred… in Thailand. The elephant pin had three heads: one to the right, one to the left, and one to the front. He gave me this pin, I'm 8 years old… and I'm crying. What does this all mean?
MORGAN:	Awwww! Because you're too tall!
LEE:	He said, "I want you to look to the right, to the left, and I want you to look forward. You never look back." Did I appreciate it then? *No, I was being fired! I'm looking back!*
MORGAN:	Awwww! "I'm eight!"
LEE:	I just remember: the St. James Theater is on 44th Street, and at the end of 44th and Eighth Avenue is a staircase to go down to the subway. So, I was just about to walk down the staircase with my mother with all of my things. I looked back to the marquee, and I said, "I'll be back."
MORGAN:	Yes!
LEE:	"Iiiiiii'm coming back!"
MORGAN:	Yes.
LEE:	My mother is looking at me and says, "Oh come *on!*"
MORGAN:	That's awesome. Graciela Daniele kept saying in her interview, "I said, okay!" That's her thing. So your tagline is "I'm coming back."
LEE:	I played the St. James Theater three times after that. *Flower Drum Song*… then I did *Mr. President* there with Peter Gennaro… then *My One and Only* as Associate Choreographer for Tommy Tune. So, four times total.
MORGAN:	Well, since you mentioned him… I want to ask you about representation of Asian and Asian American people on Broadway and in musical theatre, because we've seen it go through a lot of change. Right. And in terms of you coming up through *The King and I* with this wonderful mentor of Yul Brynner – who's a Russian man playing a Siamese king – right? We saw Jonathan Pryce originate the role of the "Engineer" in *Miss Saigon*. Now, you're in the Director's chair and the Choreographer's chair. You're behind the table on so many things. I just kind of want to know how you feel about all of it. How has the development of appropriate casting affected your process as a director? I think that's relative to what you were just talking about… not looking back… looking forward or looking to the sides, right? How do you feel about all that progress?

LEE: In the 50s and 60s, you didn't have that many Asians in theatre. Casting was not aware of authenticity. From my point of view, it was about selling tickets to keep the show running, so they got Caucasians with names to fill those roles. After the incident of Jonathan Pryce in *Miss Saigon* (1991) and the Asian community protesting, casting is much more aware of Asians playing those roles.

MORGAN: I know that you've directed *South Pacific* (1949) in recent years. Now, as a director, how do you approach all of that?

LEE: I definitely hire Asians to play those natives.

MORGAN: Understood.

LEE: I was in *Promises, Promises* and I played a waitress with a Chinese accent. People have asked, "How dare you? How could you have done that?" I said, "I was working with Neil Simon!" I wanted to be a part of the theatre. How could I get work? Most of my work in the theatre was playing kids onstage because I was only four-foot-ten. I didn't grow! I had ballet technique... I had Afro-Cuban and Kathrine Dunham technique... but I couldn't compete because you had to be 5'5" to be in the adult ensemble. You had to match the boys so they could dance with you. I would go to these auditions and hear, "Thank you very much!" I would then see that they needed kids in the show. Then, I would put my braids on, and I had all my clothes from high school. And believe it or not I would get the job! I was a part of the theatre. All I wanted to do was work! With *Bravo Giovanni*, *Mr. President*, *Here's Love*, and *Golden Boy*, I was hired as a "kid." Then they found out I could dance, and they would put me in a big number. How exciting for me! If I went to an adult audition, I would never get the job.

MORGAN: So now as a director, how does that play into the decisions that you make?

LEE: I definitely take the time to audition to see if I can have children in my shows. In my company, NAAP, we have a theatre club program for ages 8–11 at Young Wing Elementary School in Chinatown, where we train young children to make them aware of the importance of theatre. I use them in all of my productions as part of my mission. To give them the opportunities that I had. In 2004, I directed *The King and I* National Tour with Sandy Duncan. We went back to Young Wing Elementary School to audition and took 14 kids on tour for a year. What an experience they'll never forget.

MORGAN: Let's talk about *A Chorus Line* (1975). You were part of the *original* developmental workshops upon which the show is based. What does it feel like to take this show that you were a part of literally creating to so many regions, markets, and audiences throughout the years as a director and choreographer? Can you talk about that a little bit.

LEE: What an honor! Michael Bennett passed me the torch opening night, downtown, Off-Broadway. We came off the stage and he said, "Come here, come here..." I was so worried, wondering if I said my lines right. There's the actor talking. He said: you are going to take this show around the world. I had just done two flop[73] shows with him. *Henry Sweet Henry* and *Seesaw*... so I'm saying "Yeah, yeah... sure, okay..." and he said, "I'm serious. You're going to take this around the world."

MORGAN: Had you been choreographing by that point or directing at all?

LEE: Absolutely not! All I wanted to do was dance.

MORGAN: So, what did that feel like to you?

LEE: Michael and Bob Avian trained me to be their dance captain during the last 2 years of the run of *Promises, Promises*. I learned the structure of what a dance captain does. Then, I went around the United States setting his choreography in *Promises, Promises*. I was passing on Michael Bennett's choreography, but I was learning so much about how to become a director.

MORGAN: What an interesting way to work up through it.

LEE: Well, let me tell you about being a dance captain. You have to track everybody in the show's staging and choreography through charts. You have to audition newcomers and put them into the show. You have to watch the show and take notes at least three to four times a week. When someone is out sick, you have to put the covers on. You have to hold understudy rehearsals. You have to maintain the show the way the director and choreographer conceived it. In those days, people stayed until the end of their contracts because they wanted to be a part of that director or choreographer's stable of actors and dancers. If you were hired by them, you would do their Broadway shows, TV shows, or commercials.

MORGAN: Yeah, I actually trained with Gary Flannery, who was one of Bob Fosse's guys. He did the film *All That Jazz*.

LEE: This was the first time I had a home base, with Michael Bennett, even though I worked a lot before that. I was his first friend in New York because he came down in the summers from Buffalo to study with Syvilla Fort.

MORGAN: Wow.

LEE: So, years later, he said to me, "You know, when you got that show *Flower Drum Song,* you came back to the studio and you told everyone that was going to be your second Broadway show and I was *so jealous* of you! I hadn't even started yet!"

MORGAN: As a young person, I learned the *Chorus Line* opening number routine from Donna Drake[74]... who would also go around and direct productions of *A Chorus Line* all over the country...which I think is such a fascinating thing. It's one of the only shows where the original cast members are continuing its legacy in such a way. So, there's you and Donna Drake and Donna McKechnie[75] and all of these folks who are out in the world still working come back to doing *A Chorus Line*, or teach the choreography, and workshops and stuff... tell me about that...

LEE: This is what happened. I had the "book"; I had the Bible. I started helping Michael and Bob Avian to set the national companies and London. When Michael took the original company to California, he spent the time with me teaching every aspect of the show. Michael did not like to fly, and he said he was working on other projects, which gave me the opportunity to direct and choreograph all of the companies around the world. Ten years later, Michael sold the rights to stock and amateur theaters.[76] I said to them, since it's going to go to regional theaters, I think the original company should have the opportunity to direct and choreograph their show, so I set out to do a workshop with them and give them the bible.

MORGAN: Wow.

LEE: Sammy Williams went off to Greenville, South Carolina. Patricia Garland went out to California. They had "the book."

MORGAN: Wow. So, it was *you*. You're the reason!

LEE: *A Chorus Line* was becoming a machine. Somebody had to be in control of it. We had companies in New York, London, San Francisco, Los Angeles, Chicago, Australia, Stockholm, on and on. So, I couldn't perform anymore; but I promised Michael and Bob that I would be here to represent them. And I told the original cast, "I will always represent *you* authentically because I'm part of "the line" also." The most important thing for me now that Michael and Bob have passed away is to do as many companies and train as many people as possible to keep their legacy alive.

MORGAN: So, you're directing humans playing roles that are based on real humans. Art imitating life, imitating art imitating life. I mean, what is that? That's strange.

LEE: What I do at the auditions for each character is I get everyone who is coming in for that role and sit them down. We talk about the background and their characters. Now, as an actor, *you* need to build on that. When it comes to Connie, I tell them my story and their eyeballs are falling out. After an hour, they say, "I gotta play *you?!* And you're sitting in front of me?" I tell them that's another Connie. I mean, that's not me now.

MORGAN: Yeah, it's three times removed, right?

LEE: Yeah, absolutely. Well, it's still difficult for them.

MORGAN: Oh, I'm sure. They have to get over the nerves of thinking, "Holy crap, she's *right in front of me*!" All of those layers which leads me to this: How do you as an adult, especially in that choreographer's chair and director's chair, deal with the pressures of the Broadway industry producers, revenue, the commercialism of it all, the expectations? How do you cope with that? Do you thrive on it?

LEE: I think I thrive on it. To me, there's no difference between Off-Broadway, Broadway, or regional theatre… you have all the same pressures. Except it's millions of dollars on Broadway, and it's not as much money in regional theatre; but the responsibilities of getting the show on are exactly the same, whether I'm working on Broadway or in Atlanta. The quality is the most important thing. What *is* Broadway? I bring all of my experience from Broadway – my training and the choreographers I've worked with – to you. So, all of the countries that I get to do *A Chorus Line* with, whether it's Stockholm or Málaga with Antonio Banderas, get a first-class production. In all of the shows I work on, we're striving for excellence. How do I do that? I do a workshop. So, if I go to Chile and they're all actors and singers, I work on their dancing. With the dancers, I work on their acting and singing. We work hard to make them triple threats. So, if you go on YouTube and see the Chilean company, you would never know they weren't dancers before *A Chorus Line*. They were actor-singers. You see their legs? I was there from nine in the morning until midnight with them.

MORGAN: Would you say that you're the kind of person that wants to get the job done? If it means a little extra time on the front end or just trying to figure out how to get from point A to point B…?

LEE: Yes, I am there to get the job done! If the actors make the sacrifice to come in early or stay late, I am there with my associates and assistants. It's called "after school" or "before school."

MORGAN: Since musical theatre is such an American art form, I think the American theatre industry takes it for granted that it's a part of our culture. However, around the world, they don't have the same kind of access to training or the same kind of exposure to how to make it work. It sounds like you've made it part of your life's mission to take it around the world, too.

LEE: Well, absolutely. In 1976, they did not have musical theatre schools like they do now in London where we were doing our first international company. Michael held workshops before the auditions and rehearsals.

MORGAN: What I'm hearing is: Broadway is not a place. It is an expectation of excellence. It is a standard of excellence, yes?

LEE: The standard of excellence is Broadway, as far as *I'm* concerned.

> The standard of excellence is Broadway, as far as *I'm* concerned.

MORGAN: I love that. Let's break away from *A Chorus Line*. When you work on other shows, or you direct or choreograph, either something you've never done before or one of those other pieces… how do you balance where your storytelling – your perspective – comes in versus what you know about the piece… meaning, the preexisting expectations of perhaps what the show should look like, sound like, and feel like? Where do you lie on that spectrum?

LEE: Well, let me tell you… For 18 years I was the resident choreographer for the Washington Opera and worked with Placido Domingo, Pavarotti, and Jose Carreras… The Three Tenors. Opera is so different; but, because I came from the theatre, in my choreography, whether I'm doing *Merry Widow*, *Turandot*, or whatever, it's all about storytelling in the choreography. I have to ask the dancer, "*Why* are you doing that dance? What *are* those steps?" I started to really distinguish between dancing and telling stories. I learned to ask these questions from *A Chorus Line*. For every single step, there's dialog. That's the difference between a Michael Bennett show that I do and other people looking at a tape because they don't know why she's doing "Music and the Mirror." Why is she dropping to the floor, then coming up and rolling the shoulders? What is that dialogue? I'm not just kicking my foot! Why is that foot going up there, you know? In every single moment, there's dialogue in all the choreography. They say when you can't speak, then you sing. And when you can't sing, you dance.

MORGAN: Yes, absolutely.

LEE: I am still so passionate about *A Chorus Line*. Why? Because it's a university. University *Chorus Line*.

MORGAN: *A Chorus Line* University.

LEE: We're *paying* you to learn. You take all of that and you take it to the next show. What are you learning? You're learning to be a triple threat performer and getting paid to do it. I just took a company to Tokyo, and I would say 75–80% of the cast had just graduated from a university. They have all this wonderful training and I said, "Now you're going to University *Chorus Line*."

MORGAN: They should get a certificate. There should be a certificate.

LEE: You learn to be a collaborator. You learn to listen because you're standing on that line for 2 hours. If you're thinking about washing your hair and what you're going to eat, I know it and I stop you right there. You have to be in the moment, in the moment, in the moment. Because when you get out there [to do the solo work], if somebody's yawning behind you... no. You have to give *all* your attention to the person who's speaking. So that when you step forward, they give you all of their attention. It's called listening. That's collaborating.

MORGAN: *And* discipline, yeah.

LEE: Discipline and collaboration. You learn about your spacing on stage. That's what *A Chorus Line* is about because in order to make the formations, you are on a specific number and seam.

MORGAN: That's really a beautiful sentiment of establishing discipline... there's a layer of expectation in terms of honoring the original material... and then there is, of course, the layer of humanity... really trying to find that balance in the room and lead people to it. I think it is really unique and special.

LEE: Yes, it is *A Chorus Line* University. It makes you prepared for any situation whether it is television, film, or Broadway. You carry your lessons with you.

MORGAN: Do you like both directing *and* choreographing? Do you like wearing both hats, or do you prefer to wear one or the other?

LEE: I think there's no other way. There is no other way when there's choreography and staging. I think that's why you have [Bob] Fosse and [Jerome] Robbins becoming directors when they did. The arc is completed. I'm not saying that directors don't know what the choreographers are doing, because you're collaborating. If you're doing both, you know when it stops and when it starts.

MORGAN: It's also tough when the jobs are separate. You don't know what they're going to bring into the room until you see it. Then, you have to respond to it.

LEE: With Fosse, Bennett, and Robbins, it never stops. The acting is *through* the dancing. The dialogue comes *through* the singing and the dancing. It's all one cloth. I think that it's very important that I direct *and* choreograph.

MORGAN: Right. Same with Stroman, Marshall, and Daniele! How do you engage in self-care for yourself? You know... stamina... longevity. You're working now at a particular age, and you seem to be going at fairly full steam, even on this tail end of a pandemic. What kind of rituals, routines, and boundaries have you created for yourself?

LEE: Well, first of all, what I did was I created the official *A Chorus Line* warm-up. It is 1 hour and is done before rehearsals and before every show. It is for toning, to keep you in shape, and prevent injuries for the show. I lead it and that's how I stay in shape. I travel so much that staying home is rejuvenating enough for me.

MORGAN: Amazing. What would you tell someone who wants a career in this work who is, perhaps, a woman or a person of color, or belongs to another under-represented demographic?

LEE: You need to show up, represent, and never give up. I mean, now we're getting more help because diversity is "in." If you want to be in film, go to California. If you want to be in theatre, come to New York. You need to take any job where you can learn. Wherever you can direct… wherever you can choreograph… wherever you can practice your craft… because the theatre is about *doing*. You can sing in your bathroom forever, but if you can't get out in front of the audience and hear the feedback then it isn't fulfilling. As artists, we need a fire in our belly. That's the thing that I think has kept me going all these years. That little kid coming in early, going around the stage and signing in. I haven't lost her. I give it to everyone that comes to train with me in order to survive in the theatre.

MORGAN: That's beautiful. Tell me about your next steps. What's next for you?

LEE: All these years, I have trained these actors and dancers around the world. I was sitting in South Africa. I was helping them form a company to go into the townships to talk about AIDS through theatre and humor. I thought, I haven't helped my *own* community. Here I am, helping people all over the world… At the closing night of *The King and I* with Sandy Duncan, I asked my two assistants, Nina Zoie Lam and Steven Eng, "Where do these talented Asian-American people go when the show closes?" They said they are waiting for the next *Miss Saigon*, *South Pacific,* or *The King and I.* There's no work for them. So, I said, "We need to be doing something." So, we formed a company: NAAP.[77] Why *can't* we do *Oklahoma*, *Carousel* and *Hello, Dolly*? As an example, Asian countries produce musical classics with all-Asian casts. So, that's what we set as our mission. To give Asian American actors a platform to show their talents. In the past 10 years, we have formed a musical theatre club with 35 kids in Chinatown, as well as a choir. As a part of our mission, we make sure that they are used in our productions.

MORGAN: I also see on your website for NAAP that you support *new* musicals. New musical development?

LEE: What we do is called "Discover." We take musicals from new composers and cut them down to 30-minute versions. We have Asian directors and casts. The next step is to encourage them to continue to develop them after we give them the platform and feedback.

MORGAN: That's beautiful. "Discover and Rediscover." What a cool comparison… to RE-discover.

LEE: "Rediscover" are the big musicals like *Cinderella*... rediscovering the show with an Asian lens. My dream is to eventually expand our repertoire to plays.

MORGAN: That's wonderful. Representation is important. I think it must happen in different ways in order to bring it all the way to the marker that you want it to be. Sometimes it's about taking risks.

LEE: For most of my shows, my goal is to include the NAAP kids, the choir, and the professional actors together. Sometimes we have a cast of over sixty people. There is no other company that has that many Asian American actors together on stage at once.

MORGAN: Amazing. So, now you're opening doors and you're building your own buildings for people.

LEE: I formed this company to bring my communities together and give them opportunities. That's my mission now. It's my way of life: to prepare the next generation to continue our legacies and keep theatre alive.

Notes

1 Deer, Joe. *Directing in Musical Theatre: An Essential Guide* (London: Routledge, 2017), 288.
2 Marty, Paulette. *Contemporary Women Stage Directors: Conversations on Craft* (London: Methuen Drama, 2019), 279.
3 Coleman, Bud and Judith A. Sebesta, eds. *Women in American Musical Theatre* (North Carolina: McFarland & Company Inc. Publishers, 2008), 183.
4 Ibid, 185.
5 Ibid, 191-193.
6 The Teatro Colón – a professional opera house located in Buenos Aires, Argentina, since 1857: https://teatrocolon.org.ar/en/theater.
7 Eva Perón (1919-1952) – First Lady of Argentina.
8 "Corps de ballet" – group of ballet dancers, usually not principals, who dance together throughout the piece like an ensemble.
9 George Balanchine – famous choreographer (1929-1983). See https://www.nycballet.com/discover/our-history/george-balanchine/.
10 "Léonide Massine" *Wikipedia*. Updated January 23, 2023. See https://en.wikipedia.org/wiki/L%C3%A9onide_Massine.
11 The Ballets Russes – Major French ballet company in operation from 1909-1929 with a touring company.
12 "Panamericana Television" *Wikipedia*. Updated January 3, 2023. See https://en.wikipedia.org/wiki/Panamericana_Televisi%C3%B3n.
13 Roland Petit. See https://www.britannica.com/biography/Roland-Petit.
14 Jack Cole (1911-1974) – American dancer & choreographer, dubbed the "Father of Theatrical Jazz Dance"
15 Matt Mattox (1921-2013) – American dancer and protégé of Jack Cole.
16 Martha Graham (1894-1991) – American modern dancer and choreographer.
17 Merce Cunningham (1919-2009) American dancer and choreographer.
18 Steve Lawrence: Broadway performer.
19 *Hullaballo* was an American televised variety show series that ran 1965-1966 and often featured popular dances and dance styles.

184 Director/Choreographers

20 In musicals with partner dancing, choreographers will often hire a "boy" assistant and a "girl" assistant to help demonstrate both parts of the partner dances and serve as dance captains for both genders.
21 *The Milliken Breakfast Show* (1956-1980). See https://www.bonhams.com/auction/25939/lot/163/a-group-of-milliken-breakfast-show-albums/; https://www.waldorfstories.com/stories/linda-marie-fiore.
22 A luxury hotel in New York City, also famous for hosting events.
23 Bob Avian (1937-2021) - American choreographer and dancer.
24 Pre-Production – period of time before rehearsal with actors where creative team rehearses to figure out blocking, choreography, and other creative elements.
25 A racial slur to those of Latin or Hispanic descent.
26 "Oh my God" in Spanish.
27 *Ballet Hispanico* website. Accessed October 15, 2022. See https://www.ballethispanico.org/.
28 *Intar Theatre* website. Accessed October 15, 2022. See https://www.intartheatre.org/.
29 Max Ferrá (1937-2017) – Cuban-American artist and Artistic Director.
30 Jorge Luis Borges (1899-1986). https://www.newworldencyclopedia.org/entry/Jorge_Luis_Borges.
31 Astor Piazzolla (1921-1992). https://www.britannica.com/biography/Astor-Piazzolla.
32 Mel Gussow, "Stage: Borges Stories in 'Tango Apasionado'" *The New York Times*. November 10, 1987. See https://www.nytimes.com/1987/11/10/theater/stage-borges-stories-in-tango-apasionado.html.
33 Westbeth Theatre Center: professional theater in New York City. See https://westbethent.com/.
34 William Finn (b. 1952) American musical theatre composer.
35 I heard this in a church sermon at Seacoast Church (Mt. Pleasant, SC) circa 2011. I do not recall the speaking pastor. I've never found the source of the original but have seen derivatives of it in my research.
36 Susan Stroman, Interview with Amanda Wansa Morgan via Zoom, October 25, 2022.
37 Max Bialystok and Leo Bloom are the names of the lead characters of the musical *The Producers*, directed by Stroman on Broadway in 2001 and based on the 1967 Mel Brooks film by the same name.
38 The Girl in the Yellow Dress is a lead character in the musical *Contact*, directed by Stroman on Broadway in 1999.
39 Hal Prince (1928-2019) – American theatre director and producer. Prolific career.
40 Nick Hytner (b. 1956) – British theatre director, film director, and film producer.
41 Mike Ockrent (1946-1999) – British theatre director, also known for his work on Broadway.
42 Trevor Nunn (b. 1940) – British theatre director with extensive repertoire of Shakespeare's works.
43 John Kander and Fred Ebb – Musical theatre writing team behind *Cabaret*, *Chicago*, and many other works.
44 See Interview with "Mary-Mitchell Campbell".
45 Florenz Ziegfeld – producer of *The Ziegfeld Follies* from 1907-1931 and many successful Broadway musicals.
46 "Ulla" is a main character in *The Producers*.
47 Robert Wagner (b. 1933) – Tony-award-winning scenic designer with many Broadway credits.
48 Stephen Sondheim (1930-2021) - World-renowned American musical theatre composer.
49 "Interview with Hal Prince about *Cats*" Broadway The American Musical Episode 6. 13:05-13:21.
50 Andrew Lloyd Webber (b. 1948) – world-renowned British musical theatre composer.
51 Andre Bishop (b. 1948) – American theatrical producer & Artistic Director of Lincoln Center Theater since 1992.

52 Two theater spaces at Lincoln Center Theater.
53 *Center Stage* was a feature film (2000) centered around the lives of students a fictitious ballet school in New York City, featuring choreography by Stroman.
54 A film version of *Nine* came out in 2009, starring Daniel Day Lewis as Guido.
55 The "Me, Too" movement. https://metoomvmt.org/.
56 Theatrical Intimacy is in reference to actors having to portray intimate physical and/or emotional moments on stage and the practice and craft of staging those moments with care and technique. See https://www.idcprofessionals.com/.
57 Lee, Baayork. 2022. "Interview with Amanda Wansa Morgan" via Zoom, November 21, 2023.
58 "Baayork Lee" *American Masters*. Accessed November 5, 2022. See https://www.pbs.org/wnet/americanmasters/archive/interview/baayork-lee/.
59 The Majestic Theater is a Broadway theatre space on W. 44th St. In New York, built in 1927.
60 When actors arrive at a theatre, they sign in on a physical paper, posted on a callboard, so that stage management knows that they have arrived and can check the sign-in sheet if the actor cannot be physically located during a call.
61 Gertrude Lawrence (1898-1952) British American actress, original "Anna" in *The King and I*.
62 A waiting room or side room of sorts.
63 "Barre" is a warmup done *at* a ballet barre.
64 Yuriko (1920-2022) – American performer who originated the role of "Eliza" in *The King and I*.
65 92nd Street Y – a cultural and community center in Manhattan, NY.
66 Rodgers & Hammerstein Inc.: Richard Rodgers and Oscar Hammerstein created a producing group that managed their shows.
67 George Balanchine - choreographer.
68 Carol Haney (1924-1964) American dancer and choreographer.
69 Syvilla Fort (1917-1975) American dancer, choreographer, and teacher.
70 "Katherine Dunham Company" *Wikipedia*. Updated October 29, 2021. See https://en.wikipedia.org/wiki/Katherine_Dunham_Company.
71 Maria Tallchief (1925-2013) Native-American ballerina.
72 Current terms include "Native American" or "Indigenous Person."
73 "flop" – When a show does not do well financially (regardless of critical response or reception).
74 Donna Drake: original cast member of *A Chorus Line*.
75 Donna McKechnie (b. 1942) Actress. Original "Cassie" in *A Chorus Line*.
76 "stock and amateur rights" – After a show's Broadway (or West End) commercial run, the rights to the shows are sold to licensing houses so other people can produce the show regionally.
77 See https://www.naaproject.org/.

5
THE PRODUCERS

What Does a Producer Do?

If you've met a high-school drama teacher or theatre camp teacher, you've met a producer. They don't all walk around in top hats with money spewing out of their pockets. What does a producer do? What is the difference between a producer and an artistic director? Depends on who you ask. There are some common threads that include a necessity for leadership skills, organization, incredible communication skills, and a willingness to ask questions and get things done. At the Broadway level, "producer" can mean many things. Unfortunately, there isn't a delineation for an outsider as to whether a person is named a "producer" by simply investing money in a project or if they participated in the complicated process of getting a show from page to stage. There are a few hints, as shared by our subjects in this chapter. There are also two wonderful books with more detailed information on these jobs: *I Wanna Be a Producer: How to Make a Killing on Broadway or Get Killed* by John Breglio, and *The Commercial Theater Institute Guide to Producing Plays and Musicals*, edited by Frederic B. Vogel and Ben Hodges. For my intents and purposes, I will interviewed producers who engage in the work of building shows, supporting them, and actually *producing* them; versus investors or financiers who participate in the "backing" of a musical by solely writing a check and eagerly awaiting the returns. In preparation for these interviews as well as further research after them, I extracted the following quotes, which sum up the definition of what an active producer does.

Kevin McCollum, of *The Producing Office*, says:

> I have never believed that a producer's job is to raise money. That is like saying an actor's job is simply to read lines. The marginalization of a producer's role

DOI: 10.4324/9781003324652-5

in theatre today as just a money person is very destructive to the ecosystem that is musical theatre. I feel a producer's job is to help create an environment and provide the tools and philosophy that enable a new work to grow into its fullest potential. There are practical and creative realities that every good producer must navigate, but I can assure you that raising money is the last, and in many ways the easiest, one of them.[1]

Harriet Newman Leve, President of Leve Production, says:

In the early stages of getting a play off the ground, the main pressures are to secure the rights for the work, hire the director and cast, and hire the production and design team. It sounds straightforward, but it entails juggling a lot of schedules around theater availability, and at the same time finding the right mix of talents, styles, tastes, and personalities that each member of the creative and business teams are bringing to the table. [...] I also meet with the advertising and marketing team to work out what the key artwork will be for the play's poster, print ads, and playbill. While managing this initial phase of assembling the troops, I am also responsible for raising funds. [....] I see as many previews as I can. [....] I give notes on the text, the design, the performances, and other elements, and solicit comments from my two producing associates [...] I pass those to the director only.[2]

A producer usually creates a team by hiring a lawyer and a general manager (known as a GM). There are many Broadway producers who have also worked as GMs for various shows. The duties of a GM include, but are not limited to: preparing budgets, maintaining the financial books; managing payroll; working with the box office to connect all of the financial dots including ticketing prices and changes; negotiating deals with personnel; knowing the rules of all of the unions and working with them; and acting as a consultant for additional matters like marketing and public relations (PR).[3] The team may also include a PR person, team, or firm. General Managers have different jobs than stage managers, production managers, or company managers (discussed in the next chapter).

Producers tend to get a negative reputation in the eyes of the public based on portrayals in media, film, and television; however, they tend to be tough on the outside in order to get their complicated jobs done, and quite warm and caring on the inside. They have strong hearts in order to take on high risk. High risk can have a great payoff and it can also result in disappointing failure, both financially and in terms of time, hard work, and emotional investment. In reference to recruiting investors, producer Daryl Roth (she/her) says:

Please, please understand clearly this is a risky business. Do this play because you think it's important to do and have a chance and like it, or you want to support what I'm doing, or it speaks to you. Do it for the right reasons and we will all hope to get your money back for you, but we may not. Please do it because you believe in the play (or the playwright); or what the subject is; or if you just want to have some fun and you want to do something good for the cultural arts of this world. I like to say to people to consider it a donation in a way that you might donate to a theatre company in your town. Consider it a philanthropic gift to the arts.[4]

It takes guts and great empathy to make those kinds of statements and pitches to investors, all the while doing the leg work to make the show come together on the production side. The women listed in this chapter have the most bravery and *chutzpah*, as subject Jenny Gersten puts it, of all of the folks in the industry. In fact, my interview with Gersten ended up being particularly inspiring, based on my fascination with her strength, candidness, humor, and – I say this as a compliment – audacity. Her bold ability to – time and again – put herself into spaces of discomfort, to take risks, was downright inspiring. If Jenny Gersten can invite herself into a cab with Oskar Eustis to give him a 20-minute pitch as to why she should work for him at The Public, I can finish this book![5]

Notable Figures

Therese Helburn (1887–1959) was a producer and co-founder of The Theatre Guild. Her work and influence resulted in the original production of *Oklahoma*.[6]

Jean Dalrymple (1902–1998) played a major role in the development of the New York City Center [of Music and Drama] and worked as a writer, producer, manager, and press director for decades in New York theatre. For years, she worked as the Director of New York City Center Light Opera Company when it produced dozens of shows and, later, produced Broadway shows as the Executive Director of The American National Theatre and Academy (ANTA).

Lucille Lortel (1900–1999) was a theatrical producer and artistic director who produced or co-produced over 500 plays in her career. While most of the works she produced were plays (non-musicals), her imprint on the American theatre is everlasting, with her nickname being "The Queen of Off-Broadway." The Lucille Lortel Awards for Outstanding Achievement Off-Broadway were created in 1985 by the League of Off-Broadway Theatres and Producers.[7]

Nell Nugent has produced over 20 Broadway shows and served as General Manager or Stage Manager for many more, since the 1960s.

Elizabeth I. McCann (1931–2021) produced dozens of Broadway shows and served as General Manager for dozens more. Her Broadway career spanned from the 1960s until her death in 2021. Musical hits include *Hair* (2011), *Leader of the Pack* (1985), and *The Robber Bridegroom* (1976).

Barbara Whitman is an American theatrical producer having worked behind Broadway productions of *Hedwig and the Angry Inch* (Broadway, 2014), *Fun Home* (2015), and *A Strange Loop* (2002 Tony Award for Best Musical).

Rhoda Mayerson served as the Associate Producer on Broadway productions of *The Secret Garden, Smokey Joe's Café, Hairspray, The Producers*, and *The Wedding Singer*.

Paula Wagner is a producer for both film and stage, having produced the stage production(s) of *Pretty Woman: The Musical* (2019) throughout Europe.

Eva Price is a three-time Tony Award-winning producer of Broadway hits that include *Oklahoma* (2019 Revival), *Jagged Little Pill* (2019), *Tina* (2019), *Dear Evan Hansen* (2016), *and On Your Feet!* (2015). She's also produced numerous shows Off-Broadway and on tour.

Sue Frost was the Associate Producer at Goodspeed Musicals for 20 years, producing over 50 new musicals. She is a founding member of Junkyard Productions, the production company behind *Come From Away* (2017) and *Memphis* (2009).

Kristin Caskey served as a Producer on *Fun Home* (2015), *Bring it On* (2012), *Legally Blonde* (2007), and *Thoroughly Modern Millie* (2002).

Mara Isaacs and Dale Franzen were producers on the 2019 Tony-Award-winning production of *Hadestown*. Isaacs is also the founder of Octopus Theatricals, which has produced over 150 productions to date.

Carmen Pavlovic is the co-owner and CEO of Global Creatures and is behind the Broadway productions of *Moulin Rouge* (2021) and *King Kong* (2018).

Stacey Mindich, founder of Stacey Mindich Productions, produced *Dear Evan Hansen* along with over a dozen other Broadway shows including *The Bridges of Madison County* (2014) and *Catch Me If You Can* (2011).

Cynthia J. Tong is a Creative Producer working on Broadway and Off-Broadway with credits that include *Little Shop of Horrors, New York New York, The Piano Lesson*, and *Hadestown* (Co-Producer).

INTERVIEWS

Jenny Gersten
Dori Berinstein

Jenny Gersten Biography

Jenny Gersten serves as Line Producer for *Beetlejuice* on Broadway and National Tour, Executive Producer for the musical *Born for This*, Producer of Musical Theatre for New York City Center, and Interim Artistic Director of the Williamstown Theatre Festival. She sometimes produces commercially, including the award-winning Off-Broadway "pie shop" production of *Sweeney Todd*. She works with Jessica Hecht on The Campfire Project, an arts program that primarily serves Syrian and Ukrainian refugees overseas. Previously, Jenny served as Executive Director of Friends of the High Line, the Associate Producer of The Public Theater, and Artistic Director of Naked Angels. At sea, she is the Creative Producer of Virgin Voyages.

Interview with Jenny Gersten, December 1, 2022, via Zoom[8]

MORGAN: Jenny Gersten. Broadway producer and Artistic Director. Also, a producer of nonprofit theatre, commercial theatre, and all kinds of theatre. What an incredible resumé and career that you are right smack dab in the middle of. I love talking to artists that are right in the middle of the work. I'm so excited to ask you these questions and find out about how you do what you do and how you got to where you are. Let's start with the brief autobiography of how you got to where you are from, from diapers to Broadway, so to speak.

GERSTEN: Great. It's interesting: I would never qualify myself as a Broadway producer, even though I'm currently with a Broadway show in Kentucky.[9]

MORGAN: Well, what is "Broadway?" Graciela Daniele says that Broadway is a quality, a standard of excellence. Broadway can be anywhere.

GERSTEN: I grew up in a nonprofit arts household. My mother was a fairly successful modern dancer before I was born. She met my dad at a dance like Lollapalooza that he was producing at the Delacorte Theater in Central Park, back when he was the Associate Producer at The New York Shakespeare Festival, which is now known as The Public Theater.[10] After my mom had kids, she started running a nonprofit ballet company – Feld Ballet.[11] So, I grew up being shuttled around between a dance universe and a theatre universe. I would say that in my more formative, sentient years, when I was developing a brain, a lot of the dinner table conversation when they were home centered around how they were running their various nonprofits. I grew up running around The Public Theater and The Delacorte[12] as a child. When I would spend time with my dad, I was very aware of how much he loved what he did. He would stand in the back of the theater and look out at the audience enjoying the thing that he helped make and produce. Then, he'd go backstage after the bows, and everyone would hug him or he would probably hug everybody. It was such an interchange of love. They had so much respect for him, and he loved what they did so much. Not just the actors; stage managers, backstage crew… it was so profound. I think that his generosity and the beneficence of his ways really struck me, and how much he loved what he did. So, that was the drug I wanted. From very early on knew I wanted to be a theatre producer because I wanted to be like my dad and know what my dad felt.

MORGAN: What kind of training did you pursue?

GERSTEN: I quickly ruled out acting because I knew what good [acting] looked like and I don't do that. So, I quickly confirmed that I belonged exactly where I thought. When I was finishing high school and was going into college, my dad said, "You think you want a life in the theatre, but there's a lot of other things that are out there for you that we have not shown you. So, I want you to go to college and really think about the other 'ologies.'" He suggested I look at everything from archeology to zoology. I had been thinking about going to NYU for theatre. So, I went to Oberlin, and I became an archeology major. When I was home in the summer after my last year of high school – going into college – I got an internship at The Eugene O'Neill Playwrights Conference.[13] That was my first job. I got paid $100 a month. I was the Box Office Co-Manager of the Playwrights Conference, and I got to be in residence at the estate of O'Neill in Waterford, Connecticut. There were twelve playwrights there. Lloyd Richards was the Artistic Director. He was also the AD of the Yale Rep. August Wilson was there with *The Piano Lesson*. John Patrick Shanley was there. Those were the big names. Then, there were a lot of other wonderful writers, actors, and directors there. I was seventeen and I got to be in camaraderie with professionals for the first time outside of being "Bernie Gersten's daughter" or "Cora Cahan's daughter." I got a crush on an actor, and he was leaving campus and he invited me to come see him do these plays at EST [Ensemble Studio Theatre] – which is a theatre on 52nd Street [in New York]. So, I went to EST a couple of weeks later and I saw plays by The 52nd Street Project. The guy who runs The 52nd Street Project came out on stage and he's super charismatic. He talked about what The 52nd Street Project is—an inner city youth mentoring program where actors, playwrights, and directors work one-on-one with kids from Hell's Kitchen who are in some levels of various distress create theatre. I was like, "Forget that actor! What the hell is this place?!" I fell in love with the work and I kind of fell in love with that guy. I spent several summers going back to the O'Neill as their House Manager, and I got a great mentorship from Lloyd out of that. I got to meet all these artists and I started to form my community with people that were outside of what I grew up with and have my own relationships. Then, I started pursuing an internship at The 52nd Street Project – which took a while because it was a very grassroots organization that didn't have a structure for an intern. Finally, I got to my senior year of college and I got an internship for my January term at The 52nd Street Project and they hired me upon graduation as an administrative assistant. It was a super grassroots project – three people [on staff]. I think the operating budget that year was around $50,000. It was nothing [for New York]. They had one "princess phone" that we all used to make phone calls. I turned to the Executive Director and said, "Do you need help writing grants?" because I could see she was really stressed out about all the grant writing she had to do. So, she taught me how to write grants and I started helping her with it. I was pretty good at it because I could write well. Within a year or so, they gave me a new title and a little bit of a raise, which was Director of Marketing and Development, or something like that. I wrote press releases, and I wrote grants. After doing that for a while, and working with the Board on fundraising, I started to get approached for development director jobs. I was young, in my early twenties. I realized that could make a lot of money very quickly because I understand that the turnover in development offices is high in non-profit theaters, and I have the skills and the connections because of who I am.

MORGAN: And you had the energy because you were young.

GERSTEN: Yeah. So, I figured I could be a really good development director. I started to interview for those jobs and realized that wasn't what I wanted, but it was interesting, so I thought I would pay attention to it. I started dating the Artistic Director of my organization – that guy that I fell in love with a few years back.

MORGAN: The charismatic guy who gave the curtain speech…

GERSTEN: Yeah. Fell in love. So, I had to leave that organization because we were dating; it was serious, and it was awkward. I started to figure out where I should go and how to be more of a theatre producer, because I've been doing this other stuff for a while, and I wanted to get back to professional theatre. I heard about this guy named Michael Ritchie. Michael Ritchie is a stage manager… a production stage manager… on Broadway, and he was very popular. Everybody would talk with huge energy and warm emotion about Michael Ritchie, and everybody wanted to work with him. If you were Joe Mantello, you had to have Michael Ritchie as your stage manager. If Nathan Lane was doing a play, he had to have Michael Ritchie. That list went on and on. He was in demand. Everybody spoke to what a great guy he is, and I didn't know him. He was a volunteer at The 52nd Street Project but we hadn't crossed paths. So, I called him up and I asked to have coffee with him because I had heard that he was interviewing for artistic director jobs. I didn't know anyone who did a transition from stage manager to artistic director.

MORGAN: Did your dad know him? Had your dad worked with him?

GERSTEN: He worked at Lincoln Center at the time when my dad was there. We had enough people in common. We had coffee, and I said to him, "I don't get it. You're applying for AD jobs?" He suggested that he was very liked. I mean, he never said it that way, but that was sort of the gist. I said to him, "Look, it's great that you're so well-liked and that you have all these people that you can call in favors from – famous people. They're probably all right and there's a lot to cash in on there, but you don't know anything about nonprofit structure. You don't know about Boards of Directors… you don't know about staff…"

MORGAN: I just want to paint the picture for myself. You were saying this is him as a young twenty-something woman and he is an established Broadway stage manager in his thirties or forties? I just want to get the picture…

GERSTEN: Yeah. I had been at The 52nd Street Project for about 5 years, and yeah, I have a lot of chutzpah. I said to him, "Look, you should probably consider… if you get one of these jobs, I need to get out of The 52nd Street Project because I'm dating your friend Willie … and I might be really useful to you."

MORGAN: Wow, I wish I had popcorn right now. That's great.

GERSTEN: He got an artistic director job. Actually, first, he called me up and said, "Hey, I'm going to be the Artistic Director of Naked Angels[14]… I don't think I can hire you, but I'm going to try and it's going to be tricky. Then, five or six weeks later, he told me that he wasn't going to Naked Angels because he was going to be the Producer of the Williamstown Theatre Festival[15] and wanted me to be the development director there. He wasn't going to take the title Artistic Director because he wasn't a director and they had a legacy of directors there, so he asked to be called Producer. I told him that I would raise money for him, but I wanted to be his Associate Producer, which was my dad's title for Joe Papp, and he agreed to that. That is how I got my first producing job with zero producing experience.

MORGAN: That's awesome. Williamstown is primarily a summer stock, and the staff works year-round, yes?

GERSTEN: It was a very tiny six-person staff. There was a general manager, a producer, me, a company manager, a business manager, and a part-time workshop director for the education program. Then they balloon for the summer and there's hundreds of people. Michael and I had a glorious time together. We worked for 9 years together… until 2004. I got married and had some kids. It was a great job, and we were having a blast together. We were exploding Williamstown Theatre Festival in great ways, it was doing really well, and it was really satisfying. During the year, we were working out of the New York office and then we decamped to Williamstown for the summer months, basically Memorial Day to Labor Day.

MORGAN: You're in New York during the year and you're able to continue to see theatre, make connections, and be a part of the New York community.

GERSTEN: I do that for 9 years and at the beginning of the ninth year, Mike tells me that he got another job and was going to go to L.A., and they would need to replace him and he thought I should do it. I didn't want to do it; I wanted to be invisible. I didn't want to be out front. I just wanted to enable and I'm really happy doing that. He pointed out that I knew that community really well and complimented my artistic taste said that I had demonstrated that. He thought I was a natural bridge to him leaving, carrying it on.

MORGAN: … because you watched your dad sit in the back, then go backstage…

GERSTEN: Yeah, he was Joe Papp's guy.[16] He never wanted to make a name for himself. He didn't want to be out front taking up space. He just wanted to help make the work happen.

MORGAN: You're saying an Artistic Director is more visible… a Producer is less visible?

GERSTEN: That's what I thought. It's visible and it's responsible. It's one thing to help set policy and then enact it, but another to have to speak out front about it.

MORGAN: Ah… producers don't do curtain speeches; artistic directors do. ADs also make marketing decisions, a lot of publicity-based decisions, that kind of thing. Did you take the AD job?

GERSTEN: No, no, no. I didn't get it. It was a whole thing. But, during the search, it was the first time I had to walk in Artistic Director shoes. As I was walking around in the shoes and making mock [fake] seasons and whatever else you do to apply for an AD job, I thought maybe I didn't want to be my dad. That was the first moment I had that idea.

MORGAN: This was your mid-thirties?

GERSTEN: I was 35. Then, I quit Williamstown when they hired another AD because I didn't want to work for that person, and I felt gravely disappointed. So, I was freelance and then I got to be the Artistic Director of Naked Angels. They approached me and I applied for that job.

MORGAN: Back to Naked Angels?!

GERSTEN: It was a very tiny theatre company that was hardly subsisting on anything. It was a very hard job because I was basically the only staff member, but I did get to be the Artistic Director in that I set programing and then I enacted it; I led a board; and I had to do all the financial stuff. I was sort of CEO and Artistic Director for 3 years. I would go for 6 months without paying myself because there was no money in the bank; and then there'd be money and then I would pay myself and I would try to bring other people on, and I'd mentor them. I did it and I was exhausted. I did that for three and a half years and it was really, really hard because it was such a tiny existence. I was at a luncheon at holiday time with someone who gave Naked Angels some money, a really lovely person. It was me and some college scholarship kids and Oskar Eustis, who had just been named Artistic Director of The Public Theater. I need not explain that The Public Theater was always a place that I wanted to work because that's where I spent my childhood. It was very meaningful to me, and it was very meaningful to my dad who left there under very adverse conditions, so it had all kinds of healing properties for me. When Oskar got named as Artistic Director, I thought there's no way that I would work at The Public Theater because I didn't know that guy. He had L.A. friends, friends from Trinity [Repertory Company], and I was never getting in. He had been there less than a year. He was at this luncheon where I didn't spend any time with him; but, at the end of the luncheon, we're standing in the lobby of the building where the lunch happened on the Upper East Side and I asked him if he wanted to share a cab downtown. He said yes. He knew my dad and said "Sure," so we got into a taxi together. I told him my story. I basically talked at him nonstop for like a solid 20 minutes. We got to The Public [Theater] and he didn't have his wallet, so I paid for the cab.

MORGAN: Wow. You're in front of The Public. It's right there: your *goal*. This sounds like *A League of their Own*… if your dad gets you to the try-out, you get yourself on the team, you know what I mean? The connection. I'm saying it out loud because I think sometimes young artists who want to be in leadership are afraid to use the connections they have because they feel like they're *using* them. A connection can get your resume seen… your elevator pitch – or cab pitch – gets you the job!

GERSTEN: Right. I ran into Oskar at a couple parties over the next 2 or 3 months and, by the last party, he said he wanted to make a job for me at The Public. That is how I became Associate Producer of The Public Theater (my dad's title, too). Huge moment of incredibleness. I got to work with Oskar for 3 years. After 3 years, Williamstown called, and they had gone through two artistic directors in 6 years, and they were about to retire the next one. They asked if I would talk with them, and I said I was "offer only."

MORGAN: Yes! Slam it down! Offer only!

GERSTEN: It didn't work. But… They told me that, unlike the search that I went through that was hard the last time, they had hired a search consultant and I could trust this person to take me through the

	process and advocate for me and it would not be as bad. It *did* represent trauma for me.
MORGAN:	Of course.
GERSTEN:	I said, "Okay, I'll apply." Mandy Greenfield and I were the finalists, and I got the job.[17] So, I went back to Williamstown for a second time and became the Artistic Director. I did it for 3 years and then I got this crazy offer to do another job which was run Friends of the High Line. I left Williamstown a little bit in the lurch because I'd only been there 3 years, so I did one more year *while* I was doing the High Line job.
MORGAN:	Can we pause? Were you sad to leave the dream job at The Public?
GERSTEN:	The Public was a really big job. In fact, I took on a lot. I learned a lot. I can talk so much about producing at The Public. It was fantastic. I loved it. But I think it felt better to go be the Artistic Director. I love being in service to The Public and I was really good in service to Oskar. But the Artistic Director job still felt real to me.
MORGAN:	That's interesting to know. As one is progressing through their career… I've experienced this as well… when people ask you to do something, and you know you have the capability of doing that but maybe not in *that* moment… I've said, "I need a couple more years to do some things or to learn some things or to digest some things, and then I'll be ready…"
GERSTEN:	I think so. I think there's a little bit of that… although you're never *really* ready, right? Like someone's just gotta push you off the cliff… but I do think that I notice that my career switches back and forth between being of service and being autonomous.
MORGAN:	I like it.
GERSTEN:	Because when I'm producing at The Public Theater, basically, someone hands me a project and says, "Get it done." This is true at City Center. "Here's a musical. Produce it." I say, "Great, is this what you want? Let me talk to the director. Let me see what the director wants. Let me see how the team is…" I'm of service to that team and I'm of service to the institution and everyone else is setting the agenda. But when I'm Artistic Director, I'm the CEO… I get to set the agenda. I get to make choices. It's my taste. It's my style of management that I have to follow. I can do both. I am really good at service and I'm really good at leading. In a way, being of service is better because it doesn't require the loneliness of leading.
MORGAN:	Woof. Say that. *Say that.* I've done some research on the difference between leadership and management, and you're talking about it. Sometimes you're in a position to do both. Leadership is very lonely because there's so much responsibility, which is so high risk.
GERSTEN:	Yup.
MORGAN:	High reward if things go well. Devastating…

GERSTEN: ... anxiety over failure and of letting people down or making the wrong decision; or whatever it is. You don't get to share that with anyone. Ultimately, it all rests with you.

MORGAN: Yeah.

GERSTEN: I find myself really aware of it as I move through my work and all my jobs. One minute, I'm over here at City Center, in service, and that's great. But it frustrates me when Lear [DeBessonet] tells me to do something and I don't agree with it; because if I was the Artistic Director, I would do it differently. But it's not my job to artistic direct it, it's my job to produce it.

MORGAN: I feel this. I direct and music direct. Sometimes, I'm in the music director chair and I think I would not do that like that. I can feel the tone of a room going down, but it's not my room to run. If I'm the director, that'll be my room to set a vibe in. But I'm just making the music, so I hope everybody's okay!

GERSTEN: Exactly.

MORGAN: The band's going to sound great! I'm here for the actors if they need to come talk to me. It's absolutely the opposite feeling of being in the pilot's seat as a director and thinking, "This room is my vibe, and I can feel it soaring *or* crashing." It's interesting that you like to go back and forth. Do you think that's partially related to mental health and capacity. Thinking, "Oh, I really want to do this thing right now" and then "Now, I'm ready to pivot."

GERSTEN: No. I think I'm just psychotic. [*We laughed about this.*]

MORGAN: Okay. That's fair. Look, anyone working at the level that you're working at has to have like a particular kind of mold of thick skin *and* sensitivity.

GERSTEN: Anyway, that's how I got Williamstown. That's how I went to the High Line, but that did not work well at all. It was the right decision to make at the time for various reasons, but I think it potentially hurt my reputation in the theatre industry because I couldn't really get a theater job after I left the High Line. So, people started calling me to do independent work. Up until this moment, I've been independently working. I've done some commercial producing. I had done some commercial-producing-adjacent stuff both at Naked Angels and at The Public. So, I had a good sense of what commercial producing was. Even at Williamstown, we did a little bit...

MORGAN: Well, *Hair* [2009 revival], right? You worked on that, yes?

GERSTEN: Yeah, *Hair*... *Passing Strange*... all of that... I was part of all the commercial teams. Even *Bloody Bloody Andrew Jackson* [2010]. Then this crazy thing happened last year while I was doing all this various gigging, including *Beetlejuice* [2018], City Center, and various other things when Williamstown called and said they were in trouble and they didn't know what to do. I figured I didn't have a full-time job, so technically I didn't have to leave a full-time job to help them. So, I'm back as the Interim Artistic Director for Williamstown. I was supposed to only do it for a year; I was supposed to be finished by now, so I could try to normalize my path. I'm still there because my work isn't really done there.

MORGAN: So, the City Center is not a full-time thing?

GERSTEN: It's a gig. I'm a consultant. They would like me to be full-time, but I currently can't commit to that, and they understand.

MORGAN: How old are your kids?

GERSTEN: Oh, they're grown. They're twenty and twenty-three. My mom said, "have them young." I met Willie when I was twenty-two; I started dating him when I was twenty-three; and I had kids with him by the time I turned thirty.

MORGAN: You were raising your children while you had more full-time jobs rather than gigging. So now that they're grown, you can, essentially…

GERSTEN: You make it sound like strategy.

MORGAN: I know. I think you've already established in your story that there wasn't much of a strategy and that's okay! Right?! Producers don't really have an outline of how to go about building this kind of career other than just starting. We don't have *many* named producers in the history books other than David Merrick, George Abbott, The Shuberts… what are the patterns? I think it's really important to point out to young people that there's not going to *be* a path. You can try to lay some bricks for your foundation, but you're going to have to go where the tide pushes you and say yes to getting into cabs with the Producer and offer to pay for the cab!

GERSTEN: Yeah.

MORGAN: Dori [Berinstein] talked a little bit about what producers do day to day, and that one could be a producer in name with finance, or one can be "hands-on." What kind of producer do you think you are?

GERSTEN: The producers in finance-only aren't really producers. I would never use that term. I think that is one of the biggest crimes on Broadway – allowing people who invest to call themselves "producers."

MORGAN: They're financiers.

GERSTEN: People can walk into Sardi's and say, "I'm a Producer!" or they can put it at the footer of their email… but they didn't actually make a single decision on any of those shows.

MORGAN: They're an investor, right? There's a difference.

GERSTEN: The problem is you have to finance Broadway shows for millions and millions of dollars. People don't want to be called "investors," they want to call themselves "producers," and they want that Tony Award. They want to go up on that stage.

MORGAN: How often do you find yourself the only woman at a particular table of leadership? How do you feel about that? Do you feel any particular kind of way about that? Do you ever think about it?

GERSTEN: Yes. Well... my reaction to being the only woman at the table is a bit of a f*** it attitude. I mean that it just pushes my chutzpah button. If guys are going to dismiss me, I'm just going to be a little more aggressive in the way I speak about my opinion and see if that changes the way they listen to me.

MORGAN: Mm-hmm. I like it.

GERSTEN: I mean, I was in an employment interview recently. I can't believe they asked this question. They asked me, "Have you ever been the subject of a harassment situation or witnessed harassment?" I was like, "Are you serious? I'm a woman."

MORGAN: Exactly. Yes. Duh. My drive here is actually more about representation and hearing everybody's perspective of how they digest and deal with it. Everybody's a little different. What I'm hearing is most of the women at the Broadway and commercial theatre levels have pressed on to do the work, to get there.

GERSTEN: It's so much better than it was 30 years ago. What I really have learned in these situations, when I find myself in rooms that are male dominated, is that the work isn't *as* good.

MORGAN: I'm not really turned on by a lot of golden age musicals because I've always taken issue with some of the problems in the script as they relate to sexism, racism, and misogyny, etc. However, I was always drawn to the work if Betty Comden was involved... if it was a Comden and Green Show like *Funny Girl, Gypsy, Bells are Ringing*. If Kay Swift was involved or Betty Comden, it seemed like there was at least there was just something in the work that I could relate to a little better than if they weren't. The content has a different kind of depth. What kind of projects and shows really make you tick? What are the characteristics of projects that you really want to work on?

GERSTEN: The ones that turn me upside down. When you go into a thing and you think you know what it is and you think you know what the story is. Like: "boy meets girl"... "I hate my mom"... there's five narratives, right? "I'm a Jew....I'm probably not well liked..." That's a narrative.

MORGAN: Ah... *Parade*![18]

GERSTEN: But I can attend a show like that and say, "I think I know what this is. I think I know what *Parade* is." Then, I see it and it knocks me down and when I walk out of the theater or I'm at intermission – Not only can I feel a thing – because feeling is always good and actually happens in the theatre more often than it doesn't – but actually makes me acknowledge that I not only love this piece of theatre, but I actually need to be a part of it and make sure that other people keep seeing it. I felt my whole worldview shift because of this play, or they made me see a narrative in a new light, or has taught me to empathize in a new way. It really does come down to empathy in a way that cracks me open. That's what I want. That's what I lean into. I have like three projects right now. I woke up this morning and thought about three projects that I want to commercially produce right now, which never happens. Like, I can't think of a time that's happened and I'm thinking about why I'm jazzed by them.

MORGAN: You also produce shows on cruise ships, yes? What incited that?

GERSTEN: It was during my hustle moment when I was gigging. I got a call from an agent at ICM[19] – asking if I wanted to meet with the cruise ship people at Virgin because they were starting a new company of cruise ships. They were meeting with producers and creators and he was helping coordinate. I said yes because I needed a job. I met with them for around 3 hours because they did a whole presentation. Their pitch was: we only enter an industry when we think it needs a change, and the cruise ship industry is unbelievably homogenous. They all look the same, they all act the same. They think that there's something about the adventure of the sea. They said, essentially, "We think there's something about millennials looking for experience. We think we can create that and make a cruise ship for a different generation of people. So, we are disrupting the industry by making everything about this cruise ship different than typical cruise ship; specifically, how that relates to entertainment and this idea that you can only find something at sea that you couldn't find on land. We want to make theatre. We want to make entertainment that you could only find in deepest, darkest Bushwick or Edinburgh. We want to do it with young artists who are about to be famous, and we want you to help us find them." I thought that was f***ing cool. They admitted that they were not producers, so they were coming to producers because they didn't want to produce theatre. They were asking producers to help create an artist collective to make art on our ships. I said, "That is bad ass. Where do I sign?" They wanted me to come up with one show, so I tried to come up with a pitch; but that's not really what I do. They were bringing on a lot of these artists, but they weren't producers, so they needed me to help them. I said, "If you want to really commission new work, you need an Artistic Director. You need me to be able to speak corporate to the artists because they're not going to trust you, and you need me to speak artist language back to you because you're not going to understand them." I convinced them to create

	a job for me and I became the Creative Producer for Virgin Voyages. I helped them make six shows for their line. They were going to launch the company the first week in March 2020 [it launched a few years later, when the industry resumed after the COVID-19 pandemic shutdown]! I loved working for Virgin Voyages. I had a total blast.
MORGAN:	It seems like cool stuff. It does seem different from what I think we're all used to with cruise ship entertainment. Who are the other cool female-identifying producers on Broadway that you're connected to or that we should know about? Who comes to mind when you think of other folks who are doing work like you are?
GERSTEN:	Fiona Howe Rudin, Sammy Lopez, and Ben Holtzman have a cool collective – P3 Productions for Live Entertainment.[20] Rachel Sussman[21] is really young and I think she may be badass; she just did *Suffs* (2022). She works with Diana DiMenna,[22] who is great. Barbara Whitman.[23] Then, there are British ones. Sonia [Friedman][24] is a total bad ass.
MORGAN:	How do you think the industry has changed in the pandemic? What are the pros and cons? What are the ways in which you would want to continue to see the industry to change? Perhaps: elements that you're pushing for or that you've identified need to be more commonplace.
GERSTEN:	At Williamstown, we're [currently] very focused on equity and getting rid of the exploitive practices that are part of the summer-stock model. That's been something I've been very focused on as well as pay equity, and equitable opportunity, which are two different things. How you do that when there was so much privilege assigned to your theatre festival? Not only did [one] need to know [a celebrity] potentially to get there, but also one had to fund their way.
MORGAN:	Right. Right.
GERSTEN:	So, then we were immediately excluding people and bringing people into an elitist community. What does that mean? How were we setting people up for failure there? That's the thing I have look at with Williamstown. As an industry, there's not an artistic director in this country that isn't looking at major failures of the nonprofit model right now and trying to fix their financial situation. The reliance on individuals because the foundations have left, and the corporations have left is so tricky.[25] So, we're working on enhancement models; how they change the act of producing is quite tricky. How do we balance our budget? I don't talk to a single person who's not feeling that.
MORGAN:	Yes, we are seeing this at the regional level. Every theater is currently struggling to make all of the layers work.

GERSTEN: To answer your question about how the industry has changed, I don't think we know yet. We know that something impactful has happened. We know that it's going to shake a lot of things up, and maybe that is for the best, right? I also know that we're about to enter a golden age of writing, for sure.

MORGAN: Absolutely.

GERSTEN: That is thrilling. That is one of the great benefits of the pandemic: the writing is going to be unreal. I already feel it.

MORGAN: Also, the connections, right? Prior to the pandemic, it would have taken me 3 years to get to you… but the technology and accessibility through the development of Zoom culture… But, regarding productions and seasons… I think we're going to have to be more selective. A theater can't just do a five-show season with good ol' *Guys and Dolls* and *Pippin* and the same old material because audiences are going to have to pick and choose what they go to see.

GERSTEN: That's the thing. It might be *Guys and Dolls*. That's the thing; you don't *know* what they're going to pick. Right now, what all the producers that I'm talking to are noticing is that some pieces won't fly without a celebrity because of the event of it. *Into the Woods* is [selling] great when Sara Bareilles is in it, but when you put other people in it, you've lost the *event* of it, which nobody understood back when they made the decision to put *Into the Woods* in the St. James. Daniel Craig in *Macbeth* sells well. But, I think you're right. I think audiences are really going to pick and choose. They're not going to come at the rate that they did before. We know that. There's plenty of evidence for that and no one sees that changing any time soon. That means that you have to do the impossible, which is to make it an event that you can't miss; and that is a very hard kind of producing to do.

MORGAN: What's the next step for you? You're in gig mode with some gigs more consistent than others…

GERSTEN: Yeah, I have four jobs.

MORGAN: You're going full throttle. Are you just going to keep on going at this rate?

GERSTEN: No, I'll fall down. Something's got to give.

MORGAN: What's the main piece of advice you give to an up-and-coming lady boss or someone who looks at you and wants to do what you do? How do they get there?

GERSTEN:

There's no one path. Don't forget to keep listening to your heart.

	You'll never be ready. You'll never have enough money. You'll never have enough real estate. Whatever it is that you think you're waiting for… if you think there's going to be a sign from the universe that says you're ready to have kids, get married, buy a house, whatever…? That one moment will not come. So, you just got to run into whatever it is you want to do. The moments where I have that horrible feeling in my stomach where something makes me feel so scared…? I run toward that feeling.
MORGAN:	Why do you think you run toward it?
GERSTEN:	I have no idea. I'm psychotic? I'm not saying everyone should do that, but I'm just saying that you're never going to be handed the *thing*. It doesn't come. It doesn't happen. The achievements almost never feel like victories. So, do the things that make you grow and the things that make you better at what you do. You're never going to get this moment where someone's says, "Come direct a Tony Award-winning new Broadway musical that's going to set you for life." That moment is never going to present itself like that. So, all you have to do is listen to your heart. Say, "This project is something I believe in more than anything else. I don't have the money for it and I have all these obstacles. At the end of the day, this is the thing I believe in. So, I've got to figure out a way to make it work."
MORGAN:	Last question. How do you engage in self-care? Do you have any hobbies?
GERSTEN:	I do. I have things that ground me. I have practices that help. I feel better when I exercise, but I don't do it enough. When I do, it makes me more resilient. I'm aware of that. When I meditate on a regular basis, I am more resilient. Everybody's different. I mean, I *love* working.
MORGAN:	Same. The work is gratifying, so there's satisfaction, joy, warmth, and accomplishment. It's love, right?
GERSTEN:	Love is at the center of it, for sure. I think that's right.

Dori Berinstein Biography

Dori Berinstein is a five-time, Tony-winning Broadway producer, an Olivier winner and an Emmy Award-winning director, producer, and writer of film and television. Dori's Broadway productions include: *Company* (Tony Award), *Is This A Room*, *Dana H*, *The Prom* (Drama Desk Award), *Legally Blonde* (Olivier Award), *Virginia Woolf* (Tony Award), *Thoroughly Modern Millie* (Tony Award), *One Flew Over The Cuckoo's Nest* (Tony Award), *Flower Drum Song*, *The Crucible*, *Golden Child*, and *Big and Fool Moon* (Tony Award).

As a filmmaker, Dori's award-winning work includes: *ShowBusiness: The Road To Broadway, Carol Channing: Larger Than Life, Marvin Hamlisch: What He Did

For Love (Emmy Award), *The Show Must Go On* and *The Last Blintz*. Dori also produced Ryan Murphy's adaptation of her Broadway Musical *The Prom* for Netflix. (www.dramaticforces.com)

For television, Dori directed and produced *Joshua Bell: Music at Home* (PBS – 2020); and directed, produced and created *Eavesdropping with Alan Cumming* (Oxygen), and *The Isaac Mizrahi Show* (Oxygen).

Dori executive produced and/or supervised over fifty [50] feature, special f/x and/or animated productions, including Isaac Mizrahi's award-winning documentary *Unzipped*, *Dirty Dancing* (both the feature film & TV series) and Jim Henson's *MuppetVision 3-D*. She has executive produced websites for Oprah and President Clinton. She spearheaded creative development and production for DreamWorks Theatricals and has worked as a Producer and/or an Executive for Paramount Pictures, Warner Brothers, Sony Pictures, NBC, MTV, Nickelodeon, Sesame Workshop, Oxygen Media, Vestron Pictures, and Walt Disney Imagineering.

Dori is the recipient of Broadway's Robert Whitehead Award for Outstanding Achievement in Commercial Theatre Producing and the Jacob Burns Vision Award.

She is Co-Founder and CEO of The Broadway Podcast Network, the preeminent home for Broadway-related digital storytelling. (bpn.fm), Co-Founder of The Lights of Broadway Trading Cards (lightsofbroadway.nyc) and serves on the Broadway League's Board of Governors. Dori began her professional career as an Investment Banker in Mergers & Acquisitions for Morgan Stanley.

Interview with Dori Berinstein, via Zoom, October 17, 2022[26]

I worked with/for Dori on the pre-Broadway tryout of *The Prom* in Atlanta at The Alliance in Summer 2016. While I did not see her much, our interactions were always pleasant and I was privy to some decision-making that occurred via Mary-Mitchell Campbell, who was my immediate supervisor as the Music Director. When I came to New York during Previews of *The Prom* in Fall 2018, Dori not only recognized me, but engaged in a kind and fruitful conversation, which meant a lot to me. She had a lot to think about, with a Broadway show in Previews, and acted like I had been there all along. Furthermore, when reaching out to subjects for the book, she was one of the first to respond and eagerly participate.

MORGAN: Let's start at the beginning, which is a very good place to start. On Google, I can find a bunch of credits that you have and see what a rockstar you are. However, I couldn't really find a lot of autobiographical information other than you were an investment banker at one point. Did you pull a "Jessica Vosk" and pivot into the arts from finance?[27]

BERINSTEIN: I didn't pivot into the arts *because* I was frustrated and fed up with the world of investment banking. I *dreamt* of a world in the arts. I *craved* a world in the arts. I wanted that so desperately.

	But I didn't know anybody. I had no contacts… in film, theatre, television, anything…so it took a little while to get there! When I graduated from college, I was advised by a lot of my mentors that it would be great for me to get a foundation in business and finance because it would serve me throughout my career.
MORGAN:	Was that true?
BERINSTEIN:	I do think my investment banking experience was invaluable. I'm really glad I went down that path initially. I was at Morgan Stanley[28] in Mergers & Acquisitions. I learned so much and had amazing experiences. But that choice definitely delayed my entry into the creative side of the entertainment business. With all the tremendous business and finance credentials I had (including graduate schoolwork), it was difficult to convince entertainment companies that they should hire me as a creative person. My resume did not give them reason to believe in my creative potential.
MORGAN:	I've worked in nonprofit theatre, corporate theatre, and education. In my experience, some of the best arts administrators are folks who did theatre or love the arts and then go on to study marketing, business, or finance. That's how they were able to marry the two.
BERINSTEIN:	Right.
MORGAN:	I mean, I've seen so many arts administrators, especially in the nonprofit level, who love theatre and they're great artists, but they have no training in business, marketing, or finance. It's all emotional. They're not making good business decisions.
BERINSTEIN:	Agreed! It has really been invaluable because it gave me a deep comfort level in business. I can see things through that lens, which is extremely helpful. At the same time, choosing Investment Banking to launch my career was painful in some ways. My office at Morgan Stanley was on Sixth Avenue and 50th [Street] in New York. I looked out at Rockefeller Center and NBC and Radio City Music Hall and then the Time-Life building. I wanted to be in those buildings! In the long run, it all worked out!
MORGAN:	Did you grow up doing theatre?
BERINSTEIN:	I desperately wanted to be in school shows, but I had no talent at all. I break windows.[29] I auditioned for productions anyway just to be in the room.
MORGAN:	Wow.
BERINSTEIN:	They didn't have any opportunities for people behind the curtain at all. I kept auditioning…but was never cast.
MORGAN:	High school or college?
BERINSTEIN:	High school and junior high as well. Somehow, that experience didn't dampen my passion for theatre. I was so very fascinated

206 The Producers

	with how shows come together... the behind the curtain [work] and all. My parents were wonderful. Growing up in Los Angeles, they took me to the theater all the time. I was very fortunate. I was at the Dorothy Chandler Pavilion[30] seeing all these incredible touring shows. My love for theatre was deep at a very young age.
MORGAN:	That's awesome. Who were your role models coming up in that time? Could be either from before you inserted yourself into the Broadway and film industry. It could have just been in college or high school or maybe at Morgan Stanley or the finance world or in that transition. Who were the people that you glommed onto or that set really great examples for you? Or opened doors for you?
BERINSTEIN:	Well, there were very few female role models at that time, sadly.
MORGAN:	That's okay. They don't have to be.
BERINSTEIN:	Sherry Lansing: a top executive at Paramount, was a huge influence. To this day, I believe she's the highest-ranking woman ever in the film industry. She was very inspiring to me. I read everything about and followed her career extremely closely. For as long as I can remember, I wanted to be a creator, a storyteller, in the arts...theatre, film and television.

> I've always been platform agnostic...

MORGAN:	A great term! Platform Agnostic.[31]
BERINSTEIN:	My theatre role models include Nell Nugent and Liz McCann, who were the two leading female producers when I was in college. I tried to learn everything I could about their lives, their work...and I tried very hard to meet with them. They were very busy, and a meeting never happened. However, once I became a Broadway producer, both of them took me to lunch. That meant the world to me. Nell and Liz made it clear that women could be forces in theatre too. I'm very grateful to both of them because, at the time, theatre was a white man's world.
MORGAN:	Yeah.
BERINSTEIN:	They really paved the way.
MORGAN:	How does it feel when you're in that room and you're the only gal there?
BERINSTEIN:	It doesn't faze me at all. It never has. When I was in the world of special effects there were very, *very* few women. I grew up with two brothers. I grew up as the only female on the boy's baseball

	and basketball teams. It just never held me back or impacted my work. I certainly wanted female companionship, but all-male rooms certainly didn't deter me.
MORGAN:	Do you feel a particular vibe working with creatives who are women in the room? Like Tesori? Or Nell Benjamin and Heather Hach on *Legally Blonde*? Mary-Mitchell Campbell? Does it affect that room for you at all?
BERINSTEIN:	I love it! It makes it vastly better. It makes it exciting in every way. I love working with women. In fact, Broadway Podcast Network[32] – which I started with Alan Seales 3 years ago – is 90% women. Yeah, so I love that.
MORGAN:	Can you tell me more about the Broadway Podcast Network? How did it take off? How did it end up in your lap? Was that your idea or did it come to you?
BERINSTEIN:	I was, and still am, a podcast nut. I would be driving home way up to Northern Westchester after a late night of theatre. It would be one o'clock in the morning and I'd sit in my driveway listening to a podcast for another hour because I wanted to finish the podcast I was listening to. I love podcasts but I was frustrated because I wanted to listen to theatre podcasts.
MORGAN:	Right! And for a while there were only two or three. There was the *Theatre People Podcast*...
BERINSTEIN:	Just a few, yeah. I just was desperate for more theatre content. One day, I was at Google with the cast and creative team of *The Prom* for Google Talks.[33] I met this guy named Alan Seales, who at the time was running "Talks at Google," and he had a theatre podcast. We started talking and then he invited me to be on his podcast. We talked and talked and talked and talked. By the end of it, we decided to launch a podcast network for theatre! We both felt that there was a need for storytelling about the arts and specifically *about* theatre. We both wanted to give all the great storytellers in our community the opportunity to be creative in a different way. That was 3 years ago. We now have over 150 podcasts. We've done many series and musicals and plays and soap operas and game shows; and it's been spectacular. So many great people in the Broadway community are involved.
MORGAN:	Yeah, it's really spectacular. I think that it's kind of brilliant that folks like you are able to identify where the need is. Where are we saturated in one kind of thing? Then: where is a need? Podcasts have this great feeling like we're in conversation. For some of us, it's nostalgia of our moms and dads watching Oprah or having NPR on. The medium is great and taking advantage of that medium as an education resource is great.

BERINSTEIN: Yes, podcasting is very transporting. It's a very intimate medium because it's right in your ears and you can really lose yourself to the storytelling. What we tried to do is remove the barriers to entry for people in our community – financially and technically. We give them the opportunity to record and have a platform and an audience. We have over eight point five (8.5) million downloads so far. Our audience is huge. As a new business, the pandemic was disastrous for us, obliterating our advertising income. But the pandemic also helped us tremendously because there was an explosion of listeners. The network grew very quickly. It was a wonderful thing also because we were thrilled to be able to play a meaningful role in keeping theatre alive during this very difficult time. We worked very hard to keep our community together and to keep theatre audiences engaged so shows would have an audience when the pandemic was over. It was also really satisfying and thrilling to be able to employ so many actors.

MORGAN: Well, thank you for doing that legwork. I think there's a lot of misconceptions about what producers *do*. In your words, what *does* a producer do? What are your day-to-day [activities]? Let's talk about theatre first. I know you are literally in the intersection of all of these different mediums as well. "Platform agnostic." I love it.

BERINSTEIN: A "hands-on" General Partner Broadway Producer is responsible for every moving part of a show's evolution, from day one forward. We have the full fiduciary responsibility for a show. Limited Partner Co-Producers help raise the financing for a show, and often have the option to help support the show, offering advice, often in the area of marketing and outreach. Limited Partner Co-Pros have no mandatory obligations or fiduciary responsibility.

MORGAN: So, if you throw in a percent, like six or seven percent [6 or 7%]… then when the show recoups, you get that much back of the profit back like a shareholder?

BERINSTEIN: Yes. Being a lead producer of a Broadway show is like being the CEO of that company – of the *Legally Blonde* company, of *The Prom* company. You're responsible for all the moving parts. You're supporting the director, the creative team, the entire company every step of the way from blank page to opening night. There are some producers that focus primarily on the business side. They don't get involved on the creative side. I love being involved creatively as well.

MORGAN: Like a Netflix film.[34]

BERINSTEIN: Yes, yes, yes!

MORGAN: Well, I do know that. I mean, having worked on *The Prom* [with you] as a very small part of it, back in its baby days here [in Atlanta] watching it evolve and being in the room kind of knowing, "Well, that's got to change or this is something that people are going to notice" or whatever it was… whether it was structural or timing or the building of the show… and then coming to see it in previews on Broadway … it was very heartening to see that. To see that you and Bill[35] as producers were listening and making the decisions to lead those changes [to the show]. You weren't precious about holding on to things, but just let the piece change in the way that it needed to change to serve the story moving forward. I thought that that was admirable.

BERINSTEIN: I love the creative evolution of a show. It takes time to get it right. The audience plays such a huge role. When we were in Atlanta with *The Prom* [2016], we learned so much once the show was on its feet playing in front of an audience. Along with our creative team, we paid close attention to audience reaction – what's working, what's not. You have to be open to making many changes. The show is one thing on the page…and it's another thing entirely once it's on stage in front of an audience. I love that process. It's so much fun.

MORGAN: I'll make a statement then a question. I felt like, having been in the room for that process, that those characters seemed to evolve out of the original actors that they were written for.

BERINSTEIN: Our key cast was involved early. However, by the time they joined the production, we had a full script and their characters were fully fleshed out. Certainly, each actor absolutely brought a tremendous amount to their roles and their parts continued to evolve. The objective wasn't: "Let's write a show for this group of actors." There were other actors at various points in time that were considered for the roles, with one exception – the role of Angie…the Fosse dancer. Early in the process, I remember our director Casey Nicholaw asking "Who should play Angie? Someone just like Angie Schworer!" Angie Schworer was definitely the inspiration for "Angie." We were thrilled when she agreed to step into the role.

MORGAN: I can't help but notice that many of the shows that you sign on for center a female protagonist. Is that intentional or coincidental? When one looks back on their dating life and says, "Oh. I have a type." Do you think you have an artistic "type" of show, or do you think that's just coincidence?

BERINSTEIN: That's very funny. I think that it's *not* coincidence. I'm definitely drawn to stories with female protagonists, going all the

	way back to *Dirty Dancing*.[36] I relate to those stories. I feel these are important stories to tell. I also I think they're more compelling. They're stories that mean something… that are saying something that I want said. I'm thrilled to help bring these great female characters to life.
MORGAN:	Regarding shows like *Legally Blonde* that came out when it came out (2007) and [*Thoroughly Modern*] *Millie* that came out when it came out (2002) … As our society deals with political correctness, appropriation and, you know, all of the politics and the social issues that have bubbled to the surface… Do you feel like shows should be revisited and changed not only at the Broadway level, but like at the licensing level? Or that there should be flexibility there? Or do you feel like it's more important to keep them as they were to demonstrate how it was when the show came out and this is okay. What's your take on all of that?
BERINSTEIN:	I feel that there has to be an excellent reason to revive a show. It's an opportunity to tell the story through a different lens… to update it…to "correct it" if necessary. I know that's challenging when the creators aren't around anymore. To me, it's exciting to revisit a show…and help give it new relevance, new importance.
MORGAN:	Right. Like the revival of *My Fair Lady*.[37] Just make her exit after that line.
BERINSTEIN:	Yes. My daughter, Sammi Cannold, did an amazing production of *Evita* at City Center[38] where, without changing a word, the staging conveyed a far more accurate view of who Eva Perón was. It painted a picture that was far more accurate. Consequently, it was an important story to revisit because it corrected history.
MORGAN:	That's also a really great point to make for producers and directors of how staging or how those creative decisions… costume design, scenic design… can help tell the story in a way that's off the page. We study *Evita* and *Jesus Christ Superstar* in my course on musical theatre history because they came from the same era and they both present an interpretive history of a figure. I've seen a lot of different "concepts" on those kinds of shows that either work well or really do not. That's always very interesting to me… how producers and directors say, "Well, this is the concept because we're trying to make this decision without changing the ink." Sometimes it falls flat.
BERINSTEIN:	Right.
MORGAN:	Who are the *other* cool lady or female-identifying producers of Broadway shows that we have to get to know about? Who else do you feel like has been doing the work *like* you?

The Producers **211**

BERINSTEIN: Oh, wow. Well, there are quite a few. Let's see. Sue Frost. Kristen Caskey. Mara Isaacs, Eva Price, Stacey Mindich, Lia Vollack, Barbara Whitman. They've all been doing great work.

MORGAN: Is there anyone currently who serves as your sounding board? To whom you say, "I gotta call you and ask you about this. I don't know what to do."

BERINSTEIN: I reached out to Sue Frost recently.[39] She was very helpful. Also, Music Director Mary-Mitchell Campbell. She's extraordinary.

MORGAN: How do you engage in self-care? What kind of rituals, routines, or boundaries have you created for yourself that might have changed in the pandemic? You know, I think you mentioned that you're a parent. Have you had to be a caregiver throughout this career? What are the ways in which you juggle being a lady boss and a mom and a partner? What do you do to not just burn the hell out?

BERINSTEIN: I have two kids and they're coming into their own. It's wonderful to watch them soar. I try to be the best parent I can possibly be in every way. Certainly, at times, finding and maintaining that work/life balance has been very challenging. I get tremendous joy and inspiration from both my work and parenthood. I feel very fortunate. I do tend to work non-stop…but it's because I do love it. It's thrilling! I'd say for taking care of myself… successful collaborations make me so happy. Otherwise, reading, podcasts and exercise – skiing, basketball, pickleball. Love all that! Always have.

MORGAN: Right. I go for a walk to listen to that album that we need to listen to.

BERINSTEIN: Yes, exactly.

MORGAN: Do you like to travel? Do you *like* to? I mean, you must be back and forth between New York and L.A. a lot.

BERINSTEIN: I've been traveling a great deal throughout the pandemic because I've been shooting a film that has me everywhere. I was in Dubai recently. I love traveling. It's all been for business recently…but I've enjoyed every second.

MORGAN: Right. What do you like better? Film or theatre? Which space do you like being in? Or is it apples and oranges? I get asked this a lot about directing or music directing. They're both something totally different and likable.

BERINSTEIN: I love storytelling and – going back to being platform agnostic – it doesn't matter to me what the medium is. There's just so much incredible satisfaction … just total joy…when I get to create content. Often it comes down to *who* I'm working with and what the collaboration is like? The more passionate I am about telling a particular story, the more I'm going to lose myself to it. I gravitate toward stories that excite me...stories that I feel must be told. Some of those stories are best told on stage, others on screen and some in podcast form.

MORGAN: What are your favorite podcasts that are *not* theater related? I'm a fan of *Freakonomics*, *Serial*, *Revisionist History*, and anything from Brené Brown.

BERINSTEIN: Of course, I listen to all the great podcasts on The Broadway Podcast Network. I also listen to entertainment industry podcasts like *The Powers That Be* and *The Town*. I love *Fresh Air* and *On the Media*. I love all of the *New Yorker* podcasts... *Radio Hour*. I'm a political junkie so any good podcast that takes you inside what is happening in our country and in the world, specifically what's happening in Russia and Ukraine right now.

MORGAN: Do you think the industry changed from the pandemic and have there possibly been pros? Obviously, we know the cons. Now, that we're coming back, are things going back to the way they were? Do you think that's a good thing? What do you think about all that?

BERINSTEIN: I think the world *has* changed. On the positive front, I think that it's great that people have more flexibility regarding how, where and when they can accomplish their work responsibilities.

MORGAN: Yeah, I'm able to do this book because of Zoom culture, because everybody could say "yes" to a Zoom interview. When I had the idea 3 years ago, Zoom culture wasn't a thing yet and I don't think I would have had the access to all of these amazing artists, given my geographical position.

BERINSTEIN: Totally get it. Yes, I agree. I think it's fantastic. It's quite fascinating to think about the excess travel I did in the past. When I was working with DreamWorks, I was on a project in Australia so I went to Australia often for meetings. In hindsight, I could have accomplished quite a bit of the work over Zoom.

MORGAN: Thousands of dollars [in flights]. I'm interested in how it affects the productivity of the of the work in order for us to *do* the work. So that when we're in the room, really focus on the human connection and the storytelling. Are there aspects of Broadway that you wish would change?

BERINSTEIN: I would love to see the community come together... all different areas of our community... to conduct a massive, strategic deep dive to assess how best to navigate through the myriad of challenges that our industry is confronting right now. "Collaboration" is the key word. Dealing with these issues collectively, I believe, will lead to a far more exciting and healthy future.

MORGAN:	Do you think that there's a sense of what's outside of New York – meaning the life of a show after New York and Broadway when the shows are in development? Coming from someone who works in the regions and, again, licensing houses play a big part in the ownership of the estates and the flexibility of certain things. For me, as someone who directs and music directs both professionally and in academia, when we get a script like *SpongeBob* in which Tina Landau[40] wrote this whole two page note on casting ideas saying we could feel free to figure out the keys if we want to gender-bend it…
BERINSTEIN:	Right. Thinking about a life beyond Broadway is imperative.
MORGAN:	For my students, when we did *SpongeBob*, it was the answer to their call to diversify casting and to tell *our* story because we weren't married to certain parameters of the script. The script charges the creative team to cast creatively, in regard to gender and "types"; so, we didn't have to figure out how to work around difficult casting parameters. As a writer, when I'm composing, I'm thinking about the different ways of a show having life after its world premiere. I'm thinking: *How* is someone going to do this at random theater in the middle of nowhere on a bus-and-truck tour?[41] How is this going to be done live? I think about it when all my young people want to sing stuff from *Wicked* and I'm like, "Schwartz, this was *rude.*" This brings me back to that moment in the room on *The Prom* when "Dee-Dee" *used* to sing an E-flat on the word "belt" in "Not About Me," Big #6. We came in one day, and Matt had moved it down to a B-flat and I asked him, "Why did you do that?" He said, "Because we don't need it. I don't need to make the actor do that even though Beth can." He was thinking about stamina. Longevity for me is something that shows a consideration for theatre as a medium outside of New York. You've been in the development of so many big shows that get [reproduced] a lot. Now, *The Prom* is going to get done *everywhere*. How is that a part of your consideration?
BERINSTEIN:	Oh, it's a huge part of our consideration. Using *Prom* and *Legally Blonde* as examples, we were deeply committed to making sure both shows would ultimately be performed in schools all across the country and in regional theaters. For *Prom*, we knew giving ownership of the show to kids everywhere could have a profound impact. We wanted to change hearts and minds. That was our goal.
MORGAN:	Have you seen high schoolers on TikTok? It's so heartwarming. It gives me goosebumps, you know, having been a part of some of that development because seeing these high schools start to

	do it and these regional theaters start to do it… it's going to be so special for them.
BERINSTEIN:	Recently, we had a situation where a high school – Cedar Grove High School in New Jersey[42] – wanted to cancel their production of *The Prom* because of the subject matter. A show about love, tolerance, and acceptance isn't welcome, evidently. It's been life imitating art imitating life. When our cast and our Broadway community heard about this, we organized to march down to this school with picket signs – just like in the show.
MORGAN:	What's the line? "I'm a liberal Democrat from Broadway!"[43]
BERINSTEIN:	All the liberal Democrats from Broadway. We're heading down to Cedar Grove.
MORGAN:	Oh my God, grab your Drama Desks.[44]
BERINSTEIN:	Exactly. It reinforced for all of us why we made the show and why it was extremely important to fight as hard as we did to give this show a great life. And you're one of them. We were all so motivated by the show's message about acceptance, love, tolerance. We wanted that message to get out into the world in a big way. It's so ironic… in Cedar Grove, their last show was *Chicago*, where they're glorifying…
MORGAN:	Murder.
BERINSTEIN:	Yeah! And philandering… and that's okay. I know years ago they did *Sweet Charity*…which had no pushback whatsoever.
MORGAN:	Oh, *that's* okay? *That's fine?!* [*Sweet Charity* features storylines that center around prostitution, misogyny, abuse, sexual promiscuity, and other topics that would be considered Rated-R by cinema standards.]
BERINSTEIN:	Great shows…but for *The Prom* to be that show that's vilified by that community for "content?" It's absurd. It underlines why our deep commitment to a robust life for *The Prom* after Broadway is so critical.
MORGAN:	The most important question I think that I have for you is: What kind of advice would you give to an up-and-coming lady boss? What are the skills that they need to develop? We kind of talked about finance and business, but someone's reading this and they are in college, and they see your name somewhere. They meet you in passing or they say "I want to be *that* person." What are some of the things that they need to keep their eyes and ears open about, or study?
BERINSTEIN:	A few things. One is passion. If you're passionate about telling a story…about bringing a particular show to the stage or screen, you'll figure it out. You'll do whatever it takes to make it happen. I think in theatre and in the arts, it takes that kind

of willpower, perseverance… It takes deep commitment. Second, be a great collaborator. Surround yourself with amazing people! There are so many talented people in our community. Finally: listen, listen, listen! Every project is different, and we all have so much to learn, not just from each other, but from our audience… from our cast. Create a family.

> If you're passionate about telling a story…about bringing a particular show to the stage or screen, you'll figure it out. You'll do whatever it takes to make it happen. I think in theatre and in the arts, it takes that kind of willpower, perseverance… It takes deep commitment.

MORGAN: Broadway is hard.
BERINSTEIN: Broadway *is* hard! It takes a lot of time to get a show to Broadway. You must protect and nurture your "theatre family" through the years of development, though the out-of-town work, through ramp up for opening night on Broadway, etc. Do everything you can to help your team be the best versions of themselves so they can create magnificent art that will resonate…that will change lives…that will bring joy…and that will make the world a better place.
MORGAN: That's the end of the chapter right there.

Notes

1 Hodges, Ben and Frederic B. Vogel, eds. *The Comercial Theater Institute Guide to Producing Plays and Musicals* (Milwaukee: Applause Theatre and Cinema Books, 2006), 79.
2 Ibid, 91–92.
3 Breglio, John. *I Wanna Be a Producer* (Milwaukee: Applause Theatre and Cinema Books, 2016) 25-26.
4 Vogel and Hodges, ed, 110.
5 Oscar Eustis (b. 1958) Artistic Director of The Public Theater since 2005.
6 Coleman, Bud and Judith A. Sebesta, ed. *Women in American Musical Theatre* (North Carolina: McFarland & Company Inc. Publishers, 2008), 156-159.
7 Ibid, 168-171.
8 Gersten, Jenny. 2022. "Interview with Amanda Wansa Morgan", *via Zoom*, December 1, 2022.
9 At the time of our interview, Gersten was helping open the National Broadway Tour of *Beetlejuice* (2022).
10 *The Public Theater* website. Accessed December 1, 2022. See https://publictheater.org/.
11 Feld Ballet – founded in 1973 by Eliot Feld – now exists as Ballet Tech: The NYC Public School for Dance. See https://ballettech.org/about/.
12 "Delacorte Theater" *CentralPark.Com*. Accessed December 1, 2022. See https://www.centralpark.com/things-to-do/attractions/delacorte-theater/.
13 The Eugene O'Neill Theater Center. See https://www.theoneill.org/npc.

14. *Naked Angels* website. See https://www.nakedangels.com/.
15. *Williamstown Theatre Festival* website. See https://wtfestival.org/.
16. Joe Papp (1921-1991) American theatre producer – established The Public Theater.
17. "Mandy Greenfield" *Wikipedia,* American Producer. Updated November 30, 2022. See https://en.wikipedia.org/wiki/Mandy_Greenfield.
18. As of the date of this interview, City Center – where Gersten was employed – was producing a concert version of *Parade* for their 2022 gala, which was very well-received. It was announced to transfer to Broadway in 2023, as of publication of this book.
19. *ICM Partners* website. Accessed December 1, 2022. See https://www.icmpartners.com/.
20. Greg Evans, "Producing Partners Ben Holtzman, Sammy Lopez, and Fiona Howe Rudin Launch P3 Productions for Live Entertainment" *Deadline.* April 6, 2022. See https://deadline.com/2022/04/p3-productions-ben-holtzman-sammy-lopez-fiona-howe-rudin-live-entertainment-1234994746/.
21. *Rachel Sussman* website. Accessed December 1, 2022. See https://www.rachel-sussman.com/about.html.
22. "Diana DiMenna" *Broadway World.* Accessed December 1, 2022. See https://www.broadwayworld.com/people/Diana-DiMenna/.
23. Barbara Whitman is an American theatrical producer who has won multiple Tony and Drama League Awards. See https://barbarawhitman.com/.
24. *Sonia Friedman* website. Accessed December 1, 2022. See https://www.soniafriedman.com/about.
25. Historically, non-profit theaters in America derive their income from a combination of earned income through ticket sales and contributed income from individual donors, and gifts from corporations and foundations. Often, the combined income comprises the greater percentage of the total budget. When the country is in a recession or faces hard economic times due to a pandemic or other factor, revenue goes down and costs go up.
26. Berinstein, Dori. 2002. "Interview with Amanda Wansa Morgan", via Zoom, October 17, 2022.
27. Jessica Vosk is an American stage performer, known for playing Elphaba in *Wicked* on Broadway and for her personal story of pursuing a career in professional theatre after a career on Wall Street. See https://abcnews.go.com/Entertainment/wall-street-wicked-broadway-star-risked/story?id=57937051.
28. American-based financial firm. See https://www.morganstanley.com/.
29. A reference to the stereotype that poor or shrill singing would shatter glass.
30. Live music venue in Los Angeles, CA.
31. The definition of "platform agnostic" comes from the tech world. See https://www.techopedia.com/definition/23666/platform-agnostic. However, in this context, Berinstein is referring to the many mediums through which one can digest art: theatre, film, television, internet, podcast, radio, etc.
32. *The Broadway Podcast Network.* See https://broadwaypodcastnetwork.com/.
33. Broadway's *The Prom* at Talks at Google: December 13, 2018. See https://www.youtube.com/watch?v=vKukxyF0ngo.
34. As of 2022, Netflix is a popular internet service for streaming (and producing) media.
35. Bill Damaschke, producer (b. 1963).
36. Popular American film from 1987 for which Berinstein served as a Production Executive.
37. The 2018 revival of *My Fair Lady*, directed by Bartlett Sher, featured a change to the staging that made a political statement that diverted from traditionally staged productions. See https://datebook.sfchronicle.com/theater/s-f-theater-director-bartlett-sher-shifts-my-fair-lady-from-frothy-romance-to-social-critique.
38. New York City Center is a professional arts organization and performance space. See https://www.nycitycenter.org/.
39. Sue Frost is an American theatrical producer, associated with Junkyard Dog Productions. See https://www.ibdb.com/broadway-cast-staff/sue-frost-71850.

40 See Tina Landau in Chapter 4.
41 "Bus and Truck" is a term for touring shows that are either non-union or produced by a non-profit entity that results in a lower budget, and therefore, the company traveling by a bus instead of airplanes. These tours often contain shorter runs at each location, meaning more travelling than performing. Higher scale touring productions will travel by plane and stay at a location for a longer period of time, which is easier on the performers.
42 In Fall of 2022, Cedar Grove High School faced an issue where their planned production of *The Prom* was being shut down by conservative administration and parents. As the Broadway community was catching wind of the situation and mobilizing to support the students who wanted to produce the show, the show was cleared to perform. See https://www.lgbtqnation.com/2022/10/high-school-musical-saved-prom-will-go-students-devastated/.
43 A spoken line from *The Prom* (Act 1, Scene 6).
44 The Drama Desk Awards are a New York awards focused on Off-Broadway content. There is a comedic line in *The Prom* when a character brings their Drama Desk award on a trip to tout their superiority over a colleague who brings their Tony Award.

6
MANAGEMENT

Introduction

I'm not a stage manager, but I love them, I work closely with them, and I understand them. I love all of the things that they do: paperwork, organization, structure, and serving the art in a way that is humble, all-encompassing, and irreplaceable. I have always been professionally enamored with the stage managers who know how to run a room efficiently, with authority and grace. They show up at the opening night after party to connect with the cast and company members with a bottle of booze and a smile as if they hadn't handled a whole slew of dumpster fires earlier in the day at work. My first semester at college, I ran crew for a production of *Chicago*, which was stage managed by a sophomore named Wade Handy. I was awe-struck with how this college student – the same age as some of his peers and younger than some of them – loudly and crisply gave commands to the cast in rehearsal; seemed to glide through paperwork, notes, and cues with our very respected professors who were on their feet directing and choreographing; then was the first person to greet me at the door of the late-night party. I truly admired him for the way that he was able to switch gears and the way that the actors respected him. It inspired me to take on leadership roles among my peers while still in college as a music director and director. Perhaps I, too, could find that balance. I often wondered if it was a matter of organizational skills or leadership skills. Spoiler alert: it's both.

In J.P. Kotter's book *Force for Change: How Leadership Differs from Management*, he lays out differences between leadership and management. I've spent a lot of time thinking about that comparison and ended up asking our interview subjects about it. He indicates that management establishes order and consistency through planning and budgeting; organizing and staffing; and controlling and problem solving. He states that leadership establishes change and movement through

DOI: 10.4324/9781003324652-6

establishing direction; aligning people; and motivating and inspiring.[1] Stage managers engage in both. Kotter asserts: "Leadership, by itself, never keeps an operation on time and on budget year after year. And management by itself never creates significant, useful change."[2] While a team of the director, the writers, and a producer (on an original show) establishes a vision, the stage manager ensures that the vision is executed in the room and maintained after opening. They deal with logistics and interpersonal matters. They make the entire production run smoothly on stage and backstage, in pre-rehearsal, rehearsal, and in performance.[3] With a Broadway run, this could mean maintaining a show for many, *many* years. The actions of an effective stage manager, according to Lawrence Stern in his book *Stage Management (6th Edition)* include: assuming responsibility, keeping their cool, thinking ahead, and staying organized, efficient, punctual, and dependable. Sounds like the qualities of both a manager and a leader.[4]

Job Descriptions

The titles and descriptions of the stage management team vary per market (Broadway vs. regional theatre): however, our interview subjects give some insight as to why.

Production Manager – A Production Manager (PM) oversees production aspects of an entire company or season within a company. They create and maintain production schedules, working with individual show stage managers to keep rehearsal schedules current; and they align those various components. They work with a producer, general manager, and/or artistic director to maintain production budgets. They work with various parties to keep paperwork current and in alignment with a company's policies and legal structures. These topics can range from finances to union rules to royalties. A PM is mostly used at the regional level or in institutions (think: college departments) to carry out a number of organizational duties that would be hired by a general manager at the Broadway level.

Production Stage Manager – This term has yet to be clearly defined by the *Actor's Equity Handbook*. In fact, many stage managers take umbrage with the title of the union that represents actors *and* stage managers "Actor's Equity." Nonetheless, the production stage manager on a Broadway show is essentially serving as a PM for that particular show as it runs, focusing on logistics, scheduling, and organizational matters; while the stage manager focuses on managing the "room," most likely "calling" cues for the show and working with the assistant stage managers to carry out logistical tasks night to night.

Stage Manager – The stage manager runs the room. The stage manager runs the show. They are the primary leader in the rehearsal room, the technical process, and the production process when the show is running. When working on a show with actors who are members of Actor's Equity (the union), the stage manager must also be an "Equity" member, which is the case for *every* Broadway show (or "production contract"). Regional contracts vary, based on the theater's contracts with the unions. *The Actor's Equity Production League Rulebook* (2019–2022) states: "There shall be [...] no less than one Stage Manager and two Assistant Stage Managers employed in a musical production" [Section 68.A].[5]

Assistant Stage Managers – The assistant stage manager carries out a bevy of duties. While the term implies that these individuals are apprenticing by "assisting" in some way, this might be true at a regional level, but at the Broadway level, these are fully qualified individuals working as a team with the stage manager to execute the nightly tasks of running the show, working with the show crew, cast, band, and house staff. The Equity handbook indicates the presence of a "First Assistant Stage Manager" and "Second Assistant Stage Manager," to delineate tasks that each employee may or may not engage in, mostly referring to covering roles *onstage* [Section 68.G]. The numbering also refers to the hierarchy of responsibility should the Stage Manager not be present. There is additional language in the handbook about "Short-term Stage Managers," replacements, and "Temporary Stage Managers."

Additional personnel that might work with the management team at the Broadway level include but are not limited to: Child Wranglers (who manage child actors while they are at the theater), Tutors (for said child actors), Covid Coordinators (as of 2021), and Production Assistants.

Notable Figures

Lisa Dawn Cave's resume is vast. She has served as a production stage manager, stage manager, and/or assistant stage manager on over 20 Broadway shows, dating as far back as the revival of *Show Boat* in 1994. Credits include *Frozen* (2018), *Shuffle Along, Or the Making of the Musical Sensation of 1921 and All That Followed* (2016), *Fun Home* (2015), *Rocky* (2014), *The Color Purple* (2005), *Woman in White* (2005), and *Caroline, or Change* (2004).

Marybeth Abel is most known for her long run on the stage management team of *Wicked* (2004). She also served on stage management teams for *Sweet Charity* (2005 Revival), *Fosse* (1999), *Five Guys Named Moe* (1992), and *Les Misérables* (1987).

Ruth Mitchell (1919–2000) worked on over 40 Broadway shows in any of the following capacities: production stage manager, performer, production assistant, assistant director, associate producer, executive producer, and assistant to the director. She worked closely with Broadway greats Hal Prince and Jerome Robbins.

Barbara Mae-Phillips worked on Broadway shows for over 30 years with credits that include *Phantom of the Opera* (1988), *Peter Pan* (1979 Revival), and dozens of plays.

Peyton Taylor Becker has worked in various stage management roles on *Six* (2021), *The Prom* (2018), *Something Rotten* (2015), and the *Mean Girls* National Tour.

Holly Coombs has worked in various stage management roles on *Company* (2021 Revival), *Mean Girls* (2018), *Tuck Everlasting* (2016), and *Aladdin* (2014).

Jennifer Rae Moore has served on stage management teams for a dozen Broadway shows including *My Fair Lady* (2018 Revival), *The King and I* (2015 Revival), *The Bridges of Madison County* (2014), and *The Coast of Utopia Part I* (2006), *Part II* (2006), and *Part III* (2007).

Shakira Niles has served as the Stage Manager for *The Color Purple* (2015 Revival), *The Play That Goes Wrong* (2017) and *Tina* (2019); as well as Assistant Stage Manager for *Finding Neverland* (2015) and *The Gershwins' Porgy and Bess* (2012).

Karyn Meek was the Production Stage Manager for *Paradise Square* (2022) and *Natasha, Pierre, and the Great Comet of 1812* (2016); and a Production Assistant on *Fiddler on the Roof* (Revival 2004).

Tiffany Robinson has served as an Assistant Stage Manager on *MJ the Musical* (2022) and *The Cher Show* (2018), and as Stage Manager for *Motown The Musical* (2016).

INTERVIEWS

Beverly Jenkins
Amanda Spooner

Beverly Jenkins Biography

BEVERLY JENKINS, 2020 Tony Honors recipient for Excellence in the Theatre, has been managing Broadway productions for close to 30 years. Ms. Jenkins is the Production Stage Manager for the Tony Award-winning Best Musical *Hadestown*. Other shows she has worked on include *A Bronx Tale, Fully Committed, Amazing Grace, Living On Love, Holler If Ya Hear Me, Machinal, Godspell, Bengal Tiger at the Baghdad Zoo, In the Heights, Shrek: The Musical, Avenue Q, Aida, Sweet Charity, Oklahoma!, The Lion King, Bring In Da Noise/Bring In Da Funk, Miss Saigon*.

Off Broadway: *A Bronx Tale: The Musical* (Paper Mill Playhouse); *Bad Jews, If There Is I Haven't Found It Yet* (both at Roundabout).

Ms. Jenkins is on the boards of Broadway Cares/Equity Fights Aids and Beyond the Stage Door, and president of D.I.V.A., Inc: The Society for Women in the Arts. She is an adjunct professor at New York University's Tisch School of the Arts and The Conservatory at Shenandoah University. She is a proud mom, wife, and Howard University graduate.

One can listen to Beverly discuss her amazing career, being a mother of 7 (Yep. 7!) and of course, B&B: Access for Stage Managers of Color on an episode of the *Mamas Talkin' Loud* podcast.[6]

Interview with Beverly Jenkins, via Zoom, November 15, 2022[7]

MORGAN: Hello, *Miss* Beverly Jenkins. I was introduced to you on email via one of my best friends from college, Morgan Rose Johnson, who called you Miss Beverly. Is that what people call you in the biz?

JENKINS: I have graduated to a *Miss* Beverly. Yes, I have. I used to be Beverly. Yes, I accept that. It comes with age.

MORGAN: And experience, wisdom, and clout! You have this illustrious career... a prolific amount of Broadway shows: plays...musicals... comedies... dramas... epics. You have called them all.[8] You have done it all. Please tell me in a nutshell how you got from where you grew up to Broadway.

JENKINS: All right, let's start. I am a New Yorker from Queens.

MORGAN: I can hear it in your dialect.

JENKINS: Thank you. I hold on to it. They tried to beat it out of me. It's not going to happen!

MORGAN: It makes me want to listen!

JENKINS: I grew up in Queens. I always knew I would be in theatre; never even had a second thought about it. There was one time where I really thought I wanted to be an endocrinologist, because I thought that was the person who would study of why women couldn't get pregnant. That interested me because I come from a mother who every time my father looked at her, she got pregnant. I'm the ninth of twelve [12] children. I found endocrinology interesting for about seven months. It's still something that needs to be studied. But I thought *I* wanted to study it, you know...

MORGAN: to be a reproductive endocrinologist...

JENKINS: Exactly. So, that's what I thought I was going to do for a hot second. Moving on. I was always doing the shows in high school. Always, always. I went to college at Howard University[9]; I got in as a performer. In the first semester, we all auditioned for the spring musical, which was *The Wiz*. Who doesn't want to be in *The Wiz*? I was the best in my high school... so I went with all of the other kids and I auditioned. Fast forward to when they put up the cast list and I was looking down, and I knew I wasn't going to be Dorothy.... I looked in the ensemble and obviously all my friends are up there, and I don't see my name. Then, I get to the bottom and it says: "Assistant Stage Manager: Beverly Jenkins." And I'm like... "Okay!" It could have said "Props..." and I would have said, "I'm on it. You're gonna have the best props ever," just because that's how much I just needed to be around the process... it didn't matter. I also knew that I was not a trained dancer. I move very well. I am not a trained dancer. All the trained dancers filled up all those spots.

MORGAN: Yeah, gotta have that tornado!

JENKINS: Yeah, well, you know, I would have worn it out. I would have *worn it OUT!*

MORGAN: I have music directed that show. It's the most fun show to play. That funk score is so good. It's so, so good.

JENKINS: Well, *we* had Louis Johnson who choreographed the movie! He came down and choreographed and directed our show.
MORGAN: Oh, man!
JENKINS: So, I was told that as an assistant stage manager, I had to be back early from winter break, so we could have production meeting. Okay, whatever. I'm there, I'm there. So, January 2, I walk into the production meeting. I'd never been in a production meeting… had never heard about a "production meeting." Everybody's sitting around… all my professors and the folks who were in charge of tech and all that stuff. They're sitting there and they start talking about … and it really was *this*: They start talking about how the color of the cyc [cyclorama] would affect the color of the costumes. And I was thinking, "I'm sorry, *what did you just say?!*" The way that those brains started thinking about the little details… you know, as a performer, I didn't think about that. But my brain started seeing it and I was like, *This* is heaven right here! I found my place. I found *my* theater in that production meeting, and it was great.

Then, I learned what stage management was from a wonderful senior [student] named Leslie Gaskins. I believe she's in Philly. I want her to know how much she influenced me to do what I do. You would think it's always a teacher. I mean, I had a great teacher named Professor George Epting… but Leslie Gaskins was just as influential on me as Professor Epting was. I think it's important that if my story is any place that she's there. I learned about Sign-In-Sheets, and I learned about calling people when they're late. I learned about taping a floor… just all this stuff! Fast forward to the show. In my freshman year, Howard University announces that they are going to start a new concentration within the major. I was on the acting track… and they announced that they were going to do an "arts administration track" on the undergrad level. So, I figured I can learn acting almost anywhere. No one's going to tell you the secrets of the business. So, I was selected for that. The Assistant Dean, who was in charge of the program, called me in his office and talked to me, and my freshman advisor talked to me. It was very easy for me to switch over because I had already fallen in love with stage management. Also, I was looking at the actors and there's this desperation that they had that I didn't. You know.

MORGAN: Oh, I know. I made the switch, too. On the other side of the table, I can control my destiny. I feel like I'm still a part of the art and I'm serving the art rather than begging to do the art.
JENKINS: In order to do that [performing], you have to know and you *cannot* do or don't *want* to do anything else. If you're going to *make it*, you have to know that you don't want to do anything else. I wanted to help them reach the goals. So, here I am.

MORGAN: So, who were your other role models along the way? When you think about who you are today as a leader, who are some of those role models for you?

JENKINS: I had a brother – God rest his soul – my brother Michael was always supportive of me in the arts. When I was young – this is late 1960s, early 1970s – he had a garage band, and I was his go-go girl!

MORGAN: Yaaaaaas! I love that.

JENKINS: He also taught me about money because he would never let me win in Monopoly.

MORGAN: (*laughing*) In Queens? Yelling at each other in Queens.

JENKINS: Oh yeah, up late in the summer; we're up playing Monopoly.

MORGAN: Gotta get that Park Place!

JENKINS: There you go! I like the little Baltic and those little purple ones because everybody's going to turn the corner and have to pay you!

MORGAN: It's all about strategy. It's all about getting one in every category.

JENKINS: Yeah, it's a strategy.

MORGAN: What a stage manager, learning strategy like that.

JENKINS: There you go. So, I have a really good best friend named Liz Cone. I believe she was the receptionist at Allen Wasser Associates[10] – it was a general management office – and they were bringing in *Five Guys Named Moe* from the London West End for its first run on Broadway. They were specifically looking for Black stage managers to be on the team.

MORGAN: What year was that?

JENKINS: It's going to be 1991 and 1992. It was probably '91 when I applied and '92 when the show went up… '93 when it closed. She told me that I needed to send my resumé because they're looking for Black stage managers. I'm like, "Okay…" A month and a half passed. She reached out and said, "you didn't send your resumé in yet." So, finally she's like, "I'm going to kill you." So, I sit down, and I do it and I send it in. I get a call to come in for an interview. I go. I know exactly what dress I had on. I go and I interview with Marybeth Abel – who was going to be the PSM [Production Stage Manager]… she's over on *Wicked* now… she's my stage management mom… and Richard Jay-Alexander. He was the lead producer and Cameron Mackintosh's right-hand person. So, I met with them, and we talked, and I remember they asked me, "What is it you like about stage managing?" I told them that I like making the montage of all the pieces come together. What I saw was everything coming together and that I would like to make that happen. Marybeth will tell you now that once I walked out the room, they looked at each other, and said, "She's hired." I don't know what it was. I don't know what I did. They said they had to meet with other people, but they knew they were hiring me. But Richard Jay and Marybeth have always been in my life since then. They've been a great support to me. So, I was the Production Assistant on *Five Guys Named Moe* and then Marybeth left *Moe* to go back over *Les Miz* [*Les Miserables*], and I got hired as the "second" and that was my first Broadway contract. That was 30 years ago.

MORGAN: So, your first Broadway contract was on a Black show in a Black space.

JENKINS: It was on a show with all Black men in it. Once Marybeth left, it was an all-Black stage management team. The director and the choreographer were Black. But everyone dealing with money and management was white.

MORGAN: Your career includes a lot of shows that are race specific and some that are not.

JENKINS: I would say that most of my shows are actually not Black-centric.

MORGAN: Mm hmm.

JENKINS: Let me tell you a little story. So, let's go back to November of 2002. I was about 101 months pregnant [not a typo] with my third child. I was doing *Oklahoma* [2002 Revival], which had 40 cast members and there were three actors of color. One was the swing, and he was an Indian man: Rami Sandhu. We had one female in the ensemble and one male in the ensemble, and everybody else was white except for me. So, we were doing the Parade [Macy's Thanksgiving Day Parade] and my assistant, Stephen Gruse, was approached by a tall Black woman who later I found out was one of the ADs [Assistant Directors, of the MTD Parade]. This is what I saw from far away… I see her looking at him and talking to him and he pointed to me. He kept trying to clarify but she looked confused. She walked over to me, and she says, "I'm sorry. Excuse me. I'm looking for the Stage Manager for *Oklahoma*." And I said, "That's me." And she goes, "You have to excuse me a minute. I've been doing this for about ten years now, and this is the first time I've ever seen this." I said, "I know! I'm in charge of all these white people!" I knew what she was thinking. And of all shows… *Oklahoma*! Not *Hairspray*. You know? *Oklahoma*. So, I was like, "Yeah. I'm in charge."

MORGAN: How do you feel when you're in spaces with people who share your identity, either in race or gender? Does that make a difference to you? Does it *feel* different to you?

JENKINS: It does feel different because, let me tell you, I know people think that I look in a room and notice there's not a lot of women here. That's not the first thing in my head. I look to see who else has a shared culture with me. Often, I'm the person with *that* culture. Then, if I'm doing a show that has Brown people or Black people in it, I'm looked at as the expert on Blackness all of a sudden.

MORGAN: Wow.
JENKINS: All of a sudden, I'm the hair consultant, which I've done on many shows and said no, they have to pay extra for that. You know, I have had to say that.

I have a director, who I love and adore, who will just openly turn to me and ask, "Does that sound right?" And I'll say, "No, it doesn't. That sounds racist." And he goes, "I thought so." You know what I mean? But I have to give credit to them for half-hearing that something might not be right. I have been blessed to be around people who actually *do* care and are trying to do better and *are* doing better. You know, you *hire* what you see in the mirror. People are lazy.

MORGAN: Say it louder for the people in the back!
JENKINS: I'm going there. It's more than seeing that there's only two other women in the room. I'm seeing that, sometimes, I'm *the* color in the room. That's what I see more than I'm the only female.
MORGAN: Sure. How about age?
JENKINS: I'm old now. (*They both laugh.*) I'm old now. I'm 58. I'm good to go! I don't care. I'm still here. I'm breathing. I'll be 60 soon, and I'm going to celebrate, so there you go.
MORGAN: Amazing. Congratulations.
JENKINS: Thank you.
MORGAN: Who are some of your favorite collaborators? Who motivates you say "yes" to a job right away if you know they're going to be in the room?
JENKINS: Who would make me want to say "yes"? Wayne Cilento [choreographer, director, performer], who I did say "yes" to, who I'm working with on *Dancing*. I love and adore being around Wayne. Kathleen Marshall. That's my girl, Kathleen Marshall… Jerry Zaks [director] … Jason Moore [director]… Those are my four my top choice[s] because they make a great room, and they do great work. I enjoy working *with* them and I enjoy working *for* them. There's a difference. So, those are my top four directors that I can think of, right off the top of my head. I say, "Ooh! Let me see if I can fit this into my schedule!"
MORGAN: People, project, pay, right?
JENKINS: Then, there are some general management offices that when they call, I try to make it work. There's one company that I like a lot. There's one company that I asked to please *not* call me ever again.
MORGAN: It's interesting how the dynamics of working relationships sometimes mirror personal relationships in the arts. Right? How we feel walking into a room is *important* and sometimes it is just not worth whatever that dynamic is.
JENKINS: It can be soul-sucking.

MORGAN: Yeah; and if you come home at the end of every day and you feel drained because of those people, you're not going to want to go back. There's a difference between busy and stressed working with certain individuals in the business causes more stress than necessary. I don't want to be busy *and* stressed! That's not sustainable, long term, even those some folks have been working through all of that.

JENKINS: Some of us have been. But it's okay, right?!

MORGAN: You're still here! You've worked with some *real* celebrities, right? "A-Listers" like Robin Williams on *Bengal Tiger* [*at the Baghdad Zoo*], Christina Applegate in *Sweet Charity*... And now you're working with Samuel L. Jackson... [on *The Piano Lesson*, running during this interview in 2022]...

JENKINS: Samuel L... yes.

MORGAN: Right. What's that like? Dealing with their management and all that? Does that faze you at all?

JENKINS: I really deal with the *people*. I deal with the person one-on-one, more. I know their management needs things; I understand their business and what their management needs to know. Their handlers and their "people" need to know what's going on. When I'm brought into the conversation, I just give the information.

MORGAN: Here you go.

JENKINS: Take it. Run with it. Then they figure out that they're not missing a whole bunch of information anyway. When it comes to scheduling of their stuff: no problem. I enjoy working with the *people*. I enjoyed working with Christina [Applegate]. I enjoyed working with Robin [Williams]. You can't be in this position and be starstruck. You can respect people, but I respect *anybody* who comes into my space. If you give me reason *not* to respect you, I'm still going to treat you professionally. But I'm going to respect anyone who comes into my space. I just I love working with them. Jesse Tyler Ferguson, he's still a friend.

MORGAN: Yeah, well, I've found that some of these folks are where they are [in their careers] because they're *actually* lovely, and good, and professional. They've got their stuff together.

JENKINS: We are working with *people* today who might, literally, a year from now, have an Oscar in their hand. Ariana DeBose. You know what I mean? You don't know who is going to be that breakout person.

MORGAN: Right. She was the "Bullet" and now, she's an Oscar-winner.[11]

JENKINS: Treat people like people. I love my baby girl, Ariana.

MORGAN: She is amazing.

JENKINS: She works her ass off. I'll tell anyone who doubted her: she works her ass off. She really does. She always has. Robin Williams was great. You also can't have him come into the building and feel he has to be "on." He was Robin Williams: a person who's coming to do his gig. People wanted Robin to make them laugh. His job was not to make you laugh, unless you bought a ticket. Do the job and let them do their job. Respect people, you know? Christopher Jackson. I've known Chris Jackson since he was in *Lion King*... baby Chris Jackson. But he's my friend, you know what I mean? So, you work with people, and you make the space comfortable for them to come into.

MORGAN: What are the skills or personality traits that you think a stage manager or production stage manager has to have to work at the Broadway level? Other than knowing how to do paperwork?

JENKINS: Paperwork is the big thing. It's the paperwork and you have to be able to work at all these different levels. I think it's the same thing. I think that no matter what level you are, I don't change. I was just doing *Dancing* out at the Old Globe [San Diego], which is regional. I don't change how I behave. I don't treat people in my cast or management team differently because I'm working there as opposed to working on Broadway. That's not how you build a career. That's not how you learn as a stage manager. You are going to learn something new at every experience. So, what is the difference? The rules are different. That's the big thing. The rules are different; so that's why we got books! You take a second... you flip through... you read how the rules are different. It's important that you, as a stage manager, have patience. It's important that you as a stage manager kind of *like* people a little bit... maybe.

MORGAN: Technical directors don't *have* to like people. I'm married to a TD, so I can say that.

JENKINS: The stage manager *might* have to appreciate people. As a stage manager, you have to be a good listener and you have to not overreact. You have to *hear* what people are saying because maybe the words coming out of their mouth are not what they mean. *Hear* what they're saying and then react to *that*. Oftentimes, people will say one thing and then you have to work to get to the bottom of the real issue.

MORGAN: I did this leadership program last year through my university, and we talked a lot about the difference between management and leadership, which is interesting because your job title is stage *manager*. However, I personally think that a lot of leadership skills go into stage management. I'll give you a little definition that I found: "The role of management is to control a group or a group of individuals in order to achieve a specified objective. Leadership is the ability of an individual to influence, motivate, and enable others to contribute to the organization's success."[12] Do you think that a production student manager, or stage manager, is more of a leader or a manager?

JENKINS: Leader, no question. First off, that use of the word "control"... there's no need to control people. I'm not controlling anybody. It's not about control. What I liked about that statement was the phrase "to enable people" because that's where I see myself more. I've been called an enabler, in a good way. I had a roommate who was an actress and in college she would call me her fairy godmother because I made things possible. I am now a grown, grown lady. That is what I do: I make things possible. I enable the director to come into the room and direct. I enable the actors to come in and feel that the space is safe to do what they need to do. I enable management to do what they need to do so that they can get all their stuff together. I'm an enabler and I enjoy that role.

MORGAN: I forgot to ask this question earlier, but you mentioned your roommate, so I'm going to loop it in now. How do you feel like going to an HBCU impacted your career?

JENKINS: I chose to go to an HBCU because I didn't want to be in school, and not get a part, and wonder if it because I was brown. I needed to take that off the table and I needed to get an education and not have my education compromised because I was brown. So, my neighbor down the street had gone to Howard – one of my sister's best friends. But most importantly, Roberta Flack, the singer, went to Howard. If it's good enough for Roberta Flack, it's good enough for me.

MORGAN: Period. As the young people say.

JENKINS: With a "t" on the end. "Periodt."

MORGAN: I teach at Kennesaw State, which is near Atlanta, where we have HBCUs... Spelman, Morehouse, Clark Atlanta... it is interesting to see and speak with individuals who attend an HBCU vs. a PWI[13] and observe communication styles and confidence levels.

JENKINS: I never doubted that I would be working in my field. When I first got the PA [Production Assistant] job on *Five Guys Named Moe*, my friend had to beg me to send in my resumé because I was *busy!* I was traveling. It was also a world where all I saw was white people. When I think worldly, I saw white people, and then I saw a Black show or two.

MORGAN: Right.

JENKINS: I was traveling with musicians and dance companies. And I'm not talking about on a bus. I had a passport, boo! I was movin'. I was going on a plane, going to *Liechtenstein*.

MORGAN: That's it! Why would you put yourself in these spaces where you have to wonder if people are going to be rude to you or not? You can just go to Liechtenstein!

JENKINS: Oh, well!

MORGAN: She had a passport! (*laughter*) Please tell me in your own words how a stage manager does their art within the process of putting up a show, rather than it feeling like service *to* the art. Tell me about how it's *your* art.

JENKINS: I like to see the whole picture and hear what everybody needs. My art happens when I can put it together seamlessly. So, I can see it and put it together seamlessly OR sometimes I actually get to suggest if we did "X-Y-and-Z" because I can see down the line; that's the way the stage management brain should work.

MORGAN: Right. You're thinking about how you're going call the show... how is it going to track with that person having to get off for a costume change and get back on...?

JENKINS: Exactly, you track all that stuff. You weigh things like that and see it differently. The director does the same thing. That's how their brains work, you know, where they can see the full picture. That's why they're directors. My art comes into play in putting up the show; not "calling" it, because that's a whole different art, and not everyone can do that well... but in rehearsing it and putting it up and thinking about how to make things seamless so that the audience doesn't even see half of it.

MORGAN: Do you, as a production stage manager, ever get to call a show anymore?

JENKINS: I call three to four times a week.

MORGAN: Because you want to or because that's part of the contract?

JENKINS: It's not in my contract; it's just me.

MORGAN: Do you like calling?

JENKINS: Sometimes I do. Sometimes I don't because I got too many things to do, you know? But I what I like about calling is trying to do it perfect. There's always the challenge of: I'm going to call *all* the cues today!

MORGAN: Oh yeah, we love a challenge. We love when those standbys are delicious. I mean, I remember when they put up that video when they were doing the Live TV musicals like *Hairspray* or *Grease* ... did you see the video where the calling was overlaid with the television shots? I thought it was the most educational tool that we could provide stage managers because *that's* stressful! Live television... moving set... such finesse, like it's choreographed, right?

I feel the same way as a music director in that I aim to conduct a perfect show. I want to get that page turn at the right spot. I want to cue that entrance right at the end of that line and also not screw up playing with my right hand when it goes down [to the piano].

JENKINS:	Yeah.
MORGAN:	Well, how have you been a caregiver during your career? Obviously, the answer's yes... how do you juggle that?
JENKINS:	I am a step-mom to four and a mother of three. They all lived in the same house, so I'm mother of seven.
MORGAN:	Whew.
JENKINS:	I'm currently a co-caregiver, my husband really does take the brunt of the work, of my 91-year-old mother who needs help with everything. We got custody of her during the pandemic. So, my husband recently retired and he's like, I'm going to take care of mom. So, he takes care of my mom.
MORGAN:	Can I ask what he what field he was in?
JENKINS:	He was a spot op[14] ... an electrician.
MORGAN:	Did he work on your shows?
JENKINS:	We met on *[The] Lion King*. He's the only person in theater I ever dated. I never dated anybody in theater before.
MORGAN:	Yeah. Oh, blessings and curses, right?!
JENKINS:	That was 23 years ago, yep.
MORGAN:	Twenty-three years! Congratulations! Wow!
JENKINS:	So, when I had my first child, I was a single mom. I had a participating partner, but we did not live together. I lived with my sister and we would tag team taking care of Oscar. I also had great, great neighbors because I was living in the ancestral home, as my friend calls it, where I grew up. So, my neighbors next door were my parents' age and older. Sometimes if I had to leave, I would bring the baby over to them and they would watch Oscar because he was like their grandson. So, it really takes a village. I never stopped working. I [gave birth to] Oscar. March 30th is when I got "kicked out" of the theater because the prop guy said, "I'm not going to be mopping up this water when your water breaks! You've got to get out of here!" He was only sort of kidding, but they kicked me out.
MORGAN:	I'm going to say, for the record, that you're laughing, but my jaw dropped.
JENKINS:	It was all right. They kicked me out on March 30, and then on April 25, I had Oscar. The beginning of July is when I took over as the PSM for *Bring In Da Noise, Bring In Da Funk*. So, that was only a two-and-a-half-month break. Then, I started on *Lion King* and met the person who would become my husband.
MORGAN:	From the research I've done, you've been a replacement [stage manager] on a lot of shows. But then, for some shows, more recently, you've been the OG.[15]

MORGAN: Did you like the replacement aspect of coming in and taking a show and running that room that has already been formed? Or do you like being a part of the formation of the room?
JENKINS: At this stage of my career right now, I don't see myself taking over.

There aren't many opportunities for me to take over because if a PSM is going to leave... the younger stage managers on the team will bump up. So, then, there's a second place available... a first place available... so, that's where the replacement comes in.

MORGAN: What's the first Broadway show that you took the lead or the number one spot from day one on?
JENKINS: *Bengal Tiger* [*at the Baghdad Zoo*].
MORGAN: What, in your opinion, is the difference between a PSM and a Stage Manager at the Broadway level?
JENKINS: Per Equity[16] There is no such thing as a production stage manager.
MORGAN: That's what Amanda Spooner said.
JENKINS: You will not see it; it does not exist. One day, we'll break down and call it what it is: let's just call it a production stage manager. So, the difference between the stage manager and the *assistant* stage manager is that the buck stops with somebody. Somebody has to be responsible. Somebody has to set the tone for how this room is going to be run. Someone has to set the tone for the building, which I find is incredibly more important than running the [rehearsal] room, because the room is going to be run based on also the way the director wants it. Someone has to set the tone for when the company comes in that stage door. How are they going to feel? If you're crazy, they're going to be crazy. As simple as that. Set the tone.
MORGAN: Right; you have to deal with all these different personalities. How do you engage in self-care? What are your rituals, routines, and boundaries?
JENKINS: I have a mommy clause that is either is in my contract... or if it's [a producer or manager] that I know – like David Richards from RCI [RCI Theatricals] – we just have an agreement.[17] He's like, "I don't want to write it down... I'm cool because I know you," and we have a mutual respect for each other. Sometimes, I didn't have to put it in writing, but there were some companies where, I had to put it in writing: "General Management or Producer understands that said stage manager is a mother of young children and will, from time to time, have to take off to, you know, attend an important event. It is fully understood that at no time will she leave the show in jeopardy." I wasn't asking for anything special. I don't ask for extra money. I just ask that you don't question my time.

You start questioning my time? You won't see me.

Let me tell you about my experience at the Old Globe [Theater, San Diego]. Until recently, I had never worked there. When I was negotiating my contract – which is not much negotiation – there were things that I needed. I said that they would have to buy me an additional round trip ticket so I could leave and come back for my daughter's graduation from college. Also, I would be taking that week off. The person who negotiated negotiating contract with me said, "Oh, we have no problem. We can absolutely get you the plane ticket, but we'll have to check and see if everyone is okay with you being gone that long." And I said, "Okay, let me explain to you… there's my child, and then there's your play. There is no comparison. So, you tell me if I'm doing this job or not. *Those* are boundaries. I don't give a hoot. You want me or you don't. I don't have to do this show. What I *am* going to do is to be there when my child walks across that stage and gets her diploma."

MORGAN: Yeah.

JENKINS: What I'm *not* going to be doing is calling some silly little cues here in San Diego. That's not going to happen.

MORGAN: Right. You drive the decision and the conversation.

MORGAN: I just came up in a generation – I'm sure you did, too – where there was the pressure of doing *anything* for the theater. I have friends now who actually won't take shows that are in October because they acknowledge how important it is to take their kids trick-or-treating on Halloween. They're only that age for so many years and it's important that they remember their parents there for that. [Amanda] Spooner and I were talking about this; she said that her perspective changed when she became a mother. We discussed what's important and if that's going to codify your relationship with your kid with lasting memories, then go to their event. It's cultural, too, right? Here, in the South, you know, where there seems to be a bigger focus on family events. I'll have actors [college students] ask for a niece's birthday party. When I was coming through college, that was an absolute no.

JENKINS: If it ain't yours…!

MORGAN: Yeah, it had to be an emergency! But… if that's your family's culture and that's important to you and that's what you got to do… we'll figure it out. I also think the conversation around understudies has evolved in a good way. Hire them and pay them.

JENKINS: Right.

MORGAN: That leads to one of my last questions. How do you think Broadway changed because of the pandemic, for better or for worse? What are the things, at least in Broadway industry and culture, that you would hope continue to change over the next 5 to 15 years?

JENKINS: I know everybody gave a lot of lip service to: "We see you… [to People of Color] We're changing." We're doing that. It's still a slow process. It's also a dangerous process because there are still folks at the management level who are looking for people to "fill slots" with People of Color. Let's just talk stage management. During the pandemic, Lisa Dawn Cave, Jimmy Lee Smith, and I joined the lovely Kenneth J. McKee, and we started Broadway and Beyond: Access for Stage Managers of Color.[18] We've been successful with giving a platform and making it *easier*. No shame, no nothing. Just here are a bunch of stage managers that you may not have known that you could tap into. Here are stage managers of color, because we don't have as many avenues to come into this world. Here's people you would have never even thought about talking to for jobs. It's not just Broadway. It's all over: events, cruises, opera. But you can't say that you need a PSM when you haven't *trained* any PSMs for 40 years. You just can't bring someone in to be second ASM on an Off-Broadway show because they check the [diversity] boxes and make them the PSM. You have to train them up. That's not the point. You can't just put people right at the top. Right now, it's about *training* folks up. So that five or ten years down the line, you have a pool of people who are doing the job who have experience. I didn't just jump into being a PSM! It was a gradual thing. You have to learn what the job *is*. There's no shame in hiring all the PAs [Production Assistants] as People of Color. Why? Because this is the entry level job. We're going to train them up properly. So, I'm very cautious that people are hiring folks who don't have experience just because they feel some type of way about not having anyone in management of color. So, I'm hoping that the training continues. Sometimes it's not even about training; it's just about opening the door.

MORGAN: Oh yeah.

JENKINS: They have experience. Look different places for folks. You can't always just look at the college *you* went to. Look at the street. Like you said, go down to Clark Atlanta. See what's happening over there.

MORGAN: Yeah, we got a lot going on here in Atlanta. What I love about being in this community, at least in the shows that I work on and the rooms that I put myself in, is that we try to dismantle this idea that you've got to have certain kinds of credits to do certain kinds of projects. We value experience. We were casting *The Color Purple* and welcomed some real gospel singers in here. Sure, we *wanted* them to have theatre experience. In music pits, too… you *do* need to be able to read [music] score to play *West Side Story*. You don't have to be *that* good at reading score to play *The Wiz*… it's a funk score... it's mostly chords. The score looks like chicken scratch anyway. Good music directors will know the difference about not putting a person in a position and setting them up to fail if they don't have the right skills. There are flexible shows where we can do that. Then, if they don't have as much "pit" experience (maybe they play more gigs, studio work, or church work), they sit in the pit and like it and they get experience and then they maybe work a lot. Also, I say that one must put in the legwork. I think really that is missing piece that you're talking about too; the hours of mentorship and support. It means that *I'm* going to have to put in the hours to sit with that person and go through the score. Sometimes, folks just want to put the person there and see if they succeed or fail. We should say, "We are going put you here, but here are the hours that we're going to devote resources, humans, or money to help shepherd you into the process."

JENKINS: Right. Right.

MORGAN: Speaking of mentorship... what's the biggest piece of advice you have for young aspiring stage managers? How about those with marginalized backgrounds?

JENKINS: Work. Go do it. If you want to do it, do it. It's not too late to do it. It doesn't have to be, "Oh, thirty-seven years old and I'm not on Broadway, but I want to do this. How do I get there?" You know what you do? You go to your community theater, and you get some experience. Then guess what? You don't know who is working at that community theater.

You will go somewhere else, and someone will mention that there was the stage manager I knew at that community theater... let's call up this person and see if they want to come here and do this. Build the resume. Don't look for the shortcut all the time. The shortcut might come but instead of you putting in your energy into trying to get that shortcut, just get that experience. There will be no shortcut if you just keep rising and building.

MORGAN: Well, at least *then* you'll have the actual experience to do the job, as we just talked about.

JENKINS: Exactly.

MORGAN: If you take the shortcut, then you're going to get the gig but not have the experience to do the job.

JENKINS: That shortcut can lead to a *slide*, taking you right back down.

MORGAN: How quickly they rise, how quickly they fall.

JENKINS: Exactly.

MORGAN: Wow. Thank you. What an honor to get to speak with you! Thank you.

Amanda Spooner Bio

Amanda Spooner is an Equity Stage Manager and Educator, who teaches at Ithaca College and works in (and around) New York City. She has worked on and off-Broadway, regionally, on tour, in events, on immersive experiences, on opera, dance, countless readings and workshops, and in television. Her specialty is in the development of new plays and their world premieres, including Rebecca Taichman and Paula Vogel's *Indecent*. Amanda has stage-managed for Producer Daryl Roth, Barbara Broccoli, Lincoln Center Theater, Playwrights Horizons, Signature Theatre, Soho Rep, BAM, Ars Nova, Sundance Theatre Lab, The Public Theatre, American Repertory Theater, La Jolla Playhouse, Yale Repertory Theatre, Actors Theatre of Louisville, Berkeley Repertory Theatre, St. Ann's Warehouse, Williamstown Theatre Festival, Park Avenue Armory, and Westport Country Playhouse among others. She has collaborated with Vogel, Taichman, Cesár Alvarez, Les Waters, Raja Feather Kelly, Anne Kauffman, Sam Gold, Lila Neugebauer, Sheryl Kaller, Pam MacKinnon, Mark Lamos, Sarah Benson, Branden Jacobs-Jenkins, Sarah Ruhl, Anne Washburn, Michael R. Jackson, Sarah Gancher, Jordan Harrison, David Adjmi, Sarah DeLappe, and Jocelyn Bioh among others. She is the founder of Year of the Stage Manager, a grassroots campaign and virtual community for Stage Managers around the world, and serves on the Board of Directors for the Stage Managers' Association. Amanda recently finished her tenure as a TONY voter and as a member of council for Actors' Equity Association. She advocates for economic equity in professional theatre, for families in the arts, and for greater visibility for Stage Managers and spends a great deal of time on research and in discussion regarding these topics – including her ongoing support of PAAL, the Parent-Artist Advocacy League. Amanda serves on the artistic advisory boards at both Playwrights Horizons and the Signature Theatre in New York. She was named an American Theatre Magazine "Person to Watch" and was featured on the cover of Equity News with her son, among countless other articles and interviews in which she has participated. Amanda received her MFA from the Yale School of Drama, her BA from San Francisco State University, and her AA from Las Positas College.

Interview with Amanda Spooner, November 15, 2022 via Zoom

MORGAN: All right, folks, I'm here with someone who I've known for 20 years, from our many summers at Seaside Music Theater.[19] I don't remember when you came into the fold because I feel like you were always there. My first summer there was 2001.

SPOONER: My first summer would have been 2004.

MORGAN: Ah, *Beauty and the Beast* and hurricanes summer. Well, it was a good summer because that was the summer where I was comfortable enough to *host* parties. Party time, excellent.

SPOONER: And party we did.

MORGAN: And party we did. Amanda Spooner. Not only have we known each other for many years, but we share the same namesake. We are of similar age and of similar attitudes. I fell in artistic love with you early on because of your ability to balance being a boss in the spaces that you had to be a boss in, but being truly authentic, chill, and approachable in other spaces. When I was a young performer, I didn't know I was going to end up on the other side of the table. However, I really started to pay attention to stage managers when I was a young actor and the ones who could manage the balance the ability to tell people to kindly hush up in rehearsal, but then be able to relax with everyone back at the artist complex. Someone who could really turn it on and turn it off. That's something that I felt like you were able to do so early on, and I was in admiration of it. Can you tell me the amazing story about how you got into Yale?

SPOONER: Sure. I didn't even know where Yale was when I applied for it, but I applied for the grad program to have an MFA in Stage Management.[20] I had decided to pursue my MFA despite the protestations from my own undergrad faculty who weren't in support of the idea. They were wonderful; they simply were not stage management professors. I was also in San Francisco, where theater functions in a different way, in general. I applied to nine different programs because I didn't know who was going to want me. I didn't know what it was about, but I *did* know that I had to have some more formal training in order to participate in the hub of the industry in New York City. I had done an Off-Broadway show and I knew that much.

MORGAN: Did you know, at the time, that grad school was the trajectory for people who wanted to teach? I knew I wanted to teach eventually, so grad school right after undergrad seemed like a good idea for me. Sure, I wanted more training, and I knew eventually I wanted to teach college, so having the [degree] would be beneficial.

SPOONER: It was two parts for me. I knew I needed more training because I had done a show with Donna Drake[21] in New York City in the winter of 2005 (or 2006) and I had worked at Seaside [Music Theater], so I had been around people who knew what the norm was for the industry in New York City. I knew that I had a deficiency in how the theatre industry worked. I also knew that an MFA was going to unlock doors in the future for me if I wanted to teach. I really loved my teachers as a kid, and I really love learning. I think it comes from this sense of curiosity [from my dad] that I adopted early on, as a kid. So, with Yale, I had already done some early interviews and had a bunch of offers. I'd already done my Columbia interview: That was where I thought I would go because it was in New

York City, and I had a really great interview there. It was so great, that I ended up smoking cigarettes with the person who interviewed me after my interview. We had all these drag queens in common and her office was messy like my desk, and I felt a real affinity with her. I learned shortly thereafter that I didn't understand how the money works at Columbia. I realized that I can't be in *that* much debt and work in theater.

MORGAN: Louder for the people in the back!

SPOONER: It's unfortunate. In the early 2000s, there was nobody saying to me: there actually is this financial balance that you have to find. You have to be able to afford to pursue the thing you actually want to pursue, which has a lot of financial privilege attached to it. This was likely at the root of why my undergrad professors were not wildly supportive of grad school. I am just glad that I had the privilege of other full ride offers through U/RTA[22] and the foresight to ask about it before I said yes. I was really committed to Columbia. So, I went up for my Yale interview and the campus and experience is intimidating. They dismantled that a lot under the guidance of James Bundy, but I think that there is this archaic sense of importance and grandeur. The architecture radiates it. I also think I was a cynical 22-year-old "Know-It-all," so you have to remember there's like a lot of alchemy, or lack thereof, going on there. I didn't like it much when I was visiting. The only person that I really had a fondness for that I met while I was there for my interview was the woman who was the server in the restaurant of the hotel I was staying in. I was the only person in the restaurant, and she didn't have ranch dressing, so she strained blue cheese because that was as close as she could get to ranch dressing. She was just so dedicated to me having ranch dressing on my salad and I loved her. I felt so much comfort from eating with her. She was so lovely. The morning of my interview, I woke up and was getting ready and I had hot rollers in my hair, and the Chair of the program called me and said that I needed to come in early to observe a class before my interview. I had ordered room service for breakfast, and I remember that my impulse was to be overwhelmed by the schedule change, because it was quite a change. But I remember like truly saying, "F*** it." I had this offer from this other place I want to go. Spoiler alert: I ended up going to Yale. Later, I realized that there is a way to harness that feeling of importance, to let it act as a gravitational pull to bring more excellence out of you than you thought you had, while also trying to not subscribe to the essence of it.

MORGAN: Well, I think it's joy *and* confidence. I've felt that way when doing some of these interviews with some of my role models. There have been many circumstances during these conversations that have reminded me that we're just like two gals talking about what we do. We *get* to do this, right?

SPOONER: Yes, I *got* to go to this institution that had all these tools and gave me resources that I wouldn't get at other places. Was I just super cynical of it before I went? Yes. Was I suspicious of it before I went? Probably. I was raised on cable television and Pop Tarts, and some of my classmates weren't. I felt really intimidated and was lacking in self-confidence. I went to my interview, and by the time I got in there, I figured whatever is going to happen is going to happen. It's like going on a date and saying, "Look, I'm hot and there are other people who are waiting to date me, so we'll see how this goes." I went into the interview, and I actually really enjoyed meeting James Mountcastle and Mary Hunter. They interview you as a pair, and one of them is clearly playing good cop and one of them bad cop - although they will deny it to this day, but it is so obvious. Mary – the bad cop – said, "What do you do to relieve stress during Tech Week?" I said, "Honestly…lately… especially this summer… I've been prank calling places like McDonald's and trying to make reservations." There was just this silence in the room and they both started laughing, which is funny because she was trying to be *so* serious. One of them asked me why, and I said because it's funny and it usually makes the other person who answers the phone laugh.

MORGAN: Some context to the young readers. This was a big thing that we used to do in this era. There were these websites – like Ebaumsworld[23] – that had these comedic sound boards with soundbites that you could use for prank calls… the voices of Judge Judy and Miss Cleo.

SPOONER: Oh yeah… Crank Yankers[24]… it was a big deal, and you can't really do it nowadays. This all showed me that it's okay to be a human and have fun and not take yourself so seriously. I think it's around the time that I started to solidify the idea for myself that you can take the work seriously, but you don't have to take yourself seriously. There was some conflict over that sort of philosophy when I was in school. There were some people who really wanted me to take myself more seriously. I'm grateful for them because I think that I was selling myself short sometimes. Sometimes, *they* were taking *themselves* too seriously. There is a balance. At the end of the day, I'm awfully glad I went to Yale. I had a great time there, and I'm glad that I ultimately decided to go because I thought, "Well, this place seems to know what they're doing." It's the place that makes you most uncomfortable (versus being unsafe). Being uncomfortable is probably where you should be as opposed to going somewhere that's ultimately going to put you $150,000 in debt.

MORGAN: My undergrad made me very uncomfortable, but my grad experience made me super comfortable. That's how I balanced things out. I left undergrad thinking it was always going to be a rat race for me because I'm not a skinny performer... I don't dance like these other girls... it was such tunnel vision of thinking that I'll always be fighting to at least get into the ensemble. Then, I went to a grad program that was so excited about me as a human and my talents coming into that program. They treated me so well – it was such a flip – that I felt like it was the balance I needed by the time I was finished with all that education; to know what it feels like to be in both positions. In undergrad, if I wasn't given opportunities, I made them with peers. Who wants to be in my club? Let's do this show... let's go make something! I got to experience both, and I think that's important for young artists to feel or know both at some point.

SPOONER: The truth is: at any point you only know what you know. I got really interested in this idea that these seeds get planted and you just have to accept that they're going to blossom later whether you agree with them or not. As you get more context, they come into fruition. I actually have an apple seed [tattoo] on my wrist that I got it in honor of the chair of the stage management program at Yale, for Mary Hunter's retirement, because I think that a lot of our relationship was about her planting seeds. She did it so gracefully and gently. She would plant these seeds that eventually blossomed and came into fruition. I went with an apple seed because of education. You have to relax into that and believe that this is all going to come together and produce something that will grant me the autonomy to choose what I want to take and use and whatever.

MORGAN: Who else were your role models coming up through the ranks?

SPOONER: Well, who isn't a role model? I'm so open to the people around me, that I think I borrow something to do or not to do from every single person I meet. I'm the kind of person who stays in touch with her Lyft drivers, or the person who helps me at Enterprise Rental Car in Boston. I really love people, for better or worse.

A specific human who stands out is Earl Weaver.[25]

MORGAN: Yes! Earl was my college grad school professor as well, and I worked for him for a year as his Teaching Assistant.

SPOONER: He is one hell of a feminist and I always appreciate that about him. What is important to understand about our relationship is that I went to community college after high school, and I had graduated high school early. Not because I was a stellar academic, but because it was clear that when I had switched from private middle

Management 241

MORGAN: school to public high school in California. I was bored out of mind. I sort of went off the rails as a teenager. I'm grateful for that, actually, because I spent a lot of that time with a huge variety of human beings and, while my adventures probably stressed my parents out, I was lucky to be able to come out the other side safely. I just am so grateful for how those years shaped who I am, so I think it was an education in itself. Then, I went to community college right after high school because that was the logical next step for me if I was going to go to college at all. Wendy Wisely, who recently passed away, knew how to take my teenage attitude, and turn it into confidence. Then, Earl [Weaver] saw something in me that I couldn't possibly even begin to identify in myself: which was that I could actually pursue stage management as a profession. The thing that will always stand out to me when I think about Earl is that there was just no question for him. When I was sleeping through his 9AM classes, he would call my personal room line at my parents' house in front of the class and be like, "Hey Princess, are you going to come to class today?" [My email address at the time contained the phrase "Princess Spooner"].

SPOONER: Earl made me feel like they [the theatre department] were the lucky ones to have me, and that was a big deal after my time at Florida State. Earl made me feel like someone in that building really believed in me. It snowballed and then others believed in me, too. Earl would invite me into spaces to do things because he knew I could. He called me a "dancer" at one point, which took me aback because it wasn't a part of my identity, but I had worked so hard to get better at it. He just made me believe it.

Take your work seriously, but don't take yourself that seriously.

Find someone like Earl Weaver who takes you seriously. He actually helped me get my first professional theatre job and he was patient with me in all the ways. I was raised in a mid-sized town about 40 minutes outside of San Francisco. That was the limit of my worldview. I didn't even understand what I was capable of, or what was possible. Other people who were influential in this pivotal part of my life included Donna Drake, who was in the original cast of *A Chorus Line* (1975) and then went on to have a really wonderful directing and choreography career. We worked with her at Seaside [Music Theater]. She used to reference *Peter Pan* a lot. She's really drawn to the idea that if you believe you can fly, you can fly; just stop messing around. It was awesome to be influenced by someone who was a woman in the business in the latter part of the 20th century; who saw it from all sides; and who figured out how to be this force of nature.

MORGAN: She sure is kind, tough, and direct!

SPOONER: She let me stay at her apartment, she hired me for jobs, and she influenced the hiring of me for jobs I was not ready for yet, but in a good way. Just like for Earl, it was no question for her. What an act of kindness. She taught me: Strength is in the communal ties that we make and the connective tissue between people lifting each other up, yet not coddling people. She definitely doesn't coddle, but she's loving.

> Strength is in the communal ties that we make and the connective tissue between people lifting each other up.

MORGAN: Right. Love without honesty is meaningless. Honesty without love is mean.

SPOONER: That is a great quote.

MORGAN: I think about it when teaching the young people how the industry works. Some educators simulate it for them so they don't learn the hard way when they get there, but then that can feel abusive. So, if we could all be operating from that place of trying to be honest and loving. There is a way to say "That was bad. Let's go back and do it again" without saying "You suck." There's a kind and firm way to say, "Let's go back and do it again."

SPOONER: You can only do that if you found some deliberate way to build trust with people and it's clear. I make a point of saying that this is academia and that is different from the fully professional world. I can't, as a human who's a loving and naturally comforting human, stand the idea of you going into the fully professional world not knowing that these things were headed your way. The way that we teach them at Ithaca College is to give them a modular skill set. Instead of teaching you how to be a really great stage manager according to recipe cards and step-by-step paint-by-numbers, we focus on building this modular skill set, so that when you find yourself overwhelmed in an unfamiliar situation, you can rely on the comfort of that skill set. Developmentally, when you're between the ages of 18 and 25, you're still emotionally learning and processing how to be accountable for certain things in your life that you're not ready to be accountable for. I can look back at the people in my life and realize that these were people that I villainized

MORGAN:	because it was convenient for the narrative that suited me. I look back to see them actually as role models in ways that are paying off in more dividends later on.
MORGAN:	Yes, they wanted you to succeed. Any other role models?
SPOONER:	Trauma Flintstone, who is my drag mom in San Francisco; I used to perform as a Faux Drag Queen when I was in undergrad. It was my last experience on the performance side of things. I work now exclusively, 99.9% of the time, in new work development, whether it's plays or musicals. The main element is the script being the focus, but then change being born of the thing that you started with. I think working with drag performers – particularly drag queens – and performing as a faux drag queen myself – which is a woman playing a man playing a woman – really informed my skill set to be able to be in a room where things are changing so much. Richard Winchester and Mark Sargent, who are two producers that I worked with, are also on the list. Last, my parents are wonderful. They had a lot of influence on me as a human in good ways and in ways that I'm still learning from.
MORGAN:	Can you tell me in your own words: At the Broadway level, what is the difference between a production stage manager and a stage manager?
SPOONER:	It's a tricky question. I'll tell you everything that I think is true about this topic, and then somebody else will tell you something different. It's like resumé advice. You ask ten people, you get 12 different answers. As far as Actors' Equity – the union – is concerned, there are stage managers and there are assistant stage managers. In the case of a musical, there are stage managers, first assistant stage manager, and then further assistant stage managers on the Broadway. Production Stage Manager – typically in my experience on Broadway – is a title that the *originating* Stage Manager – the person who holds the Stage Manager contract – is considered. The Production Stage Manager. It has more gravity. But even as I say that, it sounds inaccurate – the truth is that it's a title that elevates the position without having to pay more for the labor.
MORGAN:	At the regional level, there's a production manager and a stage manager and it makes us think that it's someone in between that's like doing production management *things* on that particular production as the Stage Manager. It insinuates that like they might not call the show, but they're doing all of the paperwork, scheduling, and coordinating.
SPOONER:	I spend more time in the developmental part of things, so *occasionally* I'll accidentally end up on Broadway. If I were going to write an autobiography, that's what it would be called.

MORGAN: "Accidentally on Broadway."
SPOONER: There's nothing like doing a Broadway show. It's very special. However, I spend more time downtown developing stuff. Someone like Lisa Dawn Cave or Beverly Jenkins might then become the production supervisor or have this role that they play when something like *Frozen* goes international. They have this encyclopedia of knowledge of everything about the show.
MORGAN: They become a consultant.
SPOONER: I think the best stage managers or production stage managers have that kind of knowledge about whatever show they're working on. When we did *Annie* [in 2004], I drove across the country with my dad and I would trade off driving while I was reading all the stuff I printed from the internet about *Annie* or like reading books about Annie. I was so interested.
MORGAN: Ah yes, printed alongside your MapQuest directions to get across the country.
SPOONER: That is real. I feel like we had a Rand McNally Atlas. I realized that if you allow yourself to have a wide but not deep understanding of what's going on, it's going to help you do your job. I love it. That's maybe just me, but as a PSM, I think that's helpful. When I first did *Sing Street* on Broadway [that didn't *open* on Broadway because of the pandemic], I was on the "first assistant stage manager contract" and they called me "Stage Manager." That scenario in particular makes the most sense because I actually was charge of the deck: that is my jurisdiction. I was doing a job that has a lot of responsibility and autonomy associated with it. I had been the Production Stage Manager for that show Off-Broadway, so it made sense for me to be called the Stage Manager.
MORGAN: I struggle with the word "assistant" because, to a layman, it suggests that they are apprenticing the stage manager, where, in truth, they have completely different responsibilities and duties. I'm glad you brought up being "on the deck," because as a director, our school structure is that the stage manager is maintaining paperwork and they're going to call the show. They're in the booth; that's their domain. Our ASMs are backstage, and on a big musical, one is in charge of costume tracking, and one is overseeing props.

I love your statement of having a wide but not necessarily deep understanding. As a director, I attempt to develop a wide understanding of the show and its details in pre-production; then, once we get into rehearsals, I hand that paperwork to those ASMs and give them jurisdiction over managing that area. I trust y'all. Let me know if you have any questions or if we have to figure something out. I love walking into tech and seeing totally different paperwork because that's their area of expertise by the time we get to that point. To me, the workload is equal, but different. The term "Assistant" suggests that they are *assisting* the Stage Manager and they're doing something different.

SPOONER: Well, it *is* different and there is somewhat of a swath of people getting interested in the title Associate Stage Manager. If you look at like design teams, there is an *Associate* Lighting Designer. If you look at music direction, you see "associates." With any community, I think what I find from my perch on the internet, that some people who've been doing it longer seem to take more of an issue with that title changing. People want to be seen and heard. There's a place for traditionalists, right? It's like in drafting. A lot of students aren't learning hand drafting anymore. When I designed the BFA program for stage management at the college where I work, it was important to me that they were taking these classes where they learn how to hand draft, and they certainly still are. You can see over time and curricular revisions that it's turning into something that's digitized. Nothing really beats learning how to hand-draft because then you get on your hands and knees (assuming you're able to) and put tape on the floor and understand that. I understand the associate stage manager thing; that's fine. It gives people more autonomy, just like associate lighting designers. I'll be tech-ing a show, and I'll look over on day three of tech and there's the associate lighting designer sitting in the driver's seat, which is all well and good and great for them. I have no problem with that at all. They're given the keys to the car because the designer has to be somewhere else. That's totally fine. I would love to feel that way about stage manager.

MORGAN: The sharing of power doesn't bother me in any way. I think we're also trying to strike the balance of inundating people's work–life balance. Trying to establish that is a struggle in our industry because of trying to find that balance of power dynamic and institutional knowledge. That's a whole thing that plays into all of those conversations.

SPOONER: I have some students and colleagues claim that hierarchy is bad. The hierarchy of decision-making, alone, is not a horrible thing to have. It's okay for someone to still have responsibility on signing off on things. How do they rise to that occasion of responsibility? Who are the people who are being given responsibility? Those are questions that we should be asking, but I don't think there's anything inherently wrong with having a production stage manager who carries more responsibility than the rest of the team, but there is still this assumption that that person is accessible for all of everybody's urgent needs. It's fun to watch colleagues of mine say

	no to things and put boundaries up. There's seemingly a shortage of stage managers right now, which is fascinating. I know (literally) thousands of stage managers. [Producers] hope that I can help find who's available for them and do that labor for them. I'm happy to do that labor and be helpful, but I certainly don't want to be a gatekeeper in that way. I'm trying to figure that out. It is a marketable skill – especially for stage managers – to be able to push back in a gentle way. Some of them are pushing back in a harsher way.
MORGAN:	Let's talk about "The Year of the Stage Manager"[26] Facebook group.
SPOONER:	I get nasty messages from people every once in a while, asking how I can allow certain things to be posted. There are some people who are leaders in our industry that somehow missed the whole conversation that was happening in 2020 and 2021. They show up in a Facebook group that's dedicated to celebrating and uplifting stage managers and educating people about what stage managers do; and they're looking for people to work for free and *not* calling it volunteering. That's their bad. People wonder why I let people make posts in the group that are under minimum wage. I allow it because of the education that happens in the thread.
MORGAN:	Right. Let it happen.
SPOONER:	Producers post stuff in there [from really reputable institutions] that don't have appropriate pay or compensation. People will comment, resulting in an education in the thread. I think *some* people are being snarky because they feel passionately about it, and you can't really fault people for that. There are some people who don't have all the information. That's happening a lot now on Broadway. There's consternation happening in companies that want change, but they didn't totally know how it was working in the first place. You have to figure out how the whole thing has *been* functioning in order to change it. There's a growing number of stage managers who have all these opinions about how the business works, and they have a lot of power in the conversations. There's always the court of public opinion. It's why I make my students watch *The Devil Wears Prada*, because I think there's such key scenes. I'm not saying that Miranda Priestly is doing things right, but the thing that Miranda Priestly relies on is that there is this whole industry that's been functioning in that way.
MORGAN:	Yeah, the *sweater* scene.
SPOONER:	The sweater scene is the key scene. Even if they don't watch the whole movie, that's the key scene. You have an opinion about things, and you're entitled to it, but you don't even know what's going on, and in fact, you're wearing it. You're a part of it. It's an important part of understanding how things work in academia

	and beyond. It's about knowing the difference between the two. You are entitled to your opinion, you should draw boundaries, and you should develop your own value system. But there's a whole industry that's been turning before you landed on that planet, and it's going to keep turning if you decide to leave. You need to figure out why it turns. What makes it turn, so you can try and change something about that.
MORGAN:	Let's talk about your work as an educator. You work in academia, at Ithaca College. Tell me how you got into that and how do you balance that with a full time actual professional career?
SPOONER:	I had always wanted to teach. I taught as an adjunct professor at Rider University in New Jersey while I was living and working in Manhattan. I was blessed – I still am – to have a very busy career as a stage manager. As an adjunct professor, especially in the schools around New York City, there's an understanding that you're going to continue working and that your professional engagements are going to show up in your curriculum. That balance is more supported in schools around New York City because it's the norm. When I was doing *The Wolves* at Lincoln Center,[27] someone had sent me a job posting about Ithaca College. I was familiar with Ithaca College because so many people I had worked with professionally – young people in New York City, who were excellent – had attended Ithaca. It was an opportunity to be their first Assistant Professor of Stage Management. Part of taking that job was also assuming the responsibility of designing the BFA, because they had not had a BFA for Stage Management before that. I was interested in that because I thought there were some things that are conventional in the curriculum of a lot of programs that were being precious about what is foundational and necessary to stage management education. I wanted to investigate that and do some research about what might be different about our program. When I interviewed, it was the first formal educational interview I had been through, where you have to do a sample class and that sort of thing.
MORGAN:	Right. We were both fairly young, coming into higher education. That interview process is a mystery until you do it.
SPOONER:	It's cold and unlike theatre. There are so many ways in which your artistry as stage manager or director gets reduced to these things on paper. There's still stuff that I don't understand about academia.
MORGAN:	You are full time there?
SPOONER:	I am full time. I live in Ithaca. My husband is a manager for software engineering and software development. He's always worked from home, so we have been lucky. We have a son who's six now; he was born in 2016.

MORGAN: He is the coolest kid that ever walked the actual physical earth.
SPOONER: He is truly the best. He was a year-and-a-half-year old when I applied to the job and my husband wanted to move out of the city. We lived in a one-bedroom apartment with a toddler, so that was a lot. I applied and did the interview, and it reminded me of applying for grad school because I didn't know if they would want me. They made me an offer and it took some time to figure out. They wanted me to start right away, but I was doing a show at Ars Nova that I wanted to finish.[28] So, we figured it out and we have been here for four-and-a-half years. When I work in the city, I rent an apartment down there.
MORGAN: You just did a full run of a show Off-Broadway – *Sing Street*.
SPOONER: Originally, in the Fall of 2019, I had subs covering for me at school because for half of the semester, I ended up doing *Sing Street*. I had worked on it as a lab that summer and then they hired me at New York Theater Workshop in the Fall of 2019. It was Off-Broadway, and then it transferred to Broadway. So, in the Spring, I taught my classes as quarter classes, so I was able to do it in the Spring (of 2020). Then, of course, everything shut down on our first day of tech. Then we went for some time, not really knowing what was going to happen with the show. Then, this last summer (2022), the Huntington (which is a LORT Theater in Boston) produced it with commercial enhancement.[29] The goal is to take it back to Broadway. It's a joy working on it. We did that run in Boston that just closed in the middle of October and then my class started right after that. So, it's been working out. I think the school is smart to support me in that because there's several students and alumni who've already been hired to work on *Sing Street* in various capacities. It definitely influences the way I teach and the way I design and run the program. A lot of people want to know how I do both, and it's hard and it's a lot of work. At the end of the day, if I didn't think it benefited the students, I wouldn't do it. I still think it *does* benefit the students. That's why I stick to my guns on that. Often people want to know how I am a parent to a six-year-old and do it.
MORGAN: How do you manage all of that?
SPOONER: It's a privilege to be married to someone who works from home.
MORGAN: I recall your kid being pretty present during the process for *Indecent* (Broadway, 2017). You posted some social media posts about how Paula Vogel[30] knew him and he was present for a lot of that. Do you think that having a child like changed the way you work as a stage manager? Or were you already operating with that much grace and understanding for working parents?

SPOONER: No, absolutely not. I was awful to working parents before I had a child. I was *so* not understanding at all about events like a kindergarten costume parade. It is tricky from an authoritative standpoint. We're not supervisors as stage managers, but we have a lot of perceived authority, and we have a lot of responsibility and gatekeeping of who can do what and when. We end up becoming the person who decides, in conjunction with the director and often the producer, what "life things" are more important than the work.

MORGAN: Right. It used to be a no-brainer. Grandma's funeral? Excused. Concert tickets? Not excused. But… what if your mom bought you concert tickets to Lizzo six months ago and maybe she's driving in from four hours away to take you to that concert? Or your parents bought you a trip to Disney World for an unofficial family reunion and you're going to see your cousins that you haven't seen in a decade? I mean, that's hard.

SPOONER: It's really hard. Over the years, I have figured out what I think is right, although ask me in two years. The actors have to tell me what the important thing is and what's not. That's where trust comes in. You have to build trust. I do that with my students, too. You're going to have to tell me what you need because it's your education and it's your investment of your time and your money. Come to class or don't come to class. You're going to create more labor for me having to catch you up and it's going to be limited resources for you in that regard. Same thing with the people who are in casting. But, having a kid is actually what made me realize that there were plenty of parents that I was not flexible with because *I didn't* think a kindergarten costume parade was a reason to miss rehearsal, at the time. That's part of learning and not being too hard on my past self about that. Occasionally, you're going to meet somebody who makes decisions that are totally self-centered and not about the thing that they have been hired to do. Most of the time, that's not what happens. Not in my experience. Most of the time people take their job seriously. Also, there are cultural aspects of someone else's life that I'm not going to understand.

MORGAN: Absolutely, family means different things to different people.

SPOONER: I grew up in the generation of *City Slickers*.[31] You remember that movie?

MORGAN: Oh yeah! *City Slickers II* is even better!

SPOONER: That's what my husband said! There is a scene between Billy Crystal and Jack Palance that's – Spoiler alert – right before Jack Palance's character – Curly – dies. In this scene, Jack Palance says, "There is this *one thing* that life is all about. *One* thing." Billy Crystal's character asks him, "What's the one thing?" Jack Palance says, "You have to figure it out" and then he dies. So, it becomes obvious throughout the rest of the movie that the *one thing* is family. We were raised in this generation where we believe that this guy has enough privilege, ability, and mobility to drop *everything* he's doing for two weeks and go and chase cows. It's sort of absurd. It's so funny to me that there is the *one* thing and then nothing else matters. You still have to pay the bills and we live in a capitalist society! What I *wish* he had said was, "There's one thing you could *prioritize* over all these other things, but all those other things actually *don't go away*." When I had my son, I wondered if I should stop working. Financially, we were spending more on finding babysitters than I actually make as a stage manager. I thought it would be easier by being in academia, but I realized I should probably keep working professionally. The tectonic plates always shift around. I thought that it could be that my "one thing" is my son. But... he's going to get older, and I think he should be raised by a parent who actually still has a desire pulsing through her veins to be an educator, to create theater, and to be a project manager in the performing arts. The arts make her feel alive and give her a sense of purpose outside of being his parent. I'm glad that my parents had pursuits that weren't totally centered on me. It's not possible for everyone to do that.

MORGAN: Yeah, it's case by case.

SPOONER: So, I've got some notes, Curly!

MORGAN: Let's circle back to "The Year of the Stage Manager." You started this Facebook group in 2020 called "The Year of the Stage Manager" before the pandemic; this was just a thing that you were going to do. But then, because of the pandemic and the shutdown and then a reckoning around equity and inclusion and race, this group extended into all these other conversations about equity and inclusion on a grander scale within the theater community. It ballooned into this significant community. Now, it's called "The Year of the Stage Manager: The Afterglow" and has over 12,000 followers. It connects many artists and educators in our industry. It has threads on it that are valuable about educational topics, job postings, etc. You chime in there as an administrator often. How did that come about and how do you feel about the impact of that group, its threads, and its work now as a resource? How do you feel about where it started and where it is now in Fall of 2022?

SPOONER: The reason it started is because I had been organizing these events in person in New York City for stage managers to share space with each other. When I first started working in New York City, there was this seemingly impenetrable cloud of mystery that surrounded having a career in New York City. There's no welcoming kiosk that gives you a pamphlet on how to do that. I met a lot of nice people, but it still seemed overwhelming and daunting. Theaters would give me a free space to do this because they loved stage managers and they don't know how to show that love and gratitude. So, I got a space and 35 stage managers or so would come together and talk about a topic… or do stage manager professional speed dating… all sorts of things.[32] But it was all very central to New York because that's where I was. I would occasionally go on social media, primarily Facebook, and say "You know, I really wish that people understood X, Y and Z about stage management, because I think if they did, they would approach us differently and collaborate with us differently, and it would be better for everyone." I hoped for a virtual space for topics and questions that kept an eye on a positive outcome – even if it was just for one year. Celebrating stage managers and educating ourselves and people about what we do could be a really helpful tool and very simple. A virtual space, like a Facebook group, is a great space for these conversations to happen. But it had planned obsolescence in it. If it makes people uncomfortable, including some stage managers, for us to be the center of anything, why don't we say that it has planned obsolescence for the year of 2020? It was going to be this finite amount of time that stage managers are central to the conversation.

I think there was a misstep there – pandemic aside. If you're going to create some sort of social movement – which is in some ways what it ended up being – you have to give it time. A year actually isn't long *enough* to do it. I think that was an inherent mistake. 2020 was chosen because it was the hundred-year anniversary of stage managers being explicitly recognized in the notes and archives of [the union]. Even though stage managers have been a part of the union since 1913, the first time that they were explicitly recognized was in 1920. The hope was that Equity was going to get on board with it. I jumped into it and then, the pandemic happened. Actually, I think in some ways, it was really beneficial to have "Year of the Stage Manager" happening during the shutdown because we had a captured attention, a pretty big audience, and people who in our business weren't necessarily working all the time. We had a lot of events and I'm sad that there's not a video archive of all of them. Other days, I'm actually glad because I think it was captured in a time and place where it was and should remain. Year of the Stage Manager really set out to be just a space to celebrate stage management and learn more about what stage managers do. It ended up being a space where a lot of people did a lot of learning about mistakes that are made constantly in our business of theater and the process of making theater. I get unsolicited messages from people all the time that are say, "I would have never asked for a raise if I didn't see people talking about it or encouraging me in this group." There are many producers in there and many influential stage managers in there. There are a lot of people in there that are listening. I think that's important for people to remember about that space. I'm proud of it. The big lesson for me is: if you're going to lead something, you don't get to have an opinion.

MORGAN: Whew. Say that.

SPOONER: I know. That was hard because I really have a lot of opinions about stage management.

MORGAN: That's why you post so many questions! I'm always wondering if you're doing research or poking a bear or posting what popped in your head...

SPOONER: All of those things. I have to present it as a question, and I don't get to have an opinion. I once expressed a hard-core opinion about something in Equity elections and there were stage managers who left the group. They decided the whole group was toxic because I had this very specific opinion as an administrator of the group.

MORGAN: That can be high risk. You have to be the Facilitator. That's tough.

SPOONER: That's okay though. I don't mind it. It made it so that I was learning more outside my own experience because I was forced to.

MORGAN: For the up-and-coming young people who want stage manage, what are the skills you think they really need to like keep on their radar? Perhaps talk about management and leadership. Do you think production stage manager is more of a leader, or a manager, or both? What are the elements of leadership that make an effective stage manager?

SPOONER: I think the biggest thing that stage managers can learn is how to be a leader *while* they manage. How do you influence joy and inclusivity? How do you genuinely influence humanity in what you're doing? I had a student ask why being humane is the goal. I pointed out: because so many things have been so inhumane for so long. Sometimes people say that I'm being dramatic. I don't think it's dramatic that I'm in the shower washing conditioner out of my hair with my phone in a Ziploc bag, answering emails while my infant is in a car seat on the floor. Those are pretty inhumane conditions. This was expected of me to keep up with the working culture, in the industry. Some people will say, "Well, that's you." I say, "No, that's us."

MORGAN: In education, as a mentor to my stage managers, I often have to remind them to take their actual break, drink water, and take care of themselves. If you can't function, *we* can't function. If we need to take a longer break, we'll take a longer break. It's coming from a bigger umbrella.

SPOONER: I never really stopped working on projects. Even when the pandemic started, I was working on Zoom and as soon as it was happening again in person, we went right back to it. Everyone's aware that things need to change, but there is a lot of doublespeak happening, especially in certain environments where it's clearly more performative than it is in other environments. There's an inherent lack of understanding of both sides of the coin. People who were in year-round, salaried positions and are producing theatre, have either gotten really far away from their own experience or have never had their own experience of being a freelancer. Conversely, there are a lot of freelancers who don't understand how the *business* currently works at all. We commit to this idea that things need to change, but there is a missing step of actually being educated (formally or informally) about what's happening on both sides of the chasm.

MORGAN: Yeah, there are folks screaming for change but there's a lot of finger-pointing about how everybody else needs to change their side as opposed to changing one's own. Listening is important. A lot of it goes back to what we were saying about doing the legwork. It takes time and effort to try to arrive at a solution to like problems that are simply engrained in our work through the systems that we didn't create.

SPOONER: Most of the time, people are repeating what they were taught or they're clinging to old ideals. Also, we're always in a state of triage where we're making theater – whether it's commercial theater or nonprofit theater. The conversation about eradicating "ten out of twelves" has some folks asking us how we *possibly* function? Well, we're going to figure it out because we always do.

MORGAN: Right. What are the things we agree on? Let's start with what we agree on and then parse out the ways in which this format works. I use the phrase "Option Three" a lot, when there's a disagreement. This group wants one thing, and the other group wants something else. What's option three? What's the option that no one has brought to the table? I want to hear them. Let's get some more ingredients on the table before we make the casserole. Perhaps put more ingredients on the table and let's see if it's going to work.

SPOONER: That's what makes you such a great professional and educator. It's knowing that there's something we can do. It seems to be human, just to fall into the habit of binary.

"What is option three?" is brilliant and simple. It's really elegant in that way. That's good advice for stage managers. How does leadership show up in your work as a manager?

How can you be a leader as a human? How can you be a leader in the work you do? How can you be a leader in the institutions in which you participate? Learning when to listen. I think it's knowing that there's probably a third option. It's important to recognize what we are doing and then stop for a second, take a pause and ask, "*Why* do we do this?" Why do we send reports to certain people but not actors? Why do we take on the responsibility for when something goes wrong and automatically apologize for it? More and more people are learning how to be anti-racist and how to be anti-oppressive. I think taking that pause and asking ourselves why we do certain things that we take for granted as a habit that's been formed in the industry is good.

MORGAN: Sometimes decisions can feel like it's going to be "nothing or nuclear" when it comes to consequences. Sometimes, if we take ten minutes and go to option three, we can figure out something in between. If a colleague says something in a room that's really problematic, we gently call a ten-minute break, pull that colleague aside to be able to address the situation by asking, "What did you mean by that?" It doesn't require a full rehearsal being dismissed, but it does it might require us to just take a breath and that it is so counter to our aforementioned culture of pushing through. Let's take a pause and then we'll assess what we need to do next.

SPOONER: I think one of the most powerful tools for stage managers to acquire is to take a pause. You can also take a pause if you realize that you are dying emphatically on a hill that perhaps you don't need to die on. If it seems like you care more than the producers and the director about a certain thing, maybe just take a step back and ask yourself why you care more about this thing. Is it because somebody is being pressured to do something that feels unsafe? Then you should communicate that.

MORGAN: Yeah, as a music director, I'll often fight for something if I feel like it's going to impact my time or our process, based on my experience. I'm just trying to set myself up for not crashing and burning based on my live-and-learn moments. I'll circle back to option three and say, "let's try it." If it's something new and there's a lot of resistance in the room, I ask if we can try it. Maybe it will work. Maybe it won't work.

SPOONER: There's more room for that in academia or in professional regional theatre or the nonprofit environment. In the commercial end of it all, everything is being reduced to resource consumption. In commercial theatre, it's very much in the foreground of what decisions are going to *cost* us, so there's not a lot of room for trying things. Culturally, there's not a lot of room for reimagining how things can be done. I think that's tricky.

There's a missing piece. A lot of people – including myself – are not deeply educated on how the producing of commercial theater works. As somebody who participates in it, I should know something about it if I'm going to have an opinion about how it affects my participation. It's important to know, as a stage manager, that every single project and every single group of people (whether it be in a non-profit environment or a commercial environment) is always going to be different. New trust in relationships needs to be built. It's going to have to launch in a way that's specific to the people involved and the thing that you're doing. It's also going to deserve its own attention using your modular hard and soft skills. How do you combine them in a way to rise to the occasion of that specific project? The second that you feel like you've found a recipe card that you can walk into a room and paint-by-numbers, you're missing something, no matter what age you are. I guess that's where we should end it.

Notes

1. J.P. Kotter. *A Force for Change: How Leadership Differs from Management* (New York: Free Press), 3–6.
2. Ibid, 7.
3. Lawrence Stern. *Stage Management: Sixth Edition* (Massachusetts: Allyn and Bacon 1998) 1.
4. Ibid, 7–15.
5. "Section 68.A" *Actor's Equity Association: Agreement and Rules Governing Employment Under the Equity/League Production Contract*, Actor's Equity Association (New York: AEA, 2019).
6. *Broadway and Beyond: Access for Stage Managers of Color* website. Accessed January 10, 2023. See https://www.broadwaybeyondaccess.com/.
7. Beverly Jenkins, interview with Amanda Wansa Morgan via Zoom, November 15, 2022.
8. "Calling a show" – a stage manager calls cues to light, sound, and projection operators as well as to deck crew and additional personal. It is a highly orchestrated procedure, intricately timed to the show.
9. Howard University – Historically Black University (HBCU) located in Washington, DC.
10. Theatre Management Company, also known as Foresight Theatrical, website. See https://www.ibdb.com/broadway-organization/alan-wasser-associates-76146.
11. While she had other prior Broadway credits, DeBose was known in the Broadway community for her work as the featured ensemble part of the "bullet" in the original cast of the hit musical *Hamilton* (2015).
12. Nikita Duggal. "Leadership vs Management: Understanding the Key Difference" *simpl¡learn* website. Last updated January 25, 2023. See https://www.simplilearn.com/leadership-vs-management-difference-article.
13. PWI: Predominantly White Institution.
14. Spotlight operator.
15. Original.
16. Actor's Equity Association – the union for actors *and* stage managers.
17. As of 2023, David Richards is the President of RCI Theatricals. See https://www.rcitheatricals.com/ourteam.
18. *Broadway and Beyond: Access for Stage Managers of Color* website. Accessed January 10, 2023. See https://www.broadwaybeyondaccess.com/.
19. Professional Equity theatre in Daytona Beach, Florida. Open from 1970s to 2008.
20. Master of Fine Arts.

21 Cast member in original Broadway cast of *A Chorus Line*. Director and Choreographer. See https://www.ibdb.com/broadway-cast-staff/donna-drake-77936.
22 Auditions for graduate schools for theater. See https://urta.com/.
23 *eBaum's World* website. Accessed November 15, 2022. See https://www.ebaumsworld.com/.
24 Comedic television show featuring puppets (2002-2007). See https://en.wikipedia.org/wiki/Crank_Yankers.
25 American director, choreographer, performer, and professor.
26 *The Year of the Stage Manager* website. See https://yearofthestagemanager.com/home.
27 "The Wolves" *Lincoln Center Theatre*. See https://www.lct.org/shows/wolves/.
28 NYC-based non-profit arts organization. See https://arsnovanyc.com/.
29 League of Resident Theatres. See https://lort.org/.
30 American playwright (b. 1951). Pulitzer Prize winner.
31 A 1991 comedic, western film starring Billy Crystal, Jack Palance, and Daniel Stern.
32 Sounds like the way Maestra got started, doesn't it?

7
THE RESOURCES

Introduction

The women in this book have talked a good deal about where they've come from and the paths that led them to where they are in the business. My hope is to give you some resources to create your own pathways with their perspectives, and with resources in this chapter and listed throughout the book.

Training: Graduate School

Graduate school is a great idea *if* you see yourself wanting to teach in higher education someday. Yes, it's a great idea if you want additional education and mentorship; however, there are many options and opportunities for further education (the fancy term is "professional development") that a more modest investment of time and money. If you see yourself wanting to teach in higher education *and* hoping to get more education in a focused field, then look into graduate school.

The Terminal Degree

The "Terminal Degree" is the term used in higher education to establish the *highest* degree that one can get in that field, generally speaking.

In music – as well as *most* fields of study in the United States – the Doctorate is the terminal degree. This could mean a Doctor of Music Arts (DMA) – or a PhD – in an area of music. Even in music performance, one has a bevy of options to complete their Doctor in Music Arts (performance, pedagogy, music education), so it is considered the terminal degree of its field.

Conversely, in the theatre realm, the Master of Fine Arts (MFA) is (as of 2023) considered the terminal degree in *performance, design, playwriting,* and *direction.*

There are PhD programs for theatre (e.g., history and criticism) and/or performance studies and, therefore, the jobs in higher education suited for theatre historians and dramaturgs typically require the doctorate as the terminal degree. MFA programs focus on applied work – making the art; while PhD programs focus on theory and written scholarship as the bulk of the workload.

Most institutions of higher education in America require a terminal degree in order to occupy a *full-time, tenure-track* position. However, one could teach in higher education with, say, a graduate degree that is *not* terminal under the following circumstances: adjunct or part-time positions; full-time positions at private institutions (they answer to less regulation on account of being private); and exceptions with professional experience (subject to the decisions of the departments). In short, one *could* teach in higher education with a Master of Arts (MA) degree; however, there might not be a chance that one would be qualified for *all* of the full-time, tenure-track opportunities without the terminal degree.

There *are* individuals who occupy full-time tenure-track professorial positions without graduate degrees, but with *significant* experience in the field. They have been hired through extenuating circumstances – either the institution that they work for is private *or* their department chair or college dean found a way to make a very special argument for their hiring.

When it comes to selecting a graduate program, consider what the entire [theatre] department and the city surrounding the program offer in addition to the training itself, especially if you are a "multi-hyphenate" artist such as myself. If you are interested in directing for musical theatre, there are a few specialized programs out there; however, you could find a program that offers an MFA in Directing situated in a department that also has a strong undergraduate musical theatre program (therefore affording you the opportunity to assistant direct or even direct their musicals) or one that is located in a city which has opportunities for directing musicals in the professional or community scene.

MFA Stage Management programs are available throughout the country and many of them have wonderful curriculums and connections. Consider the same factors as mentioned earlier with the MFA in Directing programs if you desire to work exclusively in musical theatre: proximity to opportunities, connections, and community.

The path to a graduate training for a career in music direction isn't as clear as some of the disciplines listed earlier. You could certainly continue on the path of performance for an instrument, namely piano. You could also look at graduate degrees in music for conducting, composition, or vocal pedagogy. A master's in music might benefit someone who wants to teach at the high school level or someone who is happy to only be considered for adjunct positions. Unless you get into one of the specific programs designed with that career in mind, you are going to have to consider a number of factors including, but not limited to: the audition requirements; the curriculum; and opportunities in the surrounding department, college, community, and city. There are also graduate music programs for collaborative piano that have strong relationships with musical theatre programs at the same university where you might be able to negotiate an assistantship to play for musicals and musical theatre students. Otherwise, you'll be accompanying a lot of instrumental recitals and events only to turn around to play musicals thereafter. That's not the worst thing, but why not be building your knowledge of repertoire while you work toward the degree? Your best bet is to consider the entire experience of your graduate school journey by taking these factors into consideration.

Choreography, like music direction, is also an area where the training paths are varied. Is the right path for an aspiring professor who choreographs for musical theatre an MFA in Dance? It's possible. It's also possible that one considers an MFA in Directing or Acting in a program that has strong musical theatre ties or opportunities.

There are a few MFA in Musical Theatre programs in existence, and they are listed in the following.

What about for writers? Composers? Lyricists? Other than the few programs listed here, most opportunities for writers to have their work cultivated will be found through the many non-academic programs out there for developing new works. Composers could certainly look at graduate music programs in Composition. Lyricists and librettists could look at MFA Playwriting programs. However, you would need to investigate individual programs for opportunities to work specifically on musical theatre material within that program. I recommend that you research programs and their curriculums thoroughly and ask many direct questions throughout your interview process.

As of 2023, here are some programs in America that one might consider for graduate-level training in these areas:

- Penn State University offers a Master of Fine Arts (MFA) in Directing for Musical Theatre *and* an MFA in Music Directing.
- Arizona State University offers a Master of Music (MM) for Conducting with a musical theatre track. They also offer an MM in Composition, a Doctor of Musical Arts (DMA) in Composition, and other related degrees.
- Shenandoah Conservatory offers an MM in Performance (Voice), an MM in Conducting (Musical Theatre), and an MM in Pedagogy for Contemporary Commercial Music (CCM) Voice. Additionally, Shenandoah offers an *undergraduate* degree of interest – a Bachelor of Music (BM) in Musical Theatre Accompanying, and a DMA in Pedagogy (Voice) that requires candidates to study and teach various styles of vocal pedagogy that serve musical theatre training.
- San Diego State University offers an MFA in Musical Theatre which is performance based but produces artists who direct, music direct, choreograph, and write musicals.
- Boston Conservatory at Berklee College of Music offers an MFA in Musical Theatre: Musical Theatre Vocal Pedagogy. In addition, they have an MA in

Creative Media and Technology program that offers a Specialization Writing and Design for Musical Theatre
- Oklahoma City University offers an MM in Musical Theatre.
- Arizona State University offers an MM (Performance) with a musical theatre concentration.
- NYU Steinhardt offers an MM in Vocal Performance: Musical Theatre.
- NYU Tisch offers an MFA in Musical Theatre Writing, referred to as the "Graduate Musical Theatre Writing" program.[1]

Non-Graduate Training Opportunities

While most of these are geared toward supporting writers (composers, lyricists, librettists, and playwrights), there is much evidence in these interviews to suggest that working with these programs as a music director, director, choreographer, arranger, accompanist, stage manager, and in other various creative roles are keys to accessibility, networking, experience, and opportunities within the industry.

The BMI Lehman Engel Musical Theatre Workshop (New York, NY)

For many years, the "BMI Workshop" was one of the only development programs for new musicals available. Many of the subjects in this book found each other through this program or worked through this program in other ways. It was founded in 1961 by Broadway music director Lehman Engel through BMI – the music production agency – with the intent to create a free-standing training ground for musical theatre writers. The program typically runs September through June in New York City with weekly workshop classes, and is free to participants; however, they must plan to live near or within commuting distance to New York City while participating. When participants apply, they apply under a specific status: Composer, Lyricist, Composer/Lyricist, or Librettist. They then work with different writers in their "class" to find writing partners. Some teams are asked to participate in an "Advanced Workshop" after the main process is finished. The librettist workshop has a slightly different structure; however, there are some activities that group all of the participants together.

The New York Theatre Workshop and **The Manhattan Theatre Club** have many programs designed to help artists, particularly writers, develop new work.

Playwrights Horizons has programs designed to help artists, particularly writers, develop new work, including a program called **Playwrights Downtown** – an undergraduate program at NYU's Tisch School of the Arts for developing work.

Musical Theatre Factory NYC – see https://mtf.nyc/

The Public Theater accepts Synopsis Submissions through their Literary office.

National Alliance for Musical Theatre (NAMT) – https://namt.org/

NAMT hosts a yearly festival in New York (usually in the Fall) to share, develop, and celebrate new musical theatre work. They offer a bevy of resources to members, including a "Knowledge Exchange" division of their website and operations.

Their Festival Purpose and Goals state: in the short run, the Festival's goal is to connect writers with producers, extend the development trajectory of presented musicals and establish new creative partnerships. The long-term goals are to: expand the musical theatre repertoire; advance the musical theatre art form; and support the field.

Workshops and Training Programs Outside of New York City

The Reiser Lab, The Alliance Theater (Atlanta, GA)
New Musical Development at 5th Avenue Theatre (Seattle, WA)
The New Musicals Lab at Ferguson Center (Newport News, VA)[2]
New Musicals Inc. (Hollywood, CA)[3]
Musical Café: The San Francisco Bay Area Musical Theatre Development Program[4]
Goodspeed Musicals Music Direction Intensive[5]

Additional Resources

The American Federation of Musicians (Both National and NYC – based)
The Dramatist Guild
NewMusicalTheatre.com
Jonathan Larson Grants via American Theatre Wing[6]
The New Dramatists' Kleban Prize in Musical Theatre[7]

Organizations That Support Women in Musical Theatre

Maestra Music Inc. – see https://maestramusic.org/
Founded by Georgia Stitt and colleagues in 2017, this non-profit organization is a networking and education tool for female-identifying and non-binary musicians, music directors, and music team members in the musical theatre world to network and gain access to resources, both educational and professional. The membership is *free* and features access to a directory of musicians; virtual masterclasses and workshops; a student mentorship program; educational resources such as a timeline of women in musical theatre music development; virtual and in-person networking events; and more.

Maestra began as a series of informal meetings for female-identifying musicians and music directors in musical theatre to connect, network, and continue professional development in community with each other. They now host weekly events, both online and in person, through their virtual masterclass series, their mentorship program, and various other outreach events.

Maestra Mission Statement (as of 2022):

> Maestra Music Inc. provides support, visibility, and community to the women and nonbinary people who make the music in the musical theater industry. Our membership is made up of composers, music directors, orchestrators, arrangers, copyists, rehearsal pianists, and other musicians who are an underrepresented minority in musical theater. The organization's initiatives include monthly educational seminars, mentorship programs, technical skills workshops, networking events, and online resources and partnerships that aim to promote equality of opportunity and to address the many historical disadvantages and practices that have limited women and nonbinary composers and musicians in the musical theater.

The Kilroys – see https://thekilroys.org/

> The Kilroys is a collective of playwrights, directors and producers in LA and NYC who are done talking about gender parity and are taking action. We mobilize others in our field and leverage our own power to support one another.

League of Professional Theatre Women – see https://www.theatrewomen.org/

> The League of Professional Theatre Women is a membership organization for professional theater women representing a diversity of identities, backgrounds, and disciplines. Through our programs and initiatives, we create community, cultivate leadership, and seek to increase opportunities and recognition for women in professional theatre.

The Lillys – see https://the-lillys.org/

> Celebrating, funding, and fighting for women by promoting racial and gender parity in the American theater since 2010.

Broadway Women's Alliance – see https://thebroadwaywomensalliance.com/

> Dedicated to fostering community and supporting women, The Broadway Women's Alliance is a peer-to-peer networking and programming organization for female professionals on the business side of Broadway. Through a series of programming ranging from happy hours to unwind to symposiums with Broadway thought leaders, the core of this group lies in the benefits of connection, support, and empowerment we can provide each other. Membership is free, and our members include both business owners and employees representing a wide range of theatrical professions including marketers, general and company managers, theater owners, producers, press agents, casting directors, lawyers, company managers, and many more.

Women of Broadway – see https://www.womenofbroadway.com/

> Disney's Women of Broadway builds a community of women, including all those who identify as women and/or non-binary, who are working in — or fans

of — the Broadway, Off-Broadway, and professional theater industry. Each event is meant to offer an opportunity to share experiences, struggles, and victories with the goal of supporting each other to make our industry stronger.

Gender Amplified: Producer and Engineering Inclusion Initiative – see https://genderamplified.org/the-producer-and-engineer-inclusion-initiative/

A non-profit organization that aims to celebrate women in music production, raise their visibility, and develop a pipeline for girls and young women to get involved behind the scenes as music producers.

The Interval (NY) 2014–2019 – see https://www.theintervalny.com/

The Interval was a theatre publication featuring actors, writers, directors, composers, producers, and designers who are female-identifying. While it stopped publishing in 2019, the archives are available online and contain fascinating content.

Notes

1 "NYU Tisch: Graduate Musical Theatre Writing" Accessed January 29, 2023. See https://tisch.nyu.edu/admissions/graduate-admissions/gmtw_landing?gclid=CjwKCAiArNOeBhAHEiwAze_nKJquGfyOBftiH_vf_icCe0qaqRV3A3DnMSTB19AxsD8S506xtaUYEhoCZNQQAvD_BwE&gclsrc=aw.ds.
2 "The New Musicals Lab Homepage." Accessed January 29, 2023. See https://www.newmusicalslab.com/abouttheprogram.
3 "New Musicals Inc. Homepage" Accessed January 29, 2023. See https://nmi.org/.
4 "Musical Café Homepage" Accessed January 29, 2023. See https://www.playcafe.org/musical-cafe.
5 The most recent intensive as of the publishing of this book was 2020; however, it can be safely assumed that this was impacted by the Covid-19 pandemic and that the intensive may resume. See https://www.goodspeed.org/music-direction-intensive.
6 "Jonathan Larson Grants" Accessed January 29, 2023. See https://americantheatrewing.org/program/jonathan-larson-grants/.
7 "The Kleban Prize in Musical Theatre" *New Dramatists.* Accessed January 29, 2023. See https://newdramatists.org/kleban-prize-musical-theatre.

INDEX

Note: Page references with "n" denote endnotes.

9 to 5 11
The 25th Annual Putnum County Spelling Bee 80
The 52nd Street Project 191, 192, 193

Abbott, George 198
Abel, Marybeth 220, 224–225
Ableton Live 85
Ace Detective 45
Across the Universe 144
Actor's Equity Handbook 219
The Actor's Equity Production League Rulebook 220
Actors Theatre of Louisville 236
The Addams Family 101
Adjmi, David 236
Ahrens, Lynn 8, 10, 17–18, 66, 146
Aida 80, 221
Aladdin 145, 220
Alicia Keys 101
Allan, Gabrielle 28
Allegiance 79
Allegro 101
Allen, Debbie 145
Allen, Woody 146
Alliance Theatre, The 79
Almost Famous 122
Alphabet City Cycle 45
Alvarez, César 236
Amazing Grace 221

Amélie 87, 145
American Idiot 80
The American National Theatre and Academy (ANTA) 188
American Psycho 145
American Repertory Theater 236
Anastasia 10
Anderson, Kate 34; biography 63; interview 63–75
Anderson-Lopez, Kristen 63; biography 11–12; interview 12–28
Andrews, Julie 29
And the World Goes 'Round 157
Animal Crackers, South Pacific 171
Annie Get Your Gun 146
Anselmi, Barbara 10
Anything Goes 145
Applegate, Christina 227
Arizona State University 259, 260
Ars Nova 236
Arts Ignite 101
Asare, Masi 11
Aspects of Love 143
Assistant Choreographers 143
Assistant Directors 142–143
Assistant Music Director (AMD) 82
Assistant Stage Managers 220
Associate Choreographers 143
Associate Directors 142
Associate Music Director (Associate) 82

Avenue Q 221
Avian, Bob 151, 174, 177–178, 184n23

Baby Boomers 5
Bachelor of Music (BM) 259
Bad Jews 221
Balanchine, George 159, 173, 183n9
Ballet, Feld 215n11
Ballets Russes 183n11
BAM 236
Bandstand 114
The Band Wagon 10
Bareilles, Sara 11, 202
Barnum 171
The Beast in the Jungle 157
Beauty and the Beast 236
Becker, Peyton Taylor 220
Beetlejuice 189, 197
Bells are Ringing 144, 199
Bengal Tiger at the Baghdad Zoo 221, 232
Benjamin, Nell 11, 207
Bennett, Haley 80
Bennett, Michael 171
Benson, Sarah 236
Berinstein, Dori: biography 203–204; interview with 204–215
Berkeley Repertory Theatre 236
Bernarda Alba 146
The Best Little Whorehouse in Texas 11
Between the Lines 63
Big and Fool Moon 203
The Big Boom 45
Big Fish 101, 157
Big Red Sun 45
Big River 80
Bioh, Jocelyn 236
Birch, Patricia 143
Blodgette, Kristen 79
Bloody Bloody Andrew Jackson 197
BMI Lehman Engel Musical Theatre Workshop (New York, NY) 9, 260–261
Boesch, Diana 4
Bombay Dreams 171
Book of Mormon 65
The Book Thief 63
Born for This 189
Bossypants 65, 70
Boston Conservatory 259
Botti, Susan 87
Brave 71
Breglio, John 186
The Bridges of Madison County 10, 189, 221

Brigadoon 143
Bright Lights Big City 122
Bring In Da Funk 221, 231
Bring In Da Noise 221, 231
Bring It On 11, 189
Broadway Podcast Network 204, 207
The Broadway Sinfonietta 80
Broadway Women's Alliance 262
Broccoli, Barbara 236
A Bronx Tale 221
A Bronx Tale: The Musical 221
Brown, Brené 5
Brown, Camille A. 144
Brown, Jason Robert 52
The Bubbly Black Girl Sheds her Chameleon Skin 11
Bullets Over Broadway 157
Buñuel 114
But Not for Me 158
Byrne, David 87

Cahan, Cora 191
Call Me Madam 79
Camelot 171
Camile A. Brown & Dancers 145
Campbell, Mary-Mitchell 79, 82, 204, 207, 211; biography 100–101; interview 101–114
Camp Wish No More 65
Can-Can 79
Candide 79
Cannold, Sammi 210
Carmen Jones 171
Carol, Vinnette 144
Carol Channing: Larger Than Life 203
Caroline, or Change 80, 87, 145, 220
Carousel 143, 172
Carrie 122, 145
Caskey, Kristin 189, 211
Catch Me If You Can 189
Cat on a Hot Tin Roof 145
Cats 79, 143
Cave, Lisa Dawn 220, 234
Cavett, Wendy Bobbit 80
Center Stage 158, 185n53
Central Park 63, 71
Chavkin, Rachel 1, 144
Chenoweth, Kristin 29, 40, 101
The Cher Show 221
Chicago 145, 218
Chicago Symphony 101
Childs, Kirsten 11
Child Wranglers 220

266 Index

Choir Boy 145
choreographers: additional directing team members 142–143; Assistant Choreographers 143; Assistant Directors 142–143; Associate Choreographers 143; Associate Directors 142; Choreographers 143; Dance Captains 143; important figures 143–145; interviews 145–183; overview 141–142; *see also* directors
choreography/choreographing 142, 143, 259
A Chorus Line 171, 241
A Christmas Carol 157
Chronicle of a Death Foretold 146
chutzpah 188, 193, 199
Cincinnati symphony 101
Cinderella 171
The Circling Universe 45
City Slickers 249
Clark, Hope 145
Clarkson, Kelly 101
click tracks 85
The Coast of Utopia Part I 221
The Coast of Utopia Part II 221
The Coast of Utopia Part III 221
Coconuts 171
Cole, Jack 143, 149, 150, 174, 183n14
Coleman, Bud 5
Colorado Symphony 101
The Color Purple 10, 80, 220, 221, 234
Comden, Betty 8, 10, 199
The Comedians 12
Come From Away 80, 189
The Commercial Theater Institute Guide to Producing Plays and Musicals (Vogel and Hodges) 186
Company 101, 203, 220
Composers 8, 83
Conductors 139n9
Contact 157, 184n38
Contemporary Commercial Music (CCM) 259
Cook, Pat 35, 67
Coombs, Holly 220
copyist/engraver 83
Coraline 87
Costello, Elvis 101
The Count 3.0 3–4
Covid Coordinators 220
Craig, Daniel 202
Crazy for You 157

Creel, Gavin 101
The Crucible 203
Cumming, Alan 29
Cunningham, Merce 183n15
Cynthia Meng 85, 121

Dallas Symphony Orchestra 101
Dalrymple, Jean 188
Damn Yankees 171
Dana H 203
Dance Arranger 84
Dance Captains 143
The Dancer's Life 146
Dancing 226, 228
Dangerous Beauty 122
Dangerous Game 146
Danger Year 45
Daniele, Graciela 2, 142, 144, 190; biography 146; interview 146–157
Dani Girl 114
Daryl Roth Creative Spirit Award 2
Dave 122
Dean, Carmel 80
Dear Edwina 11, 29, 36–37
Dear Evan Hansen 80, 189
Deer, Joe 141
Delacorte Theater in Central Park 190
DeLappe, Sarah 236
DeMille, Agnes 143
Dessa Rose 10, 146
Destry Rides Again 79
The Devil Wears Prada 246
Devine, Kelly 145
Diana: The Musical 80, 145
digital audio workstations (DAWs) 8, 85
DiMenna, Diana 201
directing as experiential art 142
Directing in Musical Theatre: An Essential Guide 141
directors: additional directing team members 142–143; Assistant Choreographers 143; Assistant Directors 142–143; Associate Choreographers 143; Associate Directors 142; Choreographers 143; Dance Captains 143; important figures 143–145; interviews 145–183; overview 141–142; *see also* choreographers
Dirty Dancing 204, 210
Disney, Roy 34
Doctorate degree 257–258
Doctor of Musical Arts (DMA) 257, 259

Doctor Zhivago 10
Dodge, Marcia Milgrom 144
Don't Bother Me, I Can't Cope 11, 144
Dorothy Chandler Pavilion 206
Dot 157
Double Feature 158
Drake, Donna 237, 241
Drama Desk Awards 217n44
Dreamgirls 80
The Drowsy Chaperone 11

Eavesdropping with Alan Cumming 204
Ebb, Fred 2
Eisner, Michael 34
Elegies, A Song Cycle 146
Ellmann, Nora 4
Engel, Lehman 9, 79, 260
Ensemble Studio Theatre (EST) 191
Epting, George 223
Escape to Margaritaville 145
Esparza, Raul 101
Eugene O'Neill Playwrights Conference 191
Eustis, Oskar 188, 195, 196
Ever After 11, 38, 114
Everyone Says I Love You 146
Evita 210
experiential art 142

Fey, Tina 11
Fiddler on the Roof 87, 221
Fields, Dorothy 10
Finale 8, 67, 85
Finding Nemo the Musical 11
Finding Neverland 101, 122, 144, 221
Fine and Dandy 10
Finn, William 146, 184n34
Five Guys Named Moe 220, 224, 225, 229
Flack, Roberta 229
Flaherty, Stephen 10, 146
Fleming, Renée 87
Flora the Red Menace 157
Flower Drum Song 203
Floyd Collins 144
Flying Over Sunset 87
Footloose 144
Force for Change: How Leadership Differs from Management (Kotter) 218
For The Girls 101
For the Love of Duke 158
The Fortress of Solitude 87
Fosse 145, 220
Fosse, Bob 143, 145

Four-Track (tape recorder) 85
Franzen, Dale 189
Freakonomics 212
Freaky Friday (Rodgers) 10
Free to Be... You and Me 10
Fresh Air 212
Friedman, Michael 87
The Frogs 157
Frost, Sue 189, 211, 216n39
Frozen 11–12, 23–24, 71, 220, 244
Frozen 2 11–12, 23–24
Fryer, Rick 67
The Full Monty 87
Fully Committed 221
Fun Home 10, 188, 189, 220
Fun Home (Kron) 11
Funked up Fairy Tales 11
Funny Girl 199

Gabriel, Mike 35
Gancher, Sarah 236
Garageband 8, 67, 86
The Gardens of Anuncia 146
Gaskins, Leslie 223
The Gay Life 79
Gemignani, Paul 140n25
Genarro, Peter 143
Gender Amplified: Producer and Engineering Inclusion Initiative 263
Gershwin, George 10
The Gershwins' Porgy and Bess 221
Gersten, Bernie 191
Gersten, Jenny 188; biography 189; interview with 190–203
Girls5Eva 101
Global Creatures 189
The Glorious Ones 146
Godspell 221
Gold, Sam 236
Golden Child 203
Goldrich, Zina: biography 28–29; interview 29–45
Goldrich and Heisler: Volume One 41
Goldstein, Brent 71
The Goodbye Girl 146
Good News 10
graduate school 257
Graham, Martha 183n15
Grant, Amy 101
Grant, Micki 11
Grease 69, 143, 230
The Great American Mousical 29
The Great Comet of 1812 114

Green, Amanda 11
Greenfield, Mandy 196
Grigsby, Kimberly 46; biography 87; interview 87–100
Grishman, Emily 83
Groban, Josh 101
Grody, Andrea 114
Guettel, Adam 10, 87, 144
Gustafson, Karen 79
Guys and Dolls 202
Gypsy 171, 199

Hach, Heather 11, 207
Hadestown 144, 189, 221
Hair 188, 197
Hairspray 140n15, 189, 230
Hall, Carol 11
Hall, Katori 11
Hamilton 9, 85
Hands on a Hardbody 11, 80
Hanggi, Kristin 144
Happiness 157
Hardy, Jeff 17
Harrison, Jordan 236
Head Over Heels 80, 87
Hedwig and the Angry Inch 188
Heisler, Marcy 11, 28
Helburn, Therese 188
Hello Again 101, 146
Hello Dolly! 172
Henson, Jim 204
Here Lies Love 87
High Fidelity 11
Hilty, Meghan 29
Hodges, Ben 186
Holler If Ya Hear Me 221
Hollman, Mark 17
Hollywood Romance 28–29
Holtzman, Ben 201
Holzman, Winnie 11
Homeschool Musical 101
Honor 172
How Now Dow Jones 10
Hudes, Quiara Alegría 11
Hullaballo 183n19
Hunter, Mary 144
Hushion, Casey 145
Hytner, Nick 184n40

ICM 200
If/Then 80, 122
If There Is I Haven't Found It Yet 221
Indecent 236
in-ear monitors 86

Ingrouille, Carrie-Anne 145
Internet Broadway Database 2, 83
The Interval (NY) 263
interviews 87–139; director/choreographers 145–183; management 221–255; music team 87–139; producers 189–215
In the Heights 11, 221
Into the Woods 145, 172, 202
The Isaac Mizrahi Show 204
Isaacs, Mara 189, 211
Is This A Room 203
It Shoulda Been You 10
I Wanna Be a Producer (Breglio) 186

Jackson, Chris 228
Jackson, Christopher 228
Jackson, Michael R. 236
Jackson, Samuel L. 227
Jacobs-Jenkins, Branden 236
Jagged Little Pill 144, 189
Jay-Alexander, Richard 224–225
Jelly's Last Jam 80, 145
Jenkins, Beverly: biography 221; interview with 221–235
Jesus Christ Superstar 171, 210
Jesus Christ Superstar Live in Concert 145
John Legend 101
Johnson, Catherine 11
Joseph and the Amazing Technicolor Dreamcoat 63
Josepher, Laura 9
Joshua Bell: Music at Home 204
Joy 145
Junie B. Jones 11, 29
Junkyard Productions 189

Kaling, Mindy 65
Kaller, Sheryl 236
Kander, John 2
Katzenberg, Jeffrey 34
Kauffman, Anne 236
Kelly, Raja Feather 236
Kennesaw State University 1, 13, 15, 229, 245
Kerrigan, Kait 11
key 2/keyboard 2 87
The Kilroys 262
King, Carole 51, 101
The King and I 79, 171, 221
King Kong 189
Kiss Me Kate 79, 145
Kitt, Tom 87
Kosky, Barrie 87

Kotter, J. P. 218–219
Kron, Lisa 11
Kummer, Clare 9

LaChiusa, Michael John 146
La Grosse Valise 79
La Jolla Playhouse 236
Lambert, Lisa 11
Lamos, Mark 236
Landau, Tina 144, 213
Lane, Nathan 192
Lapine, James 87
The Last Blintz 204
The Last Two People on Earth: An Apocalyptic Vaudeville 157
Latarro, Lorin 145
Lawrence, Gertrude 185n61
Leader of the Pack 188
leadership 5–6; and management 218–219; and women 1
League of Professional Theatre Women 262
A League of their Own 195
Lee, Baayork 142; biography 171–172; interview 172–183
Lee, Jennifer 11
Legally Blonde 11, 189, 203, 207, 208, 210
Leigh, Carolyn 10
Leon, Kenny 141
Les Misérables 220
Leve, Harriet Newman 187
Leve Production 187
Librettists 8
libretto 8
Liechtenstein 229
The Light in the Piazza 87
Lights of Broadway Trading Cards 204
The Lillys 2–3, 262
Lincoln Center Theater 236
The Lion, The Unicorn and Me 87
The Lion King 144, 221
Little Dancer 158
Little Fish 146
A Little Night Music 143
A Little Princess 71
Little Shop of Horrors 48, 189
Little Women 144
Living On Love 221
Liza – Live from Radio City Music Hall 158
Loesser, Frank 80
Logic 8, 67
LogicPro 86
Lopez, Bobbie 38
Lopez, Sammy 201
Lortel, Lucille 188

Lucille Lortel Awards 188
Lynne, Dame Gillian 143

Macbeth 202
Machinal 221
Mack and Mabel 171
MacKinnon, Pam 87, 236
The Mad Show 10
Mae-Phillips, Barbara 220
Maestra Mission Statement 262
Maestra Music Inc. 261
Mainstage 84–85
Majestic Theater 185n59
Mamas Talkin' Loud 221
Mamma Mia 11, 80
management 218–255; interviews 221–255; job descriptions 219–220; overview 218–219
The Manhattan Theatre Club 260
A Man of No Importance 10
Mantello, Joe 192
Marie Christine 146
Marshall, Kathleen 87, 145, 181, 226
Marvin Hamlisch: What He Did For Love 203–204
Marx, Jeff 38
Mary Poppins 114
Master of Arts (MA) degree 258
Master of Fine Arts (MFA) 257, 259
Master of Music (MM) 259–260
Matilda 64, 70
Mattox, Matt 149, 183n15
Mayer, Michael 87
Mayerson, Rhoda 189
Mazzie, Marin 145
McBride, Julie 80
McCann, Elizabeth I. 188
McCann, Liz 206
McCollum, Kevin 186
McDonald, Audra 29, 80
McKee, Kenneth J. 234
McLaughlin, Sarah 51
McMillin, Scott 9
Mean Girls 11, 101, 114, 145, 220
Meek, Karyn 221
Memphis 189
Merrick, David 198
Merrily We Roll Along 114
Merritt, Stephin 87
The Merry Widow 49, 158
Messe, Daniel 87
metronome "app"/tempo 86
MIDI 84, 86
MIDI-capable programming 84

Mighty Aphrodite 146
Milazzo, AnnMarie: biography 122; interview 122–139
The Milliken Breakfast Show 184n21
Mindich, Stacey 189, 211
Minnelli, Liza 137, 146
Miracle Brothers 11
Miranda, Lin-Manuel 9
Miss Saigon 171, 221
Mitchell, Brian Stokes 145
Mitchell, Joni 51
Mitchell, Ruth 220
Mizrahi, Isaac 204
MJ the Musical 221
Moore, Jason 226
Moore, Jennifer Rae 221
Morissette, Alanis 51
Morrison, Greg 11
Mosaic 45
Motown The Musical 221
Moulin Rouge 80, 189
Moulin Rouge! The Musical 145
Mr. Saturday Night 11
Mrs. Doubtfire 145
MTV 204
MuppetVision 3-D 204
Murphy, Ryan 204
MUSE (Musicians United for Social Equity) 101
The Musical as Drama 9
Musical Theatre Factory NYC 260
Musical Theatre Works 139n12
Music Arranger (Arranger) 84
Music Assistant 83
Music Director (MD) 81–82
music glossary 85–87
The Music Man 79, 157
Music Supervisor 82
music team: Assistant Music Director (AMD) 82; Associate Music Director (Associate) 82; composer 83; copyist/engraver 83; interviews 87–139; job descriptions 80–85; Music Arranger (Arranger) 84; Music Assistant 83; Music Director (MD) 81–82; music glossary 85–87; Music Supervisor 82; notable figures 79–80; Orchestrator 84; personal perspective 78–79; Programmers 84–85
My Fair Lady 210, 216n37, 221
My Lifelong Love 45
My Love Letter to Broadway 101

The Mystery of Edwin Drood 146
Mystic Pizza 145

Naked Angels 193, 194–195, 216n14
Nashville Symphony 101
Natasha, Pierre, and the Great Comet of 1812 144, 221
National Alliance for Musical Theatre (NAMT) 260–261
National Asian Artists Project (NAAP) 171–172
NBC 204
Netflix 204
Neugebauer, Lila 236
A New Brain 146, 171
New York City Center 188, 216n38
New Yorker 212
New York Musical Festival (NYMF) 8
New York New York 189
New York Shakespeare Festival 146, 190
New York Theatre Workshop 260
New York Women's Foundation 2
Next to Normal 122
Nicholaw, Casey 209
Nickelodeon 204
Niles, Shakira 221
non-graduate training opportunities 260
non-profit theaters 216n25
Norman, Marsha 10
noting 86
Nugent, Nell 188, 206
Nunn, Trevor 184n42
NYU Steinhardt 260
NYU Tisch 260

Ockrent, Mike 184n41
Octopus Theatricals 189
O'Flaherty, Michael 50
Oklahoma! 16, 29, 143, 149, 157, 162, 172, 182, 188, 189, 221, 225
Oklahoma City University 260
Olaf's Frozen Adventure 63, 70, 75
Oliver! 172
Once on This Island 10, 80, 122, 144, 146
Once Upon a Mattress 10
One Flew Over The Cuckoo's Nest 203
On the Media 212
On Your Feet! 189
Orchestrator 84
Osborne, Joan 51
Oxygen Media 204

The Pajama Game 145
Papp, Joe 193, 194

Index   **271**

Parade 143, 199
Paradise Square 11, 221
Park Avenue Armory 236
Pasternak, Barbara 37
Paulus, Diane 144
Pavlovic, Carmen 189
Penn State University 259
Perfectly Frank 80
Performing in Contemporary Musicals 9
Perry, Katy 101
Peter Pan 10, 220
Phantom of the Opera 143, 220
Photograph 51 158
piano-conducting 81–82, 86–87
The Piano Lesson 189, 191
Picnic 157
Picoult, Jodi 72
Pilot, Genevieve 79
Pippin 144, 202
Pirates 146
The Pirates of Penzance 146
platform agnostic 206, 208, 211, 216n31
The Play That Goes Wrong 221
Playwrights Downtown 260
Playwrights Horizons 236, 260
Poehler, Amy 65
Porgy and Bess 80, 144, 145, 171
POTUS: Or, Behind Every Great Dumbass Are Seven Women Keeping Him Alive 157
The Powers That Be 212
Pre-Production 86, 184n24
Pretty Dead Girl 122
Pretty Woman: The Musical 189
Price, Eva 189, 211
Prince of Broadway 157
Prince, Hal 150, 160, 166–167, 184n39, 220
producers 186–215; Broadway 187; interviews 189–215; negative reputation 187; role of 186–188; team 187; *see also* directors
The Producers 157, 184n37, 189
The Producers: The Movie Musical 158
Production Assistants 220
Production Manager (PM) 219
Production Stage Manager 219
Programmers 84–85
The Prom 79, 101, 114, 145, 203, 204, 207, 209, 213, 214, 217n42, 220
public relations (PR) 187
The Public Theater 190, 196, 236, 260

QLab 86
A Quiet Revolution 45
Quinn, Anthony 146

Radio Hour 212
Ragtime 10, 144, 146
Ratatouille: The TikTok Musical, Kimberly Akimbo, and *TINA* 80
Redfield, Liza 79
regional theater: gender representation in 2–5
Reinking, Ann 145
Resnick, Patricia 11
Revisionist History 212
Richards, David 232
Richards, Lloyd 191
The Rink 146
Ritchie, Michael 192, 193
Rittman, Trude 79
Rivera, Chita 146
Road Show 101
The Robber Bridegroom 188
Robbins, Jerome 139n8, 143, 148, 156, 159
Robinson, Tiffany 221
Rock of Ages 144, 145
Rocky 145, 220
Rodgers, Mary 8, 10
Rodgers and Hammerstein 79, 143, 171
Roth, Daryl 187, 236
Rudin, Fiona Howe 201
Ruhl, Sarah 236
Russell, Brenda 10
Russell, John Morris 48

Samantha Spade 45
Samsel, Elyssa 34; biography 63; interview 63–75
San Diego State University 259
Sankoff, Irene 10
The Scarlet Pimpernel 80
Schmidt, Macy 80
Schmigadoon 80
Schoolhouse Rock 36
Schulman, Susan 144
The Scottsboro Boys 157
Seales, Alan 207
Seaside Music Theater 16, 29, 236–237, 241
Sebesta, Judith A. 5
The Secret Garden 10, 66, 71, 144, 189
The Secret Life of the American Musical: How Broadway Shows are Built 9
Segovia, Yolanda 80
Sergeant Blue 9

Serial 212
Sesame Workshop 204
session singer 86
SFX 50, 86
Shankel, Lynne 79
Shanley, John Patrick 191
Sheik, Duncan 87
Shenandoah Conservatory 259
Sher, Bartlett 87
Show Boat 157, 220
ShowBusiness: The Road To Broadway 203
The Show Must Go On 204
Shrek: The Musical 10, 221
Shuffle Along: Or the Making of the Musical Sensation of 1921 and All That Followed 220
Shy: The Alarmingly Outspoken Memoirs of Mary Rodgers 10
Sibelius 8, 67–68, 83, 85, 86
Signature Theatre 236
Silverman, Leigh 87, 144
Simon, Lucy 10, 66
Singin' in the Rain 10
Sing Street 244, 248
Sisco, David 9
Six 145, 220
"The Small House of Uncle Thomas" 79
Smile 10
Smith, Jimmy Lee 234
Smokey Joe's Café 189
Snow Child 45
Society of Stage Directors and Choreographers 144
Soho Rep 236
Some Like It Hot 101
Some Lovers 122
Something Rotten 220
Sondheim, Stephen 9, 101, 114
Songs for a New World 46
Songs From an Unmade Bed 87
Sony Pictures 204
The Sound of Music 79, 144
South Pacific 79
Spelman, Katie 145
Spider-Man: Turn Off the Dark 87
The Spongebob Musical 80, 144, 213
Spooner, Amanda 232; biography 236; interview with 236–255
Spring Awakening 46, 87, 122
Stacey Mindich "Go Work in Theater" Award 2
Stacey Mindich "Go Write a Musical" Award 2
Stacey Mindich Productions 189

Stage Management (6th Edition) (Stern) 219
Stage Manager 219–220
St. Ann's Warehouse 236
Starcrossed 50
Steel Pier 157
Steppenwolf Theatre Company 144
Stern, Lawrence 219
Stevie Wonder 31, 101
Stick Conducting 86
Stitt, Georgia: biography 45; interview 46–63
"stock and amateur rights" 185n76
Strange Faces 114
A Strange Loop 188
Stroman, Susan 142–143; biography 157–158; interview 158–171
subbing/subs 87
Suessical 10
Suffs 201
Sundance Theatre Lab 236
Sunday in the Park with George 145
Sunset Boulevard 79
Superhero 122
Sweeney Todd 101
Sweet Charity 220, 221, 227
Swift, Kay 10, 199
Swing! 144

Taichman, Rebecca 236
Take Five... More or Less 158
Tauriello, Dena 139n10
Taylor, James 101
Taylor Corbett, Lynne 144
Taymor, Julie 87, 144
Telaio: Desdemona 87
terminal degree 257–260
Tesori, Jeanine 10, 50, 66, 87
Theatre for Young Audiences (TYA) 139n13
The Theatre Guild 144, 188
TheatreWorksUSA 139n13
Theatrical Intimacy 185n56
This Ordinary Thursday 45, 46, 52
Thoroughly Modern Millie 10, 189, 203
Thou Shalt Not 157
Timbers, Alex 87
Tina: The Tina Turner Musical 11, 189, 221
Titus 144
tokenism 4
To Kill a Mockingbird 87
Tong, Cynthia J. 189
TONY voter 236
The Town 212
Tuck Everlasting 101, 220

Tune, Tommy 143, 174, 175
Tutors 220
Twillie, Christie Chiles 80
Twine, Linda 80

The Unauthorized Autobiography of Samantha Brown 11
Unzipped 204

Vestron Pictures 204
Viertal, Jack 9
Violet 10, 144
Virginia Woolf 203
Virgin Voyages 201
The Visit 146
Vogel, Frederic B. 186
Vogel, Paula 236
Vollack, Lia 211
Vosk, Jessica 101, 216n27

Wagner, Paula 189
Wagner, Robert 184n47
Waitress 11, 144, 145
Walker, Sheilah 80
A Walk on the Moon 122
Walt Disney Imagineering 204
Warner, Judith 4
Warner Brothers 204
Washburn, Anne 236
The Water 45
Waters, Les 236
Weaver, Earl 240–241
Webber, Andrew Lloyd 79, 143, 167, 184n40
The Wedding Singer 189
Westbeth Theatre Center 184n33
Westport Country Playhouse 236

West Side Story 114, 139n8, 234
Whitman, Barbara 188, 201, 211
Wicked 11, 220
Wildcat 79
Williams, Robin 227
Williamstown Theatre Festival 158, 193, 216n15, 236
Wilson, August 191
Winnie the Pooh 11
The Wiz 222
Wolfe, George C. 87
The Wolves 247
Woman in White 220
women: and leadership 1; pay gap between men and 1; write musical theatre 9–11
Women in Musical Theatre 5
Women of Broadway 262–263
The Women's Leadership Gap: Women's Leadership by the Numbers 4
Wonderful Town 145
workshops and training programs 261
writer(s): music and lyrics 9; overview 7–8

Yale Repertory Theatre 236
Yee, Ann 145
Yes, Please 65
Young Frankenstein 157
You're a Good Man Charlie Brown 143
Yuriko 185n64

Zaks, Jerry 226
Zervoulis, Meg 79; biography 114; interview 114–122
Ziegfeld, Florenz 184n45
Zipprodt, Patricia 2
Zorba 146

Printed in the United States
by Baker & Taylor Publisher Services